S7150

Trade Policy and Economic Integration in the Middle East and North Africa

The recent globalization trends have revived a long-standing interest in regional integration in the countries of the Middle East and North Africa (MENA). Despite numerous attempts to encourage economic integration in MENA in the past few decades, there is broad consensus that progress has been painfully slow and the record of economic integration in this region has been largely beset by failure. This book examines the impact of recent changes in the world economy on trade policy within the MENA region and its economic relations with the rest of the world. It considers regional integration and prospects for trade blocs; trade liberalization and economic restructuring; resource endowments and employment trends; and changes in economic boundaries, especially as a result of labour migration and regional conflicts.

Hassan Hakimian is Senior Lecturer in Economics at Cass Business School, City University, London. He specializes in the economic development of Middle Eastern countries with special reference to Iran. His main areas of interest include: globalization, demographic transition, and international trade and MENA's water resources. He has published widely and has extensive experience of consultancy in Asia and Africa.

Jeffrey B. Nugent is Professor of Economics at the University of Southern California, Los Angeles. He specializes in Development Economics and especially on the following issues and aspects: institutions, international trade and capital flows, agriculture, demographic behaviour, reforms, economic modelling, the effects of income inequality, investment, foreign aid and economic planning in all regions of developing countries.

The Political Economy of the Middle East and North Africa
(Series editor: Hassan Hakimian)

1 **Trade Policy and Economic Integration in the Middle East and North Africa**
Economic boundaries in flux
Edited by Hassan Hakimian and Jeffrey B. Nugent

Trade Policy and Economic Integration in the Middle East and North Africa

Economic boundaries in flux

Edited by Hassan Hakimian and Jeffrey B. Nugent

RoutledgeCurzon
Taylor & Francis Group
LONDON AND NEW YORK

First published 2004
by RoutledgeCurzon
11 New Fetter Lane, London EC4P 4EE

Simultaneously published in the USA and Canada
by RoutledgeCurzon
29 West 35th Street, New York, NY 10001

RoutledgeCurzon is an imprint of the Taylor & Francis Group

Typeset in Times New Roman by
Newgen Imaging Systems (P) Ltd, Chennai, India
Printed and bound in Great Britain by
MPG Books Ltd, Bodmin

British Library Cataloguing in Publication Data
A catalogue record for this book is available
from the British Library

Library of Congress Cataloging in Publication Data
A catalog record for this book has been requested

ISBN 0–415–30266–8

Contents

Figures

Maps

Tables

Contributors

Elizabeth Bailey is an Agricultural Economist and Project Officer at the International Centre for Agricultural Research in the Dry Areas (ICARDA), Aleppo, Syria.

Ali H. Bayar is Professor of Economics at Université Libre de Bruxelles and is the CEO of EcoMod Network in Brussels, Belgium.

Ghazi Ben-Ahmed is a Research Fellow at Université Libre de Bruxelles and at EcoMod Network in Brussels, Belgium.

Paul de Boer is Professor of Economics at Erasmus University, Rotterdam, and Research Fellow at EcoMod Network in Brussels, Belgium.

Jacques Charmes is Professor of Economics at the University of Versailles Saint Quentin en Yvelines (France), Centre of Economics and Ethics for Environment and Development (C3ED).

Dipak Dasgupta is an Economist in the Middle East and North Africa Region of the World Bank, Washington, DC, USA.

Xinshen Diao is an Economist at the International Food Policy Research Institute (IFPRI), Washington, DC, USA.

Leila Farsakh is a Research Fellow at the Centre for International Studies, MIT, Cambridge, MA, USA.

Sofiane Ghali is Assistant Professor of Economics at the Faculté des Sciences Economiques et de Gestion de Tunis, Université de Tunis-El Manar, Tunisia.

Patricia Goldey is a Rural Sociologist in international rural development, School of Agriculture, Policy and Development, University of Reading, UK.

Behrouz Hady Zonooz is Associate Professor of Economics at Allameh Tabatabaie University, Tehran, Iran.

Hassan Hakimian is a Senior Lecturer in Economics at Cass Business School, City University, London, UK.

Gwyn E. Jones (now retired) was a Rural Sociologist and Extension Specialist in international rural development, School of Agriculture, Policy and Development, University of Reading, UK.

Nu'man Kanafani is Associate Professor of Economics at the Department of Economics and Natural Resources, The Royal Veterinary and Agricultural University, Copenhagen, Denmark.

Jennifer Keller is an Economist in the Middle East and North Africa Region of the World Bank, Washington, DC, USA.

Zelal Kotan is an Assistant Economist in the Research Department of the Central Bank, Turkey.

Malika Abdelali-Martini is Socio-Economist/Rural Development and Gender Analysis specialist at the International Centre for Agricultural Research in the Dry Areas (ICARDA), Aleppo, Syria.

Rania Miniesy is a graduate student, Political Economy and Public Policy, University of Southern California, Los Angeles, CA, USA.

Pierre Mohnen is Professor of Economics at the University of Maastricht and a Fellow at the Maastricht Economic Research Institute on Innovation and Technology (MERIT), Netherlands.

Mustapha Kamel Nabli is Chief Economist in the Middle East and North Africa Region of the World Bank, Washington, DC, USA.

Jeffrey B. Nugent is Professor of Economics, University of Southern California, Los Angeles, CA, USA.

Karen Pfeifer is Professor of Economics at Smith College, Northampton, MA, USA and an editor of *Middle East Report*.

Serdar Sayan is an Associate Professor of Economics and Executive Manager of the Centre for European Union Affairs at Bilkent University, Ankara, Turkey.

T. G. Srinivasan is an Economist in the Middle East and North Africa Region of the World Bank, Washington, DC, USA.

Sübidey Togan is Professor of Economics and Director of the Centre for International Economics at Bilkent University, Ankara, Turkey.

Marie-Ange Véganzonès-Varoudakis is a Researcher at CNRS, CERDI, Clermont Ferrand, France, and Economist in the Middle East and North Africa Region of the World Bank, Washington, DC, USA.

Erinc Yeldan is Professor of Economics and Chair of the Department of Economics at Bilkent University, Ankara, Turkey.

Tarik M. Yousef is Assistant Professor of Economics in the School of Foreign Service at Georgetown University, Washington, DC, USA.

Preface and acknowledgements

The recent globalization trends have revived a long-standing interest in regional integration in the countries of the Middle East and North Africa (MENA). Despite numerous attempts to encourage economic integration in MENA in the past few decades, there is broad consensus that progress has been painfully slow and the record of economic integration in this region has been largely beset by failure.

This book examines the impact of recent changes in the world economy on trade policy within the MENA region and its economic relations with the rest of the world. It considers regional integration and prospects for trade blocs; trade liberalization and economic restructuring; resource endowments and employment trends; and changes in economic boundaries, especially as a result of labour migration and regional conflicts.

The recent revival of regionalism in MENA countries – dubbed the 'New Regionalism' – has been bolstered, on the one hand, by attempts at broader economic reforms and the adoption of outward-oriented economic strategies and, on the other hand, by renewed interest in economic integration with the outside world, especially with Europe. These forces have combined in recent years to set the region's economic boundaries in flux.

This book is the result of a joint initiative by the Middle East Economic Association (MEEA) and the School of Oriental and African Studies (SOAS), University of London. To mark the twenty-fifth anniversary of MEEA's foundation, we organized an international conference – MEEA's first European conference – in London University in the summer of 2001. The theme of the conference was 'Global Change and Regional Integration: The Redrawing of the Economic Boundaries in the Middle East and North Africa (MENA)'. The aim was to provide an opportunity for outstanding scholars and researchers from the region and beyond to address MENA's economic challenges in a global setting, specifically looking at ways in which the changing patterns of trade, investment and finance, and labour flows were likely to influence the region's economies as they entered the twenty-first century.

The works in this volume all draw from contributions to that conference and reflect closely its objective of fostering wide-ranging debate from multiple perspectives. This led to a unique gathering of researchers and experts from many countries and institutions – from the World Bank and the IMF to academics and researchers from MENA, Europe, and the United States – to share in and debate their latest research findings. The outcome of the debate is presented in this volume in five parts examining different aspects of MENA's economic integration in a broad regional and international context.

We would like to thank the Ford Foundation's regional office in Egypt and the SOAS Research committee for providing partial financial assistance. This was essential for encouraging participation from the MENA region itself. We are grateful to SOAS for hosting the conference and to Dr Sarah Stewart and the staff of the Centre for Near and Middle East Studies at SOAS for administrative support.

The project owes a great deal to our MEEA colleagues for their support and encouragement. Among them special thanks are due to Professor Mine Cinar, MEEA's President, and other Board members, whose names we need not list here.

The completion of the book has been greatly facilitated by the dedicated editorial assistance of Marianna Volpi who went through the various chapters which had such varied styles and authorship, and tried to maintain consistency and completeness. Her contribution is highly valued.

Needless to say that the views expressed and any errors contained in individual contributions are the responsibility of the authors and not their respective institutions or any other party.

We would like to dedicate this book to the cause of peace in the region, as another war has just 'ended'. Although it is hard to remain optimistic when adversities escalate so rapidly, we remain hopeful that both the people of the Middle East shall overcome the many adversities they face and the rest of the world will finally treat the region and its people with the respect and dignity that they deserve.

Hassan Hakimian and Jeffrey B. Nugent
August 2003

Introduction

Hassan Hakimian and Jeffrey B. Nugent

Under the combined impacts of globalization and regionalization, the economic boundaries between different nations have been in considerable flux for several decades. Thanks to its long history of attempts at greater economic integration and its pivotal role in world energy supplies, the Middle East and North African (MENA) countries have been far from immune to these forces. In the Arab world, regional integration has been a frequently stated policy goal, acting as a yardstick for evaluating the achievements of post-independence nationalism. Elsewhere in the region, too, there is a rich history of attempts at economic integration. Yet, despite numerous initiatives at the regional and sub-regional levels and hundreds of bilateral agreements, there is broad consensus that progress has been painfully slow and the record of economic integration in the MENA region is largely beset by a catalogue of failures.

In recent years, two distinct trends have emerged among MENA countries. Following the failure of region-wide trading initiatives in the earlier postwar period, the first trend (in the 1980s) was to increase efforts to integrate at the sub-regional level. Indeed, the 1980s witnessed the creation of the Gulf Cooperation Council (GCC) in 1981 (involving Bahrain, Kuwait, Oman, Qatar, Saudi Arabia, and the United Arab Emirates) and the Arab Maghreb Union in 1989 (involving Algeria, Libya, Mauritania, Morocco, and Tunisia).

The second trend – beginning in the 1990s – has been the gradual liberalization of MENA's trade with the rest of the world. Some of this was at the multilateral level after the completion of the Uruguay round. But, an even sharper boost to trade liberalization was the Euro-Med initiative between the European Union and the southern Mediterranean MENA countries. This initiative aims to create a free trade area in the Mediterranean region by 2010 and does not focus *per se* on intra-MENA trade.

The recent revival of regionalism both within and outside of MENA – dubbed the 'New Regionalism' – has been bolstered, on the one hand, by attempts at broader economic reforms and the adoption of outward-oriented economic strategies and, on the other, by renewed interest in economic integration with the outside world, especially with Europe.

This book examines the impact of recent changes in the world economy on trade policy within the MENA region and its economic relations with the rest of the world. It considers regional integration and prospects for trade blocs, trade liberalization and economic restructuring, resource endowments and employment trends, and changes in economic boundaries, especially as a result of labour migration and regional conflicts.

As a background to establishing how far MENA's economic boundaries have been changing in recent years, we attempt to identify the extent to which fundamental reforms have been undertaken and to examine the impacts of these reforms and why and how the experience may or may not have met expectations.

With or without trade reforms, the products of many sectors are not traded internationally. Services have long been an example of non-traded goods but, with the increasing relative importance of agricultural subsidies and other barriers to trade in agriculture, many agricultural products have become non-traded. The goods and services produced by the informal sector are also often non-traded. Yet, the labour markets of these sectors are often extremely important as far as employment is concerned. How have trade agreements and other measures of international cooperation affected labour flows and the composition, character, and level of employment in these activities? What are the implications for future trade arrangements for MENA country labour markets? What are the challenges ahead with new trade arrangements among MENA countries and between them and the European Union and other countries?

Another issue of considerable and special importance to the region is the relationship between political and economic boundaries. The dominant view is that the relationship is complementary. In other words, attempts to liberalize political relationships between nation states are likely to increase trade and factor flows among them. In the context of the Middle East, this has led to considerable optimism that movements toward promoting peace in the Middle East such as the Oslo Accords would have the effect of freeing up economic flows between Israel and its neighbours including the Palestinian territories. Yet, reality has taken a sad toll on such overly optimistic expectations. Moreover, as several chapters in this volume demonstrate, every actual or proposed policy change (or international treaty) is likely to have economic winners as well as losers: this implies that attempts to settle international disputes may not necessarily lower domestic conflicts and result in full implementation of agreements – a simple fact of manifest relevance to the MENA region.

The theory of international economic integration generally assumes away implementation failures and the unilateral imposition of non-tariff barriers to trade of various sorts once an agreement has been reached. Yet, implementation failures have been endemic to trade and other agreements within the MENA region. How should this be taken into account? While the theory of economic integration has dealt with polarization effects, it has not dealt with asymmetries in the power to directly limit internal product and factor mobility within one or more potential trading partners such as the Israeli security actions have in the Palestinian territories. Where international disputes are incompletely resolved and asymmetries in political and/or military power exist, the result can be very unequal benefits of any actual or potential economic integration. Since trade in commodities can serve as a substitute for trade in factors of production, the freeing of trade in commodities can result in less trade in factors and hence possibly less economic integration overall. This, too, is an issue that has not been adequately treated in the theory of economic integration.

One complicating factor of special relevance to the MENA region has been the continuation – arguably aggravation – of minor and major conflicts among countries of the region, each with regional and international implications. Unlike much of the rest of the world, which seems to have benefited from the 'peace dividend' in the post-Cold War era, the MENA region continues to suffer from lack of democracy, wars, and various forms of external shocks ranging from economic sanctions and blockades to outright military incursions. The Israeli–Palestinian conflict is as heated as ever and indeed has become more violent over time. As we write this introduction, the war against Iraq has just started against wild claims and raised expectations about the future of Iraq and the region at large. Yet, the prospects for resolving this conflict are as fuzzy as the logic used to justify it – not to mention the process used to trigger the war itself. With major national and regional resources tied up in such conflicts in MENA, the prospects for the region's economic and political integration appear as distant as ever.

While some of the trade and labour market policy issues discussed here are so important as to have received considerable attention in recent years, most of these have been from the standpoint of an individual author or international organization. Similarly, for the issues of conflict and power, there have been few studies interweaving conflicts and trade and other policy reforms in the MENA region and fewer still that use a number of different perspectives.

Given the complexity and controversy surrounding them, it is our belief that greater attempts must be made to represent a wider variety of viewpoints than is usually found in such work. The Middle East Economic Association is an organization of scholars representing a wide range of approaches and functional and geographic specializations. The present volume takes advantage of a number of the more relevant papers presented at the First European Conference of the Middle East Economic Association held at the School of Oriental and African Studies of the University of London in July 2001. As the reader will see, the papers represent an unusually diverse set of perspectives and viewpoints. Indeed, a wide variety of analytic models is used in these papers, ranging in complexity from descriptive case studies to relatively large-scale, regression-based gravity and real exchange rate models, linear programming (or activity analysis) models, and simulation-based computable general equilibrium models.

While much of the attention in the volume is devoted to the regional picture for MENA as a whole, the struggles of individual countries with trade strategy and reform are not neglected. Indeed, the volume includes detailed analyses of the more interesting and important case studies from the region, such as Iran, Syria, Tunisia, Turkey, Kuwait, Israel, and the Palestinian territories.

The presentation is divided into five parts. Part I consists of a single chapter by Dasgupta, Keller, and Srinivasan providing a comprehensive overview of both the extent to which MENA has engaged in economic reforms during the 1990s and their apparent effects on growth and employment. The chapter makes a serious attempt to distinguish the effects of the partial and tentative reforms from those of falling oil prices. The latter have, of course, had a generally depressing effect on growth throughout the region, even among non-oil exporting countries. The results show that those MENA countries that have achieved somewhat greater diversification away from oil and reformed earlier than the other countries of the region have performed somewhat better than the others. Among the different types of reform, the authors argue that progress has been greater on macroeconomic reforms involving inflation and exchange rates and most recently on private capital flows than on structural reforms involving product and labour markets. They also show that there has been an overall improvement in performance during the 1990s compared to the 1980s. They argue that this may be due to the modest but not negligible reforms operating through improvements in total factor productivity, at least relative to the decline in total factor productivity experienced in the preceding decade.

Part II consists of three chapters devoted to assessing the relative merits of different types of actual or projected trade and exchange rate policy reforms. One of the great debates facing the region is whether to concentrate on trade reforms designed to increase intraregional trade or those designed to increase trade with Europe and the rest of the world. To a large extent, the answer to this question depends on whether or not actual trade within the region or between MENA and the European Union is greater or less than would be expected on the basis of natural factors such as country size, distance, language differences, and factor endowments incorporated in a 'gravity' model. In contrast to some alternative estimates in the literature based on less complete data and specifications, in Chapter 2, Miniesy, Nugent, and Yousef show that intra-MENA trade is considerably smaller than would be expected on the basis of their gravity model. As a result, they show that a free trade agreement known as the Greater Arab Free Trade Agreement which would be as comprehensive, strong, and completely implemented as that within the European Union, could more than double this trade. Trade with some other regions such as the European Union is also less than would be expected but some with other regions such as the Less Developed Countries (LDCs) is larger than would be expected on the basis of the same natural factors captured by the gravity model.

Chapter 3 by Nabli and Véganzonès-Varoudakis shows that, despite the aforementioned improvements by MENA countries in dealing with inflation and macroeconomic instability and decreasing exchange rate overvaluation in the 1990s, considerable overvaluation still persists among several MENA countries. It is shown that such overvaluation decreases the competitiveness of MENA exports and domestic production and reduces its growth performance. The authors measure the extent of overvaluation (or more generally *misalignment*) by comparing the actual exchange rate with the equilibrium exchange rate predicted by their model based on data from 53 countries including ten MENA countries. They show that exports of manufactures have been adversely affected by the extent of such overvaluation.

A very different modelling approach to issues of trade arrangements with the rest of the world is presented in Chapter 4. This chapter by Bayar, Ben-Ahmed, de Boer, Diao, and Yeldan makes use of a multi-region, multi-sector, dynamic computable general equilibrium model of the world economy to focus on the long-term effects on MENA countries of various alternative policy scenarios. Although income distribution effects are suppressed by focusing in each country on a single representative consumer, the results show the sensitivity of the results to the character of liberalization. For example, the effects of trade liberalization with the European Union are likely to be much more favourable to MENA countries if the trade liberalization measures include the liberalization of the presently important non-tariff barriers and serve to bring about a more competitive environment. The authors also show that the simulations reveal the likelihood of major kinds of disequilibria such as trade deficits and unemployment, suggesting the need for MENA countries to be ready to make suitable adjustments to these disequilibria.

Part III is devoted to individual country experiences with restructuring, the price competitiveness of exports, trade strategy, and its relation to industrial development. Chapter 5 by Ghali and Mohnen represents an innovative approach to identifying comparative advantage and the relative scarcity (in social opportunity cost terms) of different types of labour and their contributions to economic growth in the Tunisian economy. Tunisia is one of the few MENA countries to have been somewhat successful in exporting some manufactured goods. The approach used is a linear programming or activity analysis model with given constraints and objectives that is used to identify the optimal factor allocations and the 'shadow' prices of these factors both before and after the structural adjustment programme of 1986. The sectors with comparative advantage are found to be hotels and tourism, financial services, transport and communications, construction materials, glass, and food. Even though structural adjustment has moved the economy in the direction of making greater use of skilled labour, there remains excess supply for this type of labour and a negative rate of return to such education, suggesting that further policy actions are needed.

Turkey is another MENA country that has made progress in penetrating international markets in manufacturing. Indeed, Turkish exports in the manufacturing sector grew many-fold after trade and other reforms were introduced, but its exports remain quite concentrated both by country of destination and product, making these exports vulnerable to demand and policy changes of various sorts. In Chapter 6, Kotan and Sayan compare the competitiveness of Turkish exports in the manufacturing sector to the European Union with those East Asian countries that constitute its major competitors in these markets. They estimate the responsiveness of Turkey's market share to relative prices in each of several commodity groups, ranging from traditional exports such as textiles and clothing to newer non-traditional Turkish exports like electrical machinery and power-generating machinery. Their results show the degree of competitiveness of the respective markets and then use these results to evaluate the likely effects of a customs union between Turkey and the European Union.

Chapter 7 by Zonooz examines three hypothesized harmful effects of Iran's continuing reliance on oil exports combined with Import Substituting Industrialization (ISI) long after these policies have been abandoned in much of the rest of the world. The first effect examined concerns the effect of ISI on progressively raising the foreign exchange requirements for its sustenance. The second effect concerns the allegedly deleterious effect of the protection offered to support ISI industries on static allocative efficiency. The third concerns the adverse effect of oil exports cum ISI on dynamic efficiency. Evidence for all three adverse effects is presented. While already evident in the pre-Revolution period, the non-sustainability of the oil exports cum ISI strategy has been rendered even sharper by both the choice of the Revolutionary regime to lower oil exports and the international isolation that Iran has experienced during much of the post-Revolution period. Indeed, the latter has increased the extent of rent-seeking behaviour and allocative inefficiency while at the same time depriving Iran of the technology transfer and institutional evolution that would have taken place in the absence of its increasing international isolation.

Part IV consists of two chapters focusing on three of the non-traded sectors mentioned above, namely, self-employment, the informal sector, and traditional agriculture. These sectors are quite naturally strongly affected by trade strategies and market reforms of various sorts and are of special importance as far as employment is concerned. Since these sectors are also ones where females are playing relatively greater roles in the labour force around the world, the focus in both chapters in this part is on employment, the organization of work, and female labour force participation.

In Chapter 8, Charmes provides a broad overview of female labour force participation, especially in self-employment and the informal sector across the countries of the MENA region. Some distinctly different patterns are found in different sub-regions and countries. For example, Charmes finds that, while most other MENA countries have experienced rapidly increasing female labour force participation, Iran and Turkey have not. Female labour force participation rates also vary considerably across countries of the region, being especially high for the lowest income countries of the region, followed by the Mashreq countries, and being especially low for the GCC countries with the highest levels of per capita income. While as in other LDCs, self-employment and informal sector employment have been growing rapidly in most countries of the MENA region, such growth has been slow in Iran and Turkey and has actually been negative in GCC countries. Contrary to the general pattern in developing countries, the increase in informal sector employment has not been due to that sector's feminization, implying that the increased female labour force participation in MENA countries has been solely attributable to the rising share of females in formal sector employment and especially that in the public sector. Although the data are rather weak, the only component of the informal sector in which the female share seems to be rising is in home-based work or 'putting out' work. Charmes points to very different sources for the explanation of the two areas of rising female labour force participation. In the case of formal sector employment, especially that in the public sector, the rising trend seems to be due to rising educational attainment of women and affirmative action programmes of government. But, in the case of home-based informal sector employment, the driving force seems to have been globalization.

In Chapter 9, Martini, Bailey, Jones, and Goldey take advantage of detailed field studies from north-western Syria to examine the changes in the agricultural labour force and the organization of labour. Agricultural production in this region has been influenced by several important changes, rising demand for off-farm employment of males, commercialization-induced changes in cropping patterns that have had the effect of intensifying land use throughout the year, and mechanization, which has decreased the need for male labour for heavy work, allowing female labour to be substituted for male labour in many but not all tasks. The increasing specialization and differentiation of tasks has also induced different modes of labour use to emerge, some of it in groups or labour gangs.

Part V consists of three chapters that deal with the aforementioned relationships between international conflicts and integration, political and economic boundaries, and the sources of changes in economic boundaries and the problems therein. These issues are, of course, of special relevance and importance for the MENA region. Chapters 10 and 11 focus on boundary issues (Kuwait and Palestine), Chapter 12 on the economic challenges posed by genuine integration efforts (Turkey), and Chapter 13 on those posed by those integration efforts that are 'less than genuine', meaning that not all pre-conditions for genuine integration have been satisfied (Palestine).

In Chapter 10, Pfeifer discusses the effects of the 1990–1 Gulf War on the Kuwaiti economy. Historically, Kuwait's economic dilemma has revolved around the need to diversify its economy away from oil exports without losing its cultural and social integrity. Painful and costly as Iraq's invasion and occupation of Kuwait was in 1990, the crisis and subsequent liberation offered the Kuwaiti government and its people a unique opportunity to reinvigorate their economy and to creatively redefine their external and internal economic boundaries. However, Pfeifer argues that the policies pursued in the decade after liberation neither achieved these goals nor restored sustainable economic growth. Instead, Kuwait has intensified its current and future dependence on the oil sector and on the United States, adjusting its external boundaries to accommodate this policy choice. Furthermore, it has rigidified its internal social boundaries instead of relaxing them as part of a reform that might have diversified the economy and enhanced non-state economic activities.

She further argues that the resolution of Kuwait's economic dilemma may require a paradigm shift in economic thinking, involving a fundamental redefinition of external and internal economic boundaries. Externally, a return to the model of Kuwait's more diversified pre-oil economy, and a more balanced and healthy relationship to the world economy than it has experienced during 1991–2001, may entail deeper and more extensive regional economic integration than the GCC can provide. Internally, the key to promoting development on both the demand and supply sides of the domestic growth equation, and indeed securing Kuwait's integrity, may entail the Kuwaitization of persons rather than jobs; that is, a reversal of the policy toward expatriate labour extant since the mid-1980s.

Farsakh in Chapter 11 demonstrates that, when one country has the ability to unilaterally impose non-tariff barriers to both internal and external factor mobility on its integration partner, the result can be rather catastrophic for the welfare of the partner. In particular, she demonstrates the enormous differences in effective integration between the Palestinian territories of the West Bank and Gaza Strip (WBGS) between the pre-1990 and post-1990 periods. In the former, while there was almost no progress toward political settlement, product and labour markets were both relatively open between the WBGS and Israel. The WBGS ran a trade deficit that was financed largely by its growing supply of surplus labour to the Israeli labour market. The economies of both entities grew quite rapidly. Yet, with the advent of the peace process throughout much of the 1990s, labour flows dropped off and especially recently have become extremely volatile, varying with the whims of Israeli decision-makers, border guards, and the *intifada* clashes. At a time in which Palestinians had become heavily dependent on Israel for disposing of their surplus labour, Israel prevented Palestinian workers from entering Israel and even from moving from one place to another within the WBGS. The result was an increase in the unemployment rate among Palestinian workers to over 28 per cent and a reduction in per capita WBGS GDP by some 27 per cent in 2001 alone (and reportedly even further more recently).

As indicated above, one of the major trade-liberalization initiatives facing MENA countries is the prospect of forming customs unions or even full integration with the European Union. Chapter 4 paid some attention to the implications of this for the MENA region in general in the case of agricultural trade and Chapter 2 looked at the potential trade impacts of a customs union with the European Union compared to, or in addition to, one among MENA countries. Neither of these chapters paid much attention to the several problems that MENA countries would have to address in order to take advantage of such an opportunity. In Chapter 12, however, after identifying some of the substantial benefits of full integration with the European Union, Togan identifies in considerable detail the challenges that would have to be met for Turkey to achieve its current goal of full integration with the European Union. He argues that the greatest difficulties are likely to arise from adoption of the Common Agricultural Policy, the liberalization of services, the attainment of macroeconomic stability, and meeting the stringent environmental standards of the European Union.

Chapter 13, by Kanafani, picks up where Farsakh leaves off with regard to the relationship between the peace process and economic integration between the WBGS and Israel. Kanafani's focus is on that part of the Oslo Peace process that involves economic relations between Israel and WBGS. While many have blamed the failure of the peace process on implementation failure, Kanafani suggests that the failure was more fundamentally a design failure. For peace to succeed, he argues that the economic relations would have to foster mutual prosperity and a more fair distribution of the benefits of peace and integration.

Because the political design was obscure, partial, and temporary, so too were the blueprints for economic relations. The result was a high degree of uncertainty that undermined the process. Disputes on the economic side proliferated and complicated the resolution of political disputes. The basic outcome was a failure to allow Palestinians to prosper under the arrangements. This failure is attributed to four more specific failures: (i) inability to prevent Israel from unilaterally cutting off its labour market to Palestinian workers; (ii) the absence of an independent enforcement mechanism or means of arbitrating disputes arising during implementation; (iii) a trade regime that was at the same time unnecessarily complex in its structure, imprecise, and unfair; and (iv) the absence of any mechanisms for redistributing unequal gains from integration.

Starting from their unequal levels of development, there were two mutually re-enforcing flaws in the system. First, the uncertainties about product markets and the future economic prospects in the WBGS undermined the incentives for investment in the WBGS that might have attracted funds from Israel and abroad. Second, the failure to prevent Israel from closing its labour markets to Palestinian workers increased Palestinian unemployment and lowered disposable income, undermining the viability of many economic activities and causing a serious economic depression. These effects have bred resentment and desperation among the Palestinian masses. Hence, according to Kanafani, the only way for peace to be achieved is to satisfy the aforementioned prerequisites for satisfactory economic relationships.

All in all, we hope that the depth and breadth of the contributions in this volume – as outlined above – will be a welcome addition to the ongoing debates on economic development and integration in the MENA region at a time when the challenges the region faces show no sign of relenting.

Part I

Past trends and future prospects for growth in MENA

1 Reform and elusive growth in the Middle East – what happened in the 1990s?*

Dipak Dasgupta, Jennifer Keller, and T. G. Srinivasan

1 Introduction

Achieving faster economic growth is a major economic objective and undertaking economic reform provides a main rationale for attaining this objective. The 'Washington consensus' of the early 1990s has long advocated a certain set of core reforms as essential in a rapidly globalizing world: minimum standards of macroeconomic stability, and structural reforms to foster openness and an appropriate investment environment. But since the late 1990s, questions are being asked as to whether these reforms are having their intended effects. Despite apparent reforms – albeit not to the same extent in all countries and areas – the growth performance of many developing countries and regions has often been disappointing. Countries in the Middle East and North Africa (MENA) region are no different in their experiences with reform and growth in the past decade.

The political and social implications of reforms and the expected economic growth outcomes are crucial to the success of reform efforts. This is especially critical in the MENA region because of its prevailing unemployment problem. The region's labour force has grown by about 2.8 per cent a year in the 1990s – roughly the highest rate in the world – while job opportunities have been lagging. Although rapid labour force growth can be a 'demographic gift' in the right circumstances, it can also create enormous social problems in the face of lagging job opportunities. Formal unemployment rates in the region (outside of the Gulf Cooperation Council or GCC countries) now average close to 25 per cent, the second highest in the world.[1] In some countries – Algeria, Iran, Syria, Libya, Yemen – as much as one-third of the labour force is unemployed. Even the GCC economies, with comparatively low unemployment rates of about 5 per cent on average, have begun to experience growing unemployment among their national populations. The absence of growth combined with rapidly rising unemployment has also coincided with falling real wages in the region – as is to be expected. Consequently, the crisis of growth in the MENA region since the 1980s has translated into an 'unemployment crisis', which could spill over into a larger poverty crisis (which the region has so far managed to avoid in most places because of the presence of formal/informal and implicit or explicit social safety nets). Unemployment often impacts young jobseekers the most, contributing to a potentially explosive social situation. Unemployment rates for those under 25 are about twice as high as national averages in Algeria and Tunisia, and as high as two and a half to three times higher in Lebanon and Iran. But this age group is also better educated; hence, unemployment may also potentially be a powerful force for change and a spur to further reforms.

In this context, the main purpose of this chapter is to understand the actual relationship, if any, between reform and growth in the MENA region, especially in the 1990s, benchmarked against the performance of other developing regions and countries. Since the large fall in international oil prices in the mid-1980s, most MENA countries have experienced a marked slowdown in their growth and/or suffered macroeconomic crises. This has forced the adoption of widespread economic reforms and restructuring (albeit to varying degrees) to re-establish stability and to diversify such economies away from oil and from a public sector to a private sector-led growth.

Yet, to many observers within and outside the region, the pay-offs in terms of accelerated growth in the region have been elusive. Regional Gross Domestic Product (GDP) growth averaged 3.2 per cent a year over the 1990s, higher than in the 1980s (2.7 per cent a year), but still not the rebound one might have wished, or expected, to see following a decade of stagnation. On a per capita basis, economic growth averaged less than 1 per cent a year.[2] Outside the Gulf economies, growth has been somewhat healthier, averaging 3.5 per cent per year, but remains weak on a per capita basis. This leads us to ask the following questions: Were the reforms inadequate? Were they directed at the wrong areas? Or does exclusive focus on reforms miss acknowledging some other vital ingredients for faster growth – such as improved governance, the role of market institutions, the end of conflict, and favourable geography? This chapter attempts to provide an evaluation of these broad questions.

The structure and principal conclusions of the chapter are as follows: Section 2 examines the relationship between oil prices and aggregate growth to set the context for understanding the factors that affect growth outcomes. Section 3 measures the actual reform effort and its intensity in the diversified economies of MENA. A variety of indicators are used to approximate the choice of policies and instruments (rather than outcomes, which are often wrongly used to measure policy effort). It will be seen that MENA countries have indeed undertaken sizeable reform efforts, but the main area of progress is in macroeconomic stability (expenditure reductions, lower inflation) rather than in core structural reform. In terms of structural reforms (trade policy, private investment environment), MENA countries are latecomers, with significant policy moves in this area only happening from the mid-1990s onwards. This applies to all of the countries we would classify as diversified economies (Morocco, Egypt, Tunisia, and Jordan), which are rated in the chapter as slow or gradual reformers.

Section 4 then turns to a detailed discussion of the sources of growth in MENA from an accounting perspective, and focuses on both trends in factor accumulation and total factor productivity, and their qualitative effect on the extent of reform undertaken. Four main conclusions emerge. First, reform has indeed had a significant growth pay-off, as average annual per capita growth switched from a negative −0.7 per cent in the 1980s to a positive 1 per cent in the 1990s – a swing or turnaround of nearly two per centage points. Second, virtually all or more of this has come from a dramatic turnaround in total factor productivity growth, which was a huge negative −2 per cent a year in the 1980s and improved to a small negative −0.3 per cent in the 1990s. In six out of the ten countries in the region, indeed, total factor productivity (TFP) performance improved relative to the world performance. Third, the principal reason that growth has still not taken off within most of the MENA region (from a supply-side point of view, and abstracting from the income effects of lower oil prices) is the collapse in factor accumulation, especially physical capital. Public investment has certainly fallen, as to be expected with fiscal adjustments. But equally, private investment has neither taken up the slack nor responded vigorously to reforms. In the 1990s, investment has declined dramatically, and without exception, across the region. Fourth, preliminary evidence using cross-country regression panel data including the MENA countries seems to suggest that the macroeconomic reform effort has had the greater positive (and significant) association with improvements in aggregate growth and in total factor productivity. By contrast, the 'Structural Reform Index' shows no significant or discernible impact so far. However, this work needs to be extended and examined much more carefully, before any definite conclusions can be drawn. Finally, countries that rank high on an index of sustained total factor productivity growth appear to be those that are successful in rapid diversification, openness, and macroeconomic stability, while countries at the bottom tend to be those that are relatively heavily reliant on primary resources, relatively un-diversified, and subject to larger macroeconomic volatility.

The findings in the chapter represent work in progress and should be seen as a contribution to more careful testing and analyses in future research and debates.

2 Oil prices and growth in the MENA region

Oil has an unusual degree of importance for MENA countries. Three different typologies can be constructed. The first consists of the core set of OPEC oil producers (Bahrain, Kuwait, Oman, Qatar, Saudi Arabia, and the United Arab Emirates – the so-called GCC states), whose economies are dominated by oil and whose objective function is arguably to maximize long-run oil prices and rents in global energy markets. The second comprises larger and more populous OPEC oil exporters (Iran, Algeria, Syria, and Iraq), whose economies are also dominated by oil, but whose objective functions are more diverse (in diversifying their economies away from oil). The third is the set of diversified economies (Egypt, Morocco, Jordan, Yemen, and Lebanon), whose oil exporting sectors are either relatively small or non-existent, but which are still relatively reliant on oil markets either directly as exporters or indirectly for regional export markets for traded goods or labour (worker remittances) and capital inflows from richer regional oil exporting countries.

Real oil prices (measured in $1990 per barrel) collapsed after 1985 and reached a new low in the late 1980s, before recovering modestly in the aftermath of the

1990 Gulf War (see Figure 1.1). Following that, oil prices again fell steadily during much of the 1990s, reaching a low in 1999 (of less than $10 a barrel). Only since the closing months of 1999 have oil prices recovered sharply, to reach $30 per barrel. Much of the period under examination has, therefore, been one of a dramatic fall in oil prices in real terms.

What has been the relationship between such trends in oil prices and regional GDP growth, differentiated by the three different typologies described above? For the region as a whole, the relationship is mixed, as shown in Figure 1.2. More precisely, during the 1970s until 1988 (the period when oil markets were heavily cartelized), it is possible to identify a counter-cyclical relationship – rising oil prices matched by falling GDP growth and vice versa. Since the late 1980s, though, that relationship has broken down and we see a shift to a closer positive relationship. But how far is this aggregate picture different according to the three types of MENA countries?

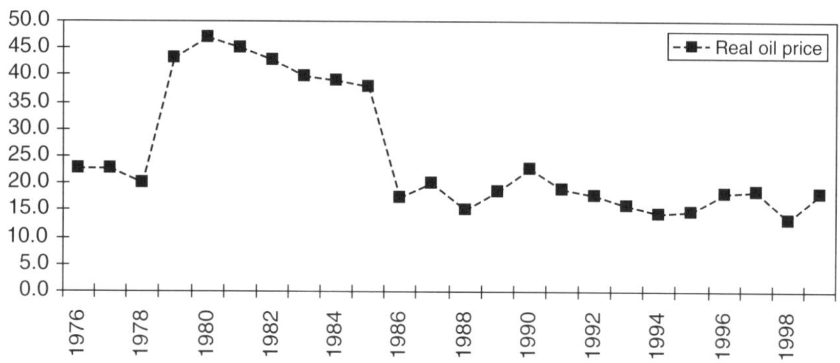

Figure 1.1 Real oil price (1990 $/bbl), 1976–2000.

Source: World Bank.

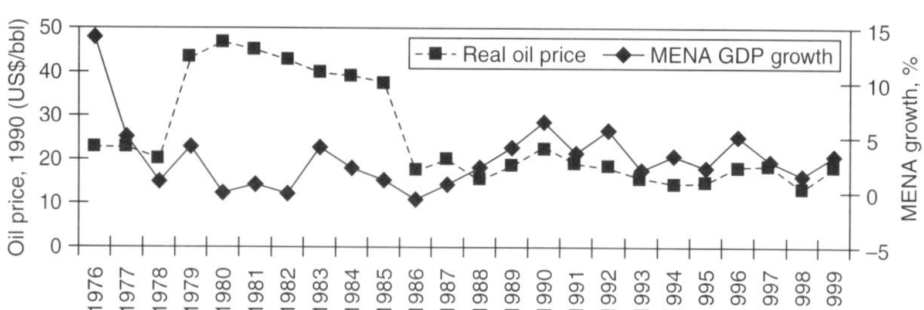

Figure 1.2 Real oil price and MENA growth, 1976–99.

Source: World Bank staff estimates.

Three separate patterns can be seen. First, GCC oil producers continue to exhibit the overall pattern, that of a counter-cyclical GDP growth relationship with oil prices between 1976 and 1988 – as would be expected since longer-term cartel producers restrict oil supplies (lowering GDP growth) to raise prices and vice versa. However, when the cartel is pressured beyond a point, they reverse, as is evident in the period since 1988 (see Figure 1.3). Second, for non-GCC oil exporters, there is a clear, close, and positive relationship between oil prices and GDP growth throughout, as higher oil prices permit faster growth and vice versa (and some free-riding on cartel behaviour, Figure 1.4). Third, for the diversified economies, falling oil prices caused collapsing GDP growth until the late 1980s, but since then, there has been a promising trend of disassociation between oil prices and GDP growth, with the latter picking up moderately despite a continuing decline in oil prices (Figure 1.5).

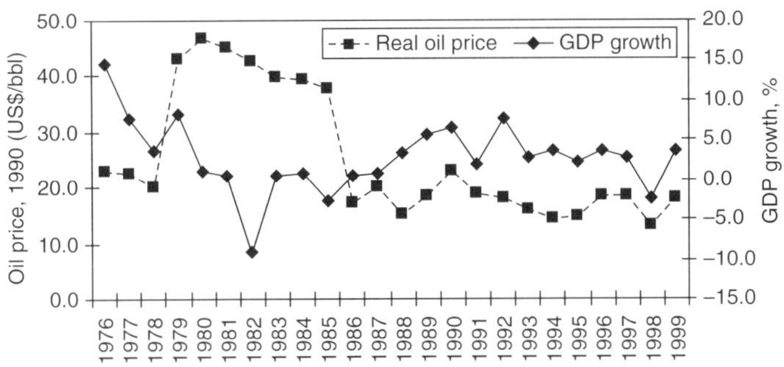

Figure 1.3 Real oil price and GCC growth, 1976–99.

Source: World Bank staff estimates.

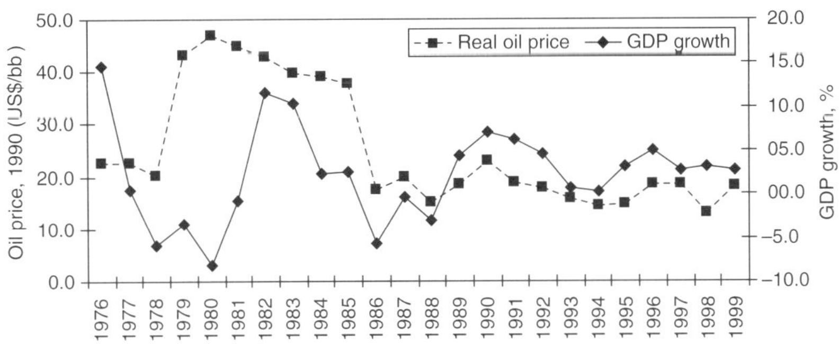

Figure 1.4 The correlation of oil prices and GDP growth in non-GCC oil producers, 1976–99 (Algeria, Iran).

Source: World Bank staff estimates.

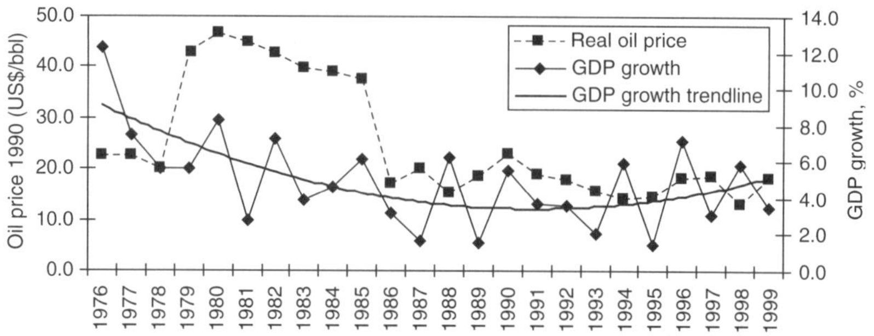

Figure 1.5 Oil prices and non-GCC diversified economies' growth, 1976–99.

Source: World Bank staff estimates.

3 Measuring reform effort in MENA

3.1 The framework

Nearly two decades after the start of structural reform programmes supported by the international financial institutions and the donor community, reaching a consensus on the effect of these programmes on growth has proven elusive. A critical step in such an evaluation exercise is the measurement of structural reform efforts. To date, there have been three broad approaches to measuring reforms. Initially, the early studies distinguished only between the presence or absence of structural reform programmes and proceeded to evaluate their effect on growth via 'with' or 'without' comparisons. Often, the researchers used the number of loans or scale of adjustment lending as indicators of the intensity of structural reform efforts (see McGillivary 1999 for a short survey of empirical methodologies for this approach). Unfortunately, even when used in an econometric regression to separate out the influences of external factors, these measures fail to adequately reflect the varying reform intensities in different countries, resulting in possibly differentiated payoffs. Later, outcome measures, under different components of reform programmes such as outward-orientation, came to be used, as these datasets are easier to assemble (e.g. Easterly *et al.* 1997). However, the outcome measures approach fails to distinguish between reform efforts by the government and the response of economic agents to these reforms. The response of the agents to reform inputs in itself is a legitimate object of study, and therefore a failure to distinguish between reform input and outcomes is a serious shortcoming. The third and last approach seeks to directly measure structural reform policy inputs, and this is the one we adapt for the current study. The earliest example of direct measures of policy reform efforts was in Agarwala (1983), which focused on price distortions in 31 developing countries by means of seven indicators in three areas of foreign exchange pricing, factor pricing, and product pricing. More recent research studies following this approach are listed, together with the indicators used, in Srinivasan (2001).

Identifying what constitutes structural reform is important for putting together a set of policy indicators that can be monitored. In broad terms, structural reforms can be defined as the set of policies that increase an economy's market orientation. Structural reforms are a large set of policies that came to be termed the 'Washington consensus' by Willamson (1990). Williamson provided a convenient overview of ten policy areas for *government action*. According to him, these can be grouped under 'macroeconomic prudence, outward orientation and domestic liberalization':

- fiscal discipline,
- public expenditure quality,
- tax reform,
- interest rate liberalization,
- competitive real exchange rate,
- freer trade,
- fostering FDI,
- privatization,
- deregulation,
- property rights.

Leaving aside macroeconomic prudence as the subject matter identical with macroeconomic stabilization, we are left with outward orientation and domestic liberalization as the two key components of structural reform. Research on construction of structural reform indices have implicitly followed the Washington consensus typology, but emphasized in greater detail particular sub-components and different weights to derive a composite indicator based on the developing country region under investigation. For example, Lora (1997) and Morley *et al.* (1999) emphasize financial indicators in their work on Latin America, while Dicks-Mireaux *et al.* (1998) and Bonaglia *et al.* (2000) in their work on Sub-Saharan Africa, and De Melo *et al.* (1996) on transition countries, stress public enterprise reform, price controls, and state intervention in marketing.

For the current study, in its initial phase, we have identified four components: Trade Policy, Tax Policy, Real Exchange Rate Overvaluation, and Privatization (see Srinivasan 2001 for more details). We opted for a parsimonious set of components because we wanted to assemble indicators for as many countries as possible with a view to comparing MENA countries with all other developing countries.

3.2 Progress of structural reform in MENA

MENA reforms were the last to start among the four regions of MENA, East Asia and Pacific (EAP), Latin America and the Caribbean (LAC), and South Asia (SA),[3] in the current phase of structural reforms, initiated in the mid-1980s.

MENA's reform index did not, accordingly, show a strong pick up until 1994, compared, for example, to LAC, whose reforms had a steady pace from 1985; EAP, where reforms gathered momentum after 1990; and South Asia, which witnessed dramatically accelerated reforms after 1990. Also, the pace of reforms has been slower in MENA than other regions. As a result, the regions ahead of MENA in 1985 (East Asia and Latin America) have raced further ahead as shown in Figure 1.6. Those who were behind MENA in 1985 (South Asia and possibly Europe and Central Asia) have closed in.

How representative is our Structural Reform Index for MENA? The MENA index used in the discussion below is the average of four reformers among developing MENA countries – Egypt, Jordan, Morocco, and Tunisia. Building a comprehensive picture of reform indicators for the rest of developing MENA (i.e. excluding high-income countries of GCC) is difficult. But the available reform indicator evidence on these countries suggests that their addition would not alter the force of arguments made in the current study for MENA. On trade policy reforms, for example, most recent available estimates of average import tariff rates for six developing MENA countries not included in this study (Algeria, Iran, Lebanon, Libya, Syria, and Yemen) amounts to 24 per cent (Oliva 2000). If measures of non-tariff barriers were also included then the excluded countries would significantly worsen the reform index as they continue to have very high non-trade barriers (NTBs), compared to the MENA economies included. In other dimensions of reforms, such as privatization (excluding the oil sector), or removal of price controls in the economy or taxation reform, the late reformers in developing MENA countries, such as Syria, Libya, or Iran, have a long way to go to catch up with the rest of the world. Therefore, we conjecture that if we include reform measures for all countries of MENA, the aggregate measure would look considerably worse.

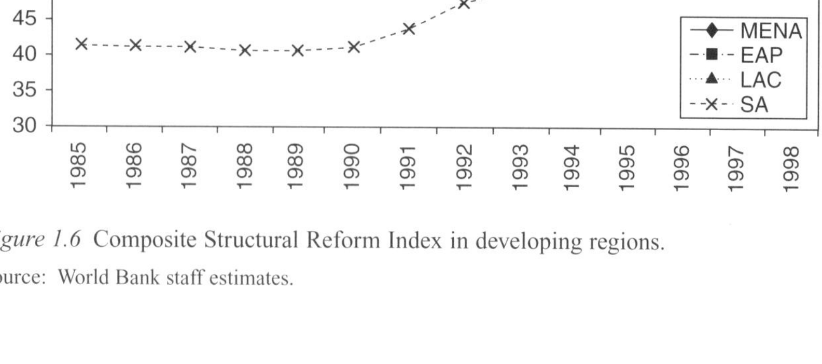

Figure 1.6 Composite Structural Reform Index in developing regions.

Source: World Bank staff estimates.

This weak pace of reforms in MENA is because of slow progress in all components of structural reforms, excluding real exchange rate overvaluation. With regard to trade policy reforms, measured by the un-weighted average tariff rate, the MENA region is the second worst among the four developing country regions, averaging around 24 per cent. The LAC region, which had a higher tariff rate than MENA in 1985, has cut it rapidly to about 10 per cent in 1998, marginally lower than EAP (Figure 1.7).

Tax policy is measured by two sub-components: highest marginal tax rates on individuals and corporations. In terms of highest marginal individual income tax rate, there is not as much divergence among countries in 1998 as there was in 1985. The MENA region has closed the gap considerably by bringing the tax rate down to 35 per cent, progress indeed as it used to be the highest taxed (57 per cent) region among the four regions compared (Figure 1.8).

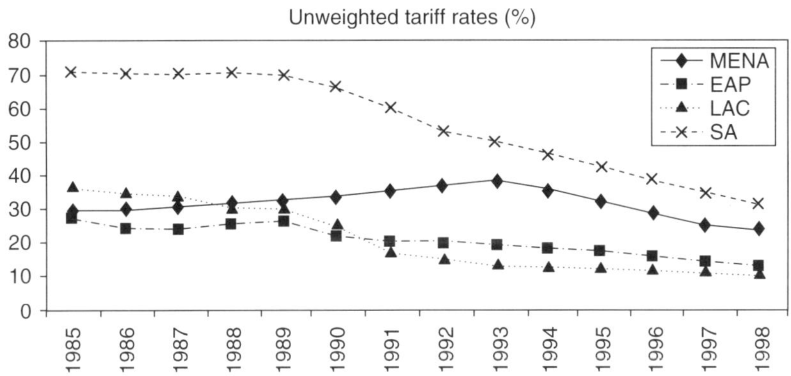

Figure 1.7 Comparative trade policy indicators among developing regions.

Source: See Appendix A.

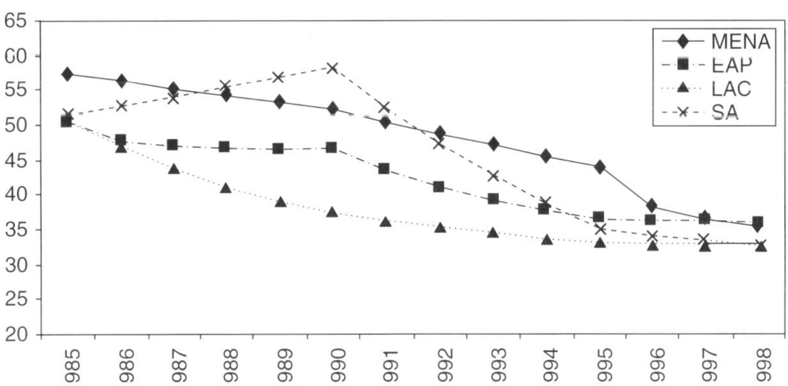

Figure 1.8 Highest marginal tax rate on individuals among developing regions (%).

Source: See Appendix A.

In terms of the highest marginal corporate tax, the MENA region continued to be the second worst in 1998, as it was in 1985 (Figure 1.9). Although for the region as a whole the index was on a declining trend, some countries like Egypt actually moved in the opposite direction until 1990. Only the LAC region has aggressively moved to match the 30 per cent corporate tax average in EAP.

In terms of privatization, measured by the cumulative privatization proceeds expressed as a ratio of GDP, the MENA region has made the least progress of all four regions, with its ratio averaging around 3 per cent in 1998, some 50 per cent below LAC (Figure 1.10).

In terms of real exchange rate overvaluation, as measured by David Dollar's overvaluation index (Dollar 1992), the MENA region compares well, exhibiting little overvaluation compared to the strong under-valuation noted in the case of

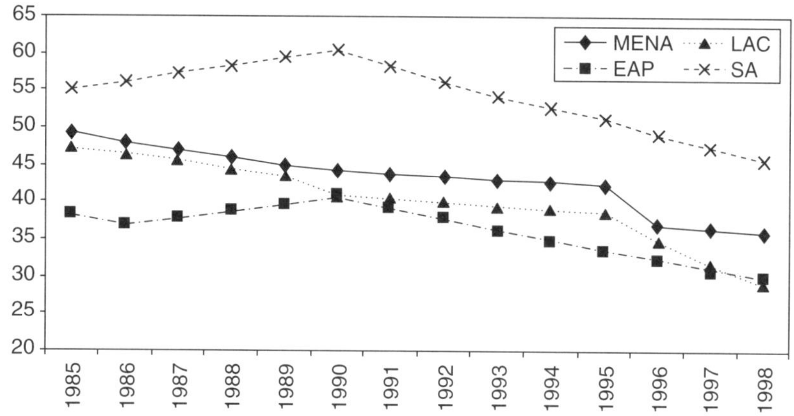

Figure 1.9 Highest marginal corporate tax rate among developing regions (%).

Source: See Appendix A.

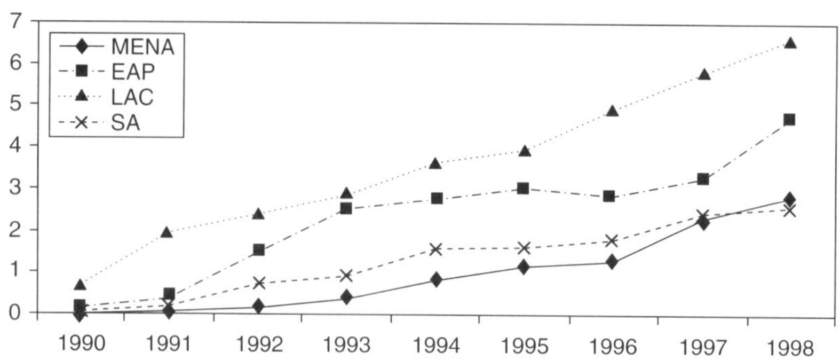

Figure 1.10 Privatization proceeds among developing regions. Cumulative proceeds from privatization to GDP rates (%)

Source: See Appendix A.

EAP or South Asia. However, good indicators of real exchange rate overvaluation are hard to come by, and the strength of MENA reformers (excluding Tunisia) in this regard does not accord well with exchange rate regimes dominated by fixed pegs to the US dollar for most of the period under investigation. However, an important conclusion to emerge from the comparison in movements of this index in Figure 1.11 is that the MENA region largely corrected the overvaluation episode that occurred in the late 1980s, while the SA region has remained relatively undervalued to both LAC and MENA.

How does the *pace of reform* in MENA countries compare, individually (as against the regional average discussed before) with others? The countries that are relatively advanced in this sense in the MENA region (Egypt, Jordan, Morocco, and Tunisia) are in the bottom two-thirds of all developing or transition countries in terms of their cumulative liberalization effort since 1985. Comparing countries keeping their starting positions on the reform index in 1985, MENA reformers can be classified as either gradual or slow reformers. Figure 1.12 shows the ranking of *change* in composite reform index between 1985 and 1998 for 27 countries across the developing world. Of the four reformers in MENA, two (Jordan and Tunisia) fall in the bottom third, and two (Morocco and Egypt) fall in the middle third.

Another way to compare the reform performance of countries is to track the pace of reforms against their starting levels and the average for all reformers. Table 1.1 makes such a comparison. Morocco started off as below average in 1985 and continues to be below average in 1998, falling under the group of 'slow reformers'. The other three from MENA (Egypt, Jordan, and Tunisia) had above average reform indices in 1985 but slipped below average in 1998 as they turned out to be 'gradual reformers'. Concerning the pace of reforms and growth outcomes, it is important to remember the additional factors that facilitate or disadvantage a country's growth performance. For instance, in some countries of the 'early reformers' group

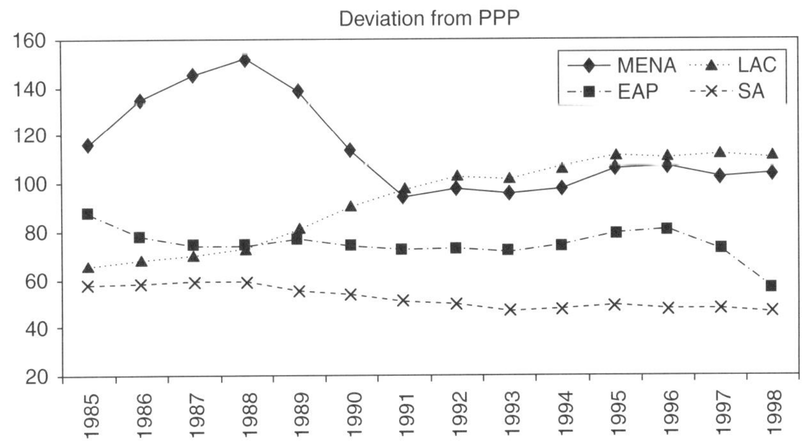

Figure 1.11 Real exchange rate overvaluation in developing regions.

Source: See Appendix A.

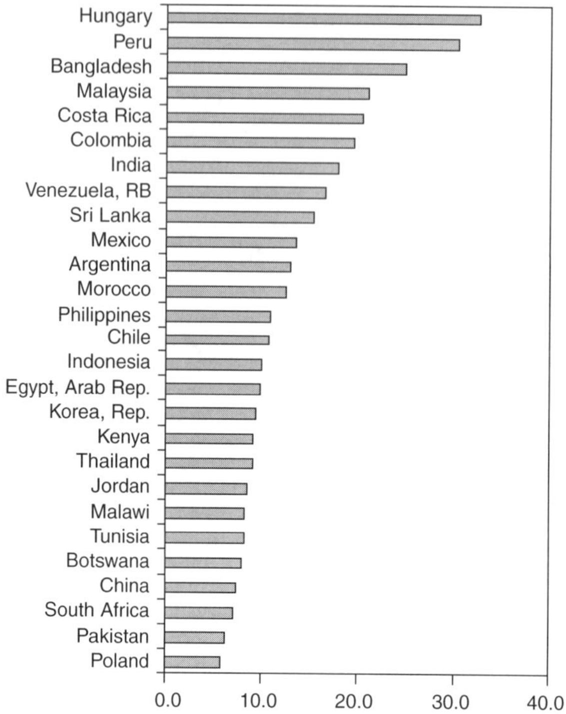

Figure 1.12 Change in Composite Reform Index, 1985–98.

Source: World Bank staff estimates; see Appendix A for Structural Reform Index (SRI).

Table 1.1 Pace of structural reforms in developing countries

		1998 Structural Reform Index level	
		Above average	*Below average*
1985 Structural Reform Index level	Above average	*Early reformers*	*Gradual reformers*
		Argentina	China
		Botswana	Egypt, Arab Rep.
		Brazil	Jordan
		Chile	Korea, Rep.
		Hungary	Malawi
		Indonesia	Poland
		Malaysia	South Africa
		Mexico	Thailand
		Philippines	Tunisia
	Below average	*Intense reformers*	*Slow reformers*
		Colombia	Bangladesh
		Costa Rica	India
		Peru	Kenya
		Venezuela, RB	Morocco
			Pakistan
			Sri Lanka

Source: World Bank staff estimates.

(such as Indonesia or Argentina) the weak financial regulatory environment has precipitated financial crises stripping away years of growth. Although Colombia, Peru, and Venezuela are counted among intense reformers, their weak performance possibly has its origins in weak governance. The varied growth performance of countries under the general group of 'gradual reformers' alludes to the strengths of spillover effects emanating from location in a region of dynamic growth or not. While the East Asian countries in this group – China, Korea, Thailand – or even Poland and Tunisia – reaped the benefits of location to major growing markets, Jordan and South Africa suffered because of slow-growing regional economies. Among slow reformers, a common characteristic appears to be their slow speed of integration with the rest of the world. India is an exception in the group, having achieved high growth despite the slow pace of reforms. It has benefited from the large size of its domestic market, which has undergone deregulation.

Contrasting the pace of reforms with the realization of real per capita GDP growth rates (Figure 1.13), we see a pattern that indicates that higher growth performance has largely been concentrated among gradual and early reformers.

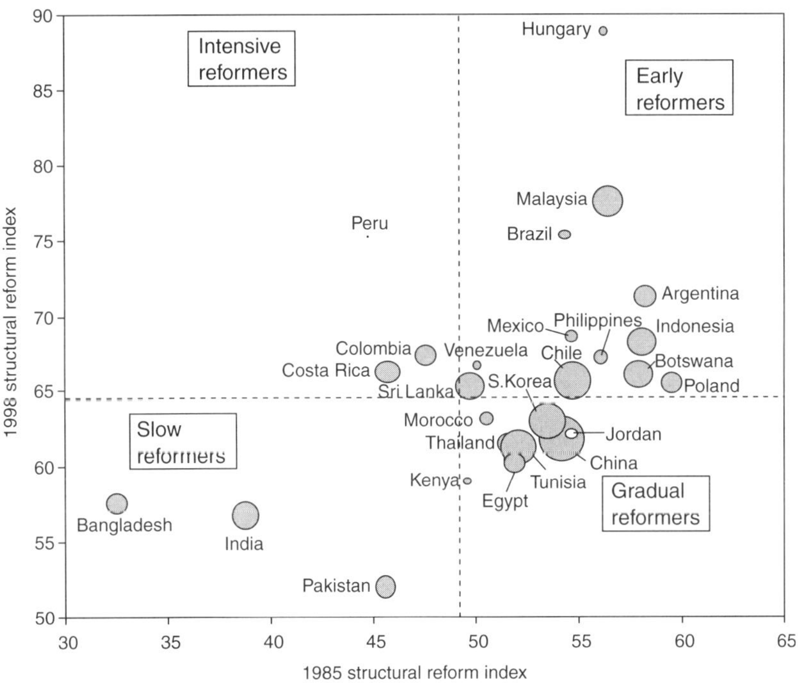

Figure 1.13 Pace of reforms and per capita GDP growth.

Source: Staff estimates based on own computations and World Bank Databases.

Note

The size of bubbles are scaled proportionately to per capita GDP growth rate. China has the largest bubble corresponding to its 8.2 per cent growth rate. Jordan has negative growth rates shown in inverse colour and is hidden behind China's.

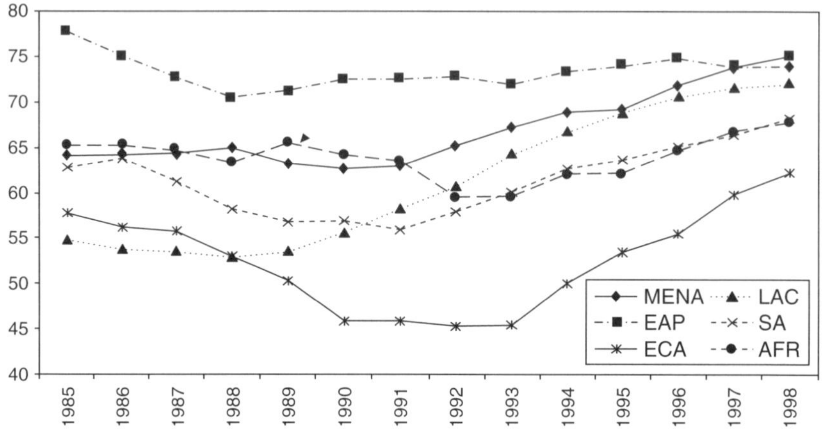

Figure 1.14 Composite index of economic stabilization by regions.

Source: World Bank staff estimates.

Note
LAC, Latin America and the Caribbean; MENA, Middle East and North Africa; EAP, East Asia and Pacific; AFR, Sub-Saharan Africa; ECA, Europe and Central Asia; SA, South Asia.

3.3 Positive signs

Although the preceding analysis of MENA's reform performance may sound gloomy, there are two positive signs that auger well for the strengthening of reforms and higher growth in the MENA region. First, MENA countries (the four reformers) have done very well in terms of economic stabilization, a prerequisite for reforms and a key component of the Washington consensus. MENA reformers have risen to the top position in the field of economic stabilization by lowering inflation, ending black exchange rate markets, and narrowing current account deficits. Figure 1.14 shows that the MENA region has maintained its good record of economic stabilization and has managed to move to the top position among all four regions – even edging marginally past East Asia.[4]

The second positive sign is that investor evaluation of the MENA region is responding favourably to the improvements in structural reforms. As shown in Figure 1.15, the institutional investor credit rating average for MENA countries (the same four reforming countries as used in the construction of Structural Reform Index) improved, in keeping with the acceleration of reforms since 1994.

4 Sources of growth in MENA

As indicated above, over the past decade the MENA region has taken a number of steps to overcome the macroeconomic imbalances and structural impediments that prevailed throughout the 1980s. Starting in the late 1980s, several countries in the region – Morocco and Tunisia, and soon after, Jordan – embarked on

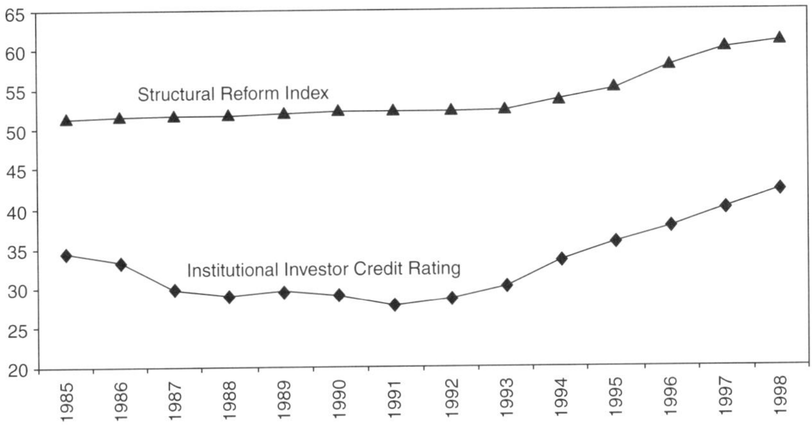

Figure 1.15 Credit rating improves with structural reforms for MENA. Structural Reform Index and institutional investor Credit Rating for MENA reformers.

Source: World Bank staff estimates based on institutional investor credit rating published twice a year in the magazine *Institutional Investor*.

far-reaching programmes of macroeconomic stabilization and policy reform. By the 1990s, nearly all of the non-GCC countries in the region had followed suit, as did several of the Gulf economies shortly after. While there has been considerable variance among economies in terms of both the speed and depth of these reforms, the overall change in policy throughout the region would seem to be a significant step forward in creating an environment in which the private sector can emerge and become an engine for higher and sustainable growth. The question remains, though, what has the more than decade-long process of macroeconomic and structural reform actually achieved to date?

A cursory examination of growth rates in the region over the last decade would appear to yield disappointing results. GDP growth over the region averaged only 3.2 per cent a year over the 1990s,[5] higher than in the 1980s (2.7 per cent a year), but not the rebound one that would have been desired following a decade of stagnation. Still, the *turnaround* in growth outcomes on a per capita basis is significant: from a negative −0.7 per cent a year to a positive 1 per cent in the 1990s (Table 1.2).

The decomposition of this growth performance between factor accumulation and productivity growth is also important. Indeed, a careful examination of the total factor productivity growth performance is especially important. As has been pointed out by Easterly and Levine (2001), the bulk of the cross-country differences in growth rates of GDP per capita are not the result of factor accumulation, but of differences in TFP growth. Decomposing accurately factor accumulation and productivity growth components is notoriously difficult. For the present study, Keller (2001) has undertaken a careful assessment, using other benchmarks, especially Bosworth *et al.* (1995; see methodology, appendix 1.2).

Table 1.2 GDP per capita growth over the 1980s and 1990s: MENA region

	GDP per capita (1995 US$)			*Average annual growth*	
	1980	*1990*	*1999*	*1980–90*	*1990–99*
Algeria	1,692	1,638	1,573	−0.3	−0.4
Egypt, Arab Rep.	731	971	1,194	2.9	2.3
Iran, Islamic Rep.	1,421	1,330	1,610	−0.7	2.2
Jordan	1,715	1,436	1,468	−1.8	0.2
Morocco	1,114	1,310	1,368	1.6	0.5
Syrian Arab Rep.	1,071	956	1,242	−1.1	3.0
Tunisia	1,641	1,823	2,394	1.1	3.1
Yemen, Rep.	315	315	281	0.0	−1.3
Bahrain	12,022	8,551	9,329	−3.3	1.0
Oman	3,509	5,581	5,900	4.7	0.6
Saudi Arabia	11,554	7,101	6,455	−4.8	−1.1
GDP per capita: weighted average	1,817	1,702	1,859	−0.7	1.0

Source: World Bank data.

Results: To check the consistency of our estimations with prior findings, we compared our TFP series between 1960 and 1990 with the TFP estimates of Bosworth *et al.* (1995), and found a high degree of consistency between the two series, with the relationship between the two series statistically significant at the 99 per cent level (Prob $\rho = 0 = 0.0001$) and a correlation coefficient of 0.93 between Bosworth's average TFP growth by decade and our TFP series.

In Table 1.3, estimates of TFP growth over the 1960–99 period are presented by region and decade. Prior to interpreting the TFP results for the MENA region, it is worth noting that our TFP growth estimates are, in general, low compared with others that have emerged in previous cross-country growth-accounting exercises. The TFP estimates are, in fact, highly sensitive to the assumptions underlying the production function, in particular the factor shares placed on capital and human capital. In the World Bank's 1993 study of *The East Asian Miracle* (Page 1993), for example, TFP growth estimates were based upon a factor share on capital of less than 0.2, which contributed to much higher TFP growth rates for all heavy-capital accumulating economies, such as the East Asian 'tigers' and the high-income OECD. On the other hand, as will be seen, the TFP estimates for the MENA region – in terms of country rankings, and in terms of the degree to which performance is above or below the world average – are relatively insensitive to such changes in assumptions. It is thus possible to speak about the region's performance relative to the world with some degree of confidence.

Our estimates of TFP growth for the MENA region over the 1960–90 period are largely consistent with previous findings: the region exhibited a pattern of high TFP growth in the 1960s, which declined dramatically over the 1970s and continued to decline throughout the 1980s.[6]

Table 1.3 Regional TFP growth rates, by decade

Region	*1960s*	*1970s*	*1980s*	*1990s*
Sub-Saharan Africa	0.1	−1.3	−1.3	0.0
East Asia and the Pacific	1.2	0.7	2.3	4.0
Latin America and the Caribbean	1.3	0.8	−2.4	−0.1
South Asia	0.0	−0.7	2.0	1.6
High income/OECD	1.7	−0.4	0.7	0.1
Middle East and North Africa	2.4	−1.4	−1.3	0.0
Early reformers	2.5	0.9	−1.0	0.0
Later reformers	1.9	−4.0	−0.9	0.4
GCC	4.7	−3.8	−4.5	−1.4
World average	1.1	0.0	1.2	2.0

Source: World Bank staff estimates.

Note
In the 1960s, the GCC figure reflects only Saudi Arabia. Regional averages weighted by population.

In the 1960s, MENA's per capita economic growth performance was the highest in the world, averaging 4.6 per cent per year. Fuelled by revenues from oil exports, worker remittances, and external financing flows, the region began a two-decade period of massive public investment in infrastructure, health, and education, which in this early period of development was able to translate into high growth. In addition to high levels of accumulation spurring growth, TFP growth over the 1960s was also high, with large-scale public investments in critical infrastructure generating a significant growth response.

In the 1970s, going by growth figures alone, MENA was still in the middle of a growth 'heyday', with GDP growth averaging 5.7 per cent a year. But the underlying conditions spurring growth in the 1970s represent a serious and negative departure from the previous decade of high growth and productivity. To begin, the 1970s was marked by an increase in the rate of physical capital accumulation per labourer of more than 60 per cent, and a near doubling of the rate of human capital accumulation per labourer. Over the 1970s, the MENA region realized the highest rates of growth of *both* physical capital per labourer and human capital per labourer. Despite this immense increase in accumulation, on a per labourer basis, growth actually declined, on average by close to 2 per cent a year. Thus, during the 1970s there were two large and yet conflicting growth dynamics for the region: investment was being undertaken at record levels (all things equal, increasing the region's growth potential), while at the same time these investments were increasingly experiencing poor returns, in terms of growth.

By the 1980s, as international oil prices slumped in the wake of global overproduction, these economic gains became unsustainable and the region's countries witnessed slow or even negative per labourer growth rates. With deteriorating macroeconomic balances and growing debt burdens, and despite heavy external assistance (which permitted high public expenditure for several more years), investments declined dramatically, with the rate of growth of the physical capital stock per labourer in the 1980s cut by almost three-fourths from the previous decade.

This decline in accumulation was almost without exception, with every country in the region but Kuwait experiencing a dramatic fall in this significant economic indicator between the 1970s and 1980s, and almost every economy experiencing a similar decline in TFP. Only Iran and Oman saw actual improvements in total factor productivity between the 1970s and 1980s. Negative productivity growth was most prevalent in the oil-producing economies of the region – both within the GCC economies as well as Algeria. Because our TFP estimates are a reflection of factor efficiency, the degree to which capital is underutilized will be heavily reflected in the ensuing TFP growth measurements. This feature is of particular importance for these economies, since as oil prices collapsed in the 1980s, there was a significant effort on the part of oil producers to prop up oil prices by restraining oil production. Nevertheless, even in the non-oil producing economies, widespread declines in productivity were witnessed in almost every country. With both massive declines in accumulation and corresponding declines in TFP for most countries, the MENA region experienced a collapse of economic growth per labourer (Table 1.4).

By the late 1980s, the 'lost decade of growth' prompted a handful of countries in the region – Morocco and Tunisia, and soon after, Jordan – to embark on programmes of macroeconomic stabilization and policy reform. By the 1990s, nearly all of the non-GCC countries in the region had followed suit, as did several of the Gulf economies. The reasoning, of course, was to create an environment in which the private sector could emerge and become an engine for higher and sustainable economic growth, crucial for employment creation.

How has the region fared in the 1990s? To understand the developments over the decade, we again turn to growth decomposition. In Table 1.5, we present the MENA region's changes in accumulation, productivity, and growth, relative to global changes, to evaluate how changes over the decade within MENA compare to the rest of the world. For clarity, the table does not present GDP and TFP growth over the 1990s, but rather the change in average GDP, factor, and TFP growth between the 1980s and 1990s (thus if an economy moved from an average GDP per labourer growth of 2 per cent a year in the 1980s to 5 per cent a year over the 1990s, the change in GDP growth per labourer over the decade is 3 per cent). Further, these growth rate changes are evaluated with respect to worldwide growth averages, in order to separate out the effects of changes in the worldwide utilization of capital or labour (global recessions or booms) from the MENA region's specific improvement in accumulation and utilization of capital and labour in the production process.

The countries are presented in order of the change to their average TFP growth per labourer between the 1980s and 1990s. Countries falling below the worldwide average growth of TFP of 0.75 per cent a year then appear below the worldwide figure.

Table 1.4 GDP per capita growth and growth of accumulation and productivity by region, 1960–90

Region	*Decade*	*Growth of GDP per labourer*	*Growth of physical capital per labourer*	*Growth of human capital per labourer*	*TFP growth*
Sub-Saharan Africa	1960s	1.8	3.8	0.4	0.1
	1970s	0.6	4.2	0.3	−1.3
	1980s	−0.9	−0.1	0.7	−1.3
	1990s	0.3	0.0	0.5	0.0
East Asia and Pacific	1960s	2.1	1.1	0.8	1.2
	1970s	3.3	5.3	0.9	0.7
	1980s	5.6	6.7	1.0	2.3
	1990s	7.5	7.8	0.6	4.0
Latin America and the Caribbean	1960s	2.9	3.1	0.6	1.3
	1970s	2.9	4.3	0.6	0.8
	1980s	−1.7	0.2	0.9	−2.4
	1990s	0.6	0.6	0.8	−0.1
High income/OECD	1960s	4.4	5.8	0.5	1.7
	1970s	1.8	3.6	1.4	−0.4
	1980s	1.8	2.3	0.3	0.7
	1990s	1.3	2.2	0.5	0.1
South Asia	1960s	2.2	4.0	0.6	0.2
	1970s	0.6	1.9	1.0	−0.7
	1980s	3.6	2.7	0.9	2.0
	1990s	2.9	2.1	0.8	1.6
MENA	1960s	4.6	4.9	0.5	2.4
	1970s	2.6	7.9	1.5	−1.4
	1980s	0.4	2.1	1.4	−1.3
	1990s	0.7	−0.3	1.2	0.0
World	1960s	2.7	3.2	0.6	1.1
	1970s	2.2	4.1	1.0	0.0
	1980s	3.2	3.8	0.8	1.2
	1990s	4.0	4.1	0.7	2.0

Source: World Bank staff estimates. Regional averages weighted by population.

Table 1.5 lists, using an easily understood presentation, the extent of improvements that have occurred for the MENA economies, relative to the world. At the top of the list of improved productivity growth is Syria, which in the 1990s benefitted from both improved oil production and agricultural performance, and an aid windfall during the Gulf War (this allowed it to undertake key growth-enhancing infrastructure investments, such as the purchase of power stations and a telephone network). Three of the four countries we have termed the 'early reformers' (Jordan, Tunisia, and Egypt) also experienced better than average increases in average TFP growth between the 1980s and 1990s (and greater improvement in TFP growth than was experienced in the United States).

Table 1.5 Change in MENA's growth and TFP growth between the 1980s and 1990s

Country	*Change in average GDP growth per labourer*	*Change in average factor accumulation growth per labourer*	*Change in TFP growth*
Syria	2.54	−3.06	4.24
Jordan	1.07	−6.27	4.00
Saudi Arabia	5.69	5.20	3.77
Kuwait	9.11	7.64	2.17
Egypt	−0.99	−5.65	1.67
Tunisia	0.84	−1.45	1.37
Iran	0.88	−0.57	0.97
Algeria	−0.92	−3.80	0.88
Worldwide	0.74	0.24	0.75
Morocco	−1.23	−1.35	−0.77
Oman	−4.10	−3.33	−3.08

Overall, TFP growth in the region actually improved in all but two economies (Morocco and Oman), and on a relative basis, TFP performance improved relative to the rest of the world in eight out of the ten countries in the sample.

At the same time, however, due to large declines in accumulation within most of MENA (larger than average global changes in the growth of factor accumulation), the change in relative GDP growth (to the world) has not reflected the large improvements in factor allocation and efficiency (e.g. Jordan, Egypt, and Tunisia).

It is difficult to definitively interpret the substantial declines in accumulation throughout the 1990s. Public sector investments have certainly dropped off. So, in the midst of an overall factor accumulation deterioration, it could be that private sector factor accumulation is actually improving. However, it is more likely that while productivity and factor allocation efficiency has improved significantly over the 1990s, it has failed to generate a comparable private sector investment response. Country studies on the private investment response in Jordan, Egypt, and Morocco, for example, suggest weak recovery in private investment. Yet, there are also signs in some countries, such as Jordan, that private investment is shifting slowly towards traded goods sectors and away from non-traded areas such as construction, which augurs better for the future.

It is beyond the scope of this chapter to adequately analyse why the reform process, which has clearly produced an impact on the region's productivity, has failed to generate a private sector investment response in the external-oriented sectors. However, the literature on growth modelling is focusing increasingly on the role of institutions on growth (e.g. Hall and Jones 1998, Mauro 1995). Institutional factors – such as the degree of regulation, red tape, and corruption of the government – have become ever more recognized as critical factors that can either hasten or obstruct sustained economic growth.[7]

To accurately diagnose the continuing fall in MENA's factor accumulation would require a detailed analysis of the changes to both public and private investments, information that is generally lacking in the region. On the other hand, getting a grasp of the specifics behind the investment collapse within MENA might be invaluable in enabling the comprehensive macroeconomic and structural reform agenda the region has adopted to generate a more dynamic growth response.[8]

5 Conclusion

The growth performance of MENA countries reviewed in this chapter suggests that reforms in MENA remain very much a half-finished business. Reforms have clearly begun but most MENA countries are late reformers and continue to lag compared to other countries' and regions' performances. It is difficult to distinguish the effects of reforms but they may have at least contributed to reversing the large total factor productivity losses of the 1970s and 1980s. But the private investment response has been lagging and understanding the reasons behind it is a priority. For structural reform to have an effect, a strong private investment response and its redirection to the traded goods sector is essential. To understand that process, we need to devote attention to certain other questions that we do not understand well yet: factors affecting the private investment response, the export diversification response, and the geography factor (regional conflict and prospects for peace). These will be critical in our understanding of why faster growth continues to elude most countries in MENA – as indeed most other middle-income countries – despite their reform efforts. This should now form the main agenda of research on growth in these countries.

Appendix A: data sources for construction of the Structural Reform Index

1. The data for privatization receipts are taken from *World Development Indicators*.
2. The data for tariffs are taken from (i) *Trade Policy Review* (WTO) for various years and countries; (ii) *Trade Policy Reform in Developing Countries since 1985* (World Bank Discussion Paper no. 267), (iii) *Jordan: Policies and Prospects for Small and Medium Scale Manufacturing Industries* (World Bank Publication Report no. 6848-jo); and (iv) *Jordan: Strategy for Adjustment and Growth* (IMF, Occasional Paper, no. 136).
3. For individual and corporate taxes, we used (i) *Price Waterhouse Coopers*, Coopers & Lybrand Global Tax Network and (ii) *International Tax Summaries*, Deloitte Touche. Tohmatsu International, Syria, is used supplementarily.
4. The data for real exchange rate deviation from Purchasing Power Parity (PPP) are originally from Dollar (1992) extended to 1999 by research staff and downloaded from http:// www.worldbank.org/research/growth/GDNdata.htm#1

Methodology

1 The Structural Reform Index (SRI) consists of five sub-indices, that is, simple mean tariff rates, cumulative privatization receipts to GDP ratios, highest marginal corporate tax rates, highest marginal individual tax rates, and real exchange rate deviation from PPP. The composite index is built by assigning weights, one-fourth, one-fourth, one-eighth, one-eighth, and one-fourth, respectively.
2 For exchange rates' deviation from PPP, any differences from 100 are treated as equal, whether positive or negative.
3 All the data are normalized by the formula as below:

$$X_{ij} = (W - V_{jt})/(W - B)$$

Where W is the worst value for all years in all countries, V_{jt} is the value of country j in year t, B is the best value for all countries in all years, and X_{ij} is the normalized value j for year t.

The best and worst benchmarks for the raw indicators before normalization are shown below:

	Best		*Worst*	
IT	Bahrain	0.0	Thailand	85.0
CT	Nicaragua	0.0	Iran	75.0
TAR	Bulgaria	1.5	Bangladesh	106.6
PRV	Hungary	26.9	Multiple countries	0.0
PPP	ECA 4 countries	0.0	Nicaragua	5,426.6

Notes
IT highest marginal income tax rate on individuals.
CT highest marginal income tax rate on corporations.
TAR average un-weighted tariff rate on imports.
PRV cumulative privatization proceeds as a ratio of GDP.
PPP deviations from PPP exchange rate.

Appendix B: measuring factor accumulation and TFP growth contributions to aggregate growth

TFP growth estimates were made utilizing panel data of capital stock accumulation, human capital stock accumulation, and GDP growth from 1960 to 1999. Estimates of the physical capital stock for a sample of 83 economies from 1960 to 1990 come from Nehru and Dhareshwar (1993). This was created by a perpetual inventory method for investment rates for 1950 onward, with initial assumptions about the capital/output ratio and a common fixed annual geometric depreciation rate of 0.04. These capital stock data were extended to 1999 using the growth rates of constant price local currency investment from the World Bank's World

Development Indicators' database,[9] and applying similar assumptions on the depreciation rate. Capital stock estimates for another 12 economies, including four economies in the MENA region of particular interest to us, were created according to a similar methodology, using investment rates from 1960 onwards. Since we will estimate GDP growth using a panel regression approach over 10-year periods, the sample was restricted to those economies in which the capital stock could be estimated for the full 1960–99 period. This was necessary both to maintain a balanced panel, and to reduce the importance of the assumption about the initial stock in the period of analysis of particular importance to us (the 1990s).

Real GDP in constant local currency also comes from the World Bank data. The human-capital-augmented labour stock was estimated, using both labour force estimates as reported by the International Labour Organization, from the World Bank database, and estimates of the educational attainment of the adult population from Barro and Lee (2000). The functional form of human capital augmented labour has been assumed as

$$H = Le^{(r \cdot S)}$$

where L is the labour force and S the average years of schooling of the adult population, and r is the rate of return to schooling. According to international evidence, a reasonable approximation of that rate of return is 10 per cent, which we have assumed for the purposes of our analysis.

TFP growth was calculated over 10-year periods for the period 1960–99, rather than on an annual basis, to minimize the error that is inherent in current capital stock measurements. National accounts would attribute any investment expenditures made over the year, even the last day of the year, to that year's capital stock. However, it is unlikely that that investment expenditure would contribute to economic growth immediately; rather it would contribute to potential growth in the future. To reduce this lag-effect that physical capital exhibits, we calculated TFP growth based on 10-year averages. We allowed for slight variations in the years counted within a decade for both Iran and Kuwait, in order to minimize the very large impacts that came from both the Iranian revolution (which took place in 1979) and the Gulf War. For every other country in the sample, the decade of the 1970s reflects the period from 1970 to 1980 inclusive, but for Iran, it reflects 1970–9. Further, while the decade of the 1980s reflects 1980–90 for all other countries in the sample, for Iran it reflects 1979–90 – thus, 1979 data have simply been moved to the next decade's data. In Kuwait, while we have kept the decade information consistent with the rest of the sample, we removed the years 1989–92 from the analysis. Both decisions were made in an effort to make the information as much a reflection of the decade as possible. In Iran, for example, using unaltered data, the simple fact that the revolution came at the end of the decade could mask what we really would like to establish – that is, how the economy was performing throughout the 1970s (the 1980s, marked by the effects of the revolution and the Iran–Iraq war, are thus fully reflected in the 1980s). Both small changes to the dataset were made not to mine the data in any fashion, but only to better serve our purpose of evaluating the country's growth, accumulation, and productivity. Production was assumed to follow a Cobb–Douglas specification with constant returns to scale between physical and human-capital-augmented labour:

$$Y_t = A_t K_t^{\alpha} H_t^{(1-\alpha)}$$

where Y is the output, A is an index of total factor productivity, and K and H are the stocks of physical and human-augmented labour, respectively. Dividing both sides by the work force, taking logs, and first-differencing, growth of output per worker can be related as follows:

$$\ln(y_i/y_{i-1}) = \alpha \ln(k_t/k_{t-1}) + (1-\alpha)\ln(h_t/h_{t-1}) + \ln(A_t/A_{t-1})$$

To determine the coefficients on capital and human-capital-augmented labour, α and $(1-\alpha)$, the average annual rate of GDP per capita growth over the decade was regressed on average growth of physical capital per worker and human-capital per worker with a least squares trend over the entire period of available data (1960–99).

From our estimation, the elasticity of output of physical capital was estimated to be 0.49, somewhat higher than the average estimated coefficient from previous research, but within the range of accepted parameters. This may be due to the inclusion of several more developing countries than in the original Nehru–Dhareshwar physical capital stock dataset, made possible using World Bank data. At the same time, our purpose here is not to break new ground in measuring TFP, but to evaluate the region's performance in factor allocation and efficiency. Thus, we have calculated the TFP using three distinct methods of calculation of factor shares – $\alpha_k = 0.3$, $\alpha_k = 0.4$, and $\alpha_k = 0.5$ – to check the sensitivity of the region's growth performance to the assumptions made on output elasticities. Within the text of the chapter, TFP calculations are based on an elasticity of capital assumption of 0.4 across countries.

Notes

* The views expressed in this chapter are strictly the authors' and should not be attributed to the World Bank.

1 Unemployment in Sub-Saharan Africa is estimated to be about 25 per cent, but definitional differences make comparisons of unemployment rates across countries difficult.

2 The growth and per capita growth rates are weighted by population and refer to Algeria, Egypt, Iran, Jordan, Morocco, Syria, Tunisia, Yemen, Bahrain, Oman, and Saudi Arabia.

3 There are insufficient observations from 1985 to derive regional averages for ECA and Sub-Saharan Africa.

4 The composite index of economic stabilization is built using four components with equal weights: (i) fiscal balance as a ratio of GDP excluding foreign grants; (ii) current account balance as a ratio of GDP excluding foreign grants; (iii) inflation, as measured by a consumer price index; and (iv) black market premium on the exchange rate. The methodology and data sources are described in Srinivasan (2001).

5 Weighted (by population) growth and per capita growth rates for Algeria, Egypt, Iran, Jordan, Morocco, Syria, Tunisia, Yemen, Bahrain, Oman, and Saudi Arabia.
6 See Bosworth *et al.* (1995) for similar findings.
7 Surveys of existing enterprises and potential investors consistently rank the three elements of institutional capability – red tape, judiciary system efficiency, and corruption – as among the major factors determining the attractiveness of developing economies for new private investment (see, e.g. the Private Sector Assessments conducted by the World Bank for more than 40 developing economies).
8 Preliminary cross-country panel regression analysis was conducted to examine whether the reforms as measured by our indices have any statistically significant effect on growth performance and in TFP observed over the period in MENA. Although far from complete or robust, the very preliminary data and results seem to suggest some significant positive association between observed growth and TFP changes across all countries and in MENA with the macroeconomic stability index, but not necessarily with the Structural Reform Index.
9 In the case of MENA economies, where there were inconsistencies, the World Bank MENA regional database investment series was preferred.

References

Agarwala, R. (1983) 'Price distortions and growth in developing countries', World Bank Staff Working Papers, Number 575, Washington, DC: World Bank.

Barro, R. J. and J. W. Lee (2000) 'International data on educational attainment: updates and implications', CID Working Paper No. 42, Harvard: Center for International Development, Harvard University.

Bonaglia, F., A. Goldstein, and C. Richaud, (2000) 'Measuring Reform' in Braga de Macedo, J. and O. Kabbaj (eds), *Reform and Growth in Africa*, Paris: OECD.

Bosworth, B., S. M. Collins, and Y.-C. Chen (1995) 'Accounting for differences in economic growth', conference paper on 'Structural Adjustment Policies in the 1990s: Experience and Prospects', Tokyo: The Institute of Developing Economies.

De Melo, M., C. Denizer, and A. Gelb (1996) 'From plan to market', Policy Research Working Paper, 1564, Washington, DC: World Bank.

Dicks-Mireaux, L., J. Le Dem, S. Phillips, and K. Kochhar (1998) 'The policy record' in Bredenkamp, H. and S. Schadler (eds), *Economic Adjustment and Reform in Low-Income Countries*, Washington, DC: International Monetary Fund.

Dollar, D. (1992) 'Outward-oriented developing economies really do grow more rapidly: evidence for 95 LDCs, 1976–85', *Economic Development and Cultural Change*, 40(3): 523–544.

Easterly, W. and R. Levine (2001) 'It's not factor accumulation: stylized facts and growth models', *World Bank Economic Review*, 15(2): 177–219.

Easterly, W., N. Loayza, and P. Montiel (1997) 'Has Latin America's post-reform growth been disappointing?' *Journal of International Economics*, 43(3–4): 287–312.

Hall, R. E. and C. I. Jones (1998) 'Why do some countries produce so much more output per worker than others?' National Bureau of Economic Research Working Paper 6564, May.

Keller, J. (2001) 'Sources of growth in MENA', unpublished, MNSED, World Bank.

Lora, E. (1997) 'A decade of structural reforms in Latin America: what has been reformed and how to measure it', Inter-American Development Bank Office, Working Paper Green Series #348, Washington, DC.

McGillivray, M. (1999) 'Assessing the impact of economic liberalization programmes: a survey of empirical methodologies', in McGillivray, M. and O. Morrissey (eds), *Evaluating Economic Liberalization*, London: Macmillan.

Mauro, P. (1995) 'Corruption and growth', *Quarterly Journal of Economics*, 110(3): 681–712.

Morley, S. A., R. Machado, and S. Pettinato (1999) *Indexes of Structural Reform in Latin America*, Santiago: United Nations, Economic Commission for Latin America and the Caribbean.

Nehru, V. and A. Dhareshwar (1993) 'A new database on physical capital stock: sources, methodology and results', *Revista de Analisis Economico* 8(1): 37–59.

Oliva, M.-A. (2000) 'Estimation of trade protection in Middle East and North African countries', IMF Working Papers, WP/00/27, Washington DC.

Page, J. (1993) *The East Asian Miracle*, New York, NY: Oxford University Press.

Srinivasan, T. G. (2001) 'Measuring reform efforts in MENA', unpublished, MNSED, Washington, DC: World Bank.

Williamson, J. (1990) 'What Washington means by policy reform', in *Latin American Adjustment: How Much Has Happened?* Washington, DC: Institute for International Economics.

Part II

Integration patterns, trade blocs, and regional policy

2 Intra-regional trade integration in the Middle East

Past performance and future potential

Rania S. Miniesy, Jeffrey B. Nugent, and Tarik M. Yousef

1 Introduction

Recent trade initiatives in the Arab world and more generally the Middle East and North Africa (MENA) region have had different objectives: integration with Europe (the Euro-Med agreements), regional integration (the Greater Arab Free Trade Association or alternatively sub-regional integration), and even combinations of these two kinds of initiatives, such as the linking of Israel, Jordan, and Palestine with the United States. A common motivation for these initiatives is the perception that existing trade flows at the regional or global level are below what would normally be expected. The different initiatives, however, also reflect uncertainty as to which trade flows are most underdeveloped relative to what would take place in a less distorted world. Where existing flows are especially low in relation to their expected or 'natural' levels, trade promotion measures might be expected to be effective. On the other hand, if these flows are not comparatively low, this would imply that there is little potential for growth in trade and that trade promotion arrangements could prove ineffective.

The purpose of this chapter, therefore, is to seek answers to the following questions: Do MENA countries trade more or less with each other and/or with other countries than would be expected on the basis of the global patterns in trade? How effective have existing sub-regional arrangements been in stimulating trade? What factors might account for the observed deviation of actual trade patterns from the expected ones? What impact should policy makers expect from a full-fledged MENA-wide Free Trade Association?

We address these questions by examining the determinants of MENA trade flows from the perspective of a gravity model of bilateral trade patterns. The parameter values of the model are estimated on the basis of a panel of well over 100 countries for the years 1970, 1975, 1980, 1985, 1990, and 1992. Separate estimates are made for total trade, energy trade, and non-energy trade between each combination of bilateral partners. Additionally, separate sets of predictions are made based on alternative assumptions about future MENA trade patterns. The results show that in 1992 both intra-MENA and MENA trade with most non-MENA countries was quite low in relation to what would be predicted on the basis of the gravity model. While the influence of existing partial free trade arrangements among countries of the MENA region is shown to have been negligible or even negative to date, the creation of a Free Trade Agreement (FTA) among MENA countries comparable in strength to other FTAs is predicted by our model to more than double the level of intra-MENA trade.

The presentation is organized as follows: Section 2 provides historical background on economic integration in the region over the past 40 years; Section 3 reviews the patterns of MENA's trade and presents our empirical examination of the determinants of bilateral trade; Section 4 provides comparisons of actual trade patterns of MENA countries with those predicted by the model; Section 5 discusses the implications of the simulations; and Section 6 concludes.

2 The pursuit of economic integration in MENA, 1960–2000

2.1 Regionalism in MENA: old and new ideas

Greater economic integration in the Arab world has been a frequently stated policy goal and a yardstick for evaluating the achievements of Arab nationalism in the post-independence era. This has been reflected in numerous initiatives at the regional level and hundreds of bilateral agreements (El-Imam 1990). Similar aspirations have been expressed more generally in the MENA region, for example, among Iran, Turkey, and Pakistan in the Regional Cooperation for Development (RCD) and among Jordan, Israel, and Egypt following the signing of various peace agreements in the past two decades. One ambitious initiative was the Arab Economic Unity Agreement that came into effect in 1964. It established a Council on Arab Economic Unity (CAEU), which successfully negotiated the establishment of the first mini Arab Common Market (ACM), actually a partial free trade area among Egypt, Iraq, Jordan, and Syria as of January 1964, later joined by Libya, Mauritania, and South Yemen. However, Egypt's membership of both the CAEU and the ACM was suspended when the country signed the Camp David Accord with Israel in 1979. Borders between other member countries were also closed from time to time because of political frictions. The ACM was further weakened by a provision allowing member countries to list products to be exempted from the tariff and quota liberalization measures. Over time, the CAEU and ACM became less relevant and were essentially disbanded by the 1990s.[1]

The dramatic failure of region-wide trading initiatives led to new efforts during the 1980s at the sub-regional level. The most important of these was the creation of the Gulf Cooperation Council (GCC) in 1981 with Bahrain, Kuwait, Oman, Qatar, Saudi Arabia, and the United Arab Emirates. Another important sub-regional arrangement was the creation of the Arab Maghreb Union in 1989 with Algeria, Libya, Mauritania, Morocco, and Tunisia. Iraq, Egypt, Jordan, and Yemen formed an arrangement in the late 1980s that was later derailed by the Gulf War. Despite the extremely partial and incomplete implementation of trade arrangements among MENA countries (United Nations Economic Commission for Western Asia 1985), the proportion of regional trade in total Arab trade doubled between 1970 and 1985, and the intensity of trade integration increased markedly in a number of these sub-regional groupings.

More recently, the peace initiatives of the last decade provided hope that political stability, once achieved, would grant an additional stimulus to the spread of economic cooperation in the Arab world and elsewhere in the region. These hopes were further strengthened following the gradual liberalization of MENA trade regimes in the 1990s. But the biggest boost to economic integration in MENA came from outside the region – the Euro-Med initiative between the European Union and the southern Mediterranean MENA countries – and did not focus *per se* on intra-MENA trade. This initiative, which aims to create a free trade area in the Mediterranean region by 2010, has already resulted in the signing of a number of bilateral agreements between the EU and MENA countries.

Yet, because of continued protection of the agricultural sector by the European Union, the required dismantling of protection for manufacturing by MENA countries, who already suffer extremely high rates of unemployment, and the 'hub and spokes' character of the Euro-Med arrangements (Galal and Hoekman 1997, Abed 2000), these agreements are hardly seen as the complete answer to the development challenges of MENA. To counter the stagnation of intra-regional trade in the 1990s and given increasing recognition of the shortcomings of the Euro-Med agreements, Arab leaders agreed in 1997 to establish a Greater Arab Free Trade Area (GAFTA) by 2008. Beginning in 1998, the 18 signatories to this plan are required to lower bilateral tariff rates by 10 per cent annually. The time-frame for tariff reductions was subsequently shortened so that completion is now envisaged by 2004. Whether such plans can be any more successful than those in the past is by no means clear. Indeed, thus far, GAFTA, like the earlier ACM, has been weakened by the fact that each member state is permitted to exclude a certain number of both agricultural and manufactured products of its own choosing from the scope of the agreement (Zarrouk 2000a). The rapidly weakening prospects for peace in the region also do not bode well for GAFTA.

Notwithstanding the rapidly evolving policy framework for MENA's trading system and its aim for multiple objectives, research on the subject has been surprisingly limited. Specifically, the economic substance of existing research has tended to reflect the polarization of political views on MENA's trade policy. On the one hand, governments and policy makers in the region seem to take for granted the necessity of economic benefits from greater trade integration in the region even if the latter should come at the expense of multilateral trade initiatives. On the other hand, outside observers appear to discount the future role of regionalism, preferring to emphasize the benefits from global trade integration (Hoekman and Zarrouk 2000). As a result, positive economic analyses of the extent and potential of intra-MENA trade and the effects of existing arrangements have been limited to a handful of studies.[2] With a few exceptions, much of the recent economic research has focused on assessing the benefits and costs from multilateral (WTO) or cross-regional trade initiatives (Euro-Med) as opposed to those that emphasize intra-regional trade.

2.2 Why promote regionalism in MENA?

The lack of outside enthusiasm for intra-regional trade initiatives in MENA fits well with mainstream perspectives on regionalism. Traditionally, economists have been suspicious of regional trading blocs on the grounds that they may be inconsistent with the maintenance of a multilateral trade system because of their discriminatory nature and potential inefficiency (Bhagwati 1993, Bhagwati *et al.* 1999). Barring externalities, trade on an open, multilateral basis is generally believed to be welfare-improving: but the literature on regional trade arrangements (free trade areas and customs unions) has pointed to the distinct possibility that such trade can be welfare-reducing.[3] However, an important limitation of such studies is that they are static, not recognizing some important dynamic effects and some possible externalities.

Indeed, more recently, several developments have contributed to a more positive assessment of the benefits relative to costs of regional trading arrangements. Recent theoretical developments have suggested that regional trade arrangements may be much less trade-diverting and more trade-creating than generally hypothesized, when carried out in an environment of overall trade liberalization as in the 1990s (in contrast to past conditions of high protection) (Kemp and Wan 1976, Panagariya 2000). On the practical side, meanwhile, new efforts at regional integration, some including a number of the largest economies in the world, have been initiated with generally positive results. The most prominent initiative of this type was the creation of the North American Free Trade Agreement (NAFTA) between Canada, Mexico, and the United States and its possible extension southward. Among others, Bhagwati (1993) and Frankel *et al.* (1998) have debated the benefits and costs of these developments and thereby renewed interest in trade integration at both the regional and world levels. Indeed, NAFTA appears to demonstrate that trade creation outweighs trade diversion and that all member countries could share in the benefits (Al-Mashat 2000). ASEAN (an FTA and soon to be a customs union in Southeast Asia) and MERCOSUR (an FTA in the Southern Cone of Latin America) also seem to be more successful than some earlier failed efforts such as the East African Common Market, The Latin American Free Trade Association, and the Caribbean Common Market, to name but a few examples.[4]

Intra-regional trade has been shown to take the form of intra-industry trade seen in a more positive light in more recent years. Many analysts believe that greater integration among the Arab countries would bring important benefits in this respect. These benefits include greater efficiency on account of a larger market size and economies of scale. Integration may also promote a deepening of capital markets and foster foreign direct investment. Since equity markets of most Middle Eastern economies remain under-developed, one way to increase the supply of equity capital and deepen markets may be to accelerate the pace of integrating national markets into a larger regional market. Greater product variety would also enhance intra-industry trade by weakening the monopoly power of local producers. Finally, for some relatively non-industrialized and non-internationally competitive countries, a definition that covers many MENA countries, becoming successful in regional or even sub-regional trade may be viewed as a prerequisite to success or even the ability to survive in an increasingly globalized world.

In light of the renewed policy interest in regional trade within MENA and the changing perception of regionalism within the economics and policy community (Galal 2000), we believe it is crucial to provide a thorough assessment of the past performance and future potential of trade integration initiatives in the region. At a minimum, such an inquiry would provide an analytical characterization of the trends and constraints facing regional trade. More ambitiously, the analysis would shed light on the gains to be expected from the multiple objectives attached to trade policy in MENA countries, with a view to establishing policy priorities.

3 Trends and determinants of trade flows in MENA

3.1 Structure and size of trade in MENA

For the purpose of this chapter, the MENA region is defined alternatively as (i) the Arab countries of the region, based on membership in the Arab League (MENA1) or (ii) MENA2, which is MENA1 plus Iran and Turkey. The countries of both definitions of MENA share a great deal in the way of common histories and cultural characteristics but at the same time are diverse with respect to size, population, natural resource endowments, standard of living, and development trajectories. Some are primarily agricultural (Sudan, Syria, and Mauritania), others energy producing (e.g. Libya and the GCC members), and a few are industrial (Egypt and Morocco) or services oriented (Lebanon). In principle, this diversity of resource endowments could be expected to contribute to intra-regional trade.

Total exports by MENA1 countries were about US$130 billion in 1998. As shown in Table 2.1, over one-half of this went to industrial countries and another

Table 2.1 Direction of Arab trade, 1998 (in billions of US dollars)

	Exports		*Imports*	
	Value	*Share*	*Value*	*Share*
Industrial countries	72.3	54.0	113.8	67.5
Developing countries	61.5	46.0	54.9	32.5
Africa	4.0	3.0	2.8	1.7
Asia	39.0	29.1	26.4	15.7
Central and Eastern Europe	4.5	3.4	9.6	5.7
Arab countries	11.0	8.2	11.8	7.0
Western Hemisphere	1.7	1.3	3.3	2.0
Other	1.3	1.0	1.0	0.6
Total	133.8	100.0	168.7	100.0

Source: IMF *Direction of Trade Statistics*, 1998 Yearbook.

one-third to Asia. Imports totalled US$170 billion, of which about two-thirds were from industrial countries and another 15 per cent from Asia. The share of total trade (exports and imports of goods and non-factor services) in GDP has averaged around 50 per cent in the last three decades, allowing the region to score relatively high on the most common openness score (exports plus imports divided by GDP).[5] However, the level of trade integration rose in the 1970s, reaching a zenith around 1980, fell in the early 1980s, then recovered somewhat in the latter part of the decade but remained stagnant or has even declined since then (Nabli and De Kleine 2000). As a result, MENA's high share in total world exports and imports in the 1970s, which exceeded most developing regions including East Asia and Latin America, has fallen in the 1990s to a figure very close to the average for developing countries.

Intra-regional exports comprised some 8 per cent of total exports in 1998, a level that compares unfavourably with other regions. For example, intra-regional trade as a share of total trade is nearly 50 per cent higher in the Andean Pact countries than in the Arab countries, and seven times higher in the countries belonging to the European Union (Table 2.2). Moreover, the share of intra-regional trade has not grown in tandem with trends elsewhere and, in fact, fell in the 1990s. For example, while intra-MENA trade as a share of total trade increased – from 5 to 8 per cent – between 1970 and 1998, trade among the Andean Pact countries increased from 2 per cent of total trade to 11 per cent, trade among the Southern Cone countries increased from 11 per cent of total trade to 25 per cent, and trade among members of NAFTA increased from 36 per cent of total trade to over 50 per cent. Before it ceased to exist, the creation of the Central American Common Market had increased intra-regional trade of that small region from 2 per cent to some 25 per cent of total trade (Nugent 1974).

Table 2.2 Trends in intra-regional trade, 1970–98 (as a share of total exports in the region)

	1970	*1975*	*1980*	*1985*	*1990*	*1995*	*1998*
All Arab Countries	5.2	4.9	4.5	7.8	9.4	6.7	8.2
Arab countries, Iran and Turkey	6.0	5.8	6.1	8.7	10.8	7.2	8.7
Andean Pact Countries[a]	1.7	3.6	3.5	3.1	4.0	11.3	11.4
Australia and New Zealand	6.1	6.1	6.4	7.0	7.6	9.9	8.6
Southern Core Countries[b]	11.4	11.1	14.3	6.7	10.6	21.6	25.5
East Asian Economies[c]	19.2	21.3	22.4	20.7	20.7	26.4	22.2
NAFTA[d]	36.0	34.6	33.6	43.9	41.4	46.2	51.0
European Union	59.5	57.7	60.8	59.2	65.9	62.4	56.8

Sources: IMF *Direction of Statistics Yearbook*, various editions; and staff calculations.

Notes

a Colombia, Ecuador, Peru, and Venezuela.

b Argentina, Brazil, Chile, Paraguay, and Uruguay.

c China, Indonesia, Japan, Korea, Malaysia, the Philippines, and Thailand. Data exclude exports by Taiwan, Province of China.

d Canada, Mexico, and the United States.

The Arab countries can be conveniently divided into four sub-groups based largely on geographical location and production base, namely: the *Maghreb* countries (Algeria, Libya, Mauritania, Morocco, and Tunisia), the *Gulf Cooperation Countries* (Bahrain, Kuwait, Oman, Qatar, Saudi Arabia, and United Arab Emirates), the *Mashreq* countries (Egypt, Jordan, Lebanon, and Syria), and *other* countries (Djibouti, Somalia, Sudan, and Yemen). About 60 per cent of intra-regional exports – which totalled US$12 billion in 1998 – went to the GCC countries with another 25 per cent to the Mashreq countries. Beyond the Arab countries, Iran is more closely integrated with the GCC countries while Turkey is integrated within the Mashreq. Importantly, the proportion of trade within the four subgroups is significantly higher than the overall intra-MENA trade: nearly two-thirds of the Maghreb countries' exports to the Arab countries is with other Maghreb countries; three-fourths of GCC exports to the Arab countries is with other GCC countries; and one-third of the Mashreq's trade with the Arab countries is with other Mashreq countries (Table 2.3). Thus, most of the intra-Arab trade is also within the sub-regions, possibly suggesting that trade impediments are lower within the subgroups than for the region as a whole.

Table 2.3 Indicators of Intra-Arab Trade, 1998

	Exports by[a]				
	Arab countries	*Maghreb countries*	*GCC countries*	*Mashreq countreis*	*Other countries*
	Intra-regional exports, in billions of US dollars				
Export to					
Arab countries, *of which*	12.0	1.6	7.5	2.6	0.3
Maghreb	2.0	1.0	0.6	0.4	0.0
GCC	6.8	0.1	5.3	1.2	0.2
Selected Mashreq	2.6	0.5	1.2	1.0	0.0
Other	0.6	0.0	0.4	0.0	0.1
	Intra-regional exports, as per cent of exports to world				
Arab countries, *of which*	8.2	4 9	7.7	22.7	12.5
Maghreb	1.4	3.1	0.6	3.3	0.0
GCC	4.6	0.4	5.5	10.2	7.5
Selected Mashreq	1.8	1.4	1.2	8.6	0.1
Other	0.4	0.0	0.4	0.6	4.9
	Intra-regional exports, as per cent of exports to Arab countries				
Arab countries, *of which*	100.0	100.0	100.0	100.0	100.0
Maghreb	16.7	63.2	7.7	14.7	0.1
GCC	56.6	7.6	71.4	44.9	59.9
Selected Mashreq	21.8	29.1	15.6	37.7	0.8
Other	4.9	0.1	5.2	2.7	39.3

Source: IMF Direction of Trade Statistics, 1998 Yearbook.

Note

a Country groupings are – *Maghreb*: Algeria, Libya, Mauritania, Morocco, and Tunisia. *GCC* Bahrain, Kuwait, Oman, Qatar, Saudi Arabia, and United Arab Emirates. *Selected Mashreq countries*: Egypt, Jordan, Lebanon, Syria, and Sudan. *Other countries*: Djibouti, Somalia and Yemen.

3.2 Structure and size of trade in MENA

To address the central objective of this chapter, assessing past trends and future potential of intra-regional trade in MENA, we need a standard model of bilateral trade flows that will allow us to draw on the experience of the world for a reasonable period of time. The gravity model is especially attractive in this context because of its demonstrated applicability to many different kinds of countries and regions, its robustness over time, and to various different specifications.[6] According to this model, trade flows between any pair of countries should be affected by their mass (the product of their respective GDPs) as well as by the distance between them.[7] The latter is because transport and transaction costs can be assumed to rise with distance. Since factors such as exchange rate variability, common language, common colonial or other historical experience, common currency, free trade agreements, and having a common border can affect these transaction or transportation costs, all such variables can be included in the gravity model.

Recent papers by Frankel and Rose (2000) and Rose (2000) have applied the gravity model to bilateral aggregate trade flows for a large panel of 186 countries for each of the 5-year intervals between 1970 and 1990. We make use of this dataset but extend it in three important directions. First, we extend it in time to 1992, based on the international trade matrix for 1992 put together by the National Bureau of Economic Research (Feenstra *et al.* 1997). Second, we fill in several thousand observations that were missing in the original dataset with information from more recent standard international sources, especially for explanatory variables like country size, distance, and especially also for MENA countries whose coverage was rather patchy in the original data set.[8] Third, we extend it by disaggregating the trade matrices of each year from the aggregate flows constructed by Rose and colleagues into energy (specifically oil and gas flows) and non-energy subtotals.[9]

Following the recent literature, we specify the gravity model as follows:

$$\begin{aligned} \mathrm{Ln}(X_{ijt}) = {} & \beta_0 + \beta_1 \,\mathrm{Ln}(Y_iY_j)_t + \beta_2 \,\mathrm{Ln}(Y_iY_j/Pop_iPop_j) + \beta_3 \,\mathrm{Ln}\, D_{ij} \\ & + \beta_4 Cont_{ij} + \beta_5 Lang_{ij} + \beta_6 FTA_{ijt} + \beta_7 ComNat_{ij} + \beta_8 ComCol_{ij} \\ & + \beta_9 Colony_{ij} + \gamma Cu_{ijt} + \delta V(e_{ij})_t + \epsilon_{ijt} \end{aligned} \qquad (2.1)$$

where i and j denote countries, t denotes time, and the variables are defined as follows:

- X_{ij} denotes the value of bilateral trade between i and j;
- Y is real GDP;
- Pop is population;
- D_{ij} is the distance between i and j;
- $Cont_{ij}$ is a binary variable, which is 1 if i and j share a border;
- $Lang_{ij}$ is a binary variable, which is 1 if i and j share an official language;
- FTA_{ij} is a binary variable, which is 1 if i and j belong to an FTA;
- $ComNat_{ij}$ is a binary variable, which is 1 if i and j are part of the same nation;
- $ComCol_{ij}$ is a binary variable, which is 1 if i and j shared the same colonizer after 1945;

- $Colony_{ij}$ is a binary variable, which is 1 if *i* colonized *j* or vice versa;
- Cu_{ijt} is a binary variable, if *i* and *j* use the same currency at time *t*; and
- $V(e_{ij})_t$ is the volatility of the bilateral of the exchange rate between *i* and *j* in period *t*.

The source of the trade matrix data is Feenstra *et al.* (1997) for all years. This dataset is reported to cover 98 per cent of all international (broadly defined) trade. The 1970–90 values of the GDP at constant prices, distance, contiguity, common language, and other transaction cost measures are taken from Rose (2000) based on Penn World Tables (5.6), World Development Indicators, and other sources. The 1992 values for GDP, population, and other variables are taken from standard sources such as the *World Development Indicators*. Detailed sources for the earlier years are given in Rose (2000). The exchange rate volatility index was computed as the standard deviation of the first difference of the monthly natural log of the bilateral exchange rate (based on line ae from the International Monetary Fund's *International Financial Statistics* in the preceding 5 years). As in Rose (2000), the EEC/EC, NAFTA, EFTA, Australia/New Zealand, ASEAN, CACM, CARICOM, PATCRA, SPARTECA, Cartagena Agreement (Andean Group), and Israel/US Free Trade Agreements are all treated as examples of FTAs and hence signified by values of 1 in the FTA dummy variable. Significantly, Rose (2000) did not include any of the aforementioned trade arrangements among MENA countries as examples of FTAs. Presumably, this was because their importance was deemed too minimal to be treated on an equal footing with other arrangements.

As indicated by the form of Equation (2.1), the model is log-linear in the continuous variables so that the estimated coefficients represent elasticities, that is, percentage changes in the bilateral trade values with respect to given percentage changes in the continuous explanatory variables. The parameters of the dummy variables indicate the percentage change in the dependent variable attributable to a unit increase in the dummy variable (from '0' to '1'). The parameters are estimated by ordinary least squares (OLS).

Table 2.4 presents the results of estimating Equation (2.1) for total bilateral trade for each individual year and for the pooled sample. Beginning with the estimates based on the 1970 cross-section, it can be seen that, consistent with expectations of the gravity model, the effects on bilateral trade flows of the product of both the respective GDPs and GDPs per capita are positive and highly significant while the effect of distance is negative and significant. Similarly, all the transaction cost-reducing variables, such as currency union, contiguity, common language, FTA, same nation, same colonizer, and same colonial relationship, all have positive and highly significant effects on the sum of the one-way trade flows. In contrast, the effect of a transaction cost-increasing variable, exchange rate variability, is highly significant and negative.

With a few exceptions, the direction and significance of all the above findings remain the same for each subsequent cross-section. For the pooled results, the significance levels of all parameters are higher relative to the cross-sections. Indeed, rather remarkably, all coefficients are significant at the 1 per cent level in the

Table 2.4 Regression results from estimating the gravity model for total trade, 1970–92

	1970	*1975*	*1980*	*1985*	*1990*	*1992*	*Pooled 1970–92*
Currency union	0.85**	1.26***	1.08***	1.33***	1.50***	1.89	0.92***
	(0.43)	(0.41)	(0.26)	(0.27)	(0.27)	(1.42)	(0.14)
Exchange rate volatility	−0.06***	0.00	−0.06***	−0.03***	−0.01***	−0.02***	−0.04***
	(0.01)	(0.01)	(0.01)	(0.01)	(0.00)	(0.00)	(0.00)
Output	0.77***	0.81***	0.81***	0.80***	0.83***	0.79***	0.79***
	(0.02)	(0.01)	(0.01)	(0.01)	(0.01)	(0.01)	(0.01)
Output/capita	0.65***	0.66***	0.61***	0.66***	0.73***	0.38***	0.53***
	(0.03)	(0.03)	(0.02)	(0.02)	(0.02)	(0.02)	(0.01)
Distance	−1.09***	−1.15***	−1.02***	−1.05***	−1.12***	−1.09***	−1.09***
	(0.05)	(0.04)	(0.04)	(0.04)	(0.04)	(0.04)	(0.02)
Contiguity	0.48**	0.35*	0.72***	0.51***	0.63***	0.26	0.56***
	(0.21)	(0.19)	(0.18)	(0.18)	(0.18)	(0.20)	(0.08)
Language	0.57***	0.40***	0.31***	0.41***	0.55***	0.63***	0.51***
	(0.10)	(0.10)	(0.09)	(0.08)	(0.08)	(0.09)	(0.04)
FTA	0.96***	1.01***	1.26***	1.21***	0.67***	1.20***	0.88***
	(0.17)	(0.21)	(0.16)	(0.17)	(0.14)	(0.22)	(0.08)
Same nation	1.72**	1.38**	1.05**	1.79***	0.89*	1.41	1.60***
	(0.71)	(0.67)	(0.45)	(0.66)	(0.52)	(1.48)	(0.26)
Same colonizer	0.90***	0.71***	0.52***	0.47***	0.57***	0.20	0.43***
	(0.15)	(0.14)	(0.12)	(0.12)	(0.12)	(0.13)	(0.06)
Colonial relationship	2.42***	2.39***	2.27***	2.01***	1.71***	1.47***	2.04***
	(0.22)	(0.19)	(0.13)	(0.13)	(0.15)	(0.14)	(0.07)
Intercept	−18.17***	−19.41***	−19.67***	−20.79***	−22.58***	−15.65***	−17.40***
	(0.68)	(0.62)	(0.56)	(0.56)	(0.56)	(0.65)	(0.25)
Number of obs.	4,052	4,474	5,092	5,091	4,239	4,343	27,291
R^2	0.57	0.59	0.62	0.65	0.73	0.64	0.61
RMSE	2.18	2.18	2.03	1.94	1.74	1.87	2.07

Notes
Standard errors are beneath the coefficients. ***, **, and * denote significance at 1, 5, and 10%, respectively.
Dependent variable is the log of the value of trade between pairs of countries in the given years.

pooled sample. The facts that the values of R^2 based on this rather simple model are never lower than 0.57 and the values of RMSE are never more than 2.18 provide strong support for the goodness of fit for the model. Our results are broadly in line with those reported by Rose (2000). In particular, the elasticities of trade with respect to the product of GDPs and per capita GDPs, respectively, are both positive but less than unity; that with respect to Distance is -1.09, indicating that a 1 per cent increase in the distance variable would lower the trade value by 1.09 per cent. The effects of having a colonial relationship or being part of the same nation increases trade several times more than this while the effects of contiguity, common language, and same colonizer are all indicated to be smaller than a doubling. The effect of forming a free trade area (exp 0.88) between two countries is almost as large as that of forming a currency union (exp 0.92), implying a virtual doubling of trade.

Tables 2.5 and 2.6 present the results of estimating Equation (2.1) separately for energy and non-energy trade. One would expect the gravity considerations to be quite a bit weaker for energy trade than for non-energy trade. To some extent this is the case. Focusing on the pooled results of Tables 2.5 and 2.6, one can see that the R^2 is considerably lower for the energy trade of Table 2.5 than that of the non-energy and total trade in Tables 2.6 and 2.4, respectively. The effects of the contiguity and same nation dummy variables, though still positive, are no longer statistically significant. The biggest single change is in the coefficient of the FTA dummy variable, which is positive and significant for non-energy trade and otherwise for energy trade (Tables 2.5 and 2.6). Yet, in other respects the results are surprisingly similar. Indeed, the influences of the same colonizer dummy, distance, and exchange rate volatility variables are even stronger for energy trade than non-energy trade. The latter finding may be due to the fact that companies involved in shipping, refining, and marketing of oil are owned by investors or governments of the former colonial powers and that transport (other than by pipeline) of oil and especially natural gas is particularly costly.

How sensitive are such results to changes in sample size and specification? To assess the sensitivity of the results to these two changes, Table 2.7 presents the comparable results obtained when the sample size is increased to provide more complete coverage of MENA countries and three alternative specifications. The results in column 1 are the same as those presented in the last column of Table 2.4, that is, for total trade based on the pooled sample of 27,291 observations. Column 2 presents the comparable results when the observations for MENA countries are maximized, increasing the number of observations to 35,621. This specification also includes two additional variables used by Rose (2000) in some specifications, namely a dummy variable for the variable 'Landlocked' and a complementary measure for distance, that is, the sum of the geographic areas of the trading partners. Column 3 adds ONEFTA and ONECU to the specification to capture the possible trade diversion effects if only one of the trading partners is a member of the FTA or currency union. Finally, in column 4 the results are given when two additional dummy variables are included, ONEOIL and BOTHOIL, representing cases in which one or both trading partners are oil-exporting countries.

Table 2.5 Regression results from estimating the gravity model for energy (oil and gas) trade, 1970–92

	1970	*1975*	*1980*	*1985*	*1990*	*1992*	*Pooled 1970–92*
Currency union	0.28	0.87	0.35	1.38*	1.81**	3.06*	0.89***
	(0.63)	(0.72)	(0.55)	(0.73)	(0.71)	(1.82)	(0.29)
Exchange rate volatility	−0.02	−0.01	−0.08***	−0.01	−0.01**	−0.03***	−0.05***
	(0.02)	(0.02)	(0.03)	(0.01)	(0.01)	(0.01)	(0.00)
Output	0.41***	0.41***	0.57***	0.60***	0.70***	0.63***	0.53***
	(0.04)	(0.04)	(0.04)	(0.03)	(0.03)	(0.03)	(0.01)
Output/capita	0.34***	0.58***	0.52***	0.34***	0.36***	0.10	0.30***
	(0.06)	(0.06)	(0.06)	(0.06)	(0.07)	(0.06)	(0.03)
Distance	−1.17***	−1.15***	−1.07***	−1.31***	−1.44***	−1.21***	−1.23***
	(0.09)	(0.10)	(0.09)	(0.09)	(0.09)	(0.09)	(0.04)
Contiguity	−0.17	0.02	0.30	−0.27	0.31	0.67**	0.20
	(0.36)	(0.32)	(0.30)	(0.33)	(0.32)	(0.32)	(0.13)
Language	0.59***	0.17	−0.31	0.21	0.57***	0.36*	0.20**
	(0.21)	(0.21)	(0.20)	(0.21)	(0.20)	(0.20)	(0.09)
FTA	−1.08**	−1.50***	−0.38	0.40	0.16	0.43	−0.28*
	(0.51)	(0.43)	(0.38)	(0.33)	(0.29)	(0.33)	(0.15)
Same nation	−0.54	−0.61	0.27	1.88	0.73	−2.01	0.04
	(1.06)	(1.23)	(0.38)	(1.34)	(0.94)	(2.02)	(0.47)
Same colonizer	0.35	1.68***	1.70***	1.58***	1.16***	0.80**	1.07***
	(0.35)	(0.36)	(0.33)	(0.40)	(0.37)	(0.38)	(0.15)
Colonial relationship	1.01***	1.15***	0.57**	0.44	0.41	0.51	0.67***
	(0.33)	(0.33)	(0.29)	(0.29)	(0.34)	(0.31)	(0.13)
Intercept	−2.76**	−6.75***	−11.62***	−8.83***	−12.58***	−7.37***	−6.02***
	(1.36)	(1.49)	(1.35)	(1.41)	(1.42)	(1.46)	(0.57)
Number of obs.	1,523	1,753	1,904	1,830	1,606	1,805	10,421
R^2	0.21	0.20	0.25	0.25	0.36	0.30	0.24
RMSE	2.78	3.13	3.09	3.00	2.80	2.93	3.05

Notes
Standard errors are beneath the coefficients. ***, **, and * denote significance at 1, 5, and 10%, respectively.
Dependent variable is the log of the value of trade in oil between pairs of countries in the given years.

Table 2.6 Regression results from estimating the gravity model for non-energy trade, 1970–92

	1970	*1975*	*1980*	*1985*	*1990*	*1992*	*Pooled 1970–92*
Currency union	0.83**	1.13***	1.14***	1.19***	1.77***	1.99	1.01***
	(0.41)	(0.36)	(0.32)	(0.34)	(0.35)	(1.41)	(0.16)
Exchange rate volatility	−0.06***	0.01	−0.05***	−0.03***	−0.01***	−0.02***	−0.04***
	(0.01)	(0.01)	(0.01)	(0.00)	(0.00)	(0.00)	(0.00)
Output	0.80***	0.85***	0.83***	0.81***	0.82***	0.80***	0.80***
	(0.02)	(0.01)	(0.01)	(0.01)	(0.01)	(0.01)	(0.01)
Output/capita	0.61***	0.58***	0.51***	0.63***	0.74***	0.37***	0.50***
	(0.03)	(0.03)	(0.02)	(0.02)	(0.02)	(0.02)	(0.01)
Distance	−1.00***	−1.10***	−0.95***	−0.94***	−1.08***	−1.05***	−1.02***
	(0.05)	(0.04)	(0.04)	(0.04)	(0.04)	(0.04)	(0.02)
Contiguity	0.64***	0.41**	0.78***	0.63***	0.51***	0.20	0.59***
	(0.21)	(0.20)	(0.18)	(0.18)	(0.19)	(0.20)	(0.08)
Language	0.55***	0.37***	0.32***	0.36***	0.51***	0.63***	0.48***
	(0.10)	(0.10)	(0.09)	(0.08)	(0.08)	(0.09)	(0.04)
FTA	1.18***	1.09***	1.27***	1.23***	0.75***	1.23***	1.00***
	(0.16)	(0.21)	(0.17)	(0.17)	(0.15)	(0.21)	(0.08)
Same nation	0.87	1.94***	1.93***	2.69***	0.82	1.41	1.73***
	(0.77)	(0.68)	(0.73)	(0.58)	(0.62)	(1.47)	(0.29)
Same colonizer	0.91***	0.69***	0.32***	0.39***	0.56***	0.18	0.37***
	(0.15)	(0.14)	(0.12)	(0.11)	(0.13)	(0.13)	(0.05)
Colonial relationship	2.62***	2.55***	2.37***	2.03***	1.74***	1.51***	2.12***
	(0.22)	(0.20)	(0.14)	(0.14)	(0.15)	(0.14)	(0.08)
Intercept	−19.22***	−20.13***	−19.80***	−21.69***	−22.77***	−16.22***	−18.02***
	(0.69)	(0.62)	(0.58)	(0.54)	(0.59)	(0.64)	(0.25)
Number of obs.	3,984	4,350	4,872	4,890	4,071	4,337	26,504
R^2	0.57	0.60	0.62	0.65	0.72	0.65	0.61
RMSE	2.20	2.16	1.98	1.89	1.74	1.84	2.04

Notes
Standard errors are beneath the coefficients. ***, **, and * denote significance at 1%, 5% and 10%, respectively.
Dependent variable is the log of the value of trade in non-oil products between pairs of countries in the given years.

Table 2.7 Panel regressions from estimating total bilateral trade with the extended gravity model, 1970–92

	1	*2*	*3*	*4*
Currency union	0.92	0.760	0.789	0.680
	(0.140)	(0.143)	(0.137)	(0.136)
Exchange rate volatility	−0.04	−0.033	−0.032	−0.034
	(0.002)	(0.003)	(0.002)	(0.002)
Output	0.790	0.864	0.868	0.863
	(0.006)	(0.006)	(0.006)	(0.006)
Output/capita	0.53	0.068	0.066	0.076
	(0.007)	(0.007)	(0.007)	(0.007)
Distance	−1.09	−0.638	−0.628	−0.799
	(0.020)	(0.173)	(0.171)	(0.171)
Distance squared		−0.023	−0.024	−0.014
		(0.011)	(0.011)	(0.011)
Contiguity	0.564	0.876	0.875	0.860
	(0.081)	(0.081)	(0.081)	(0.081)
Language	0.51	0.650	0.650	0.685
	(0.037)	(0.036)	(0.036)	(0.036)
FTA	0.881	0.902	0.876	0.802
	(0.083)	(0.088)	(0.087)	(0.087)
Samne nation	1.602	1.254	1.277	1.301
	(0.261)	((0.247)	(0.245)	(0.244)
Same colonizer	0.430	0.588	0.583	0.585
	(0.063)	(0.045)	(0.045)	(0.045)
Colonial relationship	2.038	1.827	1.807	1.774
	(0.071)	(0.102)	(0.101)	(0.100)
Landlocked		−0.619	−0.614	−0.654
		(0.029)	(0.028)	(0.028)
Sum of geo. areas		−0.144	−0.149	−0.130
		(0.010)	(0.009)	(0.009)
ONEOIL				−0.058
				(0.026)
BOTHOIL				−1.343
				(0.077)
ONEFTA			−0.045	−0.055
			(0.023)	(0.023)
ONECU			0.087	0.037
			(0.025)	(0.025)
INTERCEPT	−17.40	−12.285	−12.353	−11.776
	(0.202)	(0.312)	(0.676)	(0.674)
N	27,291	35,621	35,621	35,621
R^2 adjusted	0.607	0.604	0.604	0.608
RMSE	2.07	2.08	2.061	2.052

Note
Standard errors are beneath the coefficients.

Note that the estimates of column 1 have slightly higher adjusted values of R^2 and slightly lower mean square errors. The main point in Table 2.7 is to show that while some of the parameter estimates are somewhat sensitive to the differences in specification, the results are very similar between the two samples and in all cases the results show the general validity of the gravity model. We refer to the column 1 estimates as the base model and the column 4 ones as the extended gravity model.

3.3 Simulating intra-regional trade potential in MENA

In this section, we utilize the above empirical results to assess the conformity of MENA's actual trade with that predicted by the gravity model. The predicted values are based on the parameter estimates from the pooled results of the extended gravity model, that is, column 4 of Table 2.7. This is done for each MENA country and for MENA as a whole, with MENA1, with Iran and Turkey, and with the rest of the world, in all cases for the year 1992. Due to the fact that missing values can make quite a bit of difference at the individual country level, but less so at the level of MENA1 as a whole, it is the MENA1 results at the bottom of Table 2.7 that are most relevant and reliable.

As can be seen, in general, actual intra-MENA trade flows for 1992 were substantially below those that would be predicted on the basis of the extended gravity model. Indeed, with respect to the Arab MENA (MENA1) countries, the actual intra-regional trade was only about 68 per cent of what might be expected on the basis of extended gravity model considerations. This would seem to indicate that, even without an institutional change such as a FTA or a currency union, there could be very considerable potential for increasing intra-regional trade by simply removing some of the obstacles to such trade. On the other hand, the actual trade of Iran and Turkey (and especially the latter) with MENA1 countries is almost 25 per cent higher than would be expected. In the case of the rest of the world, actual trade of MENA1 countries with these countries is again lower than predicted trade, but only by a little over 2 per cent. Especially low in trade with other MENA1 countries are Algeria, Egypt, Kuwait, Qatar, Saudi Arabia, Sudan, and Syria, most of which are oil-exporting countries. On the other hand, 'over-achievers' in intra-MENA trade are Jordan, Morocco, Oman, and United Arab Emirates and among MENA2 countries, Turkey.

Given the aforementioned sensitivity of the results obtained in Table 2.7 to alternative sample sizes and specifications, the last row of Table 2.8 presents the comparable actual-predicted percentages for MENA1 as a whole based on the predictions obtained from column 1 that is, the base gravity model with the somewhat smaller sample. According to these estimates, MENA1 was even more of an underachiever in 1992 as far as both intra-regional and extra-regional trade were concerned.

Table 2.9 presents comparisons of the actual versus predicted trade flows of MENA1 countries with various regions including MENA1 itself for 1980, 1985, 1990, and 1992, again based on the model and sample of column 4 of Table 2.7.

Table 2.8 Actual and predicted trade of individual MENA countries, 1992 (actual/predicted in %; predicted based on estimates from column 4 of Table 2.7)

	A. Trade with MENA1	*Iran and Turkey*	*Rest of the world*
Algeria	34	75	96
Bahrain	74	75	105
Egypt	88	32	104
Iraq	319	33	6
Jordan	139	113	112
Kuwait	19	25	42
Lebanon	426	718	1,090
Libya	91	600	25
Mauritania	—	2	140
Morocco	214	174	29
Oman	488	100	47
Qatar	24	14	43
Saudi Arabia	45	26,824	409
Sudan	16	52	54
Syria	32	19	39
Tunisia	60	71	50
UAE	244	601	124
Yemen	—	—	351
B. MENA 1	68	125	98
MENA 1 (predicted based on estimates of column 1 of Table 2.7)	45		

Table 2.9 Actual and predicted regional and multilateral trade of MENA1, 1980–92 (actual/predicted in %)

	1980	*1985*	*1990*	*1992*
MENA1	56	20	33	68
Iran and Turkey	120	154	73	125
MENA2	21	37	44	85
EU	404	111	48	67
NAFTA	693	137	137	182
OOECD	467	158	96	114
LDC	842	231	207	298
East Europe	122	94	58	49
Rest of the world	452	125	72	98

While MENA was a slight underachiever with the rest of the world, it was a substantial overachiever in 1992 with NAFTA and the LDCs and a slight overachiever also with other OECD countries (OOECD). It was an underachiever with respect to the European Union and Eastern Europe. It should be noted that the underachievement with respect to the rest of the world would have been even greater had we used the estimates of the base gravity model of column 1 of Table 2.7.

How effective have the sub-regional trading arrangements within MENA been in promoting intra-MENA trade? Table 2.10 presents the regression results

Table 2.10 Regression results from estimating the gravity model allowing for regional arrangements in MENA (pooled data, 1970–92)

	All trade	*Energy trade*	*Non-energy trade*
Currency union	0.91***	0.96***	0.99***
	0.14	0.32	0.16
Exchange rate volatility	−0.04***	−0.05***	−0.04***
	0.00	0.00	0.00
Output	0.78***	0.54***	0.80***
	0.01	0.01	0.01
Output/capita	0.54***	0.28***	0.51***
	0.01	0.02	0.01
Distance	−1.09***	−1.19***	−1.02***
	0.02	0.04	0.02
Contiguity	0.57***	0.26**	0.60***
	0.09	0.15	0.09
Language	0.48***	0.22*	0.46***
	0.04	0.09	0.04
FTA	0.87***	−0.20	0.97***
	0.09	0.16	0.10
Same nation	1.59***	0.05	1.72***
	0.27	0.62	0.35
Same colonizer	0.44***	1.04***	0.39***
	0.05	0.14	0.05
Colonial relationship	2.05***	0.68***	2.13***
	0.11	0.17	0.11
GCC	−0.53***	1.48***	−0.67***
	0.09	0.19	0.09
AMU	−0.90*	−0.90	−1.60*
	0.54	0.93	0.53
ACM	−0.10	−0.12	−0.08
	0.07	0.16	0.07
Intercept	−17.43***	−6.34***	−18.03***
	0.23	0.56	0.24
Number of obs.	27,342	10,438	26,555
R^2	0.60	0.24	0.61
RMSE	2.07	3.05	2.04

Notes
Standard errors are beneath the coefficients.
***, **, and * denote significance at 1, 5, and 10% levels, respectively.
Dependent variable is the log of the value of trade between pairs of countries.

obtained from the same sample and basic gravity model used in column 1 of Table 2.7 but with dummy variables for the GCC, AMU, and ACM included. By comparing the results for total trade in the first column of Table 2.10 with the corresponding ones from column 1 of Table 2.7, it can be seen that the addition of the three dummy variables for the sub-regional trading arrangements within MENA has virtually no effect at all on any of the parameter estimates of the basic gravity model. What is striking, however, is the difference between the coefficients for FTA and GCC, AMU, and ACM. While the former – based on the various FTA arrangements around the world (not including the intra-MENA arrangements) – is 0.87 and statistically significant at the 1 per cent level, those for the GCC, AMU, and ACM are all negative and in the case of the GCC statistically significant at the 1 per cent level.

In other words, even with these trade arrangements, the non-energy and total trade figures of the countries encompassed by these trade arrangements, for the years they were in effect, were lower than would have been predicted on the basis of the gravity model. In the case of energy trade, the effects of the AMU and ACM dummy variables are again negative (but not significant) but the GCC dummy has a statistically significant positive influence on trade. What this means, however, is, of course, nothing more than that GCC countries (which happen to be especially well endowed in energy reserves) trade more in energy than would have been predicted on the basis of the gravity model alone.

Another way of gauging the extent to which intra-MENA trade has fallen short of what would be expected were there a full-fledged and well-functioning FTA at the MENA level is to simulate the predicted trade of MENA1 countries with themselves under the assumption that FTA = 1 for those trades in which both partners are MENA1 countries. This FTA = 1 assumption for MENA1 countries would have the effect of more than doubling the level of such trade. Very similar results are obtained (though to save space these are not shown) when the comparisons between the MENA FTA-simulated and actual values are based on the summation of those predicted sets of bilateral flows based on the energy and non-energy results given in the last columns of Tables 2.5 and 2.6, respectively. The results suggest that intra-MENA trade could be increased by somewhere between 47 and 122 per cent by undertaking the measures needed to fit the predictions of the gravity model (the former is based on the column 4 estimates of Table 2.7 and the latter on column 1). It could be increased by another 147 per cent if a fully fledged FTA among all Arab countries of the MENA region were established. Because of their relatively large market sizes, intra-MENA trade could be further increased by the inclusion of Iran and Turkey into this arrangement.

4 Towards a resolution of the puzzle of intra-regional trade in MENA

What accounts for the puzzle that, despite the apparent political consensus and numerous policy initiatives, intra-MENA trade has remained significantly low in relation to what has been accomplished by FTAs or CUs that have been established elsewhere? After some growth in the proportion of intra-MENA trade between 1970 and 1990, that proportion has either stagnated or declined in relative terms in the 1990s. Various reasons have been offered in the literature to explain this low level of intra-regional trade in the Middle East. These fall broadly under two headings: policy-induced factors that have hindered trade in general, and more fundamental structural differences that tend to encourage more inter-regional rather than intra-regional trade.

Trade policy has often been cited as the main policy induced barrier to intra-Arab trade (El-Naggar 1992, El-Erian and Fischer 1996). While some countries in the region, specifically the GCC countries, maintain a relatively open trade regime, others have imposed significant barriers to trade. The average tariff for the region as a whole is higher than that of any other region, except Africa.[10] Moreover, non-tariff barriers are extensive in many countries in the region (Zarrouk 2000b). Many countries employ a variety of measures, including restrictive licensing, bans, state trading/monopolies, overvalued exchange rates and accompanying restrictive foreign exchange allocation (Nabli and Véganzonès-Varoudakis 2004), as well as multiple exchange rates to discourage imports. Not unrelated, differences in overall economic strategy and policy have also been cited as reasons why intra-Arab trade is relatively small (Allum 1998). These contrasting strategies tend to discourage intra-regional trade. Delays and costs involved in clearing customs and obtaining rebates in cases where trade taxes are exempted also fall under the rubric of policy-induced barriers.[11]

Undoubtedly, political factors, including bilateral conflicts and economic sanctions, have also impacted intra-regional trade in the Middle East (Limam and Abdalla 1999). Since 1970, there have been numerous bilateral conflicts ranging in intensity from diplomatic crises to border disputes and open wars. This is most clearly visible in the Maghreb region (Libya and Algeria versus Morocco) in the 1970s and the Mashreq region in the 1980s (Iran versus Iraq, Syria versus Lebanon). Prior to the imposition of UN sanctions, Saudi Arabia's exports to Iraq exceeded US$150 million; since then, exports have been negligible. Similarly, political differences between Algeria and Morocco reduced trade between the two neighbours from US$140 million in 1992 to less than US$100 million in 1995–6. More generally, political instability is believed to have been a major obstacle in the way of resolving trade disputes and implementing various multilateral pacts in the Middle East.

Among MENA countries as a whole, there is clearly considerable complementarity in resource endowments that should be trade promoting. Yet, at the sub-regional level in which such trade has been most intensive, the lack of product and resource complementarity has been cited as an important factor hindering intra-regional trade (Fischer 1993). The relative similarity of resource endowments at the sub-regional level has made them competitors in the same product markets (e.g. in oil, phosphates, petrochemicals, and agricultural products). At the same time, the lack of a diversified export base – particularly in manufactures – limits the opportunities for trade based on product differentiation. Thus, even though in some product lines, such as oil, natural gas, phosphates, urea, cotton, and citrus, different Arab countries produce similar goods, they are not manufactured or product-differentiated goods. Hence, neither of the two main models of international trade, the Heckscher–Ohlin model that bases trade on different factor endowments, or the intra-industry model that bases trade on product differentiation, would seem to predict sizable intra-regional trade in MENA. However, as noted above, most intra-Arab trade is within sub-regions where, presumably, the lack of product complementarity is greatest. Nearly 75 per cent of the GCC's and 65 per cent of the AMU's trade with Arab countries, respectively, takes place within the GCC and AMU.[12]

Differences in per capita income have been cited as a factor constraining intra-Arab trade (Zarrouk 1992, Fischer 1993). Richer countries prefer to import high-quality goods, which are more likely to be produced by industrial nations. While per capita income (or the level of development) is not, *per se*, a barrier to trade – otherwise, trade between Mexico and the United States would be difficult to explain – both the homogeneity of the export base among many Arab countries and income disparities have generally been cited as impediments to intra-regional trade. For example, while Egypt is an important producer of consumer goods manufactures within the region and Saudi Arabia is an important importer of such goods, Saudi Arabia's high income per capita induces it to consume higher quality manufactures from European countries instead of manufactures from Egypt.

High trade costs, including transport and communications, have also been cited as a factor constraining intra-Arab trade (Limam and Abdalla 1998). The distance and difficult geographic terrain between some Arab countries make trade links difficult. The Maghreb countries, for example, are geographically closer to Europe than to other Arab countries, making trade links easier with Europe. Even where geography does not work against regional trade, the lack of transportation networks, minimally paved roads and rail links across countries, combined with border closures and, as mentioned above, customs red tape, have all created disincentives for the movement of goods and services.[13] In some cases, such transport discontinuities reflect historical legacies predating the Second World War; in others, they are due to political instability and state controls on the development of commercial networks in the region.

5 Conclusions

We used a large panel dataset for 186 countries to estimate a gravity model of bilateral trade between 1970 and 1992. The results indicate that every MENA country had achieved less in intra-regional trade than the level predicted by the model. For the region as a whole for 1992, actual trade amounted to only between 45 and 68 per cent of the predicted level. The creation of an FTA for the region would, therefore, more than double intra-regional trade potential; hence, a well-functioning MENA-FTA devoid of the barriers to trade identified in Section 4 could raise potential trade by some five times of the actual 1992 level.

Five important points remain to be investigated. First, we have not yet examined the determinants of bilateral trade in MENA on a country-by-country basis. This could easily be accomplished by introducing a set of interactions in the gravity equation. Second, we have not investigated the relation between intra-regional and extra-regional trade and growth (along the lines of Frankel and Romer 1999). Third, since the data used in the present study stop in 1992, there is clearly quite a lot of room for updating the data and re-estimating the model on the basis of more recent data. Fourth, we have not yet been able to quantitatively assess the specific sources of the shortfalls in intra-MENA trade relative to the predicted level. Finally, even though our results show unmistakably that intra-MENA trade and with the outside world is much less than would be expected, they do not necessarily indicate that this is bad in the sense of welfare losses.[14] MENA countries are clearly much less open to trade than other countries after taking into consideration the various factors captured by the gravity model. The creation of sub-regional trade arrangements has not had a discernible positive influence in this respect. Although there exists a strong belief among scholars and policy makers that openness is good for economic performance, as numerous scholars have pointed out in recent years, the empirical support for this claim remains rather weak.

With additional data and further extensions of this research, these shortcomings should hopefully be overcome in the future.

Acknowledgements

The authors express their gratitude for considerable help in the computations by Islam Kandil, Grace Lim, and Paul Hughes and to the comments of our discussants and other participants at the First European Conference of the Middle East Economic Association in collaboration with SOAS (University of London) during 20–22 July 2001, where an earlier version of the paper was first presented.

Notes

1 The CAEU still exists, but its objectives are now much more modest and training-oriented.

2 For example, the recent volume by Hockman and Zarrouk (2000) is almost entirely devoted to non-regional trade issues in MENA. While there exists a substantial literature on regionalism in MENA, the analytical studies have been limited, among others, to Ekholm et al. (1996), Limam and Abdalla (1998), and Al-Atrash and Yousef (2000).

3 Empirical studies by Krueger (1978) and others, moreover, showed the factor intensities of intra-regional trade to be different from extra-regional trade in ways that could be considered detrimental to development and equitable distribution in developing countries. In particular, intra-regional exports were found to be more capital intensive and less unskilled-labour intensive in relatively poor, labour surplus developing countries.

4 The external tariffs of most countries in the world, including developing countries in general and MENA countries in particular, are lower now than they were in the past, suggesting that there should be less trade diversion in newly created free trade areas and customs unions than the earlier ones. One incipient regional arrangement, namely APEC,

has frequently been given partial credit for the important breakthroughs in finalizing the Uruguay Round of multilateral trade negotiations, which had long been in stalemate. APEC, moreover, has championed the idea of 'open regionalism' wherein regional and multilateral trade arrangements can clearly be complementary to one another (Krugman 1991, Bergsten 1996, Nugent 1998).

5 This measure, however, is very simplistic. It fails to consider proximity to other countries, commodity composition of trade, or any other factor. By no means can it be interpreted as solely the result of the openness of trade policy, which openness measures are usually designed to indicate.

6 Use of the gravity model has become even more popular after Anderson (1979), Bergstrand (1989), and others provided a theoretical underpinning for the gravity model. To our knowledge, the only previous studies that have used the gravity model in the context of the Middle East have been Limam and Abdalla (1998), Sayan (1998), and Al-Atrash and Yousef (2000). Their results are of limited usefulness either because they focused on aggregate trade flows for one period or utilized small samples of countries and few explanatory variables.

7 Leamer and Levinsohn (1995) attribute to the gravity model 'some of the clearest and most robust empirical findings in economics'.

8 As a result, we have 4,052 complete observations for 1970, 4,474 for 1975, about 5,090 for both 1980 and 1985, 4,239 for 1990, and 4,343 for 1992. When the data are pooled for all the years, we have a total of 27,291 complete observations. Previous analytical studies have examined intra-regional trade in MENA using small country samples, a single cross-section, or bilateral trade data limited to MENA. Our sample size, country, and time coverage, and even empirical specification, as we shall see later, represent a substantial analytical improvement in this regard.

9 Rose (2000) found the results of the basic gravity model to be strong and robust to the inclusion of other variables or alternative measures of some of the included variables. Among the additional variables were regional dummy variables, the product of the two countries' tariff rates, a dummy variable for whether one of the countries is landlocked, the sum or products of the two countries' land areas, and dummy variables for one or both countries having controls on the current account and foreign exchange surrender, and for one (or both) being an island economy. Yet, since few of these variables turned out to be either very significant or to affect the other results in any substantial way, these variables are excluded from the present specification.

10 The average tariff for Arab countries is estimated at about 17 per cent. This compares to an average tariff of 20 per cent for African countries, 13 per cent for Western Hemisphere countries, 12 per cent for Asia Pacific, 10 per cent for the Baltic, Russia, and other countries of the former Soviet Union (BRO), and 9 per cent for Europe (excluding BRO).

11 Note, for example, that only 12 per cent of private firms doing business in MENA, surveyed as part of the Worldwide Private Sector Survey used in the World Bank's 1997 World Development Report, rated the 'overall efficiency of the country's customs services as good or very good'. See Brunetti *et al.* (1997).

12 Havrylyshyn (1997) calculates a 'complementarity index' for Arab countries that shows product complementarity in the region to be broadly similar to that of other regional groupings (MERCOSUR and APEC), suggesting that there could be much greater potential for regional integration among Arab or MENA countries than is being realized at present. See also Havrylyshyn and Kunzel (2000).

13 For example, several studies have shown that the cost of transporting goods between several neighbouring Middle Eastern countries exceeds those with distant European markets.

14 For instance, environmental impacts of intra- and extra-regional trade might well be different. See Whalley (1991) and for the Middle East in particular and United Nations Economic and Social Commission for Western Asia (1999).

References

Abed, G. T. (2000) 'Trade liberalization and tax reform in the southern Mediterranean region', in Hoekman, B. and H. Kheir-El-Din (eds), *Trade Policy Developments in the Middle East and North Africa*, Washington, DC: World Bank.

Al-Atrash, H. and T. Yousef (2000) 'Intra-Arab trade: is it too little?' IMF Working Paper 00/10, Washington, DC: International Monetary Fund.

Allum, P. (1998) 'Inter-Arab trade: constraints and prospects', Paper for the Sectoral Meeting on Trade and Development Between the League of Arab States and the United Nations (Cairo, 8–11 June, 1998).

Al-Mashat, R. A. (2000) 'An empirical assessment of NAFTA: the gravity model revisited', *mimeo*, College Park: University of Maryland, Department of Economics.

Anderson, J. E. (1979) 'A theoretical foundation for the gravity equation', *American Economic Review* 69: 106–116.

Bergsten, C. F. (1996) 'Globalizing free trade', *Foreign Affairs* May/June, 105–120.

Bergstrand, J. H. (1989) 'The generalized gravity equation, monopolistic competition and the factor proportions theory in international trade', *Review of Economics and Statistics* 71: 143–153.

Bhagwati, J. (1993) 'Regionalism and multilateralism: an overview', in de Melo, J. and A. Panagariya (eds), *New Dimensions in Regional Integration*, New York: Cambridge University Press.

Bhagwati, J., P. Krishna, and A. Panagariya (1999) *Trading Blocs*, Cambridge: MIT Press.

Brunetti, A., G. Kisunko, and B. Weder (1997) 'Institutional obstacles for doing business: data description and methodology of a worldwide private sector survey', in the World Bank, World Development Report, Washington, D.C.: World Bank.

Ekholm, K., J. Torstensson, and R. Torstensson (1996) 'The economics of the Middle East peace process: are there prospects for trade and growth'? *The World Economy*, 555–574.

El-Erian, M. and S. Fischer (1996) 'Is MENA a region? The scope for regional integration', IMF Working Paper 96/30, Washington, DC: International Monetary Fund.

El-Imam, M. (1990) 'Arab economic integration between two decades', *Al Mustaqbal Al Arabi*, No. 138 (August).

El-Naggar, S. (ed.) (1992) *Foreign and Intratrade Policies of the Arab Countries*, Washington, DC: International Monetary Fund.

Feenstra, R. C., R. E. Lipsey, and H. P. Bowen (1997) *World Trade Flows, 1970–1992, with Production and Tariff Data*, Cambridge, MA: National Bureau of Economic Research.

Fischer, S. (1993) 'Prospects for regional integration in the Middle East' in de Melo, J. and A. Panagariya (eds), *New Dimensions in Regional Integration*, Cambridge: Cambridge University Press.

Frankel, J. A. and D. Romer (1999) 'Does trade cause growth?' *American Economic Review*, 89(3): 379–396.

Frankel, J. and A. Rose (2000) 'Estimating the effect of currency unions on trade and output', Working Paper W7857, Cambridge, MA: National Bureau of Economic Research.

Frankel, J., E. Stein, and S.-J. Wei (1998) 'Continental trading blocs: are they natural or supernatural?' in J. Frankel (ed.), *Regionalism of the World Economy*, Chicago: University of Chicago Press.

Galal, A. (2000) 'Incentives for economic integration in the Middle East', in Hoekman, B. and H. Kheir-El-Din (eds), *Trade Policy Developments in the Middle East and North Africa*, Washington, DC: World Bank, pp. 51–68.

Galal, A. and B. Hoekman (eds), (1997) *Regional Partners in Global Markets*, London: CEPR.

Havrylyshyn, O. (1997) *A Global Integration Strategy for the Mediterranean Countries*, Washington, DC: International Monetary Fund.

Havrylyshyn, O. and P. Kunzel (2000) 'Intra-industry trade of Arab countries: an indicator of potential competitiveness' in Hoekman, B. and J. Zarrouk (eds), *Catching Up with the Competition: Trade Opportunities and Challenges for Arab Countries*, Ann Arbor: University of Michigan Press, pp. 81–99.

Hoekman, B. and J. Zarrouk (eds), (2000) *Catching Up With the Competition: Trade Opportunities and Challenges For Arab Countries'*, Ann Arbor: University of Michigan Press.

Kemp, M. and H. Wan (1976) 'An elementary proposition concerning the formation of customs unions', *Journal of International Economics* 6, 95–97.

Krueger, A. O. (1978) *Foreign Trade Regimes and Economic Development: Liberalization Attempts and Consequences*, vol. 10, Cambridge: Ballinger Publishing Co.

Krugman, P. (1991) 'The move to free trade zones', in *Symposium of the Federal Reserve Bank of Kansas City, Policy Implications of Trade and Currency Zones*, Kansas City: Federal Reserve Bank of Kansas City, pp. 7–42.

Leamer, E. E. and J. Levinsohn (1995) 'International trade theory: the evidence', in Grossman, G. and K. Rogoff (eds), *The Handbook of International Economics*, vol. III, Amsterdam: Elsevier-North Holland.

Limam, I. and A. Abdalla (1998) *Inter-Arab Trade and the Potential Success of AFTA*, Kuwait: Arab Planning Institute.

Nabli, M. K. and A. I. De Kleine (2000) 'Managing global integration in the Middle East and North Africa', in Hoekman, B. and H. Kheir-El-Din (eds), *Trade Policy Developments in the Middle East and North Africa*, Washington, DC: World Bank, pp. 7–50.

Nabli, M. K. and M. Véganzonès-Varoudakis (2004) 'Exchange rate regime and competitiveness of manufactured exports: the case of MENA countries', chapter 3.

Nugent, J. B. (1974) *Economic Integration in Central America: Empirical Investigations*, Baltimore: Johns Hopkins University Press.

Nugent, J. B. (1998) 'APEC's impact on patterns of trade and investment flows in the region, APEC: Liberalization or Development Cooperation?' *Joint U.S.–Korea Academic Studies* 8, 145–182.

Panagariya, A. (2000) 'Preferential trade liberalization: the traditional theory and new developments', *Journal of Economic Literature* 38, 287–331.

Rose, A. K. (2000) 'One money, one market: estimating the effect of common currencies on trade', *Economic Policy*, April, pp. 7–46.

Sayan, S. (1998) *The Black Sea Economic Cooperation Project: A Substitute or a Complement to Globalization Efforts in the Middle East and the Balkans*, Cairo: Economic Research Forum.

United Nations Economic Commission for Western Asia (1985) *Economic Integration in Western Asia*, London: Frances Pinter.

United Nations Economic and Social Commission for Western Asia (1999) *Proceedings of the Expert Group Meeting on Trade and the Environment in ESCWA Member Countries*, New York: United Nations.

Whalley, J. (1991) 'The interface between environmental and trade policies', *Economic Journal*, 101, 180–189.

Zarrouk, J. E. (1992) 'Intra-Arab trade: determinants and prospects for expansion', in Said E.-N. (ed). *Foreign and Intratrade Policies of the Arab Countries*, Washington, DC: International Monetary Fund.

Zarrouk, J. E. (2000a) 'The greater Arab free trade area: limits and possibilities', in Hoekman, B. and J. Zarrouk (eds), *Catching Up with the Competition: Trade Opportunities and Challenges for Arab Countries*, Ann Arbor: University of Michigan Press, pp. 285–305.

Zarrouk, J. E. (2000b) 'Para-tariff measures in Arab countries', in Hoekman, B. and H. Kheir-El-Din (eds), *Trade Policy Developments in the Middle East and North Africa*, Washington, DC: World Bank, pp. 165–180.

3 Exchange rate regime and competitiveness of manufactured exports

The case of MENA countries*

Mustapha Kamel Nabli and Marie-Ange Véganzonès-Varoudakis

1 Introduction

Recent assessments of economic policies and performance in developing countries have underlined the importance of the management of the real exchange rate (RER). It has been shown that best performers are countries that have maintained an 'appropriate' RER – that is, one close to the equilibrium real exchange rate (ERER; see Williamson 1985, Harberger 1986, Razin and Collins 1997). In particular, all countries that have been successful in promoting manufactured exports have avoided RER overvaluation.[1]

In fact, RER misalignment – especially overvaluation – is damaging to economic performance because it decreases the profitability of production and the export of tradable goods. In this way, RER misalignment leads to a reduction in economic efficiency and a misallocation of resources. In addition, by increasing uncertainty and raising the risk of macroeconomic collapse, RER misalignment can also hinder growth by deteriorating domestic and foreign investment and contributing to capital flight. These negative effects of misalignment on growth and export performance have been shown by Edwards (1988), Cottani *et al.* (1990), and Ghura and Grennes (1993) for different groups of developing countries.

In addition to misalignment, inconsistencies among macroeconomic, trade, and exchange rate policies increase the variability of the RER – which, in turn, can affect growth. Higher RER volatility sends confusing signals to economic agents. It raises the uncertainty of long-run investments and of the profitability of producing tradable goods. The sensitivity of export performance to RER volatility has been highlighted in studies of various economies by Cushman (1993), Gagnon (1993), Ghura and Grennes (1993) and Grobar (1993).

The study in this chapter also confirms the adverse effects of RER misalignment on exports of the Middle East and North Africa (MENA) economies. We show that, during the past three decades, MENA countries have experienced substantial RER misalignment, with a net tendency towards overvaluation of their individual RERs. This has had a significant negative impact on the growth of manufactured exports, though the effect is less significant when total exports are considered. This appears to have resulted in slower economic growth, as manufactured exports have become a major force behind economic growth in developing economies, a large number of which have now successfully entered world markets.[2]

Our findings present new empirical evidence on the subject of misalignment and export growth in the case of MENA countries, on which little previous work has been undertaken. The results were obtained through the estimation of an export equation on a panel of 53 countries (see Appendix A for the list), among which ten are MENA developing economies. Our calculations cover the period 1970–80 to 1999 (the starting date varies for different countries), during which tremendous changes in trade and exchange rate policies have been observed.

The first step is to provide an accurate measure of the gap (or misalignment) between the RER and its equilibrium level (ERER). In the past, estimates of ERER and of RER misalignment have always been calculated using a reduced form approach. RER behaviour is modelled using an equation that includes both the role of fundamental factors in the medium to long term (e.g. terms of trade, investment, capital flows, trade openness), and the less persistent impact of short-term variables (e.g. macroeconomic policies, nominal devaluations). The ERER is then computed using this equation, by eliminating the effect of transitory variables and using estimates of sustainable or long-term values of the fundamental variables. This technique, pioneered by Edwards (1989), has been extended by Elbadawi (1994) and Baffes *et al.* (1997).[3]

Our approach, which is based on panel data estimations techniques, thus represents a new contribution to the study of exchange rate policy in MENA economies, since the few previous studies undertaken have generally been based on a time series approach[4] (Mongardini 1998, Domac and Shabsigh 1999, Sorsa 1999, Sundararajan *et al.* 1999, Achy 2001).[5] Our calculations have the added advantage of allowing some comparative analysis between the different regions, as well as among the MENA countries themselves.

This chapter is organized as follows. In Section 2, we present our panel data calculations of the RER's long-run equilibrium. In Section 3, we discuss the misalignment and volatility of the MENA countries' RER, compared to that of other regions. Section 4 presents our estimate of the impact of RER misalignment and of RER volatility on the export performance of the economies. We conclude that the misalignment has indeed had a negative influence on the MENA countries' manufactured exports.

2 Modelling the long-run equilibrium of the RER

The long-run equation explaining RER behaviour is based on Edwards (1994), who has developed a dynamic model of RER determination for a small, open economy with a single nominal exchange rate system. The model allows for both real and nominal factors to play a role in the short run. In the long run, only real factors – the fundamentals – influence the ERER. In this instance, the long-run relationship is specified as follows:[6]

$$\ln(e_t) = c + a_1 \ln(Inv_{i,t}) + a_2 \ln(Open_{i,t}) + a_3 \ln(TOT_{i,t}) + a_4\, Capinf_{i,t} + a_5 \ln(DebtServ_t) + \varepsilon_{i,t} \quad (3.1)$$

- e_t = bilateral RER between the country concerned and the United States, measured as the ratio of the consumption price index in the country (P_{Dt}) to the wholesale price index in the United States (P_{wt}), multiplied by the nominal exchange rate of the local currency to the US\$ (E_t). These price indices are used, respectively, as proxies of the price of non-tradable goods (P_{Dt}) and the price of tradable goods ($P_{wt}.E_t$):

  $RER_t = (P_{Dt})/(P_{wt}E_t)$

- Inv_t = investment ratio to GDP.
- $Open_t$ = indicator of trade openness, measured as the sum of imports and exports divided by GDP.

  As an improved measure of trade openness, we have substituted $Open_t$ with a policy-induced trade openness indicator (TP_t). This consists of adjusting $Open_t$ for the 'natural trade openness' of the economy, constituted by the size of the country and its distance from markets (see Frankel and Romer 1999). We have named this Equation (3.1′).

- TOT_t = external terms of trade, measured as the ratio of export to import prices (in dollars).
- $Capinf_t$ = capital inflows, calculated as the net change in reserves minus the trade balance scaled by GDP.[7]
- $DebtServ_t$ = the ratio of debt service to total exports.
- c = intercept, a_1 to a_4 = parameters, t = time index, and ε_t = error term.

Following Edwards (1989), we assume that, in the long term, an increase in the investment rate (Inv_t) results in an increase in the demand for, and relative price of, non-tradables – thus causing the RER to appreciate. This assumption implies that as the investment rate grows, investment increasingly consists of non-tradable products (e.g. services and construction), and relatively less tradable goods (e.g. equipment). This effect may also be due to the multiplier effect of the investment, which raises the aggregated demand mainly for non-tradable products.

The RER is positively affected by trade restrictions, which implies a negative sign on the coefficient of the proxy for trade openness, measured as the ratio of imports plus exports to GDP ($Open_t$). The same negative sign is expected for the improved measure of policy-induced trade openness (TP_t).

The impact of the terms of trade (TOT_t) on the RER is more ambiguous, since there are two opposite effects. That is, an increase in the relative price of exported goods to imported goods leads to an appreciation of the RER only if the income effect (which results in higher demand for non-tradables) dominates the substitution effect (which is associated with a decline in the relative cost of imported intermediate goods used in the production process of non-tradables).

An increase in capital inflows ($Capinf_t$) involves stronger demand for both tradable and non-tradable goods. Increased inflows, therefore, lead to a higher relative price of non-tradables, and conversely, appreciation of the RER – as it becomes necessary for domestic resources to be diverted towards production in the non-tradable sector to meet increased demand. On the other hand, a rise in debt service ($DebtServ_t$) – which captures the important impact of debt relief in many MENA countries – contributes to a depreciation of the RER.

The existence of this long-term relationship implies that the variables of Equations (3.1) and (3.1′) are cointegrated. It is, therefore, necessary to determine the order of integration of the series. Table 3.B1 provides the results of the Augmented-Dickey–Fuller (ADF) tests of the data for our sample of 53 countries[8] over the time period. We use the methodology of Im *et al.* (1997), which provides critical values of ADF tests in the case of heterogeneous panel data. The results indicate that the series are stationary at either the 1 or 5 per cent level, which allows us to run Equations (3.1) and (3.1′). We then use the Engel and Granger (1987) method to test for cointegration between the variables of Equations (3.1) and (3.1′). Cointegration tests are then based on the residuals of the two equations. ADF tests conclude – also using critical values from Im *et al.* (1997) – that the residuals are stationary (see Table 3.B1).

Hence, Equations (3.1) and (3.1′) describe the long-run relationship between RER and a number of fundamental variables. The equations were estimated on our panel of 53 countries of which ten are MENA developing countries.[9] The results of the regressions – using the White estimator to correct for the heteroscedasticity bias – are presented in Table 3.1. The equations were estimated using a fixed-effect methodology.[10] The estimated regressions explain a fairly large amount of the observed variation of the RER.

Estimated relationships between RER and its fundamentals are consistent with theory (Edwards 1989): an increase in investment and in capital income, or an improvement in the terms of trade, result in a RER appreciation – which indicates, in the latter case, that the income effect dominates the substitution effect. Conversely, opening an economy and an increase in debt service lead to a depreciation of the RER.

3 RER misalignment

The misalignment (MIS) of the RER is measured as the difference between the RER and its equilibrium value (ERER) expressed in percentage form:

$$\text{MIS} = (\text{RER}/\text{ERER}) - 1$$

The estimates of the long-term relationship between the RER and its fundamental determinants have been used to compute the ERER based on Equation (3.1).

Table 3.1 Estimation results of the cointegrating Equations (3.1) and (3.1′); dependent variable, $\ln(e_t)$

Variable	*Equation (3.1)*	*Equation (3.1′)*
$\mathrm{Ln}(Inv_t)$	0.09	0.11
	(2.0)	(2.3)
$\mathrm{Ln}(Open_t)$	−0.71	—
	(14.4)	—
$\ln(TP)$	—	−0.32
	—	(6.7)
$\mathrm{Ln}(TOT_t)$	0.23	0.24
	(4.9)	(4.8)
$Capinf_t$	0.45	0.5
	(4.5)	(4.7)
$\mathrm{Ln}(DebtServ_t)$	−0.18	−0.14
	(9.9)	(7.5)
Adjusted R^2	0.63	0.55
Fischer test	25.9	19.1
Hausman test	20	18.8

Source
Authors' estimations.

Notes
Student *t* statistics are within brackets. The number of observations used in Equations (3.1) and (3.1′) are, respectively, 1,092 and 1,080.
Data have been compiled from World Development Indicators, Global Development Finance, Global Development Network, and Live Data Base (World Bank).

Therefore, the sustainable or equilibrium values of the fundamental variables have to be assessed. The idea is that the deviation of the fundamental variables from their equilibrium – in addition to variations in short-term economic policy variables (see the estimation of the error correction model through Equation (3.C-1) – leads to a misalignment of the RER. The permanent values of the five fundamental variables – Inv_t, $Open_t$, TOT_t, $Capinf_t$, $DebtServ_t$ – were computed using moving averages of the series over a 3-year period. This simple method was possible because our series are stationary.[11]

Following this methodology, excessive trade protection, an unexpected appreciation of the terms of trade, an increase in investment and in capital flows, or a reduction of the debt service – set against 'normal' or long-term trends in the economy – all lead to an overvaluation of the RER. It can also be shown from the estimation of the error correction model (see Table 3.C1) that, in the short run, nominal devaluations (*Dev*), black market premiums (*BMP*), and inflation (*Infl*) explain the deviations of the RER from the ERER.

The results confirm that, during the past three decades, the MENA countries in our sample have, on average, experienced substantial overvaluation of their RERs – of around 29 per cent a year from the mid-1970s to the mid-1980s, and 22 per cent a year from the mid-1980s to 1999 (see Table 3.2). In general, the extent of overvaluation does not seem to have significantly decreased during

Table 3.2 Average misalignment and volatility

	Misalignment	*Volatility*
1975–80 (depending on country) to 1984 (% per year)		
MENA	29	7.9
Latin America	20	11.2
Africa (CFA)	61	12.7
Africa (non-CFA)	29	11.3
South Asia	43	13
South East Asia	10	5.4
1985–99 (% per year)		
MENA	22	12.4
Latin America	10	12.9
Africa (CFA)	28	14.5
Africa (non CFA)	13	16
South Asia	15	8.3
South East Asia	5	8.6

Source: Authors' calculations.

the 1990s – contrary to the Latin American, African, or Asian economies in our sample. In addition, overvaluation remains higher in MENA than in other regions, except CFA Africa (Section 4 for the experience of individual MENA countries).

On the other hand, exchange rate volatility has generally been lower in the MENA region (see Table 3.2), which can surely be explained by the less flexible exchange rate regimes of these countries. This conclusion should, however, be qualified. During the second sub-period (1985–99) in particular, the volatility of the exchange rate in the MENA region was not very different from that in Latin American countries, and was higher than in Asian economies.

4 RER management and manufactured export performance

4.1 Manufactured exports in the MENA countries

Table 3.3 presents data on the performance of some MENA countries in terms of manufactured exports. Over the last three decades, the success of these countries in increasing exports and in diversifying their economies has varied widely.

Tunisia and Jordan have been the most successful in increasing their exports of manufactures. Tunisian manufactured exports rose, on average, from 24.5 per cent of total exports in the 1970s to 75 per cent in the 1990s (4.6–21.2 per cent of GDP). Although Jordan's performance seems less impressive than Tunisia's, its increase in manufactured exports as a percentage of GDP is, in fact, comparable to Tunisia's (although Jordan's level of exports to GDP remains lower). Morocco also significantly increased its exports during the 1970s and 1980s, but these gains slowed in the 1990s.

Table 3.3 Average manufactured exports of selected MENA countries

	Algeria		*Egypt*		*Iran*		*Jordan*		*Morocco*		*Tunisia*	
	%X	*%GDP*	*%X*	*%GDP*	*%X*	*%GDP*	*%X*	*%GDP*	*%X*	*%GDP*	*%X*	*%GDP*
1970–9	3.0	0.6	27.1	3.1	2.9	0.6	25.8	1.9	16.0	2.1	24.5	4.6
1980–9	1.5	0.3	19.2	1.5	4.0	0.3	42.7	5.4	39.4	6.0	49.4	11.7
1990–9	3.3	0.8	36.6	2.4	6.6	1.5	48.9	9.5	52.9	7.5	74.9	21.2

Source: Authors' calculations.

Note
For the first sub-period, four values were missing for Iran (1970, 1971, 1972, and 1973). For the third sub-period, two values were missing for Iran (1991 and 1992) and one for Jordan (1996).

In Egypt, manufactured exports increased slowly throughout the period, growing from 27.1 per cent of total exports in the 1970s to only 36.6 per cent in the 1990s (as a percentage of GDP, in fact, they decreased from 3.1 to 2.4).

The two major oil-exporting countries, Algeria and Iran, showed the most dismal performance, with manufactured exports remaining negligible throughout the period.

4.2 Modelling exports of manufactured products

In this section, we try to quantify the cost of overvaluation for the MENA countries. As seen previously, manufactured exports should suffer from RER misalignment and volatility. We use the following model to test for these effects:

$$\begin{aligned}\ln(X_t) = {} & c + b_1 \cdot GDPgrTP_{i,t} + b_2 \ln(TOTn_{i,t}) + b_3 \ln(\mathrm{Inv}_{i,t}) \\ & + b_4 \ln(Roads_{i,t}) + b_5 \ln(H1_{i,t}) + b_6 \cdot RERVol_{i,t} \\ & + b_7 \ln(RERMis_{i,t}) + \varepsilon_t \end{aligned} \tag{3.2}$$

The model explains exports as a ratio of GDP in logarithmic form by including:

- The GDP growth rate of the trade partners ($GDPgrTP_{i,t}$), which can have a 'pulling' role in exports.
- The logarithm of the terms of trade $\ln(TOTn_{i,t})$, the improvement of which increases the profitability of production for export.
- The logarithm of the ratio of investment to GDP [$\ln(Inv_{i,t})$], which is conducive to an increase in overall production capacity, and thus to an increase in export capacity.
- The availability of core infrastructure, measured by the logarithm of the length of roads $\ln(Roads_{i,t})$ measured in kilometres per square kilometre, as well as the availability of human capital, approximated by the logarithm of the average number of years of primary schooling of the adult population [$\ln(H1_{i,t})$].
- The volatility in relative prices, approximated by the volatility of the RER (*RERVol*) and calculated as the coefficient of variation of the RER over

a 5-year period.[12] RER volatility increases uncertainty regarding the profitability of producing tradable goods.

- Distortions in relative prices, as measured by the RER misalignment (*RERMis*), where overvaluation hampers competitiveness and diverts investment out of the more productive tradable goods sectors. RER misalignment can also disrupt exports by increasing RER uncertainty.

In addition, we control for the heterogeneity of the sample by considering country dummy variables. These variables reflect differences in the quality of institutions or in endowments of natural resources – which can be the origin of large discrepancies in the natural propensity to export. The hypothesis of country dummy variables is supported by the data for manufactured exports[13] (see Table 3.4).

Table 3.4 Estimation results of the exports equations; dependent variables: $\ln(Xmanuf_t)$ and $\ln(Xtot_t)$

Variable	*Manufactured exports, ln(Xmanuf)*	*Total exports, ln(Xtot$_t$)*
$GDPgrTP_{i,t}$	2.83	1.48
	(1.9)	(2.52)
$\ln(TOTn_{i,t})$	−1.4	0.1
	(0.81)	(2.49)
$\ln(Inv_{i,t})$	0.87	0.30
	(5.8)	(8.69)
$\ln(Roads_{i,t})$	0.08	0.10
	(1.4)	(3.48)
$\ln(H1_{i,t})$	1.92	0.26
	(11.13)	(5.66)
RERVol	−0.27	−0.1
	(0.80)	(1.21)
ln(*RERMis*)	−0.72	−0.10
	(5.75)	(2.75)
Year 1974	0.25	
	(1.65)	
Year 1975	0.34	
	(1.7)	
Intercept		−1.14
		(9.05)
Adjusted R^2	0.81	0.13
Fischer test	31.7	78.3
Hausman test	12.4	0.20

Source: Authors' estimations.

Notes

Student *t* statistics are within brackets. The number of observations used in the regressions are, respectively, 816 and 964.

Data have been compiled from World Development Indicators, Global Development Finance, Global Development Network, and Live Data Base (World Bank).

A time dummy variable is also introduced for the years 1974–5, corresponding to the first oil shock.

4.3 Econometric results

Equation (3.2) was estimated on our panel of 53 countries from 1970–80 (depending on the country) to 1999, for both total exports ($Xtot_t$), and manufactured exports ($Xmanuf_t$). The idea is that manufactured exports are more sensitive to problems of competitiveness and negatively influenced by RER overvaluation. Due to missing data for some variables, the model was finally estimated on two unbalanced panels of 943 and 837 observations.[14] Results are shown in Table 3.4.

Our estimations confirm the negative impact of exchange rate misalignment on both total and manufactured export performance in the countries studied. The coefficient is rather strong in the case of manufactured exports (−0.72), and remains significant for total exports (−0.10). The weaker elasticity in the latter case can be explained by the fact that total exports of goods and services include products that are less sensitive to competitiveness, such as oil products and other primary goods, which are often owned and managed by governments.

For the MENA region as a whole, exchange rate policy explains losses in competitiveness and in manufactured exports. RER overvaluation has reduced, on average, the ratio of manufactured exports to GDP by 18 per cent a year. Manufactured exports, which averaged 4.4 per cent of GDP from 1970 to 1999, could have reached 5.2 per cent of GDP if no overvaluation had been present. These losses were more concentrated in the 1970s and 1980s than in the 1990s, due to the higher overvaluation of the currencies during those two sub-periods.

Some countries with a more diversified export base, such as Jordan and Morocco (see Table 3.5), had the highest losses due to misalignment during the 1970s and 1980s. As a result of its high level of manufactured exports, Tunisia still incurred a large loss during the 1990s despite a relatively low level of misalignment. Indeed, in these countries, RER misalignment either declined significantly or remained low during the 1990s, as the countries saw a continuous expansion in the diversification of their manufactured exports.

In the major oil-exporting countries of Iran and Algeria, the large overvaluation of the currency has certainly contributed to the low diversification of their exports away from oil. But the losses, as measured here, appear small given the low initial level of manufactured exports, which can be explained by the structure of their economies.

Our estimations fail, however, to show a significant impact of RER volatility on manufactured exports, as well as on the total exports of the countries studied. This finding does not confirm the empirical results of several studies of different groups of economies (see in particular Cushman 1993, Gagnon 1993, Ghura and Grennes 1993, Grobar 1993).

Our results also highlight the fact that total, as well as manufactured, exports are positively influenced by the GDP growth rate of the trade partners, the ratio of investment to GDP, and physical and human infrastructure (measured using, as

Table 3.5 Cost of misalignment on manufactured exports, selected MENA countries

	DZA			*EGY*			*IRN*		
	ExpM[a]	*Mis*	*Cost*[b]	*ExpM*[a]	*Mis*	*Cost*[b]	*ExpM*[a]	*Mis*	*Cost*[b]
1970–9	3	1.79	−1.7	27	1.15	−2.9	3	1.42	−0.9
1980–9	1.5	1.59	−0.6	19	1.22	−3.0	4	1.24	−0.7
1990–9	3.3	1.08	−0.2	37	1.09	−2.4	7	1.84	−4.0
1970–99	2.6	1.49	−0.8	27.6	1.15	−2.7	4.5	1.49	−1.8
	JOR			*MOR*			*TUN*		
	ExpM[a]	*Mis*	*Cost*[b]	*ExpM*[a]	*Mis*	*Cost*[b]	*ExpM*[a]	*Mis*	*Cost*[b]
1970–9	26	1.57	−10.5	16	1.49	−5.7	25		
1980–9	43	1.31	−9.4	39	1.08	−2.4	49	1.03	−1.0
1990–9	49	1.09	−3.1	53	1.10	−3.7	75	1.16	−8.7
1970–99	39.1	1.25	−7.7	36.1	1.21	−3.9	49.6	1.09	−4.8

Notes
a ExpM = manufactured exports as % of total exports.
b Cost = cost of overvaluation as % of total exports.

proxies, the length of roads and the level of primary education of the population respectively).[15]

The pulling effect of trade partners' GDP growth rate is particularly strong in the case of manufactured exports (elasticity of 2.8, almost double that of the 1.5 elasticity for total exports). This result goes in the expected direction – the income elasticity being higher for manufactured products than for other products in the economy.

The same conclusions can be drawn for human infrastructure – which improves investment profitability and competitiveness of manufactured exports much more than in other sectors of the economy. The particularly strong effect of primary education on export performance of the manufacturing sector (elasticity of 1.9, compared to 0.26 for total exports) has to be underlined. This makes education a key factor for manufacturing competitiveness in the developing world.

Manufactured exports are not sensitive to an improvement in the terms of trade, which can stimulate the export sector in general. This is, however, because terms of trade measures include prices of agricultural and mining exports and not only of manufacturing products.

5 Conclusions

In this chapter, we have shown that MENA countries have been characterized by a significant overvaluation of their currencies during the 1970s and 1980s. Overvaluation has, however, decreased in the 1990s on average, probably due to the increased flexibility of the exchange rate regime in some MENA economies, and to better macroeconomic management in others. Nevertheless, misalignment remains higher than in other regions of the world (except in CFA Africa), which may be explained by the delay of MENA countries in adopting more flexible exchange rates and in reforming their economies.

Although many economies have progressively adopted more flexible exchange rate regimes – leading to better management of their RERs – most MENA countries still have fixed or adjustable-peg exchange rate policies. Even if the shift toward a more open economy has begun in several of them, this process needs to be deepened, since the current situation reduces manufactured competitiveness and weakens the incentives for exporters to increase their presence in foreign markets. This is partly the case for oil exporting countries, which have failed to address the volatility of their economies and in which diversification of exports is still very low. This lack of trade openness also explains the low diversification of other MENA countries in the 1970s and 1980s.

Our study clearly illustrates that overvaluation has had a cost for the region in terms of competitiveness. In particular, manufactured exports have been affected by overvaluation of the exchange rate. These findings confirm recent assessments of economic policies and performance in developing countries, which underline the critical importance of the management of the real effective exchange rate. In particular, our results corroborate the findings regarding growth and manufactured exports developed by Edwards (1988), Balassa (1990), and Cottani *et al.* (1990) for different groups of developing countries.

Appendix A

Table 3.A1 List of countries in the sample

MENA	*Africa*	*Asia*	*Latin America*
	CFA	*South East Asia*	
Bahrain (BHR)	Burkina Faso (BFA)	Indonesia (IDN)	Argentina (ARG)
Algeria (DZA)	Cote d'Ivoire (CIV)	Korea, Rep. (KOR)	Bolivia (BOL)
Egypt, Arab Rep. (EGY)	Gabon (GAB)	Malaysia (MYS)	Brazil (BRA)
Iran, Islamic Rep. (IRN)	Cameroon (CMR)	Philippines (PHL)	Chile (CHL)
Jordan (JOR)	Ghana (GHA)	Thailand (THA)	Colombia (COL)
Kuwait (KWT)	Niger (NER)		Costa Rica (CRI)
Malta (MLT)	Senegal (SEN)	*South Asia*	Ecuador (ECU)
Morocco (MAR)	Togo (TGO)	Bangladesh (BGD)	Guatemala (GTM)
Syrian Arab Republic (SYR)		India (IND)	Mexico (MEX)
Tunisia (TUN)	*Non-CFA*	China (CHN)	Peru (PER)
	Botswana (BWA)	Sri Lanka (LKA)	Paraguay (PRY)
Other countries	Gambia, The (GMB)	Pakistan (PAK)	Uruguay (URY)
Israel (ISR)	Kenya (KEN)		Venezuela, RB (VEN)
	Madagascar (MDG)		
	Mozambique (MOZ)		
	Mauritius (MUS)		
	Malawi (MWI)		
	Nigeria (NGA)		
	Tanzania (TZA)		

Appendix B

Table 3.B1 Augmented Dickey–Fuller ADF unit root tests for Equations (3.1) and (3.1′)

Variable	*ADF statistic*	*(k)*[a]	*Critical value*[b]	*ADF test*
RER				
$\ln(e_t)$	−1.73	(1)	−1.69**	$I(0)$
Fundamentals				
$\ln(Inv_t)$	−1.92	(1)	−1.82*	$I(0)$
$\ln(Open_t)$	−1.69	(1)	−1.69**	$I(0)$
$\ln(TP_t)$	−3.77	(1)	−1.82*	$I(0)$
$\ln(TOT_t)$	−2.15	(1)	−1.82*	$I(0)$
$Capinf_t$	−2.79	(1)	−1.82*	$I(0)$
$DebtSev_t$				
Other variables				
Def_t	−2.43	(1)	−1.82*	$I(0)$
P	−2.76	(1)	−1.82*	$I(0)$
$Depr_t$	−3.07	(1)	−1.82*	$I(0)$
BMP_t	−2.69	(1)	−1.82*	$I(0)$
Residual of estimation				
Equation (3.1)	−20.23	(1)	−1.82*	$I(0)$
Equation (3.1′)	−18.75	(1)	−1.82*	$I(0)$

Source: Authors' calculations.

Notes

a k is the number of lags in the ADF test.

b Im *et al*. (1997) critical values (*1% and **5% levels).

Data have been compiled from World Development Indicators, Global Development Finance, Global Development Network, and Live Data Base (World Bank).

Table 3.B2 Augmented Dickey–Fuller ADF unit root tests for Equation (3.2)

Variable	*ADF statistic*	*(k)*[a]	*Critical value*[b]	*ADF test*
$\ln(Xmanuf_{i,t})$	−1.76		−1.69**	
$GDPgrTP_{i,t}$	−3.69	(1)	−1.82*	$I(0)$
$\ln(TOTn_{i,t})$	−2.15	(1)	−1.82*	$I(0)$
$\ln(Inv_{i,t})$	−1.92	(1)	−1.82*	$I(0)$
$\ln(Roads_{i,t})$	−3.65	(1)	−1.82*	$I(0)$
$\ln(H1i,t)$	−1.86	(1)	−1.82*	$I(0)$
RERVol	−2.83	(1)	−1.82*	$I(0)$
Ln(*RERMis*)	−2.24	(1)	−1.82*	$I(0)$
Residual of estimation	−3.06	(1)	−1.82*	$I(0)$

Source: Authors' calculations.

Notes

a k is the number of lags in the ADF test.

b Im *et al*. (1997) critical values (*1% and **5% levels).

Data have been compiled from World Development Indicators, Global Development Finance, Global Development Network, and Live Data Base (World Bank).

Appendix C: short-term dynamics of the RER

Since our variables are cointegrated, the short-term dynamic adjustment of the RER toward its equilibrium level can be estimated through an error correction model. The estimated equation is as follows:

$$\begin{aligned}\Delta\ln(e_{i,t}) = & -a[\ln(e_{i,t-1}) - \ln(e^{*}_{i,t-1})] \\ & + a'\Delta\ln(e_{i,t-1}) \\ & + b_1 \cdot \Delta\ln(Inv_{i,t}) + b_2 \cdot \Delta\ln(Open_{i,t}) + b_3 \cdot \Delta\ln(TOT_{i,t}) \\ & + b_4 \cdot \Delta\ln(Capinf_{i,t}) + b_5 \cdot \Delta\ln(DebtSev_{i,t}) \\ & + c_1 \cdot \Delta\ln(Inv_{i,t-1}) + c_2 \cdot \Delta\ln(Open_{i,t-1}) + c_3 \cdot \Delta\ln(TOT_{i,t-1}) \\ & + c_4 \cdot \Delta\ln(Capinf_{i,t-1}) + c_5 \cdot \Delta\ln(DebtSev_{i,t-1}) \\ & + d_1 \cdot Depr_{i,t} + d_2 \cdot Depr_{i,t-1} \\ & + e_1 \cdot Infl_{i,t} + e_2 \cdot Inf_{i,t-1} \\ & + f_1 \cdot Def_{i,t} + f_2 \cdot Def_{i,t-1} \\ & + g_1 \cdot BMP_t + g_2 \cdot BMP_{i,t-1} + \varepsilon_{2t} \end{aligned} \qquad (3.C\text{-}1)$$

Table 3.C1 Estimates of the error correction model; dependent variable: $\Delta\ln(e_t)$

Variable	*Equation (3.1)*		*Equation (3.1′)*	
	Elasticity	*Student* t	*Elasticity*	*Student* t
ε_{1t-1} [a]	−0.13	(7.29)	−0.2	(9.7)
$\Delta\ln(Inv_t)$	0.04	(1.42)	0.2	(0.78)
$\Delta\ \ln(Open_t)$	−0.27	(6.97)	−0.5	(14.53)
$\Delta\ln(TOT_t)$	0.1	(2.7)	0.1 5	(4.8)
$\Delta(Capinf)$	0.006	(1.27)	0.25	(3.8)
$\Delta\ln(DebtSev_t)$			0.02	(1.81)
$\Delta\ln(Inv_{t-1})$	0.01	(0.33)	0.03	(1.2)
$\Delta\ln(openv_{t-1})$	0.06	(1.57)	0.02	(0.5)
$\Delta\ln(TOT_{t-1})$	0.02	(0.72)	0.04	(1.4)
$\Delta\ (Capinf_{t-1})$	0.78	(1.81)	−0.33	(5.1)
$\Delta\ln(DebtSev_{t-1})$			0.04	(2.1)
$\Delta\ln(e_{t-1})$	0.06	(1.64)	0.16	(4.9)
$Depr$	−0. 22	(18.0)	−0.04	(10.9)
$Depr_{t-1}$	−0.05	(8.0)	0.006	(1.4)
$Infl_t$	0.19	(17.8)	0.04	(10.4)
$Infl_{t-1}$	0.05	(7.91)	−0.007	(1.6)
Def_{t-1}	0.05	(0.38)		
Def_t	0.05	(0.44)		
BMP_t	0.006	(2.5)	0.12	(5.5)
BMP_{t-1}	0.21	(0.86)	−0.003	(1.47)
D–W	1.74		2.03	

Source: Authors' estimations.

Notes

a ε_{1t-1} is the lagged error term of the cointegrating Equation (3.1).

Student *t* statistics are within brackets. The sample includes, respectively, 640 and 828 observations over the 1970–99 period.

Data have been compiled from World Development Indicators, Global Development Finance, Global Development Network, and Live Data Base (World Bank).

In addition to the error correction term, that is, the lagged error term of the cointegrating equation $(\ln(e_{t-1}) - \ln(e^*_{t-1})]$, and lagged variables of Equations (3.1) and (3.2) in first differences, we include indicators of fiscal policy (fiscal deficit as percentage of GDP, *Def*) and of exchange rate policy (nominal depreciation, *Depr*, and black market premium, *BMP*), as well as inflation (*Infl*). Our assumption is that the adjustment path of the RER toward its equilibrium level may be affected (accelerated or slowed down) by short-term economic policies including capital controls (for which *BMP* is a proxy), nominal exchange rate depreciation and fiscal policy, of which inflation can be a consequence. Table 3.C1 shows the estimates of the error correction model.

Nominal devaluations show a short-run impact on the RER, which is in the expected direction and significant. The change in the official nominal exchange rate (NER) hence captures the strong temporary effect that devaluation may produce on the RER due to price rigidities.

In addition, these estimations highlight the role of other short-term economic policies through a black market premium (*BMP*) and inflation (*Infl*). These variables (*Infl, BMP*), by leading to a rise in the price of non-tradable goods, appreciate the RER and lead to its overvaluation. Although the public deficit does not show a significant effect, it can be captured by the inflation variable, the effect of which is strong and which is also supposed to be a proxy for some other inappropriate policies.

Notes

* The views expressed in this chapter are those of the authors and not of their institution.

1 See, for example, Balassa (1990) and Reinhardt (1995) for empirical evidence from both developed and developing countries.

2 In fact, export diversification – through promotion of manufactured exports – is important for sustained growth for different reasons. First, income elasticity of demand is higher for manufactured goods than for primary products. In this way, growth in foreign income is expected to increase the growth prospects of a country's manufactured exports. Second, both price elasticities of demand and supply are presumed to be higher for manufactured goods than for primary commodities. This implies a stabilizing effect on the terms of trade and a more stable growth of exports over time. Third, development of the manufacturing sector produces substantial scope for dynamic productivity gains through economies of scale, learning effects, and externalities among firms and industries. See Nishimizu and Robinson (1986) for cross-country evidence, at a two-digit industry level, of positive correlation between export growth, and total factor productivity (TFP) changes.

3 An alternative methodology would be to calculate the fundamental equilibrium exchange rate – FEER – which is consistent with the external and internal equilibrium of an economy in the medium to long term. This approach assumes *ex ante* equilibrium of the balance of payments and calibration of current account balance, as well as sustainable capital flows, so as to be consistent with full employment and low inflation(internal equilibrium). The RER is assumed to converge

toward this fundamental equilibrium level in the medium to long term. This approach was developed by Williamson (1994) and, with the concept of natural real exchange rate (Natrex), by Stein (1994). Although this approach may be useful in assessing consistency between exchange rate policy and macroeconomic policy in the long run, one important drawback is that this methodology assumes a particular evolution of the fundamentals, which, in fact, may not be in line with the actual features of the economy (e.g. full employment, low inflation). In this respect, the FEER may be viewed, rather, as a normative concept. It may well be helpful to assess consistency between exchange rate policy and macroeconomic policy in the long run, but such an assessment may provide an inappropriate indicator of the distortions the economy is actually facing. Conversely, using a reduced form approach allows us to take into account an almost comprehensive range of the factors that affect the RER. This second methodology can, therefore, be viewed as a positive approach, which provides a more accurate measure of the distortions. For a comparison between the two approaches, see Clark and MacDonald (1998).

4 The comparative advantage of panel data regressions compared to time series estimations can be seen, first, in the double dimension of the sample (time series cross-section), which improves estimates by adding information; second, in the country dummy variables, which generally ask for an important degree of freedom, and improve the results of the estimations.

5 See Sekkat and Varoudakis (2002) for a panel data approach to assessing the misalignment of North African countries.

6 The short-run dynamic of the RER has also been estimated through an error correction model [Equation (3.C-1)]. Results are shown in Table 3.C1.

7 An increase in net capital inflows may result from: (i) an autonomous augmentation in foreign aid, foreign voluntary lending, or foreign direct investment (FDI); (ii) an increase in borrowing due to the removal of domestic capital controls; (iii) a fall in world interest rates; or (iv) an increase in public borrowing to finance the fiscal deficit.

8 Of which 19 are African countries (8 CFA and 11 non-CFA), 13 are Latin American, countries, 10 are Asian countries, and 11 are MENA countries (CFA stands for 'Communaute Francophone d'Afrique').

9 The countries were selected based on their level of per capita income. To preserve a kind of coherence of the sample, we generally chose intermediate-income countries so they could be compared to countries in the MENA region.

10 The use of the fixed-effect methodology is supported by the data, as shown by the Fischer test of equality of intercepts across countries, and is preferable to the random effect methodology, as revealed by the value of the Hausman test.

11 Other attempts have consisted in an 'economic' determination of these 'sustainable' levels (inspired by Edwards 1988). We took, as a sustainable value for openness, the average of the three higher values of the variable, and in the case of capital inflows, zero if the rate of growth of the economy was inferior to the international interest rate (meaning that borrowing was not sustainable). Those calculations are not shown here because they did not give better results as far as misalignment is concerned.

Our calculation of misalignment has been adjusted according to a base year, where the RER could be considered close to its equilibrium level. This has been the case especially in periods following devaluation and structural adjustment, when balance of payments were also close to the equilibrium. For example, it has been considered that RER was in equilibrium in 1989 in Morocco; 1991 and 1994–5 in Algeria; 1993–4 in Egypt; 1995 in Iran; 1992 in Jordan; and 1980, 1994, and 1997 in Tunisia. The method used to determine the probability of the RER being in equilibrium has been to identify a period of time when the difference between the observed and the sustainable value of the fundamental variables was very small.

Some more sophisticated calculations involve – when a variable has a unit root – using time series techniques introduced by Beveridge and Nelson (1981), where variables are decomposed into a random walk with a drift and a stationary component. Unlike the trend stationary model-based decomposition, this technique allows the steady-state growth path of the series to shift over time. Fluctuations around the shifting permanent path reflect cyclical effects.

12 To compute this indicator, some economists use more or less sophisticated regression techniques, such as the variance of the residual of the regression of the RER on a time trend, or an ARCH model of RER behaviour. However, from an empirical point of view, all these measures are highly correlated, and the standard deviation or the coefficient of variation measures perform as well as the more sophisticated ones (see Grobar 1993, Keen and Rodrick 1996).

13 As shown by the value of the Fischer test of equality of intercepts across countries, and by the value of the Hausman test as far as the random effect method is concerned (Table 3.4).

14 Before proceeding to the estimation of Equation (3.2), we have tested the degree of integration of the series entered into the regression, as well as the existence of a long-term relationship among them. The results of the ADF tests of the variables and the residuals of Equation (2) – using Im *et al.* (1997) critical values – are shown in Table 3.B2.

15 Surprisingly, in the case of roads, the elasticity for manufactured exports is weakly significant. This may be due to the fact that, in several MENA countries, oil exports represent an important percentage of total exports (as well as of GDP). In this case, it can be assumed that oil exports have led to the construction of good physical infrastructure.

References

Achy, L. (2001) 'Equilibrium exchange rate and misalignment in selected MENA countries', EUI Working Papers, Mediterranean Programme Series, RSC no. 2001/42.

Balassa, B. (1990) 'Incentive policies and export performance in Sub-Sahara Africa', *World Development*, 18(3).

Baffes, J., I. A. Elbadawi, and S. A. O'Connell (1997) 'Single-equation estimation of the equilibrium real exchange rate', *mimeo*, Swarthmore College (May).

Beveridge, S. and C. R. Nelson (1981) 'A new approach to decomposition of economic time series into permanent and transitory components with particular attention to measurement of the business cycle', *Journal of Monetary Economics* (7).

Clark, P. B. and R. MacDonald (1998) 'Exchange rates and economic fundamentals: a methodological comparison of BEERs and FEERs', IMF Working Paper, WP/98/67 (May), Washington, DC: International Monetary Fund.

Cottani, J. A., D. F. Cavallo, and M. S. Khan (1990) 'Real exchange rate behavior and economic performance in LDCs', *Economic Development and Cultural Change*, 39.

Cushman, D. O. (1993) 'The effects of real exchange rate risk on international trade', *Journal of International Economics*, 15.

Domac, I. and G. Shabsigh (1999) 'Real exchange rate behavior and economic growth: evidence from Egypt, Jordan, Morocco and Tunisia', IMF Working Paper, WP/99/40 (March), Washington, DC: International Monetary Fund.

Edwards, S. (1988) *Exchange Rate Misalignment in Developing Countries*, Baltimore: The Johns Hopkins University Press.

Edwards, S. (1989) *Real Exchange Rate, Devaluation and Adjustment: Exchange Rate Policy in Developing Countries*, Cambridge, MA: MIT Press.

Edwards, S. (1994) 'Real and monetary determinants of real exchange rate behavior: theory and evidence from developing countries', in Williamson, J. (ed.), *Estimating Equilibrium Exchange Rates*, Washington DC: Institute of International Economics.

Elbadawi, I. A. (1994) 'Estimating long-run equilibrium real exchange rates', in Williamson, J. (ed.), *Estimating Equilibrium Exchange Rates*, Washington, DC: Institute of International Economics.

Engel, R. F. and C. W. J. Granger (1987) 'Cointegration and error: representation, estimation and testing', *Econometrica* (35).

Frankel, J. A. and D. Romer (1999) 'Does trade cause growth?' *The American Economic Review*, 89(3).

Gagnon, J. E. (1993) 'Exchange rate variability and the level of international trade', *Journal of International Economics*, 34, (3–4).

Ghura, D. and T. J. Grennes (1993) 'The real exchange rate and macroeconomic performances in Sub-Saharan Africa', *Journal of Development Economics*, 42.

Grobar, L. M. (1993) 'The effect of real exchange rate uncertainty on LDC manufactured exports', *Journal of Development Economics*, 14.

Harberger, A. (1986) 'Economic adjustment and the real exchange rate', in Edwards, S. and L. Ahamed (eds), *Economic Adjustment Exchange Rates in Developing Countries*, Chicago: University of Chicago Press.

Im, K. S., M. H. Pesaran, and Y. Shin (1997) 'Testing for unit roots in heterogeneous panels', DAE Working Paper Amalgamated Series, no. 9526, Cambridge: University of Cambridge Press.

Keen, P. B. and R. Rodrick (1996) 'Measuring and analysing the effects of short-term volatility in real exchange rates', *Review of Economics and Statistics*, 68.

Mongardini, J. (1998) 'Estimating Egypt equilibrium real exchange rates', IMF Working Paper, WP/98/5 (January), Washington DC: International Monetary Fund.

Nishimizu, M. and S. Robinson (1986) 'Productivity growth in manufacturing', in Chenery, H., S. Robinson, and M. Syruin (eds), *Industrialization and Growth: A Comparative Study*, World Bank Research Report, Oxford: University of Oxford Press.

Razin, O. and S. M. A. Collins (1997) 'Real exchange rate misalignments and growth', NBER Working Paper, no. 6174 (September).

Reinhardt, C. (1995) 'Devaluation, relative prices, and international trade', IMF Staff Paper, no. 42.

Sekkat, K. and A. Varoudakis (2002) 'The impact of exchange and trade policy reforms on North African manufactured exports', *Development Policy Review*, 20(2).

Stein, J. L. (1994) 'The natural exchange rate of the us dollar and determinants of capital flows', in Williamson, J. (ed.), *Estimating Equilibrium Exchange Rates*, Washington, DC: Institute for International Economics.

Sundararajan, V., M. Lazare, and S. Williams (1999) 'Exchange rate unification, the equilibrium real exchange rate, and choices of exchange rate regime: the case of Islamic

Republic of Iran' IMF Working Paper, WP/99/15 (January), Washington, DC: International Monetary Fund.
Williamson, J. (1985) 'The exchange rate system', *Policy Analyses in International Economics*, no. 5, Washington, DC: Institute for International Economics.
Williamson, J. (1994) 'Estimates of FEERs', in Williamson, J. (ed.), *Estimating Equilibrium Exchange Rates*, Washington, DC: Institute for International Economics.

4 Agriculture and trade liberalization in the MENA region

Dynamic impacts of future scenarios*

Ali H. Bayar, Ghazi Ben-Ahmed, Paul de Boer, Xinshen Diao, and A. Erinc Yeldan

1 Introduction

What would be the potential economic impact of a new World Trade Organization (WTO) trade round on the agricultural trade of the countries of the Middle East and North Africa (MENA) region? The answer to this question has to take into account not only the various liberalization scenarios one can meaningfully envisage as a result of the current WTO negotiations, but also the ongoing reform efforts of the European Common Agricultural Policy (CAP), the enlargement of the European Union (EU) and the future of the Euro-Mediterranean Agreements (EMAs). A great number of divergent combinations of policies/scenarios can be envisaged and the implications of these diverse combinations are very different for the agricultural trade of the MENA countries.

For the MENA countries, agricultural production and trade is greatly affected by a variety of domestic policy interventions and other external trade and agricultural policies adopted by the region's main trading partner, the EU. The commitments that have resulted from the Uruguay Round, as well as the prospect of EU enlargement, will require further policy adjustments in the CAP in the years to come. The EU has pursued a policy of reform since 1992, based on two elements: lowering the guaranteed prices for key products and offsetting the impact of these cuts on producer incomes by means of direct payments. An even more radical reform was undertaken in 1999 – the Agenda 2000 package – to prepare the EU for enlargement and in order to take an active role in the WTO negotiations on agriculture. In fact, the Doha meeting in November 2001 set a very challenging timetable. The WTO members will have to reach agreement on new rules in order to formulate fresh commitments by 31 March 2003, so they can then submit their offers at the 2003 WTO Ministerial Meeting in Mexico.

The value of preferences granted to the Mediterranean Countries (MCs: Algeria, Cyprus, Egypt, Israel, Jordan, Lebanon, Malta, Morocco, the Palestinian Authority, Syria, Tunisia, and Turkey) depends on the level of EU import barriers to Most Favoured Nation (MFN) suppliers as well as to the extent to which agriculture is liberalized in the existing Free Trade Agreements (FTAs) with Mexico and South Africa, and forthcoming ones between the EU and its partners.

In the short run, therefore, negotiations on the extension of preferences remain an important issue for the MENA region, and in particular for the MCs, but also for the Gulf Cooperation Council (GCC) countries, which will start negotiating an FTA with the EU in 2003. However, any benefits could be of a transitory nature, as these countries would be more exposed to competition by MFN suppliers than they are at present.

2 Current agricultural trade in the MENA region

MENA countries are highly diverse in terms of their economic and geographical size, natural resource endowments, and standards of living. This region is characterized by: (i) the limited extent to which member countries have been able to eliminate or streamline administrative procedures related to trade; (ii) the fact that many countries in the region have yet to accede to the WTO (Algeria, Lebanon, Oman, Saudi Arabia, and Yemen are in the process of acceding or have shown an interest in doing so); and (iii) the weakness of intra-regional trade and the high level of tariff and non-tariff barriers, the weak complementarities among these economies and of course political tension and conflict within the region. All these factors explain the limited nature of intra-MENA trade, which remains low by all accounts. In 1998, for instance, intra-Arab exports represented only 8.2 per cent of the region's total exports.

Notwithstanding the limited significance of total intra-regional trade, De Rosa (1997) finds that intra-MENA trade accounts for 30 per cent of total exports of agricultural products. Exceptionally high percentages are reported for some prominent categories of agricultural products: barley (96 per cent); rice (88 per cent); livestock, meats and dairy products (87 per cent); and cereals (47 per cent). Intra-regional trade accounts for only 10 per cent of total agricultural imports, but, remarkably, 50 per cent for fruits and vegetables.

Table 4.1 provides average figures for total exports, exports excluding oil, total imports and the total trade balance, as well as the averages of the exchange of goods and the trade balances with the EU of the MENA countries over the period 1995–7 (excluding the Palestinian Authority for which we do not have data over the period covered). It also provides sub-regional totals for the Maghreb, other North African countries, the GCC and other countries in the Middle East.

It can be seen that total annual exports of the MENA region amount to 165.9 billion euros (€) on average over 1995–7. Saudi Arabia (€43.8 billion) and the United Arab Emirates (€18.4 billion) together account for more than one-third of this total. Total imports are €155.3 billion, one-third of which is accounted for by two countries: Turkey (€25.8 billion) and Saudi Arabia (€23.0 billion). The total trade balance shows an average *surplus* of €10.6 billion: but with oil excluded, total exports of the MENA region drop by as much as €105.1 billion to 60.8 billion! From Table 4.1 we can see that Israel and Turkey both account for a quarter of total exports excluding oil.

Table 4.1 MENA countries' volume and pattern of imports and exports (average figures for 1995–7 in billions of euros)

	Total							*With the EU*				
	Exports	*(% of MENA)*	*Exports (excl. oil)*	*(% of MENA)*	*Imports*	*(% of MENA)*	*Trade balance*	*Exports*	*(% of total)*	*Imports*	*(% of total)*	*Trade balance*
Maghreb												
Algeria	10.4	6.3	1.4	2.3	6.1	3.9	4.3	6.5	62.5	4.1	67.2	2.4
Morocco	5.7	3.4	5.7	9.4	6.2	4.0	−0.5	4.2	73.7	4.6	74.2	−0.4
Tunisia	4.0	2.4	3.7	6.1	5.2	3.3	−1.2	3.5	87.3	4.2	80.8	−0.7
Total	20.1	12.1	10.8	17.8	17.5	11.3	2.6	14.2	70.6	12.9	73.7	1.3
Other NA												
Libya	7.3	4.4	0.4	0.7	3.6	2.3	3.7	5.9	80.8	2.2	61.1	3.6
Egypt	4.3	2.6	2.1	3.5	12.3	7.9	−8.0	2.4	55.8	5.3	43.1	−2.9
Total	11.6	7.0	2.5	4.1	15.9	10.2	−4.3	8.3	71.6	7.5	47.2	0.7
GCC												
Bahrain	1.5	0.9	1.0	1.7	1.4	0.9	0.1	0.2	13.3	0.6	42.9	−0.4
Kuwait	9.5	5.7	0.4	0.7	5.3	3.4	4.2	1.4	14.7	2.0	37.9	−0.6
Oman	4.9	3.0	0.4	0.7	2.4	1.5	2.5	0.1	2.0	1.1	45.8	−0.9
Qatar	3.6	2.2	0.4	0.7	2.1	1.4	1.5	0.0	0.3	1.2	57.1	−1.2
Saudi Arabia	43.8	26.4	4.9	8.1	23.0	14.8	20.8	8.6	19.6	8.3	36.1	0.2
UAE	18.4	11.1	4.0	6.6	18.5	11.9	−0.1	1.0	5.5	6.1	33.0	−5.2
Total	81.7	49.2	11.1	18.3	52.7	33.9	29.0	11.3	13.9	19.3	36.6	−8.1
Other ME												
Cyprus	0.8	0.5	0.8	1.3	3.2	2.1	−2.4	0.4	50.0	1.6	50.0	−1.2
Iran	13.6	8.2	1.9	3.1	8.2	5.3	5.4	4.9	36.0	3.8	46.3	1.1
Iraq	0.9	0.5	0.0	0.0	0.4	0.3	0.5	0.5	55.6	0.1	25.0	0.4
Israel	15.4	9.3	15.4	25.3	18.2	11.7	−2.8	5.3	34.4	9.8	53.8	−4.5
Jordan	0.6	0.4	0.6	1.0	2.5	1.6	−1.9	0.1	16.7	1.0	40.4	−0.9
Lebanon	0.4	0.2	0.4	0.7	4.2	2.7	−3.8	0.1	25.0	2.5	59.5	−2.4
Malta	1.2	0.7	1.2	2.0	2.3	1.5	−1.1	0.6	50.0	1.6	69.6	−1.0
Syria	2.6	1.6	0.7	1.2	2.9	1.9	−0.3	1.8	69.2	1.2	41.4	0.5
Turkey	15.3	9.2	15.3	25.2	25.8	16.6	−10.5	9.9	64.7	16.0	62.1	−6.1
Yemen	1.7	1.0	0.1	0.2	1.5	1.0	0.2	0.1	5.9	0.6	40.0	−0.5
Total	52.5	31.6	36.4	59.9	69.2	44.6	−16.7	23.7	45.1	38.2	55.2	−14.6
MENA	165.9	100.0	60.8	100.0	155.3	100.0	10.6	57.4	34.6	78.0	50.2	−20.6

Sources: Comtrade (for total exchanges) and Comex (for exchanges with the EU).

Table 4.1 also presents data on MENA trade with the EU. For each country and for each group, it gives share of exports to and imports from the EU. The trade balance with the EU shows an average total *deficit* of €20.6 billion.

Viewed from the MENA perspective, trade with the EU is quite important: the share of the EU in MENA's total exports is on average 34.6 per cent. Moreover, slightly more than half of MENA's imports originate from the EU. For the Maghreb, these percentages are considerably higher: about 71 per cent of exports and 74 per cent of imports.

MENA's exports are highly concentrated in mineral fuels. Oil accounts, on average, for 63.4 per cent of total exports; for the GCC countries this share is even higher at 86.4 per cent. Other important oil exporters are: Algeria, Egypt, Iran, Iraq, Libya, and Syria.

Notwithstanding the prominence of oil in the region, agriculture remains important to most economies in MENA: the agricultural and rural population still amounts to 40–60 per cent of the total population and the agricultural sector accounts for a substantial share of total employment. Agricultural products also account for a large share of the exports of several MENA countries. The EU is a net *exporter* of agricultural products to the MCs with an average surplus of around €300 million for the period 1994–8. However, for the three countries that were scheduled for agricultural re-negotiations in 2000, the EU is a net *importer* (with an average of €830 million over that period): agricultural trade with Morocco and Israel shows a clear deficit, while trade with Tunisia is close to balance.

2.1 Agricultural exports to the EU

The MCs contributed an average of 7.3 percent to the total agricultural imports of the EU between 1994 and 1998. These originated mainly from six countries: Turkey, Morocco, and Israel were the three most important suppliers, followed by Tunisia, Egypt, and Cyprus. While Syria was a considerable cotton exporter, its other exports were low. Exports from Algeria, Lebanon, Jordan, Malta, and the Palestinian Authority to the EU were rather small: less than €30 million for the whole period. The Mediterranean countries are important suppliers to the EU, though far behind Latin America and the North American Free Trade Agreement (NAFTA), countries but ahead of Australia and New Zealand. The virtual absence of exports to the United States and Japan shows the concentration of MCs' exports to the EU. Grethe and Tangermann (1998) report that in 1995, nearly 70 per cent of farm exports from the MCs (Israel, Libya, Malta, Cyprus, and Turkey excluded) are oriented towards the EU. This concentration is the highest for Tunisia (83 per cent), Morocco (47 per cent), and Egypt (64 per cent).

Agricultural exports represent an essential proportion of total exports to the EU from the Palestinian Authority (more than 50 per cent), Morocco and Cyprus (22 per cent), and Turkey and Lebanon (around 15 per cent). For Israel and Tunisia, too, the share of farm exports is significant (12.5 and 9.4 per cent, respectively), while it is negligible for others.

Mediterranean exports are concentrated in a relatively restricted number of products: hazelnuts, citrus fruits (fresh or prepared) and olive oil. Together with grapes, potatoes, molluscs, dates, and flowers, these account for 50 per cent of all farm exports to the EU. This poor diversification of exports is representative of each single country.

An analysis of exports originating from each MC to the EU thus shows weak diversification, indicating a clear pattern of specialization. For example, two-thirds of Morocco's exports are made up of citrus fruits, tomatoes, and olives, as well as fishing products (tinned sardines and anchovies, squids and octopuses). Israel's main export goods are flowers, citrus fruits (oranges, grapefruits), fruit juices, and dates, which total 50 per cent of her exports to Europe. Except for Turkey, whose exports are relatively diversified, other countries are highly specialized.

Weak diversification is not a problem *per se*, as a tendency towards specialization in foreign trade is natural. However, heavy dependence on the European markets may be risky: once CAP is revised or once liberalization progresses, exports that have benefited thus far from high and stable prices in the European markets will face serious competition. Moroccan citrus fruits of superior quality, for example, are exported to the EU precisely because of high market prices.

2.2 Agricultural imports from the EU

MENA's agricultural imports are determined to a large extent by per capita income levels and population size. For instance, large volumes of livestock, meat and dairy products are imported by Saudi Arabia, Israel, and the United Arab Emirates and by populous countries such as Iran and Egypt.

The MCs represent an important market for European agricultural exports: on average 10.6 per cent of European exports are sold to the Mediterranean region (1994–8). Of the main EU exports, the MCs absorb 38 per cent of sugar, wheat, and flour, and 78 per cent of beef. Algeria and Egypt are among the EU's main clients, representing, respectively, the 14th and 15th largest export outlets in 1997 (European Commission 1998). Hence, the opening of these countries' markets to agricultural products is not without significance for Europe. The EU has a certain interest in achieving preferential access to these markets in order to partly compensate for the negative impact of the pending reforms aimed at reducing support measures to its agricultural sector (Uruguay Round and the restructuring of the CAP).

As with exports, imports of the MCs are concentrated in some products: more than 50 per cent of imports comprise nine product groups. Imports of sugar, wheat, milk, and flour make up one-third of total imports. It is noteworthy that certain sugar and flour imports compete with local produce in some countries (Egypt and Morocco). The structure of imports at a regional level comprises two product groups: on the one hand, produce and sub-produce of cereal origin (wheat, flour, and barley); on the other hand, produce and derived produce from bovine farming (milk, meat, livestock, and cheese). This concentration hints at a relatively similar structure of imports for the different countries of the region.

Unsurprisingly, the most populated countries of the region are also the largest importers (Algeria, Egypt, and Turkey). Being a rich country, Israel also counts amongst the large importers. Algeria distinguishes itself from the rest of the MCs because of its very weak agricultural sector: as with Egypt, it has a significant trade deficit.

Examining each country in detail, it can be seen that their major imports are quite similar. Wheat (Morocco, Tunisia, Algeria, and Egypt, one of the world's biggest importers); sugar (Israel, Turkey, Algeria, and Tunisia); beef (Egypt, Turkey, and Morocco); and, to a lesser extent, milk (Algeria and Morocco), and wheat flour (Algeria and Libya) are the most important. This situation reflects a common characteristic of all these countries, namely their incapacity to satisfy domestic demand, due to a lack of arable lands, water resources, and modern production techniques.

3 Policy analysis

Our analytical model can be used to study alternatives for preferential trade agreement blocs among the countries of the MENA region, given their existing trade patterns with the EU. As a first step we study the customs union (CU) path followed by Turkey and the EU since 1995. As Turkey has already signed a CU with the EU, we trace the new policy environment beginning from Turkish–EU trade integration. The CU agreement between Turkey and the EU, which is currently in effect, covers mainly industrial commodity trade, with agriculture and services subject to a period of grace. In our next step, we extrapolate the initial CU agreement to full trade liberalization between the two partners covering all sectors. Following that, we broaden our analysis to include issues of bilateral and coordinated trade liberalization between the MENA countries and the EU.

3.1 Overview of the analytical model

The model is based on dynamic macroeconomic theory with a multi-region and multi-sector specification, and in many ways draws upon the recent contributions of dynamic applied general equilibrium modelling by McKibbin (1993), Mercenier and Sampaïo de Souza (1994), Mercenier and Yeldan (1997), Diao *et al.* (1999), and Diao and Somwaru (2000). The world economy is disaggregated into nine regions. In each region, there are nine production sectors, each of which produces a single commodity. All the regions are fully endogenous in terms of the economic behaviour of their producers and consumers. Furthermore, in a multi-region and multi-sector global model, commodity trade flows are tracked by their geographical and sectoral origin and destination. Countries are further linked by an Armington system so that sectoral commodities are differentiated in demand and supply by their geographical origin.

Firms in each region produce goods and conduct capital investment so as to maximize the firm's valuation. Households with infinite life spans consume domestically produced and imported goods to maximize an inter-temporal utility function. Household income is consumed or saved in the form of equity in domestic firms or foreign bonds. Domestic firm equities and foreign bonds are assumed to be perfect substitutes. Through equity purchases by households, the world 'pool' of savings is channelled to profitable investment projects without regard to the national origin of savings. Technological change and population growth are exogenous and, because we could normalize all variables in per capita terms, they are assumed to be zero in the model. A full and detailed description of the model is given in Bayar *et al.* (2000) and is not reproduced here.

3.2 Simulation experiments

We organize our modelling analysis under two sets of issues. First, we look into country experiences in response to bilateral trade integration with the EU, *given that Turkey has already signed a customs union with the EU*. In this stage, we hypothesize trade liberalization in manufacturing commodity trade between the respective regions of MENA and the EU. Secondly, we envisage a policy environment where manufacturing trade is liberalized under a coordinated setting within the MENA. Here, we implement a free trade area within the MENA bloc, complemented by elimination of tariffs and tariff-like barriers vis-à-vis the EU manufacturing trade. We call the first policy environment the 'No-Coordination' scenario, and the second one the 'Coordinated FTA' scenario.

Given that most of the countries in the region have similar endowments and trade patterns with the EU, emphasis of a policy distinction between coordinated versus uncoordinated trade liberalization attempts will prove to be crucial. In our modelling analysis, we report both the static and dynamic effects of trade policy. Dynamic effects will be driven by consumers' optimization and inter-temporal consumption smoothing over a long-term horizon. In this setting, saving decisions of consumers will depend on inter-temporal macroeconomic prices such as the rate of interest and the (real) exchange rate. The saving–investment gap will be covered by the current account deficit in equilibrium, which in turn will induce optimal foreign borrowing plans for the indigenous region.

Theory suggests that the dynamic effects of both bilateral and coordinated trade liberalization attempts are subject to many factors. General equilibrium processes on the national and global level may yield conflicting forces, and the realized outcomes often depend on a host of technological factors, which are hard to account for within the context of an analytical model. In the standard Solow–Ramsey framework, transitional adjustments to long-run equilibrium are achieved solely by capital accumulation, which itself is subject to diminishing returns. Trade liberalization entails, on the other hand, adjustments that go beyond standard processes of capital accumulation. There is now increasing evidence that open economies capture significant gains in total factor productivity (TFP), especially through intermediation of foreign R&D stocks by way of capital goods imports. Empirical studies in the growth literature as outlined in the seminal works of Levine and Renelt (1992) and Frankel and Romer (1999) underscore the TFP gains due to trade liberalization. Coe *et al.* (1997), on the other hand, provide estimates of foreign R&D elasticities obtained by way of intermediate imports. Early applications of trade-driven TFP gains were modelled in De Melo and Robinson (1992) and Yeldan *et al.* (1998). Diao *et al.* (1999), on the other hand, modelled the (endogenous) growth processes of R&D-driven technological change within the context of open trade regimes.

In the current study, we utilize the framework initially laid by the above modelling exercises and regard TFP generation as an endogenous function of the increase in imports in the aftermath of trade liberalization. Formally, we model such TFP gains as a positive shock on output and investment demand, which is sustained for eight periods following the trade policy implementation.

Thus, this specification leaves us with the following matrix of possible interactions of the policy environment with technological adjustments:

Policy environment	*Technological adjustments*	
	Investment effects of K-*accumulation*	*Investment plus TFP effects*
No coordination	N-C w/ Inv effects	N-C w/ INV + TFP
Coordinated FTA within MENA	FTA w/ Inv effects	FTA w/ INV + TFP

We implement our trade liberalization experiments in two steps: first, we induce the MENA countries to eliminate the existing tariffs on imports from the EU in their *manufacturing* sectors. This policy move can be envisaged as a completely bilateral arrangement with the EU and the respective country or region. Yet, it can also be envisaged to be part of a wider policy where MENA countries take the additional step of liberalizing their trade regimes vis-à-vis each other by forming a free-trade area among themselves (the coordinated FTA scenario).

After this step, we extend our analysis to take account of trade liberalization in agricultural and services trade. We implement these new trade regimes both under the uncoordinated and coordinated FTA policy environments, and also with the distinction of investment versus investment-plus-TFP dynamic adjustments, as summarized in the policy and technology matrix above.

With the aid of these sets of policy simulations, we try to capture the individual regional macroeconomic responses and welfare changes of each individual region in response to bilateral trade liberalization with the EU. Our starting point is the macro general equilibrium of the global commodity and finance markets as of 1995. Our data come from a direct aggregation of the database of the Global Trade Analysis Project (GTAP), version 5. We implement our policy simulation experiments via parametric changes of the relevant policy parameters and trace the out-of-steady-state transitional dynamic adjustments towards a new steady state equilibrium. Thus, we rely on the laboratory characteristics of our analytical apparatus and implement these strategic policy options as discrete simulation experiments sequentially. Since our focus is mostly on the short to medium run, we choose to limit our analysis exclusively on the first 20 periods of the dynamic adjustment; yet, in principle, one can extend this time horizon and portray the whole time path of the intertemporal equilibrium towards the steady state.

We first disturb the initial equilibrium configuration by implementing, *ceteris paribus*, tariff reductions for manufacturing imports from the EU. The social welfare effects are tabulated in Tables 4.2 and 4.3. The social welfare metric is the equivalent variation of income that the representative consumer is willing to forego against the implementation of the trade policy. We differentiate both the static (upon impact) welfare effects and the dynamic path.

The interesting result is that manufacturing trade liberalization entails static welfare losses for the MENA region. Under no coordination within the MENA, bilateral trade liberalization brings a welfare loss of $43 million for Morocco, $762 million for Turkey, $595 million for the 'Rest of the ME region', and $1,454 million for the 'Rest of North Africa region'. The EU is expected to capture a welfare gain totalling $6,160 million. Even though under the coordinated FTA attempts within the MENA bloc the welfare losses are somewhat smaller, they are still negative. Here, Morocco is observed to achieve almost a balance with a minor static welfare loss of 10 million. Turkey's loss is cut by one third, whereas the remaining two regions of the MENA bloc experience comparable outcomes as

Table 4.2 Changes in social welfare under bilateral trade liberalization with no-coordination among MENA countries (in million US$ and % change)

	Upon impact[a]			
	Manufacturing trade liberalization		*Full trade liberalization*	
	Million US$	*% Change*	*Million US$*	*% Change*
Morocco	−43.0	−0.148	95.3	0.328
Turkey	−762.2	−0.499	−705.8	−0.463
Rest of ME	−595.0	−0.146	−239.9	−0.060
Rest of NA	−1,454.5	−1.072	−1,323.1	−0.977
EU	6,160.1	0.094	6,395.8	0.098

	Dynamic effects of full trade liberalization					
	Cumulative % change due to investment effects			*Cumulative % change due to investment plus growth effects*		
	Period 5	*Period 10*	*Period 20*	*Period 5*	*Period 10*	*Period 20*
Morocco	−0.403	0.383	0.879	1.444	4.698	5.782
Turkey	−0.372	−0.278	−0.221	1.466	3.953	5.234
Rest of ME	−0.612	−0.419	−0.274	1.116	2.911	3.348
Rest of NA	−1.237	−0.645	−0.304	0.748	4.083	5.228
EU	0.101	0.149	0.175	0.126	0.202	0.257

Note

a Without investment or growth effects: static welfare changes due only to reallocation of existing resources.

Table 4.3 Changes in social welfare under bilateral trade liberalization with coordinated FTA among MENA countries (in million US$ and % change)

	Upon impact[a]			
	Manufacturing trade liberalization		*Full trade liberalization*	
	Million US$	*% Change*	*Million US$*	*% Change*
Morocco	−10.1	−0.035	136.4	0.470
Turkey	−212.2	−0.139	−82.8	−0.054
Rest of ME	−518.1	−0.127	−130.6	−0.032
Rest of NA	−1398.1	−1.031	−1257.7	−0.927
EU	5,700.1	0.087	5,886.4	0.090

	Dynamic effects of full trade liberalization					
	Cumulative % change due to investment effects			*Cumulative % change due to investment plus growth effects*		
	Period 5	*Period 10*	*Period 20*	*Period 5*	*Period 10*	*Period 20*
Morocco	−0.346	0.502	1.036	1.451	4.792	5.934
Turkey	−0.273	0.012	0.163	3.389	8.402	10.947
Rest of ME	−0.588	−0.383	−0.228	1.195	3.041	3.502
Rest of NA	−1.250	−0.591	−0.211	0.450	3.486	4.581
EU	0.094	0.142	0.168	0.125	0.203	0.264

Note

a Without investment or growth effects: static welfare changes due only to reallocation of existing resources.

before. Thus, a coordinated FTA arrangement within the MENA seems to cushion the adjustment costs for Turkey and Morocco.

The downward adjustments of social welfare are the direct results of short-term (static) terms of trade effects. The initial impact of elimination of manufacturing import tariffs is a reduction in import costs and an overall deflation of the domestic price level in the MENA bloc. Thus, vis-à-vis the EU the real exchange rate, defined as the ratio of the domestic versus the EU consumer baskets, depreciates in all of the countries experiencing the tariff reduction (for an analytical exposition of this point, see Obstfeld and Rogoff 1996: chapter 4). Along with domestic prices, export prices are relatively adversely affected in comparison with their import counterparts. The adverse terms of trade are of the order of 0.2 per cent in Morocco; 0.8 per cent in Turkey; 0.5 per cent in the 'Rest of ME'; and 0.05 per cent in 'Rest of North Africa'. Under the coordinated FTAs, the adverse movements of the regional terms of trade effects are smaller; hence, the welfare losses are adjusted downwards.

When we expand our policy experiment to further trade liberalization in non-industrial sectors, Morocco experiences a welfare gain of $95 million under bilateral trade liberalization, and $136 million under the coordinated FTA scenario. Turkey experiences a worsening under no coordination, but coordinated FTA seems to minimize Turkish welfare losses. Full trade liberalization under a coordinated FTA is associated with a relatively smaller welfare loss in the other two regions of the MENA, but nevertheless static effects of tariff reduction are obviously unfavourable for the region as a whole.

These results change significantly when we account for dynamic effects. Under the coordinated FTA regime, Morocco and Turkey experience a gain in social welfare starting from period 10. These standard capital accumulation effects are complemented by TFP gains, and under this technological adjustment, trade liberalization is observed to bring sizable gains to all countries in the region. The cumulative social welfare gain expected under trade liberalization by the end of period 20 is about $2 billion in Morocco; $19 billion in Turkey; $15 billion in the Rest of ME; and $7 billion in North Africa. Comparable welfare gains for the EU reach $18 billion.

Simulation results show that with no coordination envisaged, real GDP is expected to rise at the end of 20 periods in Morocco by 2.5 per cent; 0.1 per cent in Turkey; 1.2 per cent in the Rest of ME; and 1 per cent in the North African region, if only investment effects are considered. Consideration of TFP effects boosts such expected output gains significantly. In addition, implementing an enlarged FTA within the MENA maximizes such real GDP gains. In general, Morocco seems to gain the most from trade liberalization shocks.

The output responses of the experiment are diverse and it is hard to make generalizations given the complexity of intertemporal general equilibrium effects. Yet, the surge in textiles and meat processing in Morocco and in textiles, heavy manufacturing goods and high value-added services in Turkey are clearly visible. In the short term, Moroccan textiles production expands by 0.13 per cent, and meat processing expands by 0.01 per cent. Dynamic adjustments bring positive output responses in all sectors of the Moroccan economy. Even if no FTP effects are modelled, investment demand due to reallocation of consumers' intertemporal preferences leads to an expansion of all sectors exceeding 1 per cent by period 20.

Turkish output responses are also observed to be of a comparable nature. The strongest output response comes from textiles, followed by grains and the heavy manufacturing sectors. The weakest response was observed in services and light manufacturing. In drawing a comparison between the Turkish and Moroccan dynamic results, it is interesting to note that TFP-induced output gains are stronger in Turkey. The 'Rest of the ME region' also displays strong output responses in textiles. Other manufacturing industries expand in the short run, whereas services dwindle. In the long run, investment and TFP effects bring forth very significant expansion of both heavy manufacturing and light manufacturing as well as textiles.

It is interesting to note that manufacturing trade liberalization in all four MENA regions results in contraction of primary agriculture – grains and other crops – in the short run. The static output responses due to reallocation of resources clearly favour manufacturing with the move towards an open economy pricing system. Part of this expansion is due to efficiency gains in resource allocation after lowering average tariff protection, and part of it originates from the *level effects* of increased investment expenditures that lead to expansion of the capital stock. Both exports and imports expand in all regions following trade liberalization, yet the rate of expansion in the latter typically outweighs that of the former, and the trade deficit is expected to widen. The counterpart of this deficit is the rise in the investment–savings gap in the domestic economy.

Investment response is depicted by comparisons between whether trade liberalization is conducted under coordination or no-coordination within the MENA. TFP-driven growth episodes, not surprisingly, provide strong resource pulls for capital investments. The rise in investment demand reaches 18 per cent at the end of period 20 in Morocco including TFP effects. Even in the absence of such TFP externalities, capital investments are observed to rise by 10 per cent under no coordination and by 12 per cent under the coordinated liberalization scenario. In Turkey, most of the surge in investment demand seems to be driven by TFP gains. Standard capital accumulation results in minor investment expansion. This result may be due to the fact that Turkey has already taken significant steps towards liberalizing its trade and the standard gains in intertemporal reallocation have already been realized. Thus, the expected gains from future trade reform are yet to be generated from technological adjustments via TFP shocks for the Turkish economy. The 'Rest of the ME region' also displays strong TFP-induced technological gains, which do not seem to stabilize even after 20 periods. Pure investment effects are also observed to be on a rising trend. In contrast, the North African regional response is an over-shooting in investment demand. The bang-bang[1] behaviour in the 'Rest of North Africa' region is the result of the rapid intertemporal substitution that the households face in lieu of the trade shock.

Now we return to individual responses to EU trade patterns. Under the no-coordination episode, exports to EU rise fastest in Morocco, followed by Turkey, the 'Rest of North Africa' and the 'Rest of the ME'. A coordinated FTA stance does not change these results, yet the response of Turkish exports gets closer proportionally to the Moroccan performance over the medium term. A coordinated FTA within the MENA region clearly seems to be a superior strategy in trade liberalizing experiments vis-à-vis the EU.

4 Conclusions

Some caveats on the limitations of the study are necessary before we proceed with the summary of our main findings. First, it has to be clear that with this type of methodology, no definite conclusions can be drawn about the characterization of the future path of the economy based on 'calendar' dates. The policy experiments performed are basically of a *comparative* nature and are meaningful only in relation to each other rather than revealing forecasts for the future.

Second, both consumption and production activities of the economy are modelled in very aggregate terms. The idea of a *representative* national consumer, though a common device in modern macroeconomic thinking, precludes any analysis addressing income distribution questions and may seem implausible. This specification reflects, however, our main objective in focusing mostly on the dynamics of adjustment of the macro aggregates along a transition path in response to broad policy shifts, and on processes of resource allocation, which reflect changes in production efficiency. Thus, as such, many of our insights derived from the simulation exercises do not depend on detailed considerations of heterogeneity of the private sector. In similar vein, government saving and investment behaviour are not addressed and, hence, the spill-over effects of public consumption and investment in the private sector are not captured. In the absence of empirical evidence on the nature and causes of such spill-overs (especially in the context of a developing country), we try to avoid forming arbitrary algebraic characterizations as much as possible, and avoid modelling the public sector as an optimizing agent.

Third, one has to note that the adjustment path as characterized by the simulation exercises reflect *equilibrium* relationships on a *smooth* time horizon, mainly in the absence of rigidities and/or structural bottlenecks. Thus, the speed of transitional adjustment of many variables to their respective equilibrium paths should not be taken as a measure of the global stability properties of the modelled economies, but rather as a direct outcome of the laboratory characteristics of a macroeconomic model with continuous, well-behaved functional forms. For these reasons, our results should be at best regarded as crude approximations of the long-run equilibrium effects of a variety of foreign trade policies on the current account, output, capital accumulation and the real exchange rate.

The model results reveal that the expected positive outcomes of the current CU agreement between the EU and Turkey very much depend on whether the non-tariff barriers can be eliminated and a move towards a more competitive environment be sustained. The simulation results suggest that expected gains from bilateral trade liberalizations with the EU depend crucially upon whether TFP externalities can be internalized over the dynamic adjustments towards equilibrium.

Across individual sectors, 'textiles and clothing' reveals itself as the leading exporting sector in all economies of the region that stands to have significant gains from the trade liberalization episodes. Our experiment results suggest that primary agriculture and intermediate goods utilize excessive resources in comparison with the first-best open trade arrangements. According to our analysis of the patterns of macroeconomic adjustments in response to the elimination of tariff protection, trade deficits of the region's economies are likely to increase. This in turn raises the question of how feasible access to foreign resources can be in the longer term as a way of bridging the widening trade gap.

Clearly, many of these outcomes will depend upon a host of political factors, which we cannot address satisfactorily. There is a greater degree of uncertainty about the factors that will determine the impact of enlargement of trade liberalization, or extension of the Regional Trade Agreements (RTAs) in the Middle East and the North African economies. Moreover, these outcomes will also depend on many exogenous factors, and given the complexity of issues surrounding the trade liberalization initiatives, we need a coherent framework that can take all the fundamental macrodynamic and microsectoral effects into account. We believe that the multi-region, multi-sector framework based on an intertemporal dynamic methodology presented here provides an initial step in understanding these fundamentals.

Notes

* This chapter draws in part on an early work of MEDATEAM in Brussels.

1 Bang-bang investment behaviour means that firms behave as extremists, trying to buy as much as possible or scrap as much as possible to reach their desired rate quickly. This type of behaviour makes investment highly volatile.

References

Bayar, A., X. Diao, and E. Yeldan (2000) 'An intertemporal, multi-region general equilibrium model of agricultural trade liberalization in the South-Mediterranean NICs, Turkey and the European Union', IFPRI TMD Discussion Paper, no. 56, Washington, DC: IFPRI.

Coe, D., E. Helpman, and A. Hoffmeister (1997) 'North–South R&D spillovers', *The Economic Journal*, 107(1): 134–149.

De Melo, J. and S. Robinson (1992) 'Productivity and externalities: models of export-led growth', *Journal of International Trade and Economic Development*, 1(1): 41–68.

De Rosa, A. (1997) 'Agricultural trade and rural development in the MENA: recent developments and prospects', International Trade Division Policy Research Working Paper No. 1279, Washington, DC: World Bank.

Diao, X. and A. Somwaru (2000) 'An inquiry on general equilibrium effects of MERCOSUR: an intertemporal world model', *Journal of Policy Modelling*, 22(5): 557–588.

Diao, X., T. Roe, and E. Yeldan (1999) 'How fiscal mis-management may impede trade reform: lessons from an intertemporal, multi-sector general equilibrium model for Turkey', *The Developing Economies*, 37(1): 59–88.

European Commission (1998) *The Situation of Agriculture in the European Union 1998*, Brussels: European Commission.

Frankel, J. and D. Romer (1999) 'Does trade cause growth?', *The American Economic Review*, 89(3): 379–399.

Grethe, H. and S. Tangermann (1998) 'The new Euro-Mediterranean Agreements, an analysis of trade preferences in agriculture', *mimeo*, Göttingen: University of Göttingen.

Levine, R. and D. Renelt (1992) 'A sensitivity analysis of cross-country regressions', *The American Economic Review*, 82(4): 942–963.

McKibbin, W. J. (1993) 'Integrating Macroeconomic and Multi-Sector Computable General Equilibrium Models', Brooking Discussion Papers in International Economics No. 100, Washington, DC: The Brookings Institution.

Mercenier, J. and M. Sampaïo De Souza (1994) 'Structural adjustment and growth in a highly indebted market economy: Brazil', in Mercenier, J. and T. Srinivasan (eds), *Applied General Equilibrium Analysis and Economic Development*, Ann Arbor, MI: University of Michigan Press, pp. 281–310.

Mercenier, J. and E. Yeldan (1997) 'On Turkey's trade policy: is a customs union with Europe enough?', *European Economic Review*, 41(5): 871–880.

Obstfeld, M. and K. Rogoff (1996) *Foundations of International Macroeconomics*, Cambridge, MA and London: MIT Press.

Yeldan, E., T. Roe, and S. Robinson (1998) 'Trade liberalization, accumulation and growth in an archetype model of Africa, South Asia, East Asia and Latin America', *mimeo*, Washington, DC: International Food Policy Research Institute.

Part III

Trade and restructuring

Lessons and outcomes

5 Restructuring and economic performance

The experience of the Tunisian economy

Sofiane Ghali and Pierre Mohnen

1 Introduction

In mid-1995, Tunisia made the strategic choice of becoming the first country in the Middle East and North African (MENA) region to sign a Free Trade Agreement (FTA) with the European Union (EU). In 1996, the authorities launched a vast industrial restructuring programme (*programme de mise-à-niveau*) aimed at helping Tunisian firms to bridge the gap between their current performance and the benchmark performance of their trading partners by upgrading productive capacity and human capital. The programme aimed at restructuring 2000 enterprises out of 4000 potential candidates by the end of 2001.

This initiative followed the structural adjustment programme that was put into place in 1986, which was designed to progressively dismantle the many controls on resource allocation, to privatize state-controlled enterprises, and to moderate growth in aggregate demand. In the 1980s, Tunisia was a country plagued with unemployment as high as 15 per cent, a budgetary deficit of 5.2 per cent, a continuously deteriorating current account deficit, and a large and inefficient public sector. In other words, its economy had dim prospects for future development.

This chapter analyses the evolution of the potential of the Tunisian economy from 1983 to 1996 using a general equilibrium model. By using an activity analysis model and annual data on the input–output structure of the Tunisian economy and its endowments of labour and capital, we shall determine by how much each year the Tunisian economy could have increased its level of domestic final demand expenditures (current consumption and investments in future consumption) and identify the weaknesses and potential strengths that the programme of 'mise-à-niveau' could solve or reinforce.

Labour is subdivided into five levels of qualification, where the bottom three (manual workers, machine operators, and foremen) are labelled unqualified labour and the top two (technicians and engineers/administrators) correspond to qualified labour. The model allows us to measure the scarcity of each type of labour. The model also determines the sectors where Tunisia has a comparative advantage in tradable commodities. We shall compare the structure and the performance of the Tunisian economy before and after the structural adjustment programme of 1986.

In the modern theory of economic growth, research capital and human capital play a central role (see Lucas 1988, Romer 1990, Grossman and Helpman 1991). Empirical studies, mostly confined to countries of the OECD area, have shown that indeed Research and Development (R&D) earns a high rate of return (see surveys by Griliches 1995, Mohnen 2001). As reliable data on R&D are lacking for Tunisia, we cannot test the effect of innovation on the growth performance in Tunisia. Regarding human capital, generally proxied by education, case studies are more convincing than econometric studies (see Schultz 1999, Pissarides 2000). Estimates are often insignificant and sensitive to variations in measurement and specification (Topel 1999, Kalatzidakis *et al.* 2001, Krueger and Lindahl 2001). For Tunisia, instead of using data on labour by level of education, we use data on labour by type of qualification, which can be considered as the output of education and job training. We can therefore evaluate the marginal social value of qualified versus unqualified labour and their respective contributions to output growth.

The chapter is organized as follows. In Section 2, we present our activity analysis model and explain its main properties. In Section 3, we retrace the evolution of factor utilization in Tunisia between 1983 and 1996. In Section 4, we analyse the evolution of optimal factor allocations and corresponding factor prices before and after the structural adjustment programme: in particular, we compute a rate of return on qualified labour. In Section 5, we report the results of a series of experiments with different scenarios to assess the sensitivity of our results. We conclude in Section 6 by summarizing the main conclusions and by drawing some lessons from the Tunisian experience with the structural adjustment programme. The data sources and constructions are described in an appendix.

2 The model

Suppose that there is a social planner who knows the production structure, technologies, preferences, and factor endowments of the economy, and wants to allocate resources and production in such a way as to maximize the level of domestic final demand (DFD), which includes present consumption and investment towards future consumption, both public and private. We consider a small open economy where we allow the trade deficit to equal the observed deficit.

Formally, the efficient state of the economy is obtained by solving the following linear programming problem:

$$\max_{t,s,g} (\mathrm{DFD})t$$

subject to the following constraints:

$$(V' - U)s \geq ft + Jg \tag{5.1}$$

$$(L_1 + L_2 + L_3 + L_4 + L_5)'s + (l_1 + l_2 + l_3 + l_4 + l_5)t \leq N_1 + N_2 + N_3 + N_4 + N_5 \tag{5.2}$$

$$(L_2 + L_3 + L_4 + L_5)'s + (l_2 + l_3 + l_4 + l_5)t \leq N_2 + N_3 + N_4 + N_5 \tag{5.3}$$

$$(L_3 + L_4 + L_5)'s + (l_3 + l_4 + l_5)t \leq N_3 + N_4 + N_5 \tag{5.4}$$

$$(L_4+L_5)'s+(l_4+l_5)t \leq N_4+N_5 \quad (5.5)$$
$$L_5's+l_5t \leq N_5 \quad (5.6)$$
$$\hat{K}\hat{c}s \leq K \quad (5.7)$$
$$-\pi'g \leq D \quad (5.8)$$
$$s \geq 0$$

where

$$DFD=\tilde{P}'f+\tilde{w}l$$

t = (scalar) level of domestic final demand;
s = $(n \times 1)$ vector of activity levels, where n is the number of sectors;
g = $(m_T \times 1)$ vector of net exports, where T indicates tradable commodities;
V = make matrix $(n \times m)$, indicating how much of each commodity is produced in each sector;
U = use matrix $(m \times n)$, indicating how much of each commodity is produced in each sector as intermediate inputs;
J = $(n \times m_T)$ matrix selecting the tradables;
L_i = employment of labour type i, $i = 1, \ldots, 5$, where manual workers/trainees are indexed by 1, machine operators by 2, foremen by 3, technicians by 4, and engineers/administrators by 5;
N_i = labour force of type i, $i = 1,\ldots,5$;
K = $(n \times 1)$ vector of available capital stocks in each sector;
C = $(n \times 1)$ vector of capacity utilization rates;
π = $(m_T \times 1)$ vector of world prices for tradable commodities relative to a DFD-weighted average of world prices;
D = observed trade deficit $= -\pi'(V'e - Ue - f)_T$;
e = unity vector of appropriate dimension;
$\wedge$ = diagonalization operator applicable to a column vector;
$\tilde{P}$ = $(m \times 1)$ vector of observed commodity prices, where m is the number of commodities;
f = $(m \times 1)$ vector of DFD;
l_i = (5×1) vector of employment in the nonbusiness sector for each labour type;
$\tilde{w}$ = (5×1) vector of annual labour earnings per worker by qualification in the non-business sector.

The decision variables are the level of domestic final demand (t), the sectoral activity levels (s), and net exports (g). They are determined so as to maximize DFD subject to three sets of constraints. The first set is the commodity balances (5.1), which stipulate that net production in each sector has to be sufficient to satisfy domestic final demand and net exports. The second set, (5.2)–(5.7), states that the inputs used in each sector may not exceed total disposable inputs. Capital is taken to be sector-specific. In other words, we assume putty-clay technologies. Once installed in one sector, capital cannot be disassembled and affected somewhere else. A sectoral capital constraint is binding when a sector reaches full capacity utilization. For labour, we distinguish five different types, each corresponding to a certain level of qualification and expertise. Workers can always be assigned to jobs requiring lower but not higher qualifications. For example, the work requiring administrators and engineers can only be fulfilled by workers possessing those qualifications whereas the work normally done by technicians can also be fulfilled by engineers. Part of the labour force is assigned to the non-business sector, which comprises services directly consumed by final demand (government services, services provided by non-profit institutions). The last constraint (5.8) posits that the trade deficit at optimal activity levels may not exceed the observed trade deficit. To increase their level of consumption, Tunisians can import from abroad, but only up to a certain level, which is conservatively taken to be the observed trade deficit. Without constraint (5.8), Tunisia could reach an infinite value for its objective function by importing without limits.[1] The assumption of a small open economy with exogenous world prices for tradable commodities is not unrealistic in the case of Tunisia. The observed activity levels correspond to the following values: $t=1$, $s=e$, and $D=-\pi'(V'e-Ue-f)_{\mathrm{T}}$. The observed state of the economy is thus our point of reference. Efficiency derives from full capacity utilization, optimal factor allocations across sectors, and international specialization.

Variations of this model appear in ten Raa and Mohnen (1994, 2002), and ten Raa (1995). This type of model was at one time very popular for economic development planning (see Nugent 1970), but went out of fashion with the advent of computable general equilibrium (CGE) models. Compared to CGE models, the activity analysis model is less general as it neither explicitly models substitution possibilities in consumption and production nor imperfect competition or convexities. Yet, it has a number of advantages. It is simple and transparent, it provides a competitive benchmark, and it does not require any outside estimates of production and consumption parameters nor any calibrating exercise. This model can also be seen as a macroeconomic 'data envelopment analysis' (DEA) model that determines the economy's frontier given its technologies, preferences and endowments (see ten Raa and Mohnen 2002 for more discussion on this point). But it is not a benchmarking exercise with respect to a best technology as most DEA analyses are. It should also be noticed that our analysis is short term in nature, in the sense that the optimal resource allocation that underlies the optimal solution of our activity analysis is dependent on the observed levels of technology. We do not model technological change or changes in preferences and endowments.

The decomposition of labour into five levels of qualification sheds some light onto the kind of labour shortages Tunisia has been facing and on the returns to innovation. The solution of the linear programme above yields not only a picture of resource allocations in an efficient economy, but also of the prices sustaining such an equilibrium resource allocation. To see this, consider the dual programming problem

$$\min_{p,\,w,\,r,\,\varepsilon} \; w'N + r'K + \varepsilon D$$

Subject to the following constraints

$$p'(V' - U) \leq w' L' + r'\hat{K}\hat{c} \tag{5.9}$$
$$p' f + w' l = DFD \tag{5.10}$$
$$p' J = \varepsilon \pi' \tag{5.11}$$
$$p \geq 0, \quad w_5 \geq w_4 \geq w_3 \geq w_2 \geq w_1 \geq 0, \quad r \geq 0, \quad \varepsilon \geq 0$$

where p, w, r, and ε are, respectively, the shadow prices of commodities, of the five types of labour, of the sectoral capital stocks, and of the trade deficit. By the theorem of complementary slackness, a shadow price is positive only if the corresponding constraint in the primal is binding. The shadow prices w and r denote the marginal values of an additional unit of the respective inputs. If at a certain level of qualification the labour constraint is tight, it earns a mark-up over the previous level of qualification. A sector with less than full capacity utilization earns a zero rate of return on a marginal capital investment, for the very simple reason that it has no excess demand, as unused capital is still available. The shadow price ε of the trade balance indicates the marginal value in terms of attainable DFD of an additional allowed dinar of trade deficit. Under the complementary slackness conditions, it can also be said that a sector is active only if it makes no loss. Inequality (5.9) indicates that at the optimal solution of the linear programme the prices of active sectors equal average cost, and hence that the optimal solution can be obtained as a competitive equilibrium. Condition (5.10) is a normalization condition akin to the choice of a numeraire. By equality (5.11) domestic prices for tradable commodities may differ from world prices only by a certain constant ε, which can be interpreted as the exchange rate compatible with the purchasing power parity. All quantities are expressed in constant dinars, except labour, which is denoted in man-years. Hence, all shadow prices are relative constant prices, except the shadow prices of labour, which are in constant dinars per man-year.

3 The data

The data on which we base our analysis are described in Appendix B. The concordance between industry and commodity classifications is given in Appendix A. As Table 5.1 shows, the unemployment rate has always been much higher for qualified workers (levels 4 and 5) than for poorly qualified workers (levels 1–3). For instance, in 1990, 28.7 per cent of qualified workers were out of work compared to 13.9 per cent of less-qualified workers. From 1987 onwards, about the time when Tunisia adopted the structural adjustment programme, we notice first an increase in the overall rate of capacity utilization, and second a decrease in the unemployment rate for qualified workers with an increase for less-qualified workers. There is a persistent shift from manual workers (level 1) towards machine operators (level 2) over the whole period. Poorly qualified or unqualified workers make up almost 90 per cent of the total work force. However, there was no major shift of employment composition among the qualified workers (levels 4 and 5). This high level of unemployment for qualified workers might seem unreasonable

Table 5.1 Labour composition, unemployment rates, and capacity utilization rates (selected years)

	1984	*1987*	*1990*	*1993*	*1996*
	Labour composition by qualifications (%)				
$L_1 + l_1$	28.0	26.7	25.5	25.0	23.7
$L_2 + l_2$	53.2	54.7	55.6	55.9	57.3
$L_3 + l_3$	7.8	7.9	8.2	8.1	7.9
$L_4 + l_4$	7.4	7.0	7.0	7.2	7.2
$L_5 + l_5$	3.6	3.8	3.7	3.8	3.8
	Unemployment rates (%)				
$L_1 + l_1$	11.2	12.4	13.9	14.0	14.0
$L_2 + l_2$	11.2	12.4	13.9	14.0	14.0
$L_3 + l_3$	11.2	12.4	13.9	14.0	14.0
$L_4 + l_4$	28.0	34.0	28.7	28.3	28.2
$L_5 + l_5$	28.0	34.0	28.7	28.3	28.2
Average	13.1	15.0	15.5	15.6	15.6
	Overall capacity utilization rates (%)				
	62.0	68.0	73.0	69.0	68.0

Notes
L_i employment of qualification i in the business sector.
l_i employment of qualification i in the non-business sector.

for a country that devotes a significant proportion of its national resources to human capital accumulation. It can be explained by the structure of the Tunisian economy. According to a World Bank study (2000a: vol. II, Table 2.3), 82.4 per cent of Tunisian enterprises employed less than six workers while only 1.6 per cent employed more than 100 workers, and only 12 firms more than 500 workers in 1996.

We shall now examine what would have been the optimal allocation of resources in Tunisia for each year between 1983 and 1996.

4 Results

4.1 Optimal resource allocation

Table 5.2 presents the optimal sectoral activities, that is, the optimal allocation of resources in Tunisia, for five selected years. Activity levels with a star indicate full capacity utilization. For instance, in 1984 agriculture and fishing should have operated at 34 per cent above the observed activity level under optimal allocation of resources. But even at this activity level, the sector would still not have operated at full capacity. Food processing, by contrast, would in the same year have reached its full capacity at 125 per cent above observed activity.

In Table 5.2, we notice that textile and leather, and other manufacturing would have been best discontinued for most of the time. This is simply because the capital/labour ratios are very low in these two industries. Operating at full capacity

Table 5.2 Optimal activity levels, optimal net exports, and observed net exports (selected years)

	1984			*1987*			*1990*			*1993*			*1996*		
	X	*B.T. opt.*	*B.T. obs.*	*X*	*B.T. opt.*	*B.T. obs.*	*X*	*B.T. opt.*	*B.T. obs.*	*X*	*B.T. opt.*	*B.T. obs.*	*X*	*B.T. opt.*	*B.T. obs.*
Agric. and fishing	1.34	—	—	1.35	—	—	1.62	2.8	—	1.64	32.7	—	1.11	—	—
Food process.	2.25*	26.6	—	1.70*	9.8	1.3	1.70*	14.1	—	0.00	—	5.3	1.70*	5.6	—
Const. material	2.21*	3.8	—	1.68*	1.9	—	1.68*	4.0	1.5	1.68*	2.8	0.2	1.68*	3.4	0.1
Mechan. and elect.	1.28*	—	—	1.68*	—	—	1.68*	—	—	1.68*	—	—	1.68*	—	—
Chem. and rubb.	1.61*	—	—	1.42*	—	—	1.42*	—	—	0.00	—	—	1.42*	—	—
Text. and leather	0.00	—	—	0.00	—	6.0	0.00	—	14.0	0.00	—	20.2	0.51	—	29.2
Other manuf.	0.00	—	—	1.26*	—	—	1.26*	—	—	1.33*	—	—	1.26*	—	—
Mining	1.43*	—	2.6	1.37*	—	2.6	1.22*	—	0.8	1.33*	1.7	0.5	0.00	—	2.3
Hydrocarbons	1.43*	2.8	30.0	1.37*	3.9	16.5	1.22*	—	8.0	1.33*	0.0	4.0	1.37*	—	—
Electricity	1.42	n.t	n.t	1.34	n.t	n.t	1.30	n.t	n.t	1.09	n.t	n.t	1.29	n.t	n.t
Water	1.28	n.t	n.t	1.28	n.t	n.t	1.22	n.t	n.t	1.20	n.t	n.t	1.21	n.t	n.t
Construction	1.17	n.t	n.t	1.22	n.t	n.t	1.13	n.t	n.t	1.17	n.t	n.t	1.20	n.t	n.t
Transp. and comm.	1.43*	8.5	21.0	1.37*	10.0	16.6	1.22*	9.2	17.0	1.33*	8.9	20.1	1.37*	12.5	17.6
Hot. and tourism	1.43*	15.2	46.4	1.37*	27.6	56.3	1.22*	26.8	56.3	1.33*	17.1	49.7	1.37*	26.2	48.0
Other services	1.43*	43.2	–	1.37*	47.0	0.7	1.22*	43.2	2.5	1.33*	36.9	—	1.37*	52.2	2.9
Domestic final demand		1.16			1.22			1.13			1.17			1.20	

Notes

X Optimal activity levels (observed level = 1).

* Sectors with full capacity utilization.

B.T. opt. Optimal net exports in % of total optimal positive net exports (a dash denotes a deficit).

B.T. obs. Observed net exports in % of total observed positive net exports (a dash denotes a deficit).

n.t non-tradable.

would attract to these industries substantial labour resources that would find better use in terms of value-added in other industries, such as services and food processing. Electricity, water, construction, and public works produce non-tradable commodities, which are always needed by an economy as their outputs are required by other sectors and cannot be imported. They never reach full capacity though, as their production surplus cannot be exported. Agriculture and fishing could have increased their level of operation but not to full capacity, and serve as a cushion sector to hire labour in periods of close to full capacity in other sectors. The remaining sectors of food processing, construction material and glass, mechanical and electrical goods, mining, production of hydrocarbons, transport and communications, hotels and tourism, and other services could have operated at full capacity levels.

4.2 Tunisia's comparative advantage

Table 5.2 also reveals the location of Tunisia's comparative advantage, that is, sectors in which Tunisia could specialize and become a net exporter. In the second column for each year of Table 5.2, we present a sectoral breakdown of all positive net exports at the optimal allocation of resources. We notice that the strongest potential earners of foreign exchange are hotels and tourism and other services (including trade and financial services), and to a lesser extent transport and communications, construction material and glass, and what we may call the food conglomerate (agriculture, fishing, and food processing). At the optimal solution, the first two make up for at least two-thirds of net exports, transport and communications account for about 10 per cent of total positive net exports, the food conglomerate for 15–20 per cent, and construction material and glass show a steady net export of 3–4 per cent of the total. There were no major shifts in comparative advantage over the years. The mechanical and electrical goods sector should always have operated at full capacity but not for generating net exports, as for the mining and production of hydrocarbons sectors, most of the time. Occasionally, they could achieve some net exports, but they are not sectors of real comparative advantage, but merely sectors needed to sustain economic activity.

It is interesting to compare the actual and the optimal specialization of the Tunisian economy in foreign trade (columns 2 and 3 for each year). Textiles and mining show some foreign trade where there should be none, according to our analysis. In transport and communications, and in hotels and tourism, there is more trade than we would desire, compared to other services, where there is insufficient trade. In food processing, construction materials, and glass and hydrocarbons actual trade patterns tend to move in the right direction. The most impressive evolution is that of net exports in hydrocarbons, which steadily declined and ceased to be a net export at the end of our sample as predicted by our analysis of comparative advantage.

Another study released by the World Bank (2000b) confirms our evaluation of the potential and the optimal orientation of the Tunisian economy. It reports that the growth contribution of textiles to GDP is limited by its low value addition and that Tunisia, over the years, has decreased its reliance on hydrocarbons and textiles. Finally, the study also underscores the trend towards the absorption of skilled labour away from textiles and tourism and towards the manufacture of electrical and mechanical equipment and information technology-related services.

4.3 Efficiency and shadow prices

According to our results, Tunisia could have increased its level of domestic final demand, our measure of national well-being, by anywhere between 13 and 24 per cent over the various years (see first column of Table 5.3). The higher the expansion factor, the further away the economy was from its optimal factor allocation, hence the less efficient it was. If we take the years before and after the structural adjustment programme of 1986, we notice that the economy moved closer to its efficiency frontier between 1989 and 1992, but became less efficient from 1993 on, but not to the pre-1986 levels. This result is in line with the overall evolution of the rate of capacity utilization.

In our model, labour is mobile across sectors and first gets assigned to the sector with the greatest value added until it reaches its full capacity, then to the next sector with the greatest value added until this one reaches its full capacity and so on. The wage rate for a certain type of labour is thus determined by its marginal productivity in the last sector that is activated. The marginal social value of workers of different qualifications is reflected in their shadow wages (Table 5.3). In 1983, the availability of one more worker in the economy could increase its well-being by

Table 5.3 Shadow prices of labour, capital, and foreign trade deficit (1983–96)

	t	w_1	w_2	w_3	w_4	w_5	r	ε
1983	1.20	1.61	1.61	1.61	1.61	1.61	0.22	0.78
1984	1.16	2.05	2.05	2.05	2.05	2.05	0.17	0.77
1985	1.22	2.84	2.84	2.84	2.84	2.84	0.13	0.73
1986	1.24	2.27	2.27	2.27	2.27	2.27	0.14	0.77
1987	1.22	2.53	2.53	2.53	2.53	2.53	0.12	0.75
1988	1.20	1.86	1.89	1.89	1.89	1.89	0.16	0.78
1989	1.14	2.22	2.22	2.22	2.22	2.22	0.12	0.78
1990	1.13	2.96	2.96	2.96	2.96	2.96	0.09	0.75
1991	1.14	3.11	3.11	3.11	3.11	3.11	0.08	0.72
1992	1.15	3.14	3.14	3.14	3.14	3.14	0.10	0.73
1993	1.17	3.17	3.17	3.17	3.17	3.17	0.11	0.72
1994	1.20	3.17	3.36	3.36	3.36	3.36	0.10	0.69
1995	1.17	2.50	3.44	3.44	3.44	3.44	0.10	0.72
1996	1.20	2.37	3.41	3.41	3.41	3.41	0.13	0.73

Notes

t is the optimal expansion of domestic final demand (the observed level equals 1).

w_1–w_5, the shadow prices of labour by level of qualification, are in 1,000 DT / year.

r is a weighted average of sectoral rates of return expressed in dinars of returns per dinar of capital stock.

ε the shadow price of the trade deficit is also in dinars per dinar of trade deficit.

1,610 dinars per year. The fact that higher-qualified workers did not potentially earn more than lower-qualified workers is equivalent to saying that there was no room for a wage mark-up for higher qualifications. This is indeed what we would expect given the higher unemployment rate for higher-qualified workers. Only in 1988 and then again in 1994, 1995, and 1996 was there a certain shortage of the L_2 type of labour compared to the L_1 type. Excluding the years 1988 and 1989, we notice a general upward trend in labour value. In 1996, a worker's contribution to the economy in categories 2–5 was worth 3,410 dinars per year.

As capital is sector-specific, sectors can expand only up to their full capacity. All sectors with full capacity earn a positive shadow price for their capital stock. These are the sectors that are marked by an asterisk in Table 5.2. The sectors that are either completely idle or else functioning at less than full capacity earn no marginal return on their capital stock. The weighted average rate of return on physical capital dropped from 22 per cent in 1983 to 8 per cent in 1991, rising again to reach 13 per cent in 1996. The social return on capital was lower after the structural adjustment programme, showing that the Tunisian economy invested during this period and reached rates of return closer to the normal rate. From 1992 on, capital became scarcer again, but not to the extent it was in 1983 and 1984.

The purchasing power parity, that is, the shadow price corresponding to the trade deficit (the last column in Table 5.3), has moved slightly to the advantage of Tunisia. The lower domestic prices compared to world prices, the more a given foreign trade deficit can be converted into higher consumption. In 1983, the domestic price level for tradables was 78 per cent of the world price. Since then, domestic prices have declined (and hence the purchasing power parity has strengthened) to reach 73 per cent of the world price in 1996.

4.4 Evaluation of the wage bill for qualified workers

If we multiply the number of workers in L_4 and L_5 by their respective observed wages (in constant dinars), we obtain the wage bill for qualified workers per sector. We divide each industry total by the economy's total to get the decomposition of qualified labour bill by industry. From the figures reported in Table 5.4 we see that in Tunisia, the qualified labour bill is mainly concentrated in agriculture, textiles and leather, and other services. In 1996, these three sectors made up almost 64 per cent of the total qualified labour bill. Its ratio to GDP has been relatively stable over the years, at around 6.5 per cent.

4.5 Rate of return on qualified workers

We calculate the rate of return on qualified workers by dividing the difference between the optimal and the observed labour bill for labour categories 4 and 5 by the observed labour bill for those two categories combined:

$$\text{RRD} = (w_4 L_4 + w_5 L_5)/(w_4^o L_4 + w_5^o L_5) - 1$$

Table 5.4 Percentage industrial distribution of the wage bill for qualified labour and rates of return on qualified labour (selected years)

	1984	*1987*	*1990*	*1993*	*1996*
Agric. and fishing	22.1	20.9	20.0	18.2	17.0
Food process.	2.9	2.9	3.3	3.3	3.5
Const. material	2.7	3.0	2.9	2.7	2.4
Mechan. and elect.	2.9	3.0	3.6	3.6	3.6
Chem. and Rubb.	1.7	1.9	2.1	2.3	2.9
Text. and leather	13.7	10.4	9.6	10.4	9.5
Other manuf.	3.6	3.7	3.6	3.8	4.2
Mining	1.5	1.2	1.0	0.7	0.6
Hydrocarbons	1.3	1.5	1.5	1.4	1.2
Electricity	3.0	3.0	2.9	2.7	2.4
Water	1.4	1.6	1.7	1.7	1.6
Construction	2.4	2.3	2.6	3.0	3.3
Transp. and comm.	6.1	6.1	6.0	6.0	5.8
Hot. and tourism	4.5	4.5	4.5	4.3	4.8
Other services	30.3	33.8	34.7	36.2	37.3
Total wage bill for qualified labour[a]	653.6	566.0	697.7	752.9	948.3
Total wage bill for qualified labour /GDP	7.2	5.9	6.5	6.1	6.8
Average rate of return on qualified labour	−55	−32	−31	−25	−30

Note
a Total wage bill for qualified labour: in 1,000,000 dinars of 1990.

where w_4 and w_5 are the shadow wage rates and w_4^o and w_5^o are the observed wage rates. In this way, we measure the wage premium above the actual wage that each qualified worker commands at the optimal allocation of resources. This rate of return should be interpreted as a marginal social rate of return, capturing by how much the Tunisian economy – given its structure of technology, preferences, and factor endowments – is able to increase its final demand, if it invests in an extra qualified worker. The figures reported in the bottom row of Table 5.4, which are weighted averages of the sectoral rates of return (with the observed labour costs as weights), indicate that qualified workers earned a negative rate of return throughout the sample period.[2,3] The marginal value of a highly qualified worker did not match their actual wage payment. On average, the rate of return was −47 per cent before 1990. It rose to −27 per cent on average between 1990 and 1996. The structural adjustment programme seems to have had a beneficial effect on the allocative efficiency of qualified labour.

Table 5.5 Domestic final demand (DFD) growth by sources (%)

	1983–96	*1983–6*[a]	*1986–91*[b]	*1991–6*[c]
DFD	1.90	−1.07	2.55	3.28
L_5	0.16	0.21	0.08	0.11
L_4	0.27	0.25	0.16	0.21
L_3	0.31	0.42	0.49	0.18
L_2	2.36	3.03	3.08	1.85
L_1	0.43	1.27	1.26	−0.88
Capital	−0.77	−4.76	−2.98	2.98
Deficit	−0.85	−1.48	0.45	−1.18

Notes
a Sixth 5-Year Development Plan (1982–6).
b Seventh 5-Year Development Plan (1987–91).
c Eighth 5-Year Development Plan (1992–6).

4.6 Growth decomposition

In Table 5.5, we decompose the growth rate of the optimal level of DFD into the growth attributable to each factor input. We know from linear programming that the optimal value of the primal equals the optimal value of the dual. The latter can be decomposed into the value attributable to each factor of production: the five types of labour, the physical capital stock, and the trade deficit, which can be considered as an input into the production of domestic final demand in an open economy.[4] We have computed the growth rates of optimal domestic final demand and its components over the whole period and the three sub-periods corresponding to successive 5-year plans. As Table 5.5 indicates, the pro-competitive and liberalizing structural adjustment programme introduced in 1986 obviously lead to a substantial growth in domestic final demand. The major source of growth comes from the increase in the number and rewards of machine operators. However, the improved growth performance of the Tunisian economy between the Sixth and the Eighth 5-Year Development Plan is almost entirely due to investment in physical capital.

5 Sensitivity analysis

As Nugent (1970) aptly illustrates, the gap between the observed and optimal activities and shadow prices obtained from an activity analysis model may be due to market and model imperfections. In order to evaluate the extent to which our results depend on some critical assumptions underlying the model or the data construction, we have designed a number of experiments, which we will now consider.

5.1 Mobility of capital

If we assume that capital is completely mobile across sectors rather than sector-specific, the economy becomes much more flexible in its allocation of resources.

It can then completely specialize in its sectors of comparative advantage, export those commodities and, from the export proceeds, import other required commodities for production and consumption. The prices of the tradables sustaining the equilibrium drop sharply and those of the non-tradables increase as they now become bottlenecks. The optimal attainable level of domestic final demand is much higher (around 200 per cent), and the shadow wage of the most skilled members of the labour force increases.

5.2 *Unemployment by qualifications*

We have experimented with three distributions of unemployment across qualifications, a declining rate of unemployment as we move to higher categories of specialization, an increasing rate of unemployment and a U-shaped distribution with higher unemployment rates at both ends. We have made sure that the weighted average unemployment rate is always consistent with the aggregate observed rate. The more we move towards lower levels of unemployment for a given category, the more the shadow wage in that category goes up, as we would expect.

5.3 *Mobility of labour*

We have assumed that a worker with higher qualifications can always replace a worker with lower qualifications, but not the opposite. Given this asymmetry in labour mobility, the wage rates becomes flatter and lower for low levels of qualification, because of greater labour abundance. If we make the model more rigid and allow workers to be qualified for their own job only, we then obtain quite a different pattern of shadow wage rates. It is now more likely that each labour qualification experiences some scarcity. We have recalculated the linear programme with a uniform rate of unemployment of 15 per cent across labour qualifications. The interesting finding is the evolution of labour scarcity over time. Manual workers, machine operators, and foremen earn a non-zero wage rate: foremen earn the most. However, the two most qualified categories of labour, engineers and administrators, are always in excess supply. This experiment confirms that the most qualified members of the workforce are in relative abundance. Their negative rate of return shows that workers of the two most qualified labour categories get paid above their marginal social value.

5.4 *Rate of capacity utilization*

We have experimented with different levels of uniform rates of capacity utilization across all sectors. As the overall rate of utilization increases more sectors become active. If we let the rates differ across sectors, some can expand more than others but, overall the resource allocation across sectors remains the same. As final demand must move up in the same proportion for all commodities, the expansion of final demand is affected by the differential rates of capacity utilization. The optimal expansion of domestic final demand is more or less determined by a weighted average of the inverse rates of sectoral capacity utilization, where the weights are the capital stock shares. However, the pattern of shadow prices stays relatively stable across the various experiments regarding the sectoral rates of capacity utilization.

To summarize these, the results are most sensitive to the assumptions made about factor mobility. Since we have modelled labour as being partially mobile and capital as being sector-specific, the assumptions regarding unemployment by qualifications have a greater bearing on the results than those made about sectoral capacity utilization. In our preferred scenario, where workers of higher qualifications can always do lower-qualified jobs, we notice over time some scarcity developing at the level of machine operators but not at higher levels of qualification. If we do not allow downward mobility of labour in the qualification scales, then the scarcity shows at the level of supervisors. The highest qualified workers, engineers and technicians, are never in short supply.

6 Conclusions

We have examined the structural evolution of the Tunisian economy from 1983 to 1996. By solving an optimal resource allocation problem for each year, we have located the sources of strength and identified apparent bottlenecks in the Tunisian economy. We have also assessed the possible effects of the structural adjustment programme introduced in 1986. Although our results may be sensitive to modelling errors and omissions, they are, nevertheless, consistent with other reports on the Tunisian economy and we are confident that we have identified particular weaknesses and further potentials in the Tunisian economy.

Hotels and tourism and other services (regrouped among other trade and financial services) are identified as the main sectors of comparative advantage in Tunisia, and to a lesser extent, transport and communications, construction material and glass, and the food conglomerate (agriculture, fishing, and food processing). Our analysis reveals that Tunisia reached a higher degree of efficiency in resource allocations during the Seventh 5-Year Development Plan but that efficiency decreased somewhat in the following period. Labour demand shifted slightly from lower to higher levels of qualification, raising shadow wage rates, although the highest qualified workers remained in excess supply throughout the period. The rate of return on qualified labour was actually negative but increased substantially in the second half of our sample period.

The main aim of the structural adjustment programme was to make the Tunisian economy more competitive. Indeed, we notice an increase in competitiveness that would be more evident if we allowed for greater factor mobility. However, competitiveness also operates through learning, reorganization, adoption of new technologies, and innovation so that firms can improve their management, decrease their production costs and introduce new products. Statistics reveal a high level of unemployment for highly qualified workers, and our analysis confirms the relative abundance of these types of workers in the Tunisian economy; hence their low productivity that is reflected by negative rates of return on qualified labour.

The tremendous investments in education and vocational training, with a budget share amounting to about 6 per cent of GDP and 17 per cent of government expenditure, will not come to full fruition if these high-skilled workers remain jobless. The Tunisian government has to put additional efforts in reducing the unemployment of its best workers; only then can education contribute more significantly to growth.

Appendix A: nomenclature and symbols

Abbreviations	*Commodity code*	*Industry*
Agric. and fishing	00	Agriculture and fishing
Food process.	10	Food processing
Const. material	20	Construction materials and glass
Mechan. and Elect.	30	Mechanical and electrical goods
Chem. and Rubb.	40	Chemical and rubber products
Text. and leather	50	Textile and leather products
Other manuf.	60	Other manufacturing
Mining	65	Mining
Hydrocarbons	66	Hydrocarbons
Electricity	67	Electricity
Water	68	Water
Construction	69	Construction and public works
Transp. and Comm.	76	Transport and communications
Hot. and tourism	79 + 99	Hotels and tourism
	79	Hotels, cafes, and restaurants
	99	Tourism and other stays
Other services	72 + 82 + 85 + 94	Services
	72	Commodity trade
	82	Financial services and insurance
	85	Other market services
	94	Non-market services

Appendix B: the data

We make use of Tunisia's annual input–output tables for the years 1983–96 in constant 1990 prices. At the 20-sector aggregation level, the tables are expressed in market prices and not at factor costs. Indirect taxes and subsidies are thus included in the inter-industry transaction figures. Given the unavailability of labour and capital data at a sufficient level of detail, we are obliged to aggregate our tables from 20 down to 15 sectors and commodities. The 'other services' sector regroups the commodities 'trade' (72), 'financial services and insurance' (82), 'other market services' (85) and 'non-market services' (94), and is made up of sectors (72), (82), and (85). Tourism regroups the commodities 'hotels and restaurants' (79), and 'tourism and other stays' (99), and represents sector (79). The expenditures of the 'banking services' sector have been split between the various sectors in proportion to their consumed banking services following Ben Slama *et al.* (1996).[5]

The V' make matrix is diagonal implying that one sector produces only one commodity and that each commodity is produced by only one sector. Production is measured in terms of commodities and not in terms of sectors. Output includes trade margins, and import figures include import taxes. For three commodities (electricity, water and public works) we observe neither imports nor exports. Those three commodities are therefore considered as non-tradables. World prices are measured by a weighted average of Tunisian export deflators, under the assumption of competitive world prices. Labour is divided into five types: manual workers, machine operators, supervisors, technicians, and administrators and engineers. Data on employment in the business and the non-business sectors are taken from employment and population surveys conducted by the Institut National de la Statistique (INS). Rama (1998: Table 2, p. 70) provides figures on the number of unemployed workers registered with 'L'Agence Tunisienne de l'Emploi' for three categories, qualified workers, non-qualified workers, and first-job holders. We regard first-job holders as non-qualified workers. Qualified workers are attributed to categories 4 and 5 and the non-qualified workers to the first three categories. The unemployment rate is supposed to be the same for each subcategory. Combining the figures on employed and unemployed workers, we determine the available labour force by category.[6] The total observed wage bill for all categories of workers is obtained from the national accounts (INS). The spread between the lowest and highest wages (1–5) is supposed to be uniformly distributed across the five categories. This hypothesis is by and large consistent with the various estimates of wage differentials by qualification reported by Morrison and Talbi (1996: Table 4.8).

We use the capacity utilization rates for manufacturing estimated by l'Institut d'Économie Quantitative (1996). For agriculture and fishing, we assume the rate to be the same as for the food sector. For the other non-manufacturing sectors, we take a capital stock weighted average of the rates in the manufacturing sectors.

Acknowledgements

This work was supported by the Social Sciences and Humanities Research Council of Canada. We thank Thijs ten Raa for stimulating discussions. Very helpful comments are also acknowledged from participants at the MEEA conference in London (2001), the ERF conference in Cairo (2002), and an anonymous referee.

Notes

1 The observed trade balance is introduced as a factor of production, as in the work by Diewert and Morrison (1986) and Kohli (1991).

2 We have also regressed TFP growth, with pooled data correcting or not for time and sector dummies, on a constant and the ratio of the wage bill of qualified workers over sales to get an estimate of the rate of return on qualified workers. The rate of return was never significant.

3 Negative (even significant) rates of return on human capital of the male gender are reported in the literature (see, e.g. Caselli *et al.* 1996, Kalatzidakis *et al.* 2001).

4 Since $t\,\text{DFD} = w'N + r'K + \varepsilon D$,

$$\begin{aligned} \mathrm{d}(t\,\text{DFD})/(t\,\text{DFD}) = {} & [w'N/t\,\text{DFD}]\mathrm{d}(w'N)/(w'N) \\ & + [r'K/t\,\text{DFD}]\mathrm{d}(r'K)/(r'K) \\ & + [\varepsilon D/t\,\text{DFD}]\mathrm{d}(\varepsilon D)/(\varepsilon D) \end{aligned}$$

5 We have also tried an alternative split of banking services assuming a uniform distribution of those expenditures across all sectors. This construction yielded similar results of the linear programme in terms of active sectors and optimal expansion of DFD.

6 The number of unemployed in category i ($i = 1,\ldots,5$) is computed as follows:

$$U_i = \left(\sum_{i=1}^{5} L_i/(1 - \text{ur}) \right) \cdot \text{ur} \cdot \alpha_j \cdot \beta_{ij}$$

where L stands for the number of employed workers, ur the economy-wide unemployment rate, α_j is the proportion of the total unemployed in group j (where j designates qualified or low-qualified workers, see Rama 1998), and where β_{ij} is the proportion of workers of category i in group j.

References

Ben Slama *et al.* (1996) 'Relations technologiques intersectorielles et décomposition des sources de la croissance', *Cahiers de l'I.E.Q.*, no. 12.

Caselli, F., G. Esquivel, and F. Lefort (1996) 'Reopening the convergence debate: a new look at cross-country growth empirics', *Journal of Economic Growth*, 1(3): 363–389.

Diewert, W. E. and C. Morrison (1986) 'Adjusting output and productivity indexes for changes in the terms of trade', *Economic Journal*, 96: 659–679.

Griliches, Z. (1995) 'R&D and productivity: econometric results and measurement issues', in Stoneman, P. (ed.), *Handbook of the Economics of Innovation and Technical Change*, Blackwell Handbooks in Economics, Oxford: Blackwell.

Grossman, G. and E. Helpman (1991) *Innovation and Growth in the Global Economy*, Cambridge, MA: MIT Press.

Institut d'Économie Quantitative (1996) 'Compétitivité, restructuration, diversification et ouverture sur l'extérieur des industries manufacturières et des services,' Étude stratégique no. 8, 8622/96.

Institut National de la Statistique, *Les comptes de la nation*, Tunisia, Various issues.

Kalatzidakis, P., T. P. Mamuneas, A. Savvides, and T. Stengos (2001) 'Measures of human capital and nonlinearities in economic growth', *Journal of Economic Growth*, 6: 229–254.

Kohli, U. (1991) *Technology, Duality, and Foreign Trade: The GNP Function Approach to Modeling Imports and Exports*, Ann Arbor, MI: University of Michigan Press.

Krueger, A. B. and M. Lindahl (2001) 'Education for growth: why and for whom?' *Journal of Economic Literature*, 29: 1101–1136.

Lakhoua, F. (1998) 'The Tunisian experience of "Mise à Niveau": conceptual issues and policy orientations', MDF II, World Bank, Marrakech, September.

Lucas, R. (1988) 'On the mechanics of economic development', *Journal of Monetary Economics*, 22: 3–42.

Mohnen, P. (2001) 'International R&D spillovers and economic Growth', in Pohjola, M. (ed.), *Information Technology, Productivity, and Economic Growth: International*

Evidence and Implications for Economic Development, Oxford: Oxford University Press.

Morrison, C. and B. Talbi (1996) *La croissance de l'économie tunisienne en longue période*, Paris: Centre de développement de l'OCDE.

Nsouli Saleh M., S. Eken, P. Duran, G. Bell, and Z. Yücelik (1993) '*The path to convertibility and growth: the Tunisian experience*', IMF Occasional Papers 109, Washington, DC: International Monetary Fund.

Nugent, J. (1970) 'Linear programming models for national planning: demonstration of a testing procedure', *Econometrica*, 38(6): 831–855.

Pissarides, C. A. (2000) 'Human capital and growth: a synthesis report,' Technical Paper No. 168, Paris: OECD Development Centre.

Rama, M. (1998) 'How bad is unemployment in Tunisia? Assessing labour market efficiency in a developing country', *The World Bank Research Observer*, 13(1): 59–77.

Romer, P. (1990) 'Endogenous technological change', *Journal of Political Economy*, 89(5): 71–102.

Schultz, T. P. (1999) 'Health and schooling investments in Africa', *Journal of Economic Perspectives*, 13(3): 67–88.

ten Raa, T. (1994) 'On the methodology of input–output analysis', *Regional Science and Urban Economics*, 24(1): 135–158.

ten Raa, T. (1995) *Linear Analysis of Competitive Economies*. LSE Handbooks in Economics, Hemel Hempstead: Prentice Hall-Harvester Wheatsheaf.

ten Raa, T. and P. Mohnen (1994) 'Neoclassical input–output analysis', *Regional Science and Urban Economics*, 24(1): 135–158.

ten Raa, T. and P. Mohnen (2002) 'Neoclassical growth accounting and frontier analysis: a synthesis', *Journal of Productivity Analysis*, 18(2): 111–128.

Topel, R. (1999) 'Labour markets and economic growth,' in Ashenfelter, O. and D. Card (eds), *Handbook of Labour Economics*, Amsterdam: North Holland.

World Bank (2000a) 'Tunisia–private sector assessment update: meeting the challenge of globalization, Report No. 20173-TUN, December, Washington, DC: World Bank.

World Bank (2000b) *Republic of Tunisia: Social and Structural Review 2000*, Washington, DC: World Bank.

6 Price competition between Turkish and East Asian exports in the European Union market in the 1990s

An empirical investigation*

Zelal Kotan and Serdar Sayan

1 Introduction

Turkey experienced a major export boom following the introduction of the structural adjustment programme of 1980, which entailed a decisive policy switch from protectionist import substitution policies to trade liberalization and export orientation. The value of exports increased from $2.26 billion in 1979 to $12.96 billion in 1990, rising to almost $31 billion in 2001. The composition of exports also underwent a major change, shifting away from heavy concentration in agricultural and livestock products and towards manufactured goods, principally textiles and garments, iron and steel, and food-processing products (Sayan and Demir 2003). Yet, this initial phase of diversification signalled only a change in the commodity composition of Turkish exports, rather than marking a transformation in its market concentration. Textiles and clothing, for example, significantly increased their shares in total exports, reaching about 44 per cent after 1989 (Erlat 1993). Similarly, despite a visible increase in the number of export destinations after 1980, a greater portion of Turkish exports continued to be shipped to relatively few markets, particularly the European Union (EU).[1]

Such concentration of exports with respect to markets and product categories has the potential to make the country's export receipts vulnerable to variations in the demand. Given the intensity of competition that Turkish exports face from close substitutes from other countries, increasing export receipts and market shares often involves price competition. The EU market is particularly important within this context, since it has traditionally been the major export destination for Turkish products. Yet, for most Turkish manufacturing exporters, the EU market is subject to intense competition.

In this chapter, we consider price competition between Turkish and East Asian (EA) exports of selected manufacturing products in the EU market. We conduct an empirical investigation into the nature and effectiveness of this competition, focusing on Turkish competition with EA exports. This focus is due to the importance of the East Asian countries as Turkey's main competitors in the EU market as frequently cited by the Turkish Exporters' Association during the 1990s.

For this purpose, we develop and estimate a model for a series of commodities, using data from 1990 to 1999. The model we develop is similar to that used in Merkies and Van Der Meer (1988) and relates the respective market shares of Turkish and EA exporters to relative prices charged by each country's exporters against competitors.

We analyse markets for six commodity groups: 'Textiles', 'Clothing', 'Road vehicles', 'Electrical machinery', 'Power generating machinery', and 'Telecommunications equipment'. Textiles and Clothing are intuitive choices as they have long been major export sectors for Turkey:[2] due to their weight in total exports, fluctuations in these exports can cause significant variations in Turkey's export receipts. Moreover, textile exports are known to significantly contribute to economic growth (Guerrieri and Milana 1995) and to have a potentially important role in improving a country's overall competitiveness in international markets (Daniels 1999).

Even so, the 1990s was a decade during which the relative significance of textiles and garment exports declined, while that of other categories increased (Lohrmann 2000): thus, the other commodity groups in the list were selected as up-and-coming export categories for Turkey, with the potential to replace Textiles and Clothing as the leading source of export revenue (see Appendix 6.A1 for the commodity coverage of these groups).[3] These commodities are also highly tradable goods with an increasing share in total exports of both Turkey and the EA countries as well as in world trade, especially in recent years.[4]

Our country sample includes China, Hong Kong, Republic of Korea (hereafter, South Korea), and Taiwan as the main EA group of competitors against Turkish exports in the EU markets. The selection of these countries in our sample was determined on the basis of export similarity indices calculated for Turkey vis-à-vis each of these countries.

Our analysis provides evidence that price competition is important in explaining the shares of Turkish and EA exports in the EU market, and produces useful information on relative price elasticities. We also explore ways in which the possible contributions of Turkey's proximity to the EU market as well as the Customs Union (CU) between Turkey and the EU may be evaluated with regard to the competitiveness of Turkish products.

The rest of the discussion is organized as follows. The next section provides an overview of the export performance of the product groups under consideration within the last decade. Section 3 describes the data and the framework of investigation. The results obtained are presented in Section 4. The last section concludes the chapter with a summary of the findings and suggestions for further research.

2 The performance of Turkish exports in the 1990s

The 1990s witnessed a structural change in the growth and composition of Turkey's exports. The initial export boom of the early to mid-1980s was fuelled by excess production capacity in the manufacturing sector, itself the result of a comprehensive structural adjustment programme introduced in 1980. The programme started with a devaluation and was followed by measures aimed at the liberalization of trade and financial markets. As a consequence of the contraction in domestic demand (which resulted from wage restraints), many sectors traditionally serving the domestic market looked abroad for new markets. The result was a significant increase in the value and diversity of exports, a trend that continued for most of the 1980s (Uygur 1997, Kotan and Sayan 2001).

An examination of Turkey's export performance in the 1990s, though, reveals that both export growth and the ratio of exports to GNP experienced marked fluctuations (Figure 6.1). The slow export growth of the period 1990–3 can be attributed to the overvaluation of the domestic currency. By 1994, however, growth had been restored thanks to a sizeable real depreciation of the currency.

This correspondence between high rates of export growth and real depreciations (Figure 6.2)[5] implies that export performance and real exchange rate movements are strongly correlated (Brada *et al.* 1997).

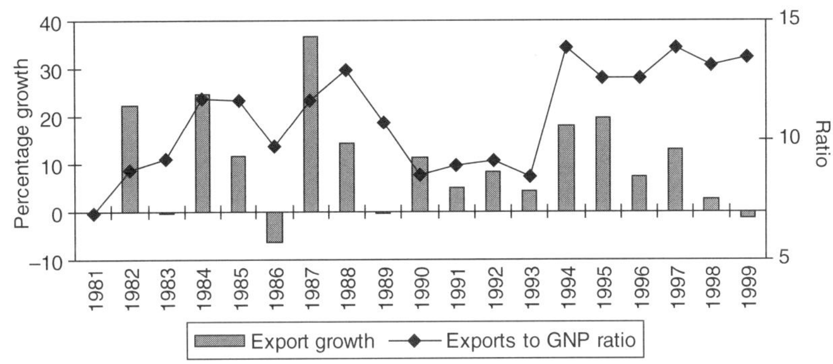

Figure 6.1 Growth of exports and exports to GNP ratio, 1980–99.

Source: SIS (2001) and CBRT (2001).

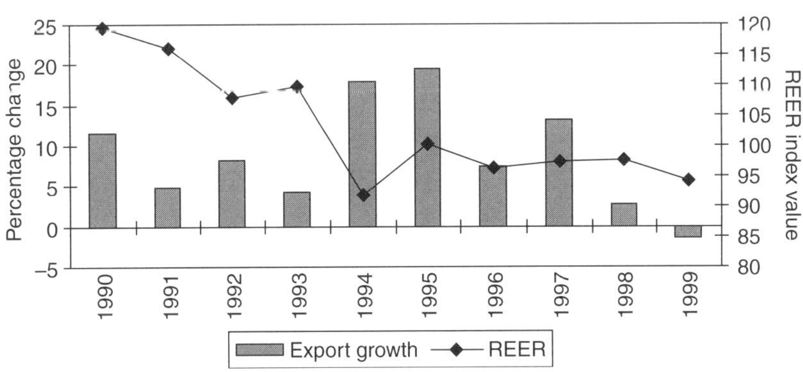

Figure 6.2 Export growth and changes in real effective exchange rate (REER), 1990–9.

Source: SIS (2001) and CBRT (2001).

Other than changes in the real value of the Turkish Lira (TL), developments in major export markets, particularly in the EU, affected Turkey's export performance during the 1990s as well. Using constant market share (CMS) analysis, for instance, Kotan (2000) shows that a slower growth of EU imports (compared to the rest of the world) during the period 1990–7 has impeded Turkish exports to some extent. The analysis in Kotan (2000) shows further that this slowdown in import demand by the EU was accompanied by a change in the composition of its imports. The EU's demand for textiles and clothing declined during the second half of this period, whereas its demand for the other product groups under consideration here increased, leading to a gradual increase of these products in total imports. The two panels in Figure 6.3 illustrate the developments in the shares of these groups in EU imports.

Since the EU is Turkey's major market, the decline in the share of textiles and clothing in total EU imports affected the performance of this leading export sector for Turkey. Even though textiles and clothing exports managed to catch up with the performance of manufacturing exports, which continued to grow faster than total exports in the 1990s, the composition of Turkish exports changed due primarily to the remarkable export performance of the other product categories we consider. The progress of Electrical machinery, Power generating machinery, Telecommunications equipment, and especially Road vehicles sectors was indeed exceptional, with the average annual growth rate of exports increasing from 20.1 per cent in 1990–3 to 41.5 per cent in 1994–9 (Figure 6.4).[6]

Turkish producers of the non-agro-based products considered here managed to increase their exports to the EU just when the EU's import demand for these products expanded. The remarkable exports growth for this group of products in fact helped counter the effects of the contraction in the Textiles and Clothing exports receipts. As a result, recent developments in the EU's demand for imports do not appear to have adversely affected Turkey's export receipts. However, heavy dependence of Turkish exports, both in terms of composition and volume, on these developments remains a cause for concern for both policy makers and exporters in Turkey.

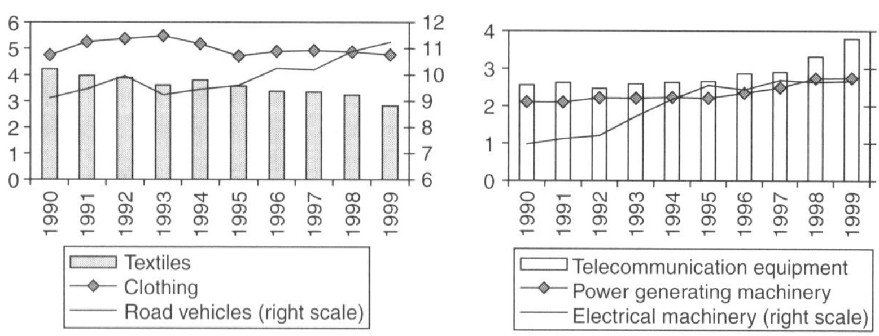

Figure 6.3 Shares of selected product groups in the EU imports (%), 1990–9.

Source: OECD International Trade Statistics CD-ROM.

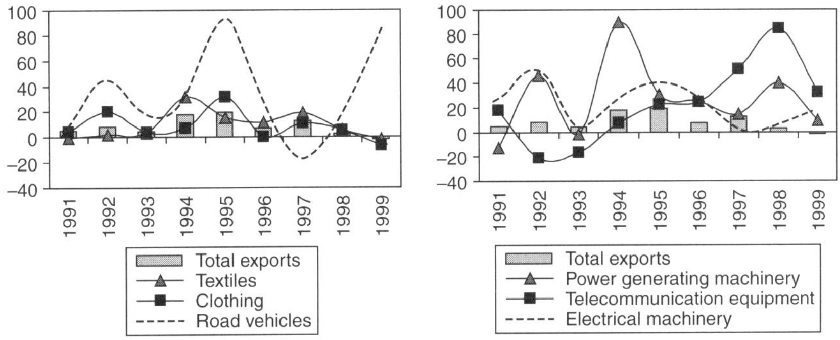

Figure 6.4 Growth rates of Turkish exports in selected sectors, 1990–9.

Source: OECD International Trade Statistics CD-ROM.

In general, concentration of exports with respect to markets and product groups has the potential to negatively affect the overall export performance of a country and its receipts. Such concentration may be particularly damaging for the exporting country, when world demand for the products in question or the total demand for imports in major markets falls (Lloyd 1994). In such cases, it may become very hard for the exporting country to maintain – let alone increase – its market share. Changes in export performance due to shifts in the degree of competitiveness, on the other hand, are easier to deal with as policy measures may be very effective in such instances. In fact, relative price disturbances may alter the competitive position of a country in the export market, having a considerable effect on overall export performance (Lloyd 1994).[7]

Assessing the competitive position of Turkish exports vis-à-vis EA exports to the EU market requires an understanding of the performance of EA exports for the product groups studied here. The next section provides evidence concerning the importance of price competition in the EU market for these products, and discusses Turkey's additional advantages of geographic proximity and CU membership with the EU.

3 Empirical investigation – the framework

In this section, we explain how we can estimate the effectiveness of price competition between Turkey and the EA countries with respect to the six product groups under consideration here.

3.1 Theoretical background

We begin our analysis by considering homothetic import demand functions resulting from a two-stage utility maximization process (Merkies and Van Der Meer 1988). In the first stage, a constant elasticity of substitution (CES) utility function is maximized subject to the import budget of the importing country (EU in this case), to be allocated between a number of commodities indexed by $k \in \{1, 2, \ldots, m\}$. The solution to this problem enables us to express M^k, the optimum demand for commodity k imports by the EU, as a function of the total demand for imports, M; the ratio of the import price index of commodity k, P^k, to the overall import price level, P; and a parameter representing the stable taste pattern of the EU, δ^k. That is:

$$M^k = \delta^k M \left(\frac{P^k}{P} \right)^{(1-\sigma)} \tag{6.1}$$

where σ is the elasticity of substitution at the top level of utility maximization.[8]

In the second stage, a utility function similar to that of the first stage is maximized subject to the budget allocated to the imports of commodity k (as determined in the previous stage) so as to determine imports from exporters of different countries. The solution to this problem yields:

$$M_n^k = \delta_n^k M^k \left(\frac{P_n^k}{P^k} \right)^{(1-\sigma^k)} \tag{6.2}$$

where n is the index for the country supplying commodity k to the EU.

Equation (6.2) shows that M_n^k, the optimum import demand for each commodity k by the EU from each exporter n, depends on the optimum level of import demand for commodity k – M^k in Equation (6.1), a price ratio, and the corresponding stable taste pattern parameter, δ_n^k. The price ratio shows the price that the exporting country n charges for commodity k relative to that commodity's average import price in the EU market. δ^k in Equation (6.2) is the elasticity parameter which, when subtracted from 1, measures the percentage change in the share of exporting country n in the commodity k imports resulting from a one per cent increase in the price charged by country n exports relative to average import price. This interpretation of σ^k follows from:

$$\mathrm{d} \ln \left(\frac{M_n^k}{M^k} \right) = (1 - \sigma^k)\, \mathrm{d} \ln \left(\frac{P_n^k}{P^k} \right) \tag{6.3}$$

Equation (6.3) indicates that when the price of commodity k exported from Turkey to the EU increases relative to the prices charged by EA exports, Turkey loses her relative price competitiveness, and hence market share, in the EU market.

To proceed with the estimation, Equation (6.2) is manipulated to convert it into the following form (Kotan and Sayan 2001):

$$M_n^k[\mathrm{d} \ln (M_n^k)] = M_n^k \left[\mathrm{d} \ln (M^k) + (1 - \sigma^k)\, \mathrm{d} \ln \left(\frac{P_n^k}{P^k} \right) \right] + \varepsilon_n^k \tag{6.4}$$

where the product of the terms in brackets with the base period values of M_n^k serves to obtain the error terms with equal variances (Kotan and Sayan 2001).

3.2 Data and estimation

Equation (4) has been estimated using data for the period between 1990 and 1999. The product coverage of each category is given in Appendix 6.A1 in terms of three-digit Standard International Trade Classification (SITC) Revision 3. Values and prices of total imports and exports were taken from IMF's *International Financial Statistics* CD-ROM. All trade data (manufacturing exports from Turkey and EA countries to the EU, as well as EU's manufacturing imports from Turkey, EA countries, and the rest of the world) are obtained from the OECD *International Trade Statistics* CD-ROM, expressed both in values and quantities. Export and import prices were calculated by dividing values by respective quantities and then indexing by the Laspeyres method.[9]

In selecting the EA countries for our sample, two criteria were used. Availability of data as well as the export similarity indices calculated for Turkey vis-à-vis China, Hong Kong, South Korea, and Taiwan (see Appendix 6.B1). The degree of similarity in the case of Textiles and Clothing was found to be high. In this category, Turkish exports turned out to have the highest degree of export similarity with exports from China and Hong Kong. Unlike the export similarities for Textiles and Clothing, however, the similarity index for Electrical machinery exports turned out to be fairly low throughout the 1990s. In addition, export similarity indices declined slightly over time in the case of Power generating machinery and Telecommunications equipment. In the case of Road vehicles, on the other hand, initially low values of similarity indices at the beginning of the 1990s significantly increased over time for all countries under consideration. For example, the export similarity index for Turkey vis-à-vis South Korea, the highest of all, rose from 2.3 in 1990 to 25.8 in 1999.

A fixed-effects model is used in the panel data estimation of Equation (6.3) using ordinary least squares (OLS) (Matyas 1995). The fixed-effects model is chosen since it estimates the model conditionally on errors using the simple OLS technique, thereby ignoring the dependence of the errors and regressors. Regardless of whether the errors that are initially assumed to be random are correlated with one or more regressors, the fixed effects estimator depends only on the deviations of the regressand and regressors from group means. The estimates remain consistent within the group, even though they may be inconsistent for the full sample (Davidson and MacKinnon 1993).

4 Empirical findings

Our empirical analysis was carried out first by considering the 1990–9 period as a whole. Two sub-periods, 1990–4 and 1995–9, corresponding to low- and high-growth periods for Turkish exports, respectively (and high and low values of real exchange rates), were then considered separately to see if there would be any differences in results across these two periods.

Panel data estimation results for the entire sample period indicate that relative prices are not significant determinants of the relative shares of the EU's total imports from Turkey, China, Hong Kong, South Korea, and Taiwan. However, separately estimating the equation for the two sub-periods leads to considerably different results. The estimates of elasticities of substitution vary widely, implying that margins for charging high mark-ups over cost in the short- to medium-run changed for exporters during the 1990s. Table 6.1 presents the panel data estimation results for each country, by period and for the relevant product groups.

It must be noted that all estimates for σ^k (the elasticity of substitution for product category k) reported in the table are statistically significant at the one per cent level and all have the expected signs.[10]

The results imply that relative prices notably affected the relative shares of Turkey, China, Hong Kong, South Korea, and Taiwan in the EU's textiles imports during the period 1990–4. In other words, when export prices in a given country increase relative to competitor countries, that country stands to lose part of its share in the EU market. The estimated values indicate that the EU's demand for imports of textiles from all countries in the sample is elastic. This is especially the case for imports from Turkey, South Korea, and Hong Kong. The R^2 values reported in the second column of Table 6.1 imply that price competition explains over 80 per cent of the movements in the relative share of Turkish exports and nearly half of the relative shares of EA exports to the EU's textiles market during the first half of the 1990s. It is further observed from the R^2 values that during the 1990–4 period, price competition better explains the share of each exporting country in the EU market than in the 1995–9 period. Thus, it appears that competition over market shares was subject to stiffer price competition in the first sub-period than in the second.

The estimation results for clothing exports reported in the third and fourth columns of Table 6.1 are similar to the results for textiles. Relatively higher prices for one exporting country will reduce its market share relative to others here too; and the elasticities declined during the 1995–9 period for all EAs. A comparison of R^2 values across the two sub-periods indicates that price competition gets relatively stiffer in the second period, for Turkish clothing exports only. The EU's elasticities of substitution among the exporters of clothing are observed to decrease somewhat after 1994, implying that the pressure of price competition diminishes in the 1995–9 period compared to the previous sub-period. The reduction in the elasticities of substitution in the second period also implies that it becomes relatively easier to charge higher mark-ups over cost, with a lower risk of losing market share.

The results reported in the fifth and sixth columns of Table 6.1 depict a similar picture for Road vehicles. R^2 values for the 1990–4 period show that price competition explains almost half of the market share for each EA road vehicle manufacturer exporting to the EU (for South Korea this ratio is as high as

Table 6.1 Estimated results for the selected product groups

Periods/ countries	*Textiles*		*Clothing*		*Road vehicles*		*Electrical machinery*		*Power gen. machinery*		*Telecom. equipment*	
	σ^k	R^2	σ^k	R^2	σ^k	R^2	σ^k	R^2	σ^k	R^2	σ^k	R^2
1990–9												
Turkey	1.008	0.09	1.090	0.08	1.192	0.25	1.028	0.17	1.168	0.20	1.015	0.07
China	1.019	0.07	1.017	0.09	1.037	0.08	1.006	0.14	1.071	0.35	1.044	0.19
Hong Kong	1.002	0.10	1.002	0.11	1.063	0.08	1.011	0.23	1.102	0.22	1.001	0.14
South Korea	1.003	0.11	1.006	0.04	1.012	0.12	1.028	0.10	1.044	0.03	1.031	0.09
Taiwan	1.000	0.10	1.005	0.08	1.005	0.07	1.009	0.14	1.011	0.13	1.015	0.08
1990–4												
Turkey	1.174	0.82	1.021	0.25	1.358	0.43	1.066	0.43	1.329	0.85	1.050	0.29
China	1.051	0.48	1.305	0.54	1.616	0.51	1.440	0.57	1.081	0.74	1.490	0.62
Hong Kong	1.187	0.57	1.193	0.39	1.370	0.37	1.073	0.43	1.091	0.43	1.043	0.35
South Korea	1.327	0.54	1.008	0.29	2.250	0.66	1.290	0.70	1.440	0.28	1.218	0.27
Taiwan	1.085	0.31	1.310	0.46	1.376	0.47	0.831	0.53	1.008	0.28	1.174	0.30
1995–9												
Turkey	1.010	0.37	1.056	0.32	1.552	0.76	1.000	0.28	1.121	0.24	1.018	0.30
China	1.006	0.35	1.001	0.41	1.022	0.25	1.001	0.40	1.054	0.53	1.023	0.71
Hong Kong	1.001	0.18	1.003	0.18	1.045	0.13	1.010	0.40	1.091	0.20	1.010	0.36
South Korea	1.021	0.32	1.005	0.07	1.010	0.19	1.010	0.17	1.090	0.28	1.039	0.30
Taiwan	1.000	0.32	1.010	0.11	1.002	0.25	1.007	0.16	1.059	0.30	1.005	0.15

two-thirds). Considerably high elasticities of substitution during the same period reveal that exporters did not have wide margins for charging mark-ups over cost. However, both the elasticities and explanatory power of price competition for EAs are observed to decline significantly after 1994. Turkey, on the other hand, became increasingly more dependent on price competition during the second half of 1990s in this sector.

The results for exports of Electrical machinery and Power generating machinery are presented in columns 7–10 of the same table. During the 1990–4 period, price competition in these two sectors explains a significant part of each exporter's share in the EU market (see the relevant R^2 values). These values are particularly high for Turkey and China in the Power generating machinery market. This is due to the high elasticities of substitution in the same period, which do not allow for wide margins between costs and prices. In the 1995–9 period, on the other hand, the influence of price competition on market shares declined considerably as seen in the reduced elasticities of substitution.

In the case of Telecommunications equipment, we do not find much deviation between the estimated elasticities of substitution of the two consecutive sub-periods (see the last two columns in Table 6.1). This implies that the nature of price competition did not change significantly during the 1990s in this sector. However, the elasticities of substitution declined in the latter period, especially for China and South Korea, giving exporters from these countries more scope to charge higher mark-ups.

An overview of the results in Table 6.1 reveals that price competition explains a greater portion of shifts in the relative shares of Turkey and EAs in the EU markets in the 1990–4 period, as indicated by generally higher R^2 values for this period. Road vehicles exports from Turkey are a notable exception, as dependence on price competition increases after 1994. In all other cases, the role of price pressures in determining market shares declines during 1995 and 1999, although the extent of the decline varies from one exporting country to another.

Increased intensity of price competition for Turkish products over the 1990–4 period is consistent with the relatively poor export performance of the country during this period when the overvaluation of domestic currency slowed export growth. In addition, despite a visible increase in the exports of products other than Textiles and Clothing, especially after 1994, Turkey did not manage to fully adapt its export structure to its growing markets and commodity groups (Lohrmann 2000). The country remained mostly a spectator while the EA countries gained a sizeable share in the world trade of those products (Noland 1997).

However, Turkish exports enjoy two potentially important advantages over their EA competitors. First, the geographic proximity of Turkey to the EU's markets and the associated transportation cost advantage is expected to enable Turkish exporters to charge relatively lower prices.[11] Secondly, Turkey's membership of a CU with the EU makes it possible for Turkish manufactures to enter EU markets free from the customs duties to which EA exports are subject.

Even though the cost advantage due to Turkey's geographic proximity to the EU would be expected to be equally applicable to exporters of all products, our examination of the differences between cost, insurance, and freight (CIF) and free on board (FOB) prices of EU imports point in an interesting direction.[12] The differences we have calculated between CIF import and FOB export prices for the product groups and countries in our sample indicate that only certain Turkish commodity exports to the EU benefit from the 'proximity' advantage. Textiles, Clothing and Road vehicles have transportation cost advantages but not the exports of Telecommunications equipment, or Electrical and Power generating machinery exports.

To illustrate this, we calculated the differences between the CIF and FOB prices of Textiles, Clothing, and Road vehicles for Turkey and EA countries in the EU markets. These are then presented in panels A–C in Figure 6.5. It can be clearly observed that the difference is markedly lower for Turkish exports compared to other countries, clearly pointing to a Turkish exporters' cost advantage in these products due to proximity factors.

When the differences between CIF import and FOB export prices of Electrical machinery, Power generating machinery, and Telecommunications equipment are considered, the situation is somewhat reversed. Panels A and B of Figure 6.6 show that price differences are higher for Turkey in some years but lower in others for Electrical machinery and Telecommunications equipment. This implies that Turkey's proximity advantage is not as strong in the case of these products as in the case of Textiles, Clothing, and Road vehicles.

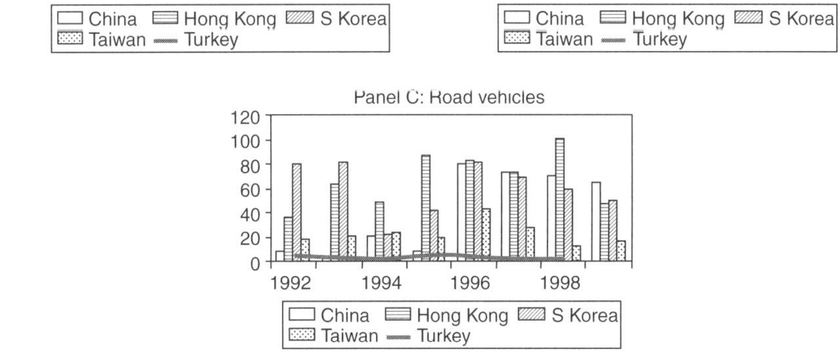

Figure 6.5 Export (FOB) and import (CIF) price differences, 1992–9. Panel A: Textiles; Panel B: Clothing; Panel C: Road vehicles.

Source: Authors' calculations based on OECD data.

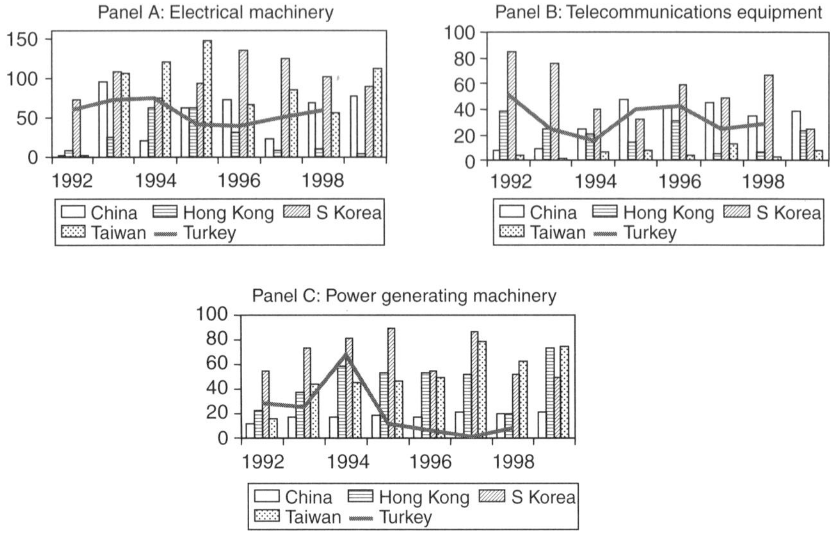

Figure 6.6 Export (FOB) and import (CIF) price differences, 1992–9; Panel A: Electrical machinery; Panel B: Telecommunications equipment; Panel C: Power generating machinery.

Source: Authors' calculations based on OECD data.

In the case of Power generating machinery, the differences between CIF import and FOB export prices for Turkey are higher during the first sub-period under consideration, but they begin to decline gradually after 1995, indicating that the cost advantage may disappear over time (Figure 6.6, panel C). One possible explanation of this phenomenon may be due to the economies of scale involved in the EA's exports to the EU (Noland 1997, Kotan and Sayan 2001). In other words, the volume of shipments may enable EA exporters to overcome Turkey's transportation cost advantages vis-à-vis EU markets.

In addition to geographic proximity, the 1996 Turkey–EU CU agreement offers an additional advantage to Turkish exports. Under this agreement, customs duties on Turkish manufacturing exports to the EU are to be phased out gradually. However, the effects of Turkey's membership in the CU on her price competitiveness cannot be explored here since the gradual nature of the reductions make the extraction of relevant information from the data very difficult.

5 Conclusions

This chapter has investigated the nature and effectiveness of price competition between Turkish and EA exports of selected manufacturing products in the EU market between 1990 and 1999. For this purpose, we estimated a model that allows relative market shares of Turkish and EA exporters in the EU markets to be determined by prices of imports from respective countries. We considered People's Republic of China, Hong Kong, South Korea, and Taiwan as Turkey's main EA competitors in the EU markets.

In our analysis, we focused on six commodity groups: Textiles, Clothing, Road vehicles, Electrical machinery, Power generating machinery, and Telecommunications equipment. The first two groups were included in the sample in view of their importance as Turkey's leading exports, especially in recent decades. As such, variations in the Textiles and Clothing exports may cause serious fluctuations in Turkey's export receipts. The latter four groups, on the other hand, have become more important for Turkey recently. Exports of these products have risen in importance in world trade too. They can potentially help improve a country's international competitiveness and, hence, prospects for growth.

The results of the panel data estimation suggested that relative price movements play an important role in determining the relative shares of Turkey and EA countries in the EU market for the product groups considered during the 1990–4 period. More precisely, our estimations confirmed that a country's share of exports in the EU markets for a particular product group is inversely related to its relative price movements. However, this dependence fell considerably in the 1995–9 period, except for Turkey's Road vehicle exports, which became more dependent on price competition after 1994.

The results also indicated that the EU's import demand for all product groups was elastic during the period 1990–4, implying that the exporters of these products would not be able to charge high mark-ups over their costs in that period. On the contrary, elasticity was lower during the period 1995–9 allowing them to charge higher mark-ups over costs without risking a significant loss in their market shares

Within this context, Turkish exporters shipping their products to the EU market were noted to have two potential advantages over their competitors from the EA countries. First, the geographical proximity of Turkey to the EU entails lower transportation costs for Turkish exports. Yet, further investigation of this issue led to the remarkable finding that the cost reducing effects of geographical proximity do not equally apply to all product groups considered. While Turkey's proximity advantage was clearly visible in the case of Textiles, Clothing, and Road vehicles, this was not so for other product groups. The explanation we offered for this asymmetry was based on the economies of scale associated with the large volumes of EA shipments to the EU.

A second advantage of Turkish exporters is thought to come from Turkey's special status vis-à-vis the EU, involving a gradual abolition of customs duties on Turkish manufacturing exports to the EU. In fact, custom duties were bilaterally reduced to very low levels or were totally abolished for certain products long before the CU agreement was put into effect in 1996 (DPT 1995). However, due to data restrictions, a full exploration of this issue was beyond the scope of this chapter.

In conclusion, our results indicate that the cost reducing effects of shorter distances and preferential customs duties on the competitiveness of Turkish manufacturing exports would not be large. The geographic proximity of Turkey to the EU markets is likely to provide some cost advantage by lowering freight costs, but such an advantage can be overcome by large volumes of shipments from countries that are not so close to the EU markets. So, proximity alone is not likely to be sufficient to give Turkey a significant edge in competition against EA exporters. In the long run, the country will have to take steps to maintain and enhance its competitive advantage in key export industries, particularly in highly price competitive world markets.

Appendix A

Table 6.A1 Three-digit SITC categories covered under the six product groups

	Textiles
261	Silk
263	Cotton
264	Jute, other textile bast fibre, n.e.s., not spun; tow
265	Vegetable textile fibres, not spun; waste of them
266	Synthetic fibres suitable for spinning
267	Other man-made fibres suitable for spinning; waste
268	Wool and other animal hair (incl. wool tops)
269	Worn clothing and other worn textile articles; rags
611	Leather
612	Manufactures of leather, n.e.s.; saddlery and harness
613	Furskins, tanned or dressed, excluding those of 8483
651	Textile yarn
652	Cotton fabrics, woven
653	Fabrics, woven, of man-made fabrics
654	Other textile fabrics, woven
655	Knitted or crocheted fabrics, n.e.s.
656	Tulles, trimmings, lace, ribbons, and other small wares
657	Special yarn, special textile fabrics, and related
658	Made-up articles, of textile materials, n.e.s.
	Clothing
831	Travel goods, handbags, and similar containers
841	Men's clothing of textile fabrics, not knitted
842	Women's clothing, of textile fabrics
843	Men's or boy's clothing, of textile, knitted, crochet.
844	Women's clothing, of textile, knitted etc.
845	Articles of apparel, of textile fabrics, n.e.s.
846	Clothing accessories, of textile fabrics
848	Articles of apparel, clothing access., excluding textile
851	Footwear
	Road vehicles
783	Road motor vehicles, n.e.s.
	Electrical Machinery
772	Apparatus for electrical circuits; board, panels
773	Equipment for distributing electricity, n.e.s.
774	Electro-diagnostic appa. for medical sciences, etc.
775	Household type equipment, electrical or not, n.e.s.
776	Cathode valves and tubes; diodes; integrated circuits
778	Electrical machinery and apparatus, n.e.s.
	Power generating equipment
711	Vapour generating boilers, auxiliary plant; parts

			Telecommunication equipment
712	Steam turbines and other vapour turbine., parts, n.e.s.	761	Television receivers, whether or not combined
713	Internal combustion piston engines, parts, n.e.s.	762	Radio-broadcast receivers, whether or not combined
714	Engines and motors, non-electric; parts, n.e.s.	763	Sound recorders or reproducers; television record.
715	Rotating electric plant and parts thereof, n.e.s.	764	Telecommunication equipment, n.e.s.; and parts, n.e.s.
716	Other power generating machinery and parts, n.e.s.	771	Electric power machinery, and parts thereof

Appendix B: export similarities

Export similarity index is defined as:

$$S(n, m) = \{\sum_k \text{Minimum}[X_k(1m), X_k(2m)]\} * 100$$

where $X_k(nm)$ is the share of commodity k in country n's exports to country m for $n = 1, 2$ (Finger and Krenin 1979). This index determines the proportion of the commodity basket of one exporter that is perfectly matched by that of the other exporter by removing the effects of the relative scale of total exports.

Table 6.B1 Export similarity indices in the EU market: Turkey versus EA countries, 1990–9

	Textiles	*Clothing*	*Road vehicles*	*Electrical machinery*	*Power gen. machinery*	*Telecom. equipment*
			Turkey versus China			
1990–9	50.40	31.76	3.15	1.78	27.85	19.26
1990–4	49.94	31.31	2.09	1.44	31.18	20.97
1995–9	50.85	32.21	4.21	2.12	24.52	17.54
			Turkey versus Hong Kong			
1990–9	48.71	31.92	2.72	0.84	39.04	14.58
1990–4	48.11	31.25	1.45	0.63	41.79	15.18
1995–9	49.31	32.59	3.98	1.04	36.28	13.98
			Turkey versus South Korea			
1990–9	34.18	26.90	13.28	0.70	13.69	18.17
1990–4	36.36	26.61	6.87	0.54	21.50	18.33
1995–9	32.00	27.18	19.70	0.86	5.88	18.02
			Turkey versus Taiwan			
1990–9	28.68	21.43	7.95	2.08	6.57	16.67
1990–4	28.65	21.09	6.81	2.02	8.55	16.81
1995–9	28.72	21.78	9.10	2.15	4.58	16.53

Source: Authors' calculations based on OECD data, period averages.

Appendix C

Table 6.C1 Statistical properties of the estimated results

Periods/ countries	*Textiles*		*Clothing*		*Road vehicles*		*Electrical machinery*		*Power gen. machinery*		*Telecom. equipment*	
	$(1-\sigma^k)$	*DW*	$(1-\sigma^k)$	*DW*	$(1-\sigma^k)$	*DW*	$(1-\sigma^k)$	*DW*	$(1-\sigma^k)$	*DW*	$(1-\sigma^k)$	*DW*
1990–9												
Turkey	−0.00776*	2.20	−0.09021*	2.29	−0.19209*	2.18	−0.02794*	2.39	−0.16797*	2.31	−0.01511*	2.16
China	−0.01883*	2.18	−0.01659*	1.80	−0.03653*	2.29	−0.00594*	1.82	−0.07051*	2.29	−0.04424*	2.09
Hong Kong	−0.00194*	2.07	−0.00203*	2.06	−0.06325*	2.39	−0.01114*	2.42	−0.10191*	1.93	−0.00083*	2.07
South Korea	−0.00301*	2.16	−0.00599*	1.55	−0.01176*	2.02	−0.02778*	2.04	−0.04404*	2.63	−0.03127*	2.13
Taiwan	−0.00020*	1.89	−0.00460*	1.91	−0.00501*	2.39	−0.00926*	2.44	−0.01115*	1.82	−0.01495*	1.98
1990–4												
Turkey	−0.17391*	2.99	−0.02099*	2.67	−0.35795*	2.40	−0.06580*	2.53	−0.32852*	2.73	−0.04977*	2.45
China	−0.05115*	2.66	−0.30453*	2.43	−0.61568*	2.35	−0.43961*	1.90	−0.08136*	2.67	−0.48989*	2.47
Hong Kong	−0.18659*	2.49	−0.19299*	2.35	−0.37005*	2.94	−0.07259*	2.69	−0.09139*	2.27	−0.04347*	2.37
South Korea	−0.32749*	2.24	−0.00850*	2.04	−1.24971*	2.72	−0.28966*	2.63	−0.43985*	2.78	−0.21760*	3.21
Taiwan	−0.08526*	2.44	−0.31015*	2.08	−0.37643*	2.29	0.16912*	3.08	−0.00799*	2.57	−0.17406*	2.66
1995–9												
Turkey	−0.00994*	2.09	−0.05614*	2.32	−0.55159*	2.44	−0.00009*	2.63	−0.12096*	2.53	−0.01752*	2.57
China	−0.00564*	2.40	−0.00126*	2.44	−0.02205*	2.28	−0.00127*	2.30	−0.05363*	2.68	−0.02308*	2.36
Hong Kong	−0.00085*	2.38	−0.00332*	2.16	−0.04492*	2.78	−0.00972*	2.72	−0.09070*	1.98	−0.00970*	2.46
South Korea	−0.02076*	2.45	−0.00525*	1.74	−0.00999*	2.56	−0.00969*	1.86	−0.08956*	2.48	−0.03902*	1.99
Taiwan	−0.00038*	2.12	−0.01027*	2.80	−0.00203*	2.32	−0.00652*	2.54	−0.05901*	1.83	−0.00534*	2.20

Notes
* denotes significance at the one per cent level.
The negative sign in the first column for each product group shows that the effect is in the expected direction for all cases. Relative prices have a statistically significant effect on the relative shares in the EU market for the exporting countries.

Notes

* This chapter is an extended and modified version of Kotan and Sayan (2001).

1 In recent decades, EU's share in Turkey's exports has been around 50 per cent, with Germany alone accounting for an average share of 20 per cent (Sayan 2000); see Erlat and Akyuz (2001) for a detailed analysis of the concentration of Turkey's foreign trade with respect to her partner countries.

2 In light of the discussion by Erlat and Sahin (1998) concerning a stricter use of the terminology of 'traditional' and 'non-traditional' exports in the literature, we deliberately avoid calling Textiles and Clothing 'traditional' exports here. We adopt instead the convention in Sayan and Demir (2003) designating Textiles and Clothing 'agro-based' sectors because of their strong backward linkages with the agricultural sector. For the sake of symmetry and convenience, we will call the other sectors under consideration here 'non-agro-based' sectors.

3 Road vehicles in particular have become one of the largest sources of exports revenue since the mid-1990s.

4 Turkey also managed to increase her share in world markets for these product categories during the 1990s (Lohrmann 2000).

5 In the period 1990–9, two firms producing passenger cars mainly for the domestic market under licences with Fiat and Renault began to look abroad for export markets (particularly to the EU and the Middle Eastern markets). The period also witnessed an inflow of automotive manufacturers from the United States (such as GM and Ford), Japan (Toyota and Honda), and Korea (Hyundai), who formed joint ventures with domestic firms to increase their exports to the EU by taking advantage of Turkey's CU agreement with the latter. This led to a significant increase in exports of passenger cars, as well as commercial vehicles, including makes that are designed and produced domestically.

6 The real value of the Turkish Lira (TL) was calculated against a currency basket consisting of 1 US dollar and 1.5 German marks. Turkish private manufacturing price indices were used to measure the domestic inflation rate, whereas foreign inflation rate was calculated using a weighted average of US and German producer price indices (with the weights of 0.544 and 0.456, respectively). A fall (rise) in the index shows real depreciation (appreciation) of the TL against the currency basket.

7 A hike in the price of an imported commodity will encourage demand substitution, aided by such advantages as lower transportation and/or insurance costs, lower tariffs, etc. In such instances, changes in relative prices of different exporters of the same commodity (or close substitutes) trigger a demand reaction.

8 See Kotan (2000) for detailed derivations of Equations (6.1) and (6.2).

9 Although there is no consensus on the choice of indexation method, the Laspeyres method is relatively more common and is thus used here (Fagerberg and Sollie 1987, Lohrmann 2000).

10 See Appendix C for a precise description of statistical properties.

11 Using a gravity model framework and based on a sample of Turkey's non-EU trade partners, Sayan (1998) and Sayan and Zaim (1998) have shown that the distance from Turkey to the country of destination is a significant factor affecting Turkish exports negatively.

12 Import and export prices are defined as inclusive of CIF and FOB, respectively. The difference between the two comes from freight and insurance charges. While freight costs are directly and positively related to the distance between exporting and importing countries, the distance affects insurance costs only as one of several factors that insurance companies consider in determining the level of risk premium to be charged.

References

Brada, J. C., A. M. Kutan, and S. Zhou (1997) 'The exchange rate and the balance of trade: the Turkish experience', *The Journal of Development Studies*, 33: 675–692.

CBRT/Central Bank of the Republic of Turkey (2001) Website at http://www.tcmb.gov.tr/

Daniels, P. (1999) 'Empirical gains from technology-intensive trade: an empirical assessment', *Cambridge Journal of Economics*, 23: 427–447.

Davidson, R. and J. G. MacKinnon (1993) *Estimation and Inference in Econometrics*, New York: Oxford University Press.

DPT/State Planning Organization of Turkey (1995) *Turk Ekonomisi'nin Rekabet Gucundeki Gelismeler*, Ankara: DPT.

Erlat, G. (1993) 'Is there a meaningful relationship between exports and industrial concentration? Case studies from the Turkish manufacturing industry', *METU Studies in Development*, 20: 43–61.

Erlat, G. and O. Akyuz (2001) 'Country concentration of Turkey's exports and imports over time', Paper presented at the *26th Annual Meeting of the Middle East Economic Association* (held in conjunction with the Allied Social Science Associations), New Orleans, January 5–7.

Erlat, G. and B. Sahin (1998) 'Export diversification of Turkey over time', *METU Studies in Development*, 25: 47–60.

Fagerberg, J. and G. Sollie (1987) 'The method of constant market shares analysis reconsidered', *Applied Economics*, 19: 1571–1583.

Finger, J. M. and M. E. Kreinin (1979) 'A measure of "export similarity" and its possible uses', *The Economic Journal*, 89: 905–912.

Guerrieri, P. and C. Milana (1995) 'Technology and trade competition in high-tech products', *Cambridge Journal of Economics*, 19: 225–242.

IMF, *International Financial Statistics*, CD-ROM, Washington, DC: International Monetary Fund.

Kotan, Z. (2000) 'Export performance of Turkey in the European Union market in comparison to South East Asian countries: *1990–1997*', Unpublished MA thesis, Department of Economics, Bilkent University, Ankara.

Kotan, Z. and S. Sayan (2001) 'A comparative investigation of the price competitiveness of Turkish and South East Asian exports in the European Union market: 1990–1997, *Emerging Markets Finance and Trade*, 38(4): 59–85.

Lloyd, P. J. (1994) 'Intraregional trade in the Asian and Pacific region', *Asian Development Review*, 12: 113–143.

Lohrmann, A. M. (2000) 'On Turkey's export performance: a decomposed constant market share analysis', *Russian and East European Finance and Trade*, 36(4): 80–90.

Matyas, L. (1995) *The Econometrics of Panel Data: Handbook of the Theory with Applications*, Boston, MA: Kluwer.

Merkies, A. H. Q. M. and T. Van Der Meer (1988) 'A theoretical foundation for constant market share analysis', *Empirical Economics*, 13: 65–80.

Noland, M. (1997) 'Has Asian export performance been unique?' *Journal of International Economics*, 43: 79–101.

OECD, *Annual International Trade Statistics*, CD-ROM, Paris: Organization of Economic Cooperation and Development.

Sayan, S. (1998) 'The Black Sea Economic Cooperation Project: a substitute for or a complement to globalization efforts in the Middle East and the Balkans?, Working Paper No. 9806, Cairo: Economic Research Forum.

Sayan, S. (2000) 'Recent developments in Turkish foreign trade', paper presented at the *Conference on the Economy of Turkey*, Tel Aviv University, Tel Aviv, June 15.

Sayan, S. and N. Demir (2003) 'Structural change in agriculture and water requirements in Turkish economy, in Lofgren, H. (ed.), *Food, Agriculture and Economic Policy in the*

Middle East and North Africa, vol. 5 of *The Research in Middle East Economics*, Amsterdam: JAI Press, pp. 289–315.

Sayan, S. and O. Zaim (1998) 'The Black Sea Economic Cooperation Project', in Rittenberg, L. (ed.), *The Political Economy of Turkey in the Post-Soviet Era*, Westport, CT: Praeger/Greenwood Publishing Group, Inc., pp. 115–136.

SIS/State Institute of Statistics (2001) State Institute of Statistics Website at http://www.die.gov.tr/

Uygur, E. (1997) 'Export policies and export performance: the case of Turkey', Working Paper No. 9707, Cairo: Economic Research Forum.

7 Trade strategies and industrial development in Iran: 1979–98*

Behrouz Hady Zonooz

1 Introduction

The performance of the industrial sector of Iran during the post-Revolution period has been weak in comparison with the preceding period. Undoubtedly, the tumultuous events of the Revolution, the ensuing war, economic sanctions and periodic oil shocks have contributed to this weak performance. However, this chapter suggests that the major factor in the emergence and continuation of the Iranian industrial sector's lacklustre performance has been the economic policies pursued by the government, particularly in the fields of trade strategy and industrial policy. This conclusion is reached following a thorough review of the effects of Iran's trade strategies on industrial sector performance during the post-Revolution period in the country.

The issue of growth-enhancing trade strategies is perhaps one of the most contentious in economics, with competing opinions roughly divided into four main camps: the neoclassicals, institutionalists, industrial strategists, and political economists.

Neoclassical economists, such as Balassa (1981), Krueger (1990), and Salvatore (1996) hold that, compared to the strategy of import substitution, export-led development leads to greater economic growth, increased exports and more rapid adoption of new technologies. Specifically, Krueger states that due to access to larger markets, the possibility of economies of scale and exposure of industries to international competition, the strategy of export development is superior to that of import substitution. Neoclassicals also commonly argue that under an import substitution strategy, rent seeking and smuggling takes root, the intensity of application of production factors is not commensurate with the abundance of such factors, income distribution becomes inappropriate and industries work at lower capacity (Krueger 1990).

Moreover, due to the importance of economies of scale in the production of intermediate and capital goods, the need for horizontal specialization in the production of machinery, and the desirability of vertical specialization (in the form of production of component parts and spare parts) on an efficient scale in the motorcar manufacturing industries, production in protected internal markets may often entail much higher costs (Balassa 1981: 18).

Although typically opposing any government intervention in the market mechanism, a number of neoclassical economists do acknowledge that market failure, which encompasses dynamic considerations, may necessitate the general promotion of industrialization. In such cases, the prescribed instruments for promotion of infant industries comprise subsidies, granted at equal rates and on a temporary basis according to the value added of the industry (Balassa 1975: 374). However, Krueger disagrees, arguing that simultaneous adoption of the policy of protection of infant industries and the granting of subsidies to export industries is not efficient in practice (Krueger 1990: 157).

Industrial strategists and institutional economists, however, disagree with the neoclassicals' view. Krugman (1986), for example, argues that in the presence of oligopoly and economies of scale, import substitution is not only compatible with export promotion, but is of unavoidable exigency toward this purpose.

Stiglitz and Dasgupta (1988) have shown that whenever there are strong possibilities for learning, there will emerge a tendency towards the appearance of dominant companies and industrial concentration. Under such circumstances, monopoly does not necessarily comprise the worst form of market structure. In those cases where the domestic industry is faced with a learning curve that is steeper than foreign competitors, protection of infant industries via trade policy is considered appropriate.

Meanwhile, Pack and Westphal (1986) argue that the secret behind the success of the Republic of Korea lies in its adoption of a dual trade policy with regard to industries with static and dynamic comparative advantage, and the special attention granted to the acquisition of technological capabilities. These authors do not view import protection policies as inconsistent with export orientation (Pack and Westphal 1986). Using a three-sector model, the possibility of simultaneous adoption of the policy of industrial protection and export promotion is demonstrated by Liang (1992).

Findlay (1978: 97) argues that the static comparative advantage of economic sectors is determined on the basis of the proportion of factors in that particular instant in time. In his opinion, since various sectors of the economy differ in the cost of resources required for development on the supply side and from the aspect of market particularities and growth potential on the demand side, selection of the leading sector is of great importance, and the long-term advantage of an economy will be in those fields where the potential for growth is greater.

Finally, political economists contend that internal and external policy orientations are not as important as the ways in which policy instruments are utilized. According to Amsden, industrial policies in the Republic of Korea are similar to other countries with late industrialization. Relative prices do not at all times reveal actual scarcity and it is due to this reason that governments manipulate prices. She holds that the selectiveness of protection policies and the relationship thereof with industrial performance is an important factor in the regulation of industrial behaviour. The rapid growth of the Republic of Korea has thus not only been due to disciplined industrial protection, but also to the institutions on which industrialization has been structured, which have been managed differently. Amsden is of the opinion that the main factors behind Korea's success have been the government's investment in the creation of physical infrastructures and training of manpower, protection of *chaebols*, the appearance of wage and salary recipient managers responsible for the application of borrowed technologies and, finally, concentration on shop-floor management that enabled optimization of technology transfers (Amsden 1989: chapter 1).

Evans believes that the type of governmental intervention depends on the structure and nature of the government itself and that only development-oriented governments are capable of intervening beneficially in an economy. In Evans' opinion, development-oriented governments enjoy internal solidarity and relative independence from the interests of influential groups. At the same time, such governments act in a collection of embedded social relations that link the government with the society (Evans 1995: 2).

So, was Iran's long-standing policy of import substitution beneficial or not to the industrial sector? Having provided the contextual background to this issue, we move on to consider how to find the answer to this question. The first hypothesis of this research is that the policy of import substitution by reliance on oil exports is essentially unstable, and even notwithstanding the destructive effects of war, economic sanctions, and oil shocks, such a policy is doomed to fail. This is demonstrated by the fact that the policy failed to lead to economizing in imports but, parallel with industrial development, demand for capital and intermediate goods actually increased. However, since there is no relationship between increases in foreign exchange requirements and oil revenues, capital accumulation and the rate of exploitation of industrial capacity was subject to continuous cyclical fluctuations, resulting in weak performance by the sector overall.

The second hypothesis is that due to the continuation of general protection policies, resource allocation efficiency has decreased. This hypothesis is tested via the calculation of the domestic resource cost (DRC) in four selected industries for 1996.

The third hypothesis is that the long-term continuation of the protection policy has resulted in the denial to Iranian industry of the dynamic advantages of export-led development. To this end, the relationship between industrial protection and the limited scope of the market, non-utilization of economies of scale, industrial concentration, and the appearance of technological inertia have been appraised from both qualitative and quantitative aspects.

In the following section, the methodology for testing these hypotheses is set out. Section 3 evaluates the performance of the industrial sector, and Section 4 analyses Iran's trade strategies and tax and credit preferences, which together constitute the financial incentive system, over a 30-year period (1968–98). The impact of trade policy on industrial development is dealt with in Section 5, where all three hypotheses are considered in detail.

2 Research methodology

The relationship between trade strategy and economic growth has been the subject of extensive empirical studies during the past two decades. In most of these studies, the export variable has been entered in the production function as a new production factor. Such models have been used both in cross-section studies between countries and in time-series studies of individual countries (Yaghmaian 1994: 1977–8). However, export-led growth theory has been questioned over its presumption of the causal relationship between exports and economic growth. Moreover, the growth of total factor productivity (TFP) in production has been attributed to structural changes in production which ensue economic growth and not to growth in exports *per se* (Singh 1995). Probably the main shortcoming of such studies, though, is that little insight is provided into *how* trade strategies affect industrial and economic growth.

It must be admitted that attempting to evaluate the effects of policies on economic performance is a forbidding task. In order to prove whether or not industrial policies have improved performance, we need to ascertain what changes would have come about in the absence of those policies. However, in practice this is not always easy or possible. Moreover, the effects of negative external shocks cannot readily be separated from those of policies. In addition, general government policies, including monetary and fiscal policies, public investment in infrastructure and human capital, affect the efficiency of trade policies and the incentive system. Hence, assessment of the consistency or inconsistency of such a collection of policies and actions is of great importance for an accurate appraisal of the effectiveness of trade policies.

Finally, it must be noted that the internal structure of the government, institutions, and existing legal frameworks affect both the nature of adopted policies as well as the efficiency their implementation. As may be noted, assessment of the effect of trade strategies on industrialization is much more complicated than fathoming its mechanism with the aid of partial economic analysis, for instance, via an econometric test of the relationship between openness of trade and economic growth.

It is due to this reason that the method adopted in the present research is of a holistic and comparative nature. It is comparative in that it deals with the comparison of the incentive system and the performance of the industrial sector between the pre-Revolution (1968–77) and the post-Revolution periods (1978–98). It is holistic in that the effects of social capabilities on the attraction of technology and technical progress have been taken into consideration. Trade orientation and openness to foreign trade comprise only one of the component factors of social capabilities: macroeconomic policies, investment in physical infrastructure and human capital, clarity of laws pertaining to property rights, the operation of the labour market, the political environment, and efficiency of the political system also affect social capabilities, probably more significantly so. Therefore, these factors have been analysed both qualitatively and quantitatively.

Four groups of industries have been selected on a case basis and closely examined. Two old industries (textile and cement) and two new industries (petrochemical and steel) have been selected and in each case, the nominal protection rate, the effective protection rate and the DRC have been calculated.

The methods of calculation of DRC, the effective rate of protection (ERP) and the incremental capital output ratio (ICOR) as well as industrial concentration have been explained in Appendix A.

3 The performance of the industrial sector: 1968–98

In order to assess industrial performance in Iran, the three criteria of industrial growth, labour productivity and industrial exports have been utilized. Data on industrial performance, industrial investment and foreign exchange and credit resources allocated to this sector are shown in Table 7.1.

It can be seen that average annual growth rate of manufacturing during 1968–72 was about 13.6 per cent declining to 1.9 per cent in the first decade after the Revolution. Although in the second decade the performance of the industrial sector improved dramatically (with annual growth rate rising to 10.8 per cent), it stayed well below that for the period before the Revolution. During 1980–97, Iran's annual industrial growth rate has not only been weaker than that of the Republic of Korea, a successful example of a developing country, but has even been lower than the average performance of developing countries as a whole (UNIDO 2000: 34, 75).

During the 1966–76 period, per capita labour productivity growth was, on average, 13.3 per cent per annum. This decreased to 2.3 per cent per annum in the 1976–86 decade and to 1.4 per cent per annum in the 1986–96 decade (Central Bank of Iran and Statistical Centre of Iran). Up to 1995, labour productivity in workshops with 50 and more employees was lower than in the pre-Revolution period and has only surpassed the latter rate during the past few years (Table 7.1).

Iran's industrial exports were minimal both in the pre-Revolution period and the first post-Revolution decade. However, following the end of the war, a visible change occurred in the value of industrial exports. Notwithstanding this fact, a comparison of industrial exports with imports of capital and intermediate goods would indicate a considerable gap in the trade balance in the industrial sector.

4 Trade strategy and the incentive systems in the industrial sector of Iran

The incentive system refers to that category of government actions and measures that influence resource allocation among industries and affect the orientation of activities between exports promotion and import substitution. In line with Balassa *et al.* (1982: 3), the incentive system has been defined in such a manner as to include both protective measures as well as credit and tax preferences.

The change in Iran's financial incentive system during the 1968–98 period is shown in Table 7.2. As with other countries pursuing import substitution, Iran's trade strategy in the past three decades has been characterized by overvaluation of the domestic currency, high customs tariffs and quantitative import restrictions.

During the first decade following the Revolution, the adopted trade policy included stabilization of the official foreign exchange rate and the application of severe quantitative restrictions on imports. The main objective of the government at the time was the prevention of a balance of payments deficit. Neither controlling domestic prices nor industrial protection was, in theory at least, at the centre

Table 7.1 The performance of manufacturing sector and investment in manufacturing in Iran, 1968–98

		Unit	*1968–72*	*1973–7*	*1978–88*	*1989–93*	*1994–8*
Performance	Average growth of value added (in constant 1982 prices)	Per cent	13.6	15.7	1.9	10.8	6.6
	Maximum value added (at constant 1982 price)	Million Rials	531.3	1,101.4	1,301.8	2,002.4	2,881.0
	Maximum labour productivity in large Industrial Establishments	×1,000 Rials	2,283 (1974)	2,768 (1977)	2,477 (1981)	2,521 (1990)	3,077 (1997)
	Maximum annual export of manufactured products (at constant 1982 prices)	Million $	102.6 (1977)	153.6 (1977)	232.7 (1988)	1,191.7 (1993)	1,588.2 (1998)
Industrial investment, foreign exchange and bank facilities available	Average annual fixed capital formation in manufacturing and mining (at constant 1982 prices)	Billion Rials	97.0	277.3	146.6	257.5	199.6
	Average annual investment of public sector in manufacturing and mining (at constant 1982 prices)	Billion Rials	n.a.	n.a.	59.6[a]	86.8	114.0
	Average annual investment of private sector in manufacturing and mining (at constant 1982 prices)	Billion Rials	n.a.	n.a.	47.3[a]	170.7	255.6
	Value of capital goods imported during the period (at constant prices)[b]	Million $	4,499.0	11,921.0	14,484.8	10,172.0	7,232.0
	Foreign exchange content of investment in manufacturing and mining per 1,000 Rials (at constant 1982 prices)	$	9.28	8.47	9.00	7.90	7.2
	Value of intermediate goods imported for manufacturing and mining[b]	Million $	13,527.5	30,718	54,058.6	29,220.0	20,011.0[a]
	Foreign exchange required per 1,000 Rials value added (in constant 1982 prices)	$	5.09	5.58	3.77	2.32	2.81
	Facilities and direct investments of Industrial and Mining (I&M) Bank in manufacturing and mining sector[c]	Billion Rials	21.7	101.5	217.8	62.5	63.0
	Share of I&M Bank in manufacturing and mining investment	Per cent	22.3	36.1	19.8	12.5	12.6

Sources: Economic Report and Balance Sheet of Central Bank of Iran, different years.

Notes

a Covers the period 1979–88.

b Adjusted by unit $ prices of exports of industrial countries (Based on IFS data).

c Adjusted by price index of investment in manufacturing and mining.

of the government's attention. In practice, however, through stringent price controls on industrial products and rationing and distribution of such goods through the official network, the government managed to keep the profit margin of domestic producers at a low level (see Table 7.2).

In the period following the Iran–Iraq War, Iran emerged from political isolation to a certain degree. During this period, pessimism about market mechanisms gave way to simplistic optimism regarding the outcome of active participation in the international division of labour, attraction of foreign capital, and less restricted operation of market forces in international trade and domestic business. Hence, the government decided to reduce the existing macroeconomic imbalances through implementation of economic adjustment policies and, as far as possible, to decrease severe distortions between border and internal prices.

In the trade policy sphere, these reforms included devaluation of the local currency, reducing quantitative import restrictions and tariffs, elimination of administrative export obstacles, continuation of the policy of exemption of export-generated income from corporate income tax, and reimbursement of customs charges and duties collected from intermediate inputs used in exports.

After the war, the government gradually ceased its policy of officially pricing industrial goods. At the same time, steps were taken to reduce the disguized subsidy rate of energy and credit preferences (Table 7.2), leading to rises in energy prices and interest rates. However, trade liberalization did not last long and it became increasingly evident that changing the industrial structure by merely relying on relative prices was not possible. Indeed, pursuance of expansionary financial policies parallel to the devaluation of the local currency and liberalization of trade resulted in a large deficit in trade balance and accumulation of foreign debts.

By the beginning of 1995, therefore, Iran faced severe exchange rate fluctuations, and it became clear that considerable short-term foreign debts had accumulated that the government was unable to honour. So new measures were adopted to control the foreign exchange market and domestic prices. This policy resulted in the administrative stabilization of the exchange rate, reinforcement of quantitative import restrictions, price controls, and restriction of bank credits.

As stated above, Iran's trade strategies, during both the pre- and post-Revolution periods, have been based on import substitution. A case study of the steel and petrochemical industries reveals that even in 1996, following the introduction of adjustment policies, the Rial revenues from the sale of their products have been greater in the domestic market than in export markets. Industrial exports were not developed in either period, restricting Iran's role severely in the current international division of labour.

This situation is, to a great extent, due to the fact that during the past few decades, the real exchange rate has not been stabilized and, therefore, the competitive capability of Iran in the world market has decreased. Although, during the recent decade, the devaluation of the national currency and purchase of export-generated foreign exchange at rates higher than the official rate by the Central Bank has rectified this problem to a certain extent, the export development of the

Table 7.2 The incentive system in Iran, 1968–98

		Unit	*1968–72*	*1973–7*	*1978–88*	*1989–93*	*1994–8*
Exchange rate	Foreign exchange gap	Per cent	8.6–12.9	8.9–13.3	29.3–1,372.0	9.9–1,583.4	60–394.6
Import barriers	Import tax per US$	Rials	16–17.4	11.6	13.9–17.8	27.3–56	108.9–309.4
	Quantitative barriers of import		Moderate	Negligible	Vast	Considerable	Vast
	Number of commodity groups import of which is prohibited	Number	Not calculated	Not calculated	637	631	680
Export incentives	Export bonus		Available	Available	n.a.	n.a.	n.a.
	Income tax exemption of export		Available	Available	Available	Available	Available
	Preferential foreign exchange rate for export		n.a.	n.a.	Available	Available	Available
Other incentives	Ratio of corporate tax to value added of manufacturing industries	Per cent	14.5	33.0	17.2	12.6	13.8
	Duration of income tax exemption	Years	5	5	5	4–8	4–8
	Nominal interest rate of bank facilities to M&M	Per cent	n.a.	9	4–10	11–18	16–19
	Real price of energy (in constant 1982 prices)						
	Kiln oil	Rials/litre	n.a.	10.1–13.8	2.9–9.2	2.4–2.5	1.7–5
	Gas oil	Rials/litre	n.a.	20.2–27.6	6.9–18.5	4.7–5.8	3.3
	Relative price of industrial products	—	1.12–1.2	1.02–1.11	0.71–0.97	0.70–0.83	0.79–0.81

Sources: Central Bank of Iran, Ministry of Commerce, Export and Import Regulations, Ministry of Energy, Annual Energy Balance Reports.

country was once again halted due to instability in foreign exchange policies in the 1995–7 period.

4.1 Nominal and effective rates of protection in selected industries

The nominal rate of protection serves to measure the degree of distortion of domestic prices from international prices. The results of calculations of the nominal rate of protection in the selected industries are indicative of the considerable distortion in domestic and foreign prices against the various rates of exchange (Table 7.3).

Table 7.4 shows our calculations of the *effective* rate of protection in the selected industries for 1996. As may be noted, the petrochemical industry enjoys the highest effective rate of protection. The first phase of Arak Petrochemical Complex reached the commissioning stage in 1993. It is expected that the learning process in this industry should have been completed during the 4-year time span. It is noteworthy that in 1996 approximately 42 per cent of the products of Arak Petrochemical Complex were exported. Nevertheless, this Complex also supplied the requirements of numerous downstream industries. Should exports be considered as an indication of the achievement of competitive capability in the petrochemical industry, the unsparing continuation of this type of protection can only exacerbate economic inefficiency, wastage of energy and scarce capital, as well as of skilled labour.

The Mobarakeh Steel Plant ranks second to Arak Petrochemical Complex in terms of effective protection. This factory reached its commissioning stage in 1992 and in 1996 approximately 9.9 per cent of its products were exported. Despite the wastage of energy and excess production capacity in 1996 (82.6 per cent), this industry has enjoyed a high effective rate of protection.

The cement industry in Iran has a long-standing history going back over 68 years. It cannot, therefore, be considered an 'infant' industry. The domestic price of cement in 1996 was less than the international price. However, due to consumption of cheap energy, it enjoys a positive effective rate of protection.

The cotton and synthetic fibres textile industry was established in Iran between the two World Wars. It would be expected that over such a long period this industry would have managed to acquire the technological capabilities and the power to compete in world markets without any protection. Although compared to the foregoing industries, this industry has enjoyed the least effective protection, it is an unhealthy industry with worn out machinery and obsolete technology. Indeed, due to the smuggling of fabrics into the country, the industry is faced with a depression in the domestic market, while its poor export performance is indicative of its lack of competitiveness in international and regional markets.

This brief review serves to indicate that industrial protection in Iran does not bear a clear logic and the pattern of protection in industries has been randomly determined. Furthermore, industrial protection has been granted for an unlimited

Table 7.3 Nominal protection rate in selected branches of manufacturing industry in Iran, 1996

	Unit	*Volume of annual sales*	*Total value of sales (million Rials)*	*Domestic price (Rials)*	*Border price ($)*[a]	*Nominal protection rate*		
						1$ = 2,480 Rials	*1$ = 3,108 Rials*	*1$ = 3,750 Rials*
1 Cotton and synthetic fibres textile[b]	Metre	110,442,536	276,125	2,500.1	0.851	18.5	−5.5	−21.7
2 Petrochemical products	Tonnes	415,820	754,053.6	1,813,412	503.89	45.1	15.8	4.2
3 Cement[c]	Tonnes	16,404,345	915,930	55,834.6	24.10	−6.6	−25.5	−38.2
4 Steel sheet products	Tonnes	1,924,296.4	1,973,982	1,025,820	283.7	45.8	16.3	−3.6

Notes
a Border price is a weighted average of export and import prices.
b Data relate to five major cotton textile producing units.
c Data relate to 19 cement-producing units out of 22 active units.

Table 7.4 Effective protection rate in selected branches of manufacturing industry in Iran, 1996

Exchange rate per $ against Rials	*Balassa method of calculation*				*Corden method of calculation*			
	Cotton and synthetic fibres textile	*Petrochemical products*	*Cement*	*Steel sheet products*	*Cotton and synthetic fibres textile*	*Petrochemical products*	*Cement*	*Steel sheet products*
2,480	24.6	653.3	306.2	426.6	22.5	339.2	177.2	190.7
3,108	−2.4	403.8	182.6	236.1	−2.2	250.5	121.2	132.0
3,750	−20.1	276.3	115.5	145.4	−19	190.5	83.3	92.1

period of time, indiscriminately and without due regards to industrial performance.

4.2 Inaccuracy of selected strategies

At the initial stage of late industrialization, import substitution is an unavoidable policy. However, immediately after attaining technological capabilities through imitation and learning supported by protection, first generation industries must be exposed to international competition, and exploit export markets in order to earn foreign exchange income. This is the successful trajectory followed by Japan, the Republic of Korea, and Taiwan.

In Iran, however, due to the abundance of oil resources, the exchange rate was kept at a low level by the government for many years, thus maintaining discrimination against industrial exports. At the end of the Fifth Development Plan (1973–7), it was clear to all that the policy of development of oil exports parallel with pursuing industrial development through import substitution would render the economy of the country vulnerable to oil shocks. Moreover, it was foreseen that due to the finite nature of oil resources, with economic development, the importance of oil in GDP would diminish sooner or later. The policy implication was a decrease in the role of the public sector in favour of the private sector, and encouragement of a non-oil export development strategy. However, following the Revolution, Iran moved in exactly the opposite direction. In the early 1980s, at a time when liberalization of trade regimes and direct foreign investment was witnessed worldwide, the Iranian government adopted an internal orientation, along with a policy of extensive intervention in economic affairs.

4.3 Internal inconsistency of governmental policies

One of the reasons behind the relative success of Iran's industrial development before the Revolution was that there was internal consistency between trade policies and the financial incentive system on one hand and other government policies on the other. However, after the Revolution, government policies have been marked by glaring inconsistencies. Despite the rhetoric of post-Revolutionary governments to develop non-oil exports, intervention in foreign exchange and domestic prices have decreased the competitive capability of domestic industries and discriminated against exports (Table 7.2).

At the same time, although domestic producers benefited from disguised foreign exchange and energy subsidies, the official pricing of their products during the first decade after the Revolution kept their profit margins low. The sharp reduction of the relative prices of industrial products during this period attests to this claim (Table 7.2).

Notwithstanding the fact that interest rates have in most years been lower than the inflation rate, in order to soften the inflationary impact of its expansionary fiscal policies, the government has often kept the ceiling on bank credits at a low level and even imposed severe quantitative restrictions on loans. As a consequence, the share of bank credits in funding industrial investments has decreased (Table 7.1). Furthermore, through obligatory allocation of bank facilities to certain projects and regions in the budget, the government has maintained discrimination against the private sector in the distribution of bank credits.

4.4 Inconsistency of policies with institutional arrangements

Efficient functioning of market forces also requires an appropriate institutional foundation.

In the period following the Revolution, the security of ownership was jeopardized by confiscation of domestic and foreign private corporations. Moreover, the Constitution restricted the scope of the private sector's activity. An undefined scope of ownership, threat of confiscation of property and the inability of the judiciary to provide timely and equitable legal judgements increased uncertainty for domestic and foreign investors and increased transaction costs.

Following the Revolution, industrial relations deteriorated, and a new Labour Law was not enacted until 1990. This did not, however, allow for workers' dismissals – reflecting the official policy of maintaining employment at any cost.

Although the Direct Taxation Act 1987 provided for tax preferences for newly established industries, it placed serious impediments to industrial investment in other areas. Repeated amendments of the Act, ambiguity in its wording, high and progressive corporate income tax, calculation of depreciation on the basis of the book value of assets, collection of tax on transfers of shares and exemption of foundations from taxation were among its numerous shortcomings.

Aside from these institutional arrangements that were clearly inconsistent with industrial development, we must also mention chronic internal political instability and tension in international relations. Unfortunately, after more than two decades after the Revolution, relations between the government and civil society and the scope, functions and powers of each have not yet been clearly defined. Absence of a clear separation between the technocratic 'body' of the government and its political 'brains', tensions spread to all planning and executive management levels, causing uncertainty and increasing investment risks in the country.

In the 1980s, tensions in international relations too were detrimental to the national economy. Compounded by external provocation, political imprudence, and ambiguity over Iran's position in the international politics and economics arena contributed to the creation of such a situation. Fortunately, after the War, in particular since 1997, the policy of friendly relations with neighbouring countries and détente in international relations has been pursued, and an appropriate foundation has been laid for the development of economic and trade relations at the regional and international levels.

5 The impact of trade policy on industrial development

In this section, the implications of trade policy on the performance of the manufacturing sector are evaluated. For this purpose, the subject is discussed under three headings pertaining to our three hypotheses.

5.1 Foreign exchange shortage consequences of import substitution

Foreign exchange shortages may be considered a logical consequence of the strategy of import substitution. Import substitution had two prominent features: technological backwardness of the industrial sector and a dependence on foreign exchange revenues generated by oil exports. Iranian industry was thus characterized by: limited manufactured exports, dependence on imports of capital and intermediate goods, purchase of technical know-how from abroad, and higher domestic product prices compared with similar foreign products.

During the course of the Fourth and Fifth Development Plans (1968–77), for every 1,000 Rials of industrial and mining investment, 9.28 and 8.47 dollars, respectively, were required for imports of capital goods (at 1982 constant prices). During the same period, for every 1,000 Rials of value-added in the industrial and mining sector, 5.09 and 5.58 dollars, respectively, were required for imports of intermediate goods (Table 7.1). The important point is that import substitution failed to achieve economies in the imports bill for industrial capital, intermediate and consumer goods – indeed, these costs eventually escalated. In addition, the industrial sector became dependent on fluctuating oil revenues (Tables 7.1 and 7.5).

In these circumstances, capital accumulation and capacity utilization were inevitably influenced by the economy's ability to sustain imports through the foreign exchange proceeds from oil exports. But the quantity and price of oil exports are both exogenous and beyond the control of the government. Moreover, since neither the volume and nor value of non-oil exports increased in line with industrial growth, there was no relationship between foreign exchange revenues and industrial performance.

During the post-Revolution period, the ratio of the aggregate value of imports and exports to gross domestic product at constant prices both decreased and became highly volatile. These fluctuations were in turn due to severe fluctuations in Iran's oil exports and lack of access to international financial resources in the 1980s. In this period, Iran was ever more closed to foreign trade, financial resources, and technology (Table 7.5).

Foreign exchange shortages also caused the overvaluation of the currency. Increases in the import bill for agricultural products and military armaments, transfers of capital abroad and administrative corruption in government purchases also intensified the foreign exchange shortage.

Lack of technological capability for the manufacture of domestically required capital equipment combined with foreign exchange shortages had an adverse effect on capital accumulation in the industrial sector (Table 7.2). Indeed, the foreign exchange shortage – itself a symptom of the malaise in the industrial sector – was behind the low rate of capital accumulation and underutilization of production capacity in this period. Reflecting this malaise, the incremental capital output ratio rose to 2.22 in the 1978–87 period (up from 1.88 during the Fifth Development Plan period; see Table 7.6).

Capacity utilization in the industrial sector too declined in the first decade after the Revolution – reaching just 40 per cent by 1988 (Plan and Budget

Table 7.5 Foreign trade and access to international financial resources, 1968–98

		Unit	*1968–72*	*1973–7*	*1978–88*	*1989–93*	*1994–8*
Foreign trade	Share of Foreign Trade in GDP[a]	Per cent	60.5–65.0	56.0–64.2	20.3–44.9	26.0–34.6	17.0–30.3
	Total balance of current account	Million $	−2132	29,978	2,275	−20,031	13,619
Access to international financial resources	Total commodity export (in current prices)	Million $	9,366	99,868	169,032	88,995	91,684
	Total commodity import(in current prices)	Million $	10,786	63,593	137,051	110,330	67,744
	Access to foreign financial resources		Available	n.a.	n.a.	Available	Available
	Government policy toward FDI		Positive	Positive	Confiscation and prohibition	Positive	Positive
	Inflow of FDI		Positive	Positive	Negative	Little	Little

Source: Economic Report and Balance Sheet of Central Bank of Iran in different years.

Note
a Ratio of total exports and import to GDP.

Table 7.6 Incremental capital–output ratio in manufacturing and mining industries, 1976–98

Years	*Duration*	*ΔKMM*	*ΔVAIM*	*ICOR2*
1968–72	5	371.4	277.5	1.34
1973–7	5	1,130.6	6,010.1	1.88
1978–88	7	437.6	197	2.22
1989–93	5	690.9	710.8	0.97
1994–8	5	981	650.7	1.5

Source: Calculated on the basis of national accounts.

Notes
ΔKMM: Increment in Capital Stock.
ΔVAIM: changes of value added.

Organization 1989: 7–23). In some main branches of industry (such as machine manufacturing), the rate was in fact as low as only 22 per cent (Plan and Budget Organization 1989).

After the war with Iraq ended, political stability improved, economic reforms were undertaken and the government tried to remove major infrastructure bottlenecks in the economy (Table 7.8). These reforms brought about greater investment incentives in both the private and public sectors. However, expanded foreign exchange supplies played a key role in improving economic performance. Quantitative import restrictions were reduced giving the private sector an opportunity to complete delayed industrial projects. With an increase in budgetary Rial revenues due to a depreciation of the national currency, the government also increased the volume of its investments in infrastructure and industrial affairs (Table 7.1). Thus, after 1988, industrial capacity utilization improved and capital accumulation in the industrial sector too rose. During this period, incremental capital output ratio contracted, indicating increased capital efficiency in comparison with the War period (Table 7.6).

In this period, import substitution also spread to intermediate and capital industrial sectors as the foreign exchange content of each investment unit in production declined (Table 7.1). This could to a certain extent be due to the start in operations of large petrochemical and steel projects, which are the main suppliers of intermediate goods for down-stream industries, combined with the increase in capacity utilization in the machine manufacturing industries. However, it is also probably due to the creation of additional industrial capacity in Iran's heavy industries, as well as an expansion of part-manufacturing capacity in the country (in particular, the motorcar industry).

After the onset of foreign debt crisis in 1993, the government resorted to import compression again. Import restrictions and circulating capital deficiencies once again increased idle capacity. However, the volume of industrial investment did not fall, as apparently during the 1994–8 period, the foreign exchange requirements for investment and industrial production declined (Table 7.1). Even so, the increase in ICOR during this period clearly reflects a decrease in the technical efficiency of production, which is itself due to a shortage of foreign exchange. Administrative stabilization of the domestic currency in the mid-1990s restricted the export growth rate of industrial products.

The experience of the past two decades indicates that Iranian economy continues to suffer from scientific and technical backwardness, combined with over-dependence on oil exports. This problem may not be overcome without an overhaul of the trade strategy and structural changes in the economy as a whole.

5.2 *Industrial protection and static inefficiency in resource allocation*

Government intervention led to substantial and significant price distortion as our calculations of the DRC indicate.

Using alternative shadow exchange rates (SERs) of Rials 2,480, Rials 3,108, and Rials 3,750, respectively, against the US dollar, all industries under study here, with the exception of the textiles, are inefficient (Table 7.7).

Table 7.7 Domestic resource cost in selected industries, 1996 (figures in Rials)

Description	*Cotton and synthetic fibres textile products*	*Petrochemical products*	*Cement products*	*Steel products*
DRC (e = 2,480)	2,971	3,262	7,715	7,885
DRC (e = 3,108)	3,153	3,562	8,227	9,113
DRC (e = 3,750)	3,338	3,869	8,750	10,206

Due to the low prices of energy vectors in Iran, energy wastage is very high in all industries investigated here. A study of nine petrochemical units in Iran has shown that their total energy consumption was 11 million barrels of oil – exceeding similar processes in the world by 3.7 million barrels (Institute of International Energy Studies 1995). In 1990, fuel consumption per ton of cement was 84 litres in Germany, whereas the equivalent figure for Iran in 1996 was 110 litres (*Cement Quarterly* 1996: 11–15). In steel production, energy consumed per ton of steel in Iran is 20 per cent more than in developed countries. Even if the direct energy consumption of the industries under study were economized by 20 per cent, their DRC (estimated at Rials 3,750 to the dollar) would reach Rials 2,860 in the petrochemical industry; however, in the cement and steel production sectors, it would remain more than the SER, decreasing only to Rials 5,775 and Rials 7,748, respectively.

5.3 *Trade strategy and long-term dynamics of growth*

Trade strategy also affects long-term economic growth through other channels. In this section, the effects of trade strategy on long-term dynamics of growth will be briefly reviewed.

5.3.1 *Trade strategy, market size, and economies of scale*

Import substitution limits industrial development to the size of the domestic market. In the second stage of import substitution in Iran, which began with the production of intermediate goods, manufacture of industrial machinery and motorcars, most investments were made with the aim of meeting domestic market requirements. However, this stage was marked by gross industrial inefficiency. In the production of intermediate goods, such as steel, petrochemicals, synthetic fibres and so forth, economies of scale are of great importance. At the beginning, production in these industries began on a low scale, which meant that unit costs for these goods were much higher than similar imported items. The costs were borne out by the downstream production units, which were consumers of these goods.

Iran's machine manufacturing industries which had been prioritized since the Fourth Development Plan, gradually lost their significance partly due to insufficient attention paid to horizontal specialization and partly through receiving non-competitive East European technologies. This was reflected in their failure to supply quality capital goods at sufficiently low prices to the market.

In the motorcar manufacturing industry, which was established approximately 40 years ago, vertical specialization in the form of manufacture of parts and components is of importance. At the same time, all successful manufacturers are based in large domestic markets and, hence, have been able to establish a successful presence in world markets. The motorcar manufacturing industry of Iran began with manufacturing for a small domestic market and, until the beginning of the 1990s, failed to form vertical specializations within the industry, remaining merely an assembly industry, reliant on importation of components and spare parts from abroad. It was only after the Vehicles Act of 1993, that vertical specialization began to occur.

5.3.2 Trade strategies and monopolistic market structures

Calculations of industrial concentration, based on the International Standard Industrial Classification (ISIC) four-digit code level, indicate that in 1996, 49 of the 141 industrial branches in Iran were characterized by monopolistic or oligopolistic market structures.

In a similar study based on similar criteria for Korea, Japan, and Taiwan, industrial concentration at the beginning of the 1980s was shown to have been higher than that of Iran. Protection of *zaibatsus* by the Japanese government (Vestal 1995) and the protection of *chaebols* by the Korean government (Amsden 1989) are recognized aspects of economic development in Japan and Korea, respectively.

There are several significant difference between these East Asian economies and Iran. First, in the East Asian case, such monopolies were owned by the private sector. Second, those monopolies benefited from economies of scale and agglomeration; and third, they were exposed to international competition. Hence, they were, and still are, involved in tough competition in order to gain market share and maintain their competitiveness in world markets (e.g. by spending considerable sums on R&D).

In Iran, most large monopolies are in the public sector and under government management. These were in general loss making, particularly during the first post-Revolution period, with their losses funded from the public purse. In most cases, these monopolies funded investment in new or development projects through the development budget and for free. Their foreign exchange requirements too were allocated administratively.

Public sector managers were, in practice, obliged to maintain the level of employment in production units. The main concern of management was therefore not improvements in the quality of products, costs reduction, imitation of new innovations, and customer satisfaction. Instead, during the course of the War, the most important function of the public sector managers was to be present at decision-making centres in order to secure their Rial and foreign exchange resources and to maintain quantitative import restrictions. In the private sector also, irrespective of the monopolistic or competitive structure of the market, private managers and employers pursued rent-seeking activities. Thus, relations with political and administrative officials and exercising influence in bureaucratic decisions were considered the most profitable activity for these managers.

During the second decade after the Revolution, the government gradually began to resist the underwriting of the government-owned companies' losses and reduced foreign exchange rationing. Thus, government and private companies were forced to secure their foreign exchange requirements through the market. Furthermore, although there were fewer restrictions on bank credits, payment of high nominal interest rates (despite the negative real rate of interest) became a heavy financial burden for these companies. For this reason, both government and private companies found that they *had* to economize on foreign exchange and Rial expenses, to seek to improve the quality of their products and to enter the world markets by enhancing their competitive capabilities. Of course, adaptation to the new situation was not a simple task. Laying off excess manpower, better utilization of production capacities, purchase of new and, in certain cases, second-hand machinery for replacement of foreign machinery, and substitution of domestic capital and intermediate goods were among the consequences of this situation. However, cyclical changes in foreign exchange and trade protection policies, randomness and irrationality of the pattern of protection among industries, political instability, and negative and positive oil shocks have created such a chaotic economic environment that in practice the adoption of strategic decisions on a purely commercial basis is impossible.

5.3.3 *Trade strategy and technological advancement*

Countries with low rates of productivity may catch up via the attraction and adoption of more advanced production technologies from high-productivity countries. However, the realization of this potential requires the possession of necessary social capabilities. Openness to world competition (Hansson and Henrekson 1994: 117, 121) is one of the determinants of social capability. This is because the more an economy is exposed to international competition, the greater the interaction with advanced technology, and hence competitiveness is augmented (Baumol 1986). The qualitative and quantitative indices of the factors determining social capabilities have been summarized in Table 7.8. The degree of openness of Iran's economy has also already been presented in Table 7.5.

The appropriate criterion for measurement of technological advancement is TFP. However, due to unavailability of valid data with respect to physical capital stocks, the labour force engaged in the industrial sector and its human capital, TFP calculations cannot be undertaken. In the absence of such required data, a comparative study of the change in per capita labour productivity during the two extended periods has sufficed (Table 7.9).

Tables 7.8 and 7.9 show that social capability before the Revolution was higher than after the Revolution. During the latter period, per capita labour productivity

Table 7.8 Determinants of social capabilities for absorbing technological achievements and enhancing economic growth

		Unit	*1968–72*	*1973–7*	*1978–88*	*1989–93*	*1994–8*
Macroeconomic indicators	Annual growth of GDP (excluding oil sector)	Per cent	10.8	13.3	+0.33	4.16	4.6
	Ratio of budget deficit to GDP	Per cent	6.4	5.1	7.4	1.5	1.7
	Range of inflation rate	Per cent	0–6.9	10–25.5	8.6–29.0	8.9–24.4	17.3–49.3
Labour market performance	Employment rigidity	Qualitative evaluation	Little	Little	Large	Large	Large
	Producers wage index at the end of each period	1982 = 100	58.8 (1974)	69.6	91.5	90.4	99.6
Human capital	Literacy rate	Per cent	28.7	47.5	61.8	74.1	79.5
	Availability of work force with university education	Qualitative evaluation	Little	Manpower shortage	Manpower shortage	Excess supply	Excess supply
	Availability of skilled labour in technical fields	Qualitative evaluation	Little	Manpower shortage	Manpower shortage	Excess supply	Excess supply
Physical infrastructures	Transportation facilities	Qualitative evaluation	Not any problem	Serious bottlenecks	Bottlenecks	Persistence of problems	Persistence of problems
	Electricity	Qualitative evaluation	Not any problem	Occasional shutdowns	Occasional shutdowns	No problems	No problems
	Access to telephone lines	Qualitative evaluation	Low penetration	Long waiting time	Long waiting time	Short waiting time	No problems
	Ports and port facilities	Qualitative evaluation	No problem	Congestion	Overloading of Bandar Abbas	No problems	No problems
Government policy toward institutions	Government policy toward private business	Out of 10	10	9	3	6	6
	Government policy toward labour unions	Qualitative evaluation					
Political environment	Political stability	Out of 10	10	9	3	7	5
	Efficiency of political system	Out of 10	10	8	3	4	4
	Relations with neighbouring countries	Qualitative evaluation	Good	Good	Very bad (war)	Moderate	Good
	Relations with Europe and Japan	Qualitative evaluation	Good	Very good	Bad	Moderate	Good
	Relations with USA	Qualitative evaluation	Good	Good	Embargo no relation	Embargo no relation	Embargo no relation

Table 7.9 Average annual growth rate of per-capita stock of capital, human capital, and labour productivity in manufacturing and mining (M&M) sectors, 1966–97

Duration	*Annual growth of K in M&M*	*Annual growth rate of human capital employed in M&M*	*Annual growth rate of ratio of employees with university education to total number of employees*	*Annual growth of labour productivity*				*Openness of economy*	*FDI (Rials)*
				Industry and mining	*Total manufacturing*	*Large industrial establishment (with 10 employees and more)*	*Large industrial establishments (with 50 employees and more)*		
1966–77	14.8	3.1	12.4	11.2	12.5	n.a.	n.a.	55.8	2,295
1977–97	2.4	4.1	5.8	2.2	2	0.9	0.5	29.4	Negligible

growth in the manufacturing and mining sector has been one-fifth of the previous period.

6 Conclusions

It may be concluded that in the period before the Revolution, the Iranian economy experienced rapid industrial growth and improvement of per capita labour productivity, based on a strategy of import substitution and promotion of oil exports. However, such rapid growth increased the foreign exchange requirements of manufacturing industries increased dependence on oil revenues.

The experience after the Revolution has shown that such an industrial structure is essentially unstable and vulnerable to external shocks, since capital accumulation and capacity utilization have been dependent on the oil revenues.

In this period, Iran's economy has been beset with static inefficiency due to extensive government intervention in the economy. Moreover, crises in the economic relationship between Iran and the developed nations and the continuation of the import substitution strategy for an extended period intensified. In this period, due to discrimination against exports and the inward orientation of the domestic industries, industrial growth was restricted to the domestic market. The resulting monopolistic structure of the domestic market was to the detriment of domestic consumers, and instead of investing in R&D and expanding in overseas markets, the vast majority of these monopolies have engaged in profiteering from rent-seeking opportunities.

Iran's industrial backwardness and her sluggish growth and development in the post-Revolutionary era are also the product of an inappropriate trade strategy and an unlimited, unconditional, and non-selective financial incentives system. At the same time, this situation is the product of the inconsistency of trade and industrial policies of the government with other economic policies and inadequate institutional and legal arrangements required for the efficient performance of market forces.

Finally, the structure of the state in Iran in the period under consideration has not been conducive to economic development. Persistent political crises and bureaucratic corruption have limited the state's capability to intervene beneficially in economic affairs.

Appendix A

Calculation of the ERP

The ERP consists of the ratio of gross value added of industry (on the basis of domestic prices) to the value added of industry at border prices, minus one. In fact, this ratio serves to indicate the amount of protection for the value added of the industry. In the present research, the two methods of Balassa and Corden have been used for calculation of the effective rate of protection (Balassa *et al.* 1982: 351–355).

The difference between the two methods lies in their different treatment of non-traded goods:

$$\text{ERP}^{\text{B}} = \frac{p_{\text{d}} - \sum_{j} a_{ji} p_{\text{d}} - \sum_{n} a_{nj} p_{\text{d}}}{p_i - \sum_{j} a_{ji} p_i - \sum_{j}\sum_{n} a_{ni} p_i r_{jn} - \sum_{w}\sum_{n} a_{ni} p_i r_{wn}}$$

$$\text{ERP}^{\text{C}} = \frac{p_{\text{d}} - \sum_{j} a_{ji} p_{\text{d}} - \sum_{j}\sum_{n} a_{nj} p_{\text{d}} r_{jn}}{p_i - \sum_{j} a_{ji} p_i - \sum_{j}\sum_{n} a_{ni} p_i r_{jn}}$$

where
p_{d} = domestic price;
p_i = border price;
a_{ji} = input–output coefficient for intermediate products at domestic prices;
a_{ni} = input–output coefficient for non-traded goods at domestic prices;
r_{jn} = direct plus indirect input–output coefficient for intermediate inputs used in producing non-traded goods at domestic prices;
r_{wn} = direct plus indirect input–output coefficient for value added embodied in the production of non-traded goods at domestic prices.

Method of calculation of DRC

DRC measures the domestic resources used for the production of one unit of foreign exchange unit in each activity. Domestic resource cost has been defined in various forms (see, e.g. Srinivasan and Bhagwati 1978: 104–106).

DRC has been used both as a criterion for identifying the trade system as well as measurement of resource allocation efficiency. We have used the following relationship for calculation of DRC:

$$\text{DRC} = \frac{\left(\text{CF}_{l1} \sum_{l1} a_{l1} L_1 + \text{CF}_{l2} \sum_{l2} a_{l2} L_2\right) - \left(\sum_{k1} a_{k1} K_1' + \sum_{k2} a_{k2} K_2\right)}{p_i - \sum_{j} a_{ij} p_l - \sum_{j}\sum_{i} a_{ni} p_i r_{jn}}$$

where
CF_{l1} = conversion factor for the wages and salaries paid for production of the product;
CF_{l2} = conversion factor for the wages and salaries of the labour force used directly or indirectly in the production of non-traded goods;
$\sum a_{l1} L_1$ and $\sum a_{l2} L_2$ = compensation of services of the labour force employed in the related industry and compensation of services of the labour force used in the production of non-traded goods, respectively;

$\sum_l a_{k1}K_1' =$ shadow price of capital services directly used in the production of the related product plus depreciation cost;

$\sum_l a_{k2}K_2 =$ value of capital services used directly and indirectly in the production of non-traded goods plus depreciation (at market prices).

The other symbols used are similar to those used in the calculation of ERP.

Method of calculation of ICOR

ICOR is used as a measure of technical and economic efficiency. Due to unavailability of data for the capital stock of industry and mining sectors, this ratio has been calculated using the following relationship:

$$K_t = K_{t-1} + I_t - \delta\, K_{t-1} = (1 - \delta)\, K_{t-1} + I_t$$

In the above relationship, δ is the annual capital depreciation coefficient, K is capital stock, and I is annual investment. For calculation of capital stock as at the beginning of the period (1965), the capital output ratio was first assumed to be 1.25 and then as 1.8. Since the result of this calculation is not so sensitive to changes in these hypotheses, the first assumption has been used. We have assumed an annual depreciation rate of 5 per cent ($\delta = 5$ per cent).

Method of calculation of industrial concentration

To measure industrial concentration, the ratio of production value of three workshops in each large industry to the total production value of the same industry has been calculated. Where this index in 60 per cent or over, it is assumed that oligopoly prevails in the market.

Acknowledgement

The author and editors are grateful to Marianna Volpi for her meticulous and substantial editorial input into this chapter.

References

Farsi sources

Baumol, W. J. (1996) 'Productivity Growth, Convergence and Welfare', Translated by Behrouz Hadi Zonooz, *Economic Research Quarterly*, Autumn (2): 53–81.

Bergstrom, V. (ed.) (1999) *Government and Growth*, Translated by Ali Hayati, Teheran: Plan and Budget Organization.

Cement Quarterly (1996) September no. 17, Tehran (in Persian).

Central Bank of Iran, *Economic Report and Balance Sheet*, various years.

Central Bank of Iran, *National Accounts of Iran*, various years, Tehran.

Central Bank of Iran, Census Results of Large Industrial Workshops, various years Tehran.

Institute of International Energy Studies (1995) *A Comparison of Energy Consumption for Production of Chemicals in Iran and Other Countries*, Office of Deputy for Research, Winter.

Krueger, A. O. (1995) *Economic Policy Reform in Developing Countries*, Translation Team, Tehran: High Institute of Planning and Development Research.

Krueger, A. O. (1998) 'Sustainable development based on export orientation: lessons from East Asia', translated by Ali Dini Torkamani and Masoumeh Saleh Amin, *Commercial Research Quarterly*, Spring (6).

Leipziger, D. (ed.) (1996) *The Experience of Development in East Asia*, Translation Team, Tehran: High Institute of Planning and Development Research.

National Iranian Petrochemical Industries Company (1997) 'Operational Report of the Iranian Petrochemical Industries for the Year 1996', Tehran.

National Iranian Steel Industries Co. (1996), *The Mobarakeh Steel Complex Financial Accounts*.

Plan and Budget Organization (1989) 'Law of the First Economic, Social and Cultural Development Plan of the Islamic Republic of Iran (1989–1993)', Tehran.

The Statistical Centre of Iran, *Census Results of Large Industrial Workshops*, various years, Tehran.

English sources

Amsden, A. H. (1989) *Asia's Next Giant, South Korea and Late Industrialization*, Oxford: Oxford University Press.

Balassa, B. (1975) 'Reforming the system of protection in developing countries', *World Development*, 3: 365–382.

Balassa, B. (1981) 'The choice of development strategy, lessons and prospects in the process of industrial development and alternative development strategies', in Belassa, B. (ed.), *The Process of Industrial Development and Alternative Development Strategies, Essays in International Finance*, Princeton, NJ: Princeton University Press.

Balassa, B. *et al.* (1982) *Development Strategies in Semi-Industrial Economies*, Washington, DC: World Bank.

Baumol, W. J. (1986) 'Productivity, growth, convergence, and welfare', *American Economic Review*, 76: 1072–1085.

Chang, H.-J. (1997) 'Institutional structure and economic performance, some theoretical and policy lessons from the experience of the Republic of Korea', *Asia Pacific Development Journal*, 4(1): 39–59.

Evans, P. (1995) *Embedded Autonomy, States and Industrial Transformation*, Princeton; NJ: Princeton University Press.

Findlay, R. (1978) 'Comment on Harberler's liberal development policy', in Meier, G. M. (ed.), *Pioneers in Development*, Second Series, Oxford: Oxford University Press.

Hansson, P. and M. Henrekson (1994) 'Catching up in industrial countries: a disaggregated study', *Journal of International Trade and Economic Development*, 3(2): 46–129.

Krueger, A. O. (1990) 'Import substitution versus export promotion in international economic policy', in King, P. (ed.), *International Economics and International Economic Policy, A Reader*, London and New York: McGraw-Hill.

Krueger, A. O. (1997) 'Trade policy and economic development – how we learn', *The American Economic Review*, 87(1): 1–22.

Krugman, M. A. (1986) *Strategic Trade Policy and New International Economics*, Cambridge, MA: MIT Press.

Liang, N. (1992) 'Beyond import substitution and export promotion: a new typology of trade strategies', *Journal of Development Studies*, 28(3): 447–472.

Pack, H. and L. E. Westphal (1986) 'Industrial strategy and technical change – theory versus reality', *Journal of Development Economics*, 22: 87–128.

Salvatore, D. (1996) 'International trade policies, industrialization and economic development', *The International Trade Journal*, 10(1): 21–47.

Srinivasan, T. N. and J. N. Bhagwati (1978) 'Shadow prices for project selection in presence of distortions: effective rate of protection and domestic resource cost', *Journal of Political Economy*, 86(1): 97–116.

Singh, A. (1995) 'The causes of fast economic growth in East Asia', *UNCTAD Review*, Geneva: United Nations, 91–127.

Stiglitz, J. E. and P. Dasgupta (1988) 'Leaning-by-doing, market structure and industrial and trade policies', *Oxford Economic Papers*, 40: 246–268.

UNIDO (2000) *International Yearbook of Industrial Statistics*, New York and Geneva: UN.

Vestal, J. (1995) *Industrial Policy and Japanese Economic Development:1945–1900*, Oxford: Clarendon Press.

Yaghmaian, B. (1994) 'An empirical investigation of exports, development and growth in developing countries: challenging the neoclassical theory of export-led Growth', *World Development*, 22(12): 1977–1995.

Part IV

Resource endowments, factor markets, and employment issues

8 Trends in informal sector employment in the Middle East

Jacques Charmes

1 Introduction

For statistical and cultural reasons, the measurement of the informal sector and especially female labour force has always been a challenging task in all regions and particularly so in the Middle East. Accurate measurement of the participation of women in informal sector activities, which are highly invisible, is an even more difficult task. After a brief review of issues relating to definitions, measurement difficulties, and methods designed to tackle these issues, this chapter focuses on the profile of women in self-employment and in informal sector employment in the Middle East in general, and in the Arab countries in particular.

2 Issues in measurement, methods, and definitions

It is common knowledge that most statistical data available from central statistical offices do not provide an appropriate picture of the actual profile of the informal sector and of the female labour force, and especially of the female labour force in the informal sector. While broadly correct, this statement needs to be qualified in the light of progress made since the end of the 1980s in the measurement of the size of informal sector in general and of female participation in the labour force in particular. The three issues of the UN's 'World's Women, Trends and Statistics' (1990, 1995, and 2000a) are important landmarks in this respect, embodying significant developments in the field.

New international definitions of labour force concepts, or revision of former concepts, have, of course, played a major role in this process, not only because they have given impetus to new data collection, but also because they have encouraged and initiated new ways and means of compiling data.

Although still debated, the international definition of the informal sector adopted in 1993 at the fifteenth International Conference of Labour Statisticians (ICLS; see ILO 1993a,b) was a considerable advance in the process of estimation of employment in the informal sector on a sound and internationally comparable basis (see Box 8.1).

Box 8.1 The international definition of the informal sector adopted by the fifteenth ICLS

For statistical purposes, the informal sector is regarded as a group of production units which form a part, within the System of National Accounts (SNA), of the household sector as unincorporated enterprises owned by households.

Household enterprises (or unincorporated enterprises owned by households) are distinguished from corporations and quasi-corporations on the basis of their legal status and the type of accounts they hold: accordingly, household enterprises are not constituted as separate legal entities independently of the household or of household members that own them, and no complete set of accounts are available which can permit a clear distinction between the production activities of the enterprises and the other activities of their owners.

The informal sector is defined, irrespective of the kind of workplace, the extent of fixed capital assets, the duration of the activity of the enterprise, and its operation as a main or secondary activity. It comprises:

1 Informal self-owned enterprises which may employ family workers, and employees on an occasional basis: for operational purposes and depending on national circumstances, this segment comprises either all self-owned enterprises, or only those which are not registered under specific forms of national legislation (factories or commercial acts, tax or social security laws, professional groups, regulatory or similar acts, laws or regulations established by national legislative bodies).
2 Enterprises of informal employers which may employ one or more employees on a continuous basis and which comply with one or both of the following criteria:

- Size of the establishment must be below a specified level of employment (defined on the basis of minimum size requirements embodied in relevant national legislation or other empirical or statistical practices: the choice of the upper size limit taking account of the coverage of statistical enquiries in order to avoid an overlap);
- Non-registration of the enterprise or its employees.

Furthermore, and for practical purposes, the informal sector may and should be restricted to non-agricultural activities. Professionals and domestic workers are included in the informal sector as far as they comply with the definitional characteristics or criteria. Home-based workers are included if they are own-account workers or sub-contracting with other informal sector units. Non-market production is excluded.

The value of this definition resides in the fact that it leans on existing practises for estimating informal employment at a national or macroeconomic level.

The statistical definition distinguishes two main components or segments of the informal sector: (i) the 'family enterprises or self-employed' (own-account informal enterprises) without permanent employees, and (ii) the 'micro-enterprises' (informal employers) with permanent employees.

Source: ILO (1993a,b).

3 Data sources and proxies

By distinguishing the self-employed (own-account workers and family workers) and the enterprises of informal employers (employers and paid employees) among the non-agricultural labour force, the new definition provides an easy means for analysing data from population censuses or labour force surveys, which are regularly published in the ILO *Yearbook of Labour Statistics* and the *UN Demographic Yearbook*. The use of proxies is still necessary, but their incidence on the global figures is negligible: the published tables, in particular the tables cross-classifying status in employment (ICSE) by industrial sector (ISIC) and by sex, generally merge employers and own-account workers. These sources do not separate permanent from non-permanent paid employees, either. Consequently, statistics presented in this chapter will distinguish between the self-employed (including own-account workers, unpaid family workers and employers) and the informal sector (which, in addition to the self-employed, comprises wage employees in informal enterprises), both excluding agricultural activities (but not rural non-farm activities).

3.1 Sources

Estimating self-employment and employment in the informal sector requires not only availability of data from population censuses and labour force surveys (or other household surveys) at various periods, but also availability of detailed published data, especially tabulations cross-classifying employment by industries (in order to exclude agriculture), status in employment, and by sex. Special issues of the ILO *Yearbook of Labour Statistics* (1990; retrospective edition on population censuses, 1945–89 and subsequent issues up to 1995, when the edition of this precise table stopped); the UN *Demographic Yearbook* (1994: tables on economic characteristics), as well as national sources available from the ILO's Bureau of Statistics have been used to compile the data for this section. They have been complemented by the ESCWA labour force statistics database and by the Statistical Abstract for Arab countries, prepared by the Arab League Secretariat

(1998), which also uses population census and labour force data. Any other estimates or projections have been ignored.

Nevertheless, data are still missing for some countries and for some periods. This does not, however, mean that no source is available, rather that the required table has not been prepared. For recent periods, secondary analyses of relevant databases could be envisaged, but this is not possible for previous periods. Our data presented in the tables hereafter have, therefore, been organized by decade. For each decade, there is generally a source for each country, even if not for the same year for all countries; the corresponding indicators have been added up and an average has been calculated for the decade. This average is a simple arithmetical non-weighted mean to avoid the undue influence of populous countries in the overall average and uses the method rehabilitated by the United Nations (2000a). For the last decade (1990s), several years were generally available for many countries; thus, a simple average has been calculated to provide the figure used for each country in the decade. Generally, the sources for this last decade are often labour force surveys rather than population censuses, which may have had an impact on the results (results are more reliable, but also less detailed and precise). In the near future, it will probably be possible to disaggregate the last decade into two 5-year periods as soon as the results of the recent labour force surveys are made available.

3.2 Proxies

Non-agricultural self-employment (defined as the sum of own-account workers, unpaid family workers, and employers) is used as a proxy for the main component of the informal sector, that is, the enterprises of own-account workers, for the following reasons. First, it has to be noted that the international definition leaves open the use of the non-registration criterion depending on national circumstances. This means that this criterion should be implemented where data on registration are available although this does not seem to be the case for most countries in the region. Second, it is obvious that a certain number of the non-agricultural self-employed could be included in the formal sector, such as professionals or start-ups. However, professionals are not excluded from the informal sector by definition and the fact that no formal or systematic registration is maintained is an argument against their exclusion. Third, why not exclude the employers from this statistics? This is because, on the one hand, statistical yearbooks most frequently merge the category of employers into the category of own-account workers and, on the other hand, the informal sector comprises employers of small-scale enterprises who are much more numerous than the employers of medium and large firms that are often incorporated. Finally, self-employment must be taken as a proxy; therefore, it is clear that the indicator is admittedly a little overestimated but this overestimation is negligible with respect to the actual bulk of self-employed activities in the informal sector.

Another question worth asking is: why non-agricultural self-employment and not self-employment as a whole (which includes agriculture)? After all, the statistics on total self-employment are much more readily available from national statistics. But the international definition of the informal sector discussed above recommends a clear separation of the agricultural sector from the informal sector. There are two reasons for this. First, the agricultural sector is obviously totally different from the informal sector in its structures and behaviour. Second, self-employment in agriculture and non-agricultural self-employment have followed completely different patterns and trends over the past three decades so that the overall indicator would hide their two different trends and would not be of great use for the analysis.

A systematic compilation of existing data in international yearbooks as well as in national sources shows a continuous increase in self-employment and informal sector employment over the past few decades (Charmes 1999a,b).

In almost all regions and countries in the world, labour force trends over the past decades have been characterized by a dramatic increase in self-employment and employment in the informal sector. Women in particular have played a key role in this process through their large-scale entry into tertiary sector labour markets (trade and services). The industrialized countries of Northern Europe, and the newly industrialized countries of Eastern and South-eastern Asia are the only exceptions to this rule. Table 8.1 illustrates these trends.

The reasons why the growth of the market economy and the globalization process have not created proportionate wage employment opportunities are diverse. On the one hand, the two oil shocks and the ensuing indebtedness were important especially for those countries that subsequently had to undertake structural adjustment programmes. On the other hand, and perhaps more importantly, globalization may have had adverse effects in economies that were not sufficiently diversified.

In this respect, the Arab world and the Middle East present specific features. First, as oil producers, most countries of the region have been less affected by the oil crises. Second, countries of Western Asia have had remarkably stable trends in self-employment (at just above 24 per cent of the non-agricultural labour force) combined with what is effectively the lowest regional female participation rates in the world (21 per cent in 1980 and 27 per cent in 1997 for Northern Africa; 28 per cent in 1980 and 33 per cent in 1997 for Western Asia; United Nations 2000a). Could this relative absence of women in the labour market explain the slower and lower expansion of the informal sector in the region?

A systematic and methodical compilation of Western Asian labour force data, comparable with those for other regions, presents an opportunity to investigate what is essentially a unique exception at world level.

4 Trends in self-employment in the Arab world and Middle East

As the main component of the informal sector, non-agricultural self-employment is a useful and significant indicator of the labour markets in developing countries. It is usually the main route by which women enter the labour market, often involving

Table 8.1 Trends in self-employment and employment in informal sector by world regions (1970–90s)

Regions	*% of self-employed in non-agricultural labour force*			*% of informal sector in non- agricultural labour force*	
	1970s	*1980s*	*1990s*	*1980s*	*1990s*
Developed regions	11.8	11.8	13.7	—	—
Eastern Europe	3.5	3.4	8.5	—	—
Western Europe	13.3	12.4	15.8	—	—
Northern Europe	9.4	6.8	8.5	—	—
Southern Europe	20.9	21.6	25.0	—	—
Western Europe	11.6	10.9	12.2	—	—
Other developed countries	10.0	10.7	10.8	—	—
Africa	28.3	48.1	54.6	55.7	66.9
Northern Africa	23.0	18.8	34.0	38.8	43.4
Sub-Saharan Africa	29.6	54.9	66.9	68.1	74.8
Eastern Africa	27.5	—	61.0	—	—
Middle Africa	34.1	58.4	72.5	—	—
Southern Africa	12.6	16.8	22.6	—	—
Western Africa	40.0	70.0	79.7	—	—
Latin America	28.8	30.2	37.8	52.3	56.9
Central America	25.1	29.9	25.4	—	—
South America	28.6	29.8	41.4	—	—
Caribbean	42.8	41.2	—		
Asia	28.6	29.7	31.9	53.0	63.0
Eastern Asia	19.9	24.6	21.0	—	—
South-eastern Asia	30.4	31.0	29.4	—	—
Southern Asia	33.4	35.3	43.7	—	—
Western Asia	24.3	23.1	24.9	—	—
World	22.6	27.6	28.4	—	—

Source: Charmes J. (1999a,b). Data have been compiled from diverse international sources on population censuses and labour force surveys and was prepared for the ILO programme 'Improving the quality of women's employment'. Averages are worked out as non-weighted means for different regions comprising 93 countries.

the sale on the market of the goods that have been processed at home. In this regard, the Arab region and the Middle East is quite heterogeneous. Various patterns can be identified in the region as a whole.

The common and widespread pattern mentioned above is very different from the experience of the Gulf Cooperation Council countries (GCC), for example, where self-employment has steadily decreased over the past three decades (down from 13 per cent of the non-agricultural labour force to 4.8 per cent). This region is, in fact, the only one in the world to have experienced such a pattern during the past three decades (see Table 8.2). Even in the newly industrialized countries of south-eastern Asia, self-employment has decreased more slowly. During the same period, the share of women in the non-agricultural labour force has steadily increased

Table 8.2 Trends in self-employment in the Middle East and least developed Arab countries (1970–90s)

Regions	*% of self-employed in non-agricultural labour force*			*% of self-employed in female non-agricultural labour force*			*Share of women in non-agricultural labour force*		
	1970s	*1980s*	*1990s*	*1970s*	*1980s*	*1990s*	*1970s*	*1980s*	*1990s*
GCC Countries	13.0	6.4	4.8	4.1	1.1	1.6	7.1	12.8	15.6
Mashreq	20.5	20.0	27.4	13.4	10.0	12.4	9.4	10.8	16.1
Maghreb	14.7	22.0	31.1	17.4	27.2	27.3	12.7	18.3	22.0
Least developed countries	33.3	36.2	41.1	46.1	59.8	41.8	8.2	15.0	23.0
Other Middle East countries	28.0	29.0	30.8	40.7	22.2	25.8	15.7	10.7	13.3

Source: Author's Compilation from database prepared for the Centre of Arab Women, Training and Research (CAWTAR 2001).

Note
Figures are non-weighted averages based on countries and years available; when various censuses or surveys are available for one country in the period (e.g. individual years in the 1990s), the average is calculated. For the same period, all countries' figures are summed up and the non-weighted average is calculated at a regional level. Each country has thus the same weight and the average provides a profile for the region. For a list of different sub-regions in this table, see Table 8.3.

from 7.1 to 15.6 per cent (Table 8.3), but still remains among the lowest regional levels in the world. In the meantime, the proportion of self-employed in the female non agricultural labour force has been decreasing (from 4.1 to 1.6 per cent); in GCC countries, new female entrants into the labour market were mainly offered wage jobs, rather than taking the initiative of creating own-account jobs.

Mashreq countries have had a slightly higher share of women in the labour force and especially in the non-agricultural labour force (16.1 per cent of the total in the 1990s), but they have also followed a different pattern with regard to non-agricultural self-employment. The latter has increased by nearly 8 percentage points across the three decades under consideration here: from 20.5 per cent in the 1970s to 27.4 per cent in the 1990s. In these countries, an increasing number of women have entered the labour force through wage jobs and as self-employed workers. In fact, the share of self-employed in female non-agricultural employment remained stable or slightly decreased (by one percentage point).

In Maghreb countries, the share of women in the labour force has reached the highest level in the region (22 per cent), but this has come about through a dramatic increase in self-employment as a whole (up from 14.7 per cent of the non-agricultural labour force in the 1970s to 31.1 per cent in the 1990s) and of female self-employment in particular (up from 17.4 to 27.3 per cent between the 1970s and the 1990s).

The experience of Iran and Turkey is very similar to the Maghreb countries with respect to the share of self-employed in the non-agricultural labour force (30.8 per cent) as well as the share of self-employed in the female non-agricultural labour

Table 8.3 Women in the non-agricultural labour force and self-employment

Regions/countries	*Share of women in the non-agricultural labour force*			*% of self-employed in female non-agricultural employment*		
	1970s	*1980s*	*1990s*	*1970s*	*1980s*	*1990s*
GCC countries	7.1	12.8	15.6	4.1	1.1	1.6
Bahrain	5.8	10.9	16.8	4.8	2.0	1.1
Kuwait	12.0	19.9	—	0.5	0.5	—
Oman	—	—	14.4	—	—	2.0
Qatar	—	10.0	—	—	0.1	—
Saudi Arabia	—	—	—	—	—	—
United Arab Emirates	3.5	10.3	—	7.1	1.7	—
Mashreq	9.4	10.8	16.1	13.4	10.0	12.4
Egypt	13.4	13.8	17.6	5.1	4.6	14.0
Iraq	8.6	10.8	—	24.7	10.8	—
Jordan	8.2	—	12.2	4.3	—	6.5
Lebanon	—	—	22.8	—	—	14.9
Palestinian Authority	—	—	—	—	—	—
Syria	7.4	7.9	11.7	19.6	14.6	14.3
Maghreb	12.7	18.3	22.0	17.4	27.2	27.3
Algeria	10.9	10.4	14.3	1.4	1.7	17.0
Libya	5.8			13.5		
Morocco		22.7	27.6		44.3	35.1
Tunisia	21.4	21.7	24.1	37.3	35.6	29.7
Least developed countries	8.2	15.0	23.0	46.1	59.8	41.8
Comoros	—	15.0	30.1	—	59.8	76.6
Djibouti	—	—	35.5	—	—	21.5
Mauritania	—	—	—	—	—	—
Somalia	—	—	—	—	—	—
Sudan	8.2	—	19.3	46.1	—	52.4
Yemen	—	—	7.0	—	—	16.7
Other Middle East countries	15.7	10.7	13.3	40.7	22.2	25.8
Iran	18.8	9.2	12.0	45.7	30.8	35.8
Turkey	12.5	12.1	14.5	35.6	13.6	15.8

Source: Author's compilation from database prepared for the Centre of Arab Women, Training and Research (CAWTAR 2001). For Comoros, see PNUD (2000).

force (25.8 per cent). However, in these two countries the share of women in the non-agricultural labour force is also the lowest (13.3 per cent). This is exhibited in a persistently low share in Turkey as well as a dramatic drop in Iran after the Islamic revolution (decreasing from 18.8 per cent in the 1970s to a low of 8.8 per cent in the 1980s before rising to 12.0 per cent in the 1990s).

Finally, the least developed countries of the region (Comoros, Djibouti, Mauritania, Somalia, Sudan, Yemen) have, as expected, exhibited an even more distinct pattern, which is very close to other African countries. Despite the fact that their share of women in the non-agricultural labour force increased by more than 15 percentage points in the past three decades, it is still quite low (23.0 per cent in the 1990s). Moreover, in these countries, more than two-fifths (41.8 per cent) of the female labour force outside agriculture is in self-employment.

Table 8.3 shows the sub-regions of the Arab world and the Middle East. In the case of Egypt, Algeria, and Tunisia, it is clear that progress in the economic participation of women started much earlier. However, in Egypt and Algeria activities of women tend to be concentrated in self-employment, while in Tunisia wage employment tends to be more prevalent, due in part at least to affirmative policies designed to feminize some professions (especially the civil service).

The relative size of self-employment in the various sub-regions explains why some countries have attempted to measure the informal sector while others have not. In the GCC countries, the continuous decrease of this category of the labour force clearly indicates that the informal sector is very small and participation of women in this sector is even smaller. The larger the size of self-employment, the greater the interest in a sector that absorbs a large and increasing part of labour surpluses; in Mashreq countries and even more in Maghreb countries, the informal sector has been estimated, sometimes regularly, and the participation of women in this sector can be measured.

5 Trends and structures of informal sector in some Arab countries

Tables 8.4 and 8.5 synthesize the results of our estimations derived from a single and harmonized methodology using data on labour force and self-employment, as well as statistics on employment in the formal sector (see Charmes 2000).

In most countries, the absolute and relative size of the informal sector has dramatically increased over the past decade. In Algeria, it represented more than 25 per cent of the non-agricultural labour force by the end of the 1980s. Tunisia has experienced the most dramatic increase: with a rise of nearly seven percentage points in 8 years, this share reached 47.1 per cent in 1997. In Morocco, the rise was more than six percentage points within only 3 years: in the urban areas in 1998, it reached 46.3 per cent of the non-agricultural labour force, a figure that would be higher at the national level. This was in sharp contrast with Egypt, where it only rose by one percentage point in 10 years (reaching 38.4 per cent in 1998). However, it is most likely that the figure for Egypt is an underestimate because it does not take into account the multiple jobs of civil servants, which should be included in the informal sector. On this basis, in fact, Charmes (1999a) has estimated that Egypt's informal sector is the largest of the three countries.

But contrary to the general trends in other regions of the world (Africa, Asia, Latin America), the increase in informal sector employment is not due to massive entries of women in this kind of employment; the share of women working in the informal sector has, in fact, decreased continuously. In Tunisia, it fell from 33.2 per cent in 1980 to 21.8 per cent in 1989 and 18.5 per cent in 1997.

Table 8.4 Structures and trends in informal sector employment in selected Arab countries and for selected years

Tunisia	*1980*	*1989*	*1997*
% informal sector in non-agricultural employment	36.6	39.3	47.1
% of women in informal sector	33.2	21.8	18.5
% of women in informal sector who are self-employed	82.2	73.2	50.6
% of women in informal sector who are paid employees	17.8	26.8	49.4
% of women in informal sector who are in industries	80.7	77.1	64.6
Morocco Urban	*1995*	*1998*	
% informal sector in non-agricultural employment	39.9	46.3	
% of women in informal sector	22.0	16.0	
% of women in informal sector who are self-employed	93.0	93.3	
% of women in informal sector who are paid employees	7.0	6.7	
% of women in informal sector who are in industries	74.4	66.5	
Egypt	*1988*	*1998*	
% informal sector in non-agricultural employment	37.3	38.4	
% of women in informal sector	13.9	14.0	
% of women in informal sector who are self-employed	61.3	66.8	
% of women in informal sector who are paid employees	38.7	33.2	

Source: For *Tunisia*, compiled by the author and S. Jomni on the basis of national statistics; for *Morocco Urban*, compiled by B. Hamdouche for ERF on the basis of national statistics; for *Egypt*, compiled by A. Al Mahdi for ERF on the basis of national statistics.

Table 8.5 Characteristics of the informal sector in some Arab countries and Turkey (selected years)

	Tunisia, 1997	*Morocco national, 1995*	*Egypt, 1998*	*Syria, 1994*	*Turkey, 1996*
% informal sector in non-agricultural employment	47.1	44.8	38.4	41.7	27.7
% of women in informal sector	18.5	29.6	14.0	10.6	9.7
% of women in informal sector who are self-employed	50.6	96.4	66.8	56.6	41.2
% of women in informal sector who are paid employees	49.4	3.6	33.2	43.4	58.8
% of women in informal sector who are in industries	64.6	85.2	—	—	—

Source: Compiled by the author on the basis of Table 8.4 and national statistics.

In Morocco, it declined from 22 per cent in 1995 to 16 per cent in 1998. In Egypt, it remained broadly stable at about 14 per cent between 1988 and 1998. In Syria, the share of women employed in the informal sector in 1994 was 10.6 per cent, while for Turkey it was even smaller at 9.7 per cent.

One of the reasons for such a different pattern, compared to world trends in informal sector employment, is that women in the Middle East tend not to be involved in trade activities and particularly in street vending (see Table 8.6). By contrast, in most other regions, informal sector growth takes place through processes of feminization and tertiarization (two phenomena that are closely linked; see Charmes 2002, ILO 2002).

In Arab countries, entry of women into the labour market does not mainly take the form of going out to the shops and workshops or to the streets as street vendors to sell what they have processed at home. Rather, they continue to work at home and their production is sold by other members of the household or are sold to traders (as in the case of the self-employed in Morocco), or to enterprises that sub-contract a part of their production (as in the case of paid employees in Tunisia, Syria, Egypt, and Turkey). The importance of wage employment in the informal sector (ranging from 33.2 per cent in Egypt to 58.8 per cent in Turkey) and/or of industrial (manufacturing) employment in the informal sector, especially concerning women, clearly illustrates the development of the 'putting out system'. This new 'old' form of organization of work relations consists of enterprises placing orders with female workers, providing them with raw materials and eventually equipment, and purchasing the goods manufactured at home on a piece-rate basis. In this case, the employers do not put the workers 'out' of the enterprise to have them working at home, but they rather maintain the workers at home, which is consistent with cultural habits.

The relative importance of female industrial employment in the informal sector is, of course, strongly related to social and family customs, which is a reason that precludes women from undertaking activities outside the home – they are expected to stay and work at home. The fact that, despite their small and often declining share in informal sector employment, they remain numerous in industries for pay or gain, means that structural adjustment policies and globalization have entailed the marketization of their products rather than their 'putting out' from the home to outside labour and commodities markets. A major issue that remains to be tackled in order to provide a better understanding of labour markets in the region is probably the measurement of such home-based work. Jordan, Palestine, and Morocco have taken steps in this direction by designing questions on the place of work in their labour force surveys (Jordan, see Nour, 2000) or by implementing time-use surveys such

Table 8.6 Proportion and characteristics of street-based workers in Tunisia and Turkey

Country (year)	*Number of street vendors*	*% of non-agricultural labour force*	*% females*
Tunisia (1984)	59,200	4.5	1.8
Tunisia (1994)	132,832	7.3	3.9
Tunisia (1997)	125,619	6.4	2.1
Turkey (2000) urban	255,000	2.4	2.7

Source: Author's calculations on the basis of national sources for 1984 and 1994 population censuses and the 1997 Labour Force Survey for Tunisia; State Institute of Statistics (2001) for Turkey.

Box 8.2 Women's time-use in Morocco, 1997–8

Time-use surveys are generally the best for a better assessment of women's work and a better measurement of their participation in the labour force and of their contribution to GDP. UNDP and the UN statistics division have recently encouraged, supported, and launched such surveys in developing countries.

One of the major findings of the Morocco survey using this approach (with a sample size of 2,776 women) is that the participation rates of 15–70-year-old women are raised substantially; 71.4 per cent in rural areas and 34.6 per cent in urban areas (i.e. equivalent to 50.6 per cent at the national level).

Another finding is that 4.5 per cent of all women who are either active or inactive (3.5 per cent in urban areas and 5.9 per cent in rural areas) undertake daily unmeasured crafts activities (for more than three and a half hours). This compares to 5.7 per cent of all women (8 per cent in urban areas and 2.7 per cent in rural areas) who undertake ordinary and measured economic activities on a daily basis (for nearly 6h). Aggregated at the national level, these figures indicate that, in terms of the number of working hours, the unmeasured craft activities performed by women are equivalent to half of their measured activities, thus underestimating their overall participation by nearly one-third.

It is clear that these activities are undertaken within homes; nearly 50 per cent of interviewed women declared that they practise the craft they have learned at home (33.1 per cent in urban areas and 63.8 per cent in rural areas).

Source: Royaume du Maroc, Direction de la Statistique (1999).

as in Palestine (United Nations, 2000b) and Morocco. Oman also implemented a time-use survey in 1999 in the income–expenditures survey that year.

Table 8.7 shows that in the 1980s, female home-based work was performed on an own-account basis in Morocco and Tunisia, but that it progressively turned to piece-rate wage employment in the 1990s; 52 per cent of female home-based workers are employees in Jordan (1999) and 9.2 per cent in Tunisia. The size of informal sector wage-employment for women in Syria (1994) is also a sign of the same trend. The progressive extension of the 'putting out system' is observed at the global level as a consequence of the globalization process; this category of the labour force is characterized by the worst conditions of work, the lowest piece-rate wages, and no social protection. These labourers are the means by which international competition implements the reduction of labour costs and gets round the labour laws and systems of labour protection. Consequently, these workers are not declared by the enterprises that hire many of them through sub-contracting arrangements by means of middlemen. They are, in fact, the 'home-workers' to which the 1996 ILO Convention on home-work refers.

Table 8.7 Proportion and characteristics of home-based workers in various Arab countries

Country (year)	*Number of home based*	*% of non-agricultural labour force*	*% Females*	*Females*					
				Employment status			*Industries*[b]		
				% own-account[a]	*% employees*	*% family workers*	*% manufacturing (textiles)*	*% trade*	*% services*
Jordan (1999)	15,000	0.7	66.7	48.0	52.0	0.0	70.0	—	—
Morocco (1982)	128,237	4.1	78.3	100.0	0.0	0.0	95.7	1.4	1.9
Tunisia (1984)	123,060	9.4	75.6	100.0	0.0	0.0	—	—	—
Tunisia (1994)	86,267	4.8	71.3	63.8	9.2	27.0	90.2 (86.4)	1.3	2.1

Sources: Author's calculations on the basis of national sources (1982 Population Census for Morocco; 1984 and 1994 population censuses; and 1997 Labour Force Survey for Tunisia; third round of 1999 Employment and Unemployment Survey for Jordan).

Notes

a Total equal to 100% means that the question on place of work only covered the own-account.

b Total does not equal 100% because other non-manufacturing industries are excluded (mining and quarrying, construction, electricity, gas, and water supply).

The underestimation of this category of the labour force is a real issue for the application of the fundamental labour standards and the extension of social protection systems.

Recent data collected by the 1997 national survey on economic activities in Tunisia provide unique insights on the structures of employment and gender gaps in wage income and micro-entrepreneurs' income. Tables 8.8–8.10 summarize the results. They will soon be completed by comparable figures in the modern sector.

Comparisons with the previous estimates of the informal sector as a whole are illuminating; while women represent only 14.6 per cent of employment in the micro-enterprise sector (which is part of the informal sector), they account for 18.5 per cent of the informal sector. While the share of paid employees in the micro-enterprise sector is 37.1 per cent, this ratio was 49.5 per cent in the informal sector. It constitutes more evidence of the trends and extension of the 'putting out' system; women in the informal sector are mainly paid employees working at home.

Table 8.9 shows gender gaps in wages. There are some important variations between the various industries. Wages are compared with the legal minimum salary, which was 180 DT per month in 1997. The gender gap is calculated by dividing female wages by male wages.

A major finding of the Tunisian survey is the estimate of the gender gap at 75.5 per cent, that is, equivalent to the ratio proposed by the UNDP Human Development Report where no data are available and also equivalent to the average of countries where data are available. It means that in the micro-enterprise sector and on average, a female paid employee earns only three-fourths of what a man earns per month.

Table 8.8 Distribution of employment by status and sex in the micro-enterprise sector, Tunisia, 1997

Status	*Women*	*Men*	*Total*	*Distribution by status (%)*		*Distribution by sex (%)*	
				Women	*Men*	*Women*	*Men*
Own-account	16,577	129,343	145,920	26.8	35.8	11.4	88.6
Employers	8,562	85,213	93,775	13.9	23.6	9.1	90.9
Associates	682	8,302	8,984	1.1	2.3	7.6	92.4
Paid employees	22,884	84,267	107,151	37.1	23.3	21.4	78.6
Unpaid family workers	11,264	31,931	43,195	18.2	8.8	26.1	73.9
Apprentices	1,656	21,309	22,965	2.7	5.9	7.2	92.8
Other	120	969	1,089	0.2	0.3	11.0	89.0
Total	61,746	361,334	423,080	100.0	100.0	14.6	85.4

Source: Institut National de la Statistique (2002).

Table 8.9 Average monthly wages in the micro-enterprise sector in Tunisia, 1997

Industries	*Women*		*Men*		*Gender gap (women's wages as % of men's)*
	In DT	*As multiple of the legal minimum salary*	*In DT*	*As multiple of the legal minimum salary*	
Food processing industries	155	0.9	222	1.2	69.8
Textiles	127	0.7	194	1.1	65.5
Clothing	138	0.8	160	0.9	86.3
Leather			159	0.9	
Wood			171	1.0	
Metal			152	0.8	
Furniture			175	1.0	
Construction			205	1.1	
Trade and car repair			154	0.9	
Wholesale trade	205	1.1	242	1.3	84.7
Retail trade	125	0.7	176	1.0	71.0
Restaurants	137	0.8	188	1.0	72.9
Transport			289	1.6	
Services to enterprises	164	0.9	218	1.2	75.2
Education	158	0.9	194	1.1	81.4
Health	161	0.9	168	0.9	95.8
Personal services	115	0.6	139	0.8	82.7
Total	148	0.8	196	1.1	75.5

Source: Institut National de la Statistique (2002).

Note

Only major industries have been included in the table, but the total includes all industries. When the number of salaried women in the industry is negligible, the cell has not been filled although data are available, because the figures are not significant.

It is in the textiles and in food processing industries that the gender gap is the widest: 65.5 and 69.8 per cent, respectively, followed by retail trade and restaurants (71 and 72.9 per cent, respectively). The gap is the narrowest in health services (95.8 per cent), clothing (86.3 per cent), and wholesale trade (84.7 per cent), followed by education services with a gender gap of 81.4 per cent. The concentration of female apprentices is, in fact, heaviest in the clothing industry with an average remuneration of only 17 per cent of the legal minimum salary. Another interesting finding is that, while male employees in the micro-enterprise sector earn 1.1 times the minimum salary, female employees earn just 0.8 times the minimum salary.

Table 8.10 shows that entrepreneurs' income is 4 times higher than the legal minimum salary and 2.2 times higher than the average wage in the formal sector. Although food processing is the most rewarding industry and is an industry where women are well represented, it is also the one where the gender gap is among the

Table 8.10 Micro-entrepreneurs' income by industry and sex, and as multiple of the legal minimum salary (SMIG) and average wage in the formal sector in Tunisia, 1997

Industrial sectors	*As multiple of SMIG*			*As multiple of the average wage in the formal sector*			*Gender gap (women in % of men)*
	Men	*Women*	*Both sexes*	*Men*	*Women*	*Both sexes*	
Industries	5.7	2.3	5.4	3.1	1.2	2.9	39.9
Food processing industries	7.3	4.3	7.1	4.0	2.3	3.9	58.8
Textile, clothing, leather	3.8	1.8	3.2	2.1	1.0	1.8	46.8
Wood industries	4.0	3.3	4.0	2.2	1.8	2.2	83.4
Metal industries	3.7		3.7	2.0	0.0	2.0	
Construction	4.8	5.5	4.8	2.6	3.0	2.6	114.4
Commerce, repairs	3.0	2.2	2.9	1.6	1.2	1.6	74.2
Services	4.8	5.3	4.9	2.6	2.9	2.7	109.9
Hotels and restaurants	6.1	3.8	5.9	3.3	2.1	3.2	61.8
Transport and communications	3.6	2.3	3.6	2.0	1.3	1.9	65.0
Personal services	2.7	2.8	2.7	1.5	1.5	1.5	101.8
Total	4.0	3.3	4.0	2.2	1.8	2.2	81.3

Source: Institut National de la Statistique (2002).

Note
Underlined figures are not significant, due to the small number of female entrepreneurs in these industries.

highest. For all activities female entrepreneurs earn about 81.3 per cent of the income of their male counterparts.

Finally, as illustrated by Table 8.5, the informal sector presents quite similar characteristics in all Arab countries examined; it represents between 40 and 50 per cent of the non-agricultural labour force (if we take account of the underestimation of Egyptian figures for previously indicated reasons) and follows an upward trend. The share of women working in the informal sector ranges from 10 to 30 per cent but follows a downward trend. At the same time, however, their share as wage employees in the industrial informal sector is either increasing (as in Tunisia where it grew from 19.8 per cent in 1980 to 49.4 per cent in the mid-1990s) or remains at a relatively high level (as in Egypt and in Syria where the share was 33.2 and 43.4 per cent, respectively). The very high share of women in the manufacturing informal sector in Morocco correlated with their low share in wage employment, indicating the existence of a sub-contracting system based on own-account workers whose production is collected by middlemen.

6 Conclusions

Despite data inadequacies and statistical problems, in this chapter we have managed to find some clear evidence regarding informal sector employment in the Arab region and the Middle East as a whole. These are summarized below:

- In all countries and all sub-regions, the share of women in the total labour force, and in the non-agricultural labour force, has dramatically increased over the past three decades, and especially so in the past two decades, except for Iran and Turkey.
- Progress has been faster in Maghreb countries and in the least developed countries of the Arab region than in the GCC and Mashreq countries. As far as the participation of women in the labour force (and particularly in the non-agricultural labour force) is concerned, sub-regions can be ranked in an ascending order as follows: 'Other' countries of the Middle East, GCC countries, Mashreq, Maghreb, and 'Least developed' countries of the region.
- Although data are not yet available for the least developed countries, the same ranking holds for the importance and pace of growth in the informal sector: GCC countries are the only ones to have experienced a decrease in self-employment and as a result of informal sector employment. The other three sub-regions of the Arab world have all followed the trends observed in the rest of the developing world: a dramatic increase in informal sector employment. Turkey and Iran ('Other countries of the Middle East') have experienced a very slow increase.
- Contrary to the general pattern in developing countries as a whole, this dramatic increase of informal sector employment is not due to its 'feminization'. The share of women in informal sector employment has decreased in all countries or remained very low. This means that in the Arab countries and in other countries of the Middle East, wage-employment in the formal sector has been the main vehicle for the entry of women to the labour market.
- In the informal sector itself, wage employment and more generally home-based work or 'outwork' in manufacturing activities represents a major category of informal sector employment for women; this category of work seems to follow an upward trend while the overall participation of women in the informal sector has been on a downward trend. However, available data are still scarce and this issue needs further research and empirical work. Furthermore, home-workers, and especially female home-workers, are not well recorded so that the underestimation of this category of the labour force is related to the general underestimation of female workers.
- The mass entry of Arab women into the labour force has taken two shapes: wage employment in the formal sector (and probably in the public sector) and wage employment in the manufacturing informal sector as out-workers (Tunisia), or market-oriented self-employment in the same manufacturing sectors of mainly textiles and clothing (Morocco). Although there is only anecdotal evidence on these trends, it is probable that they may be observable in the other countries of the Middle East as well.

- The first trend (wage employment in the formal sector) is visible in all countries and all sub-regions of the Arab world. It is a result of more affirmative policies towards women and a consequence of progress in education and training.
- The second trend (outwork or market-oriented self-employment) is a result of the globalization process, which leans on, and fits with, cultural habits, in order to reduce labour costs given international competition in global markets. In countries where structural adjustment programmes have been implemented, a means of maintaining standards of living has been found through the marketization of goods traditionally produced by women for self-consumption in their households. This process has thrown them into highly competitive world markets where labour costs are the main comparative advantage. This entry into the labour market from the bottom end has certainly been a consequence of globalization.
- Finally, the entry of women on to the labour market in the Arab region and in the Middle East operates at the upper end as well as at the bottom end; this last pattern constitutes a crucial issue related to globalization.

To conclude, globalization as a factor influencing the structures and trends of labour force and particularly the economic participation of women has played a different role in various parts of the Arab region and the Middle East in general; in all sub-regions and in most countries, entry of women into the labour force has mainly operated through formal wage employment. This is not a consequence of globalization, but is rather due to improvements in female education as well as progress in gender equality and subsequent adoption of affirmative policies and actions. At the same time, with the exception of the GCC countries, women in informal paid employment and in market-oriented self-employment have been experiencing the harsh law of global markets competing for lower labour costs and generating extremely poor working conditions. Persistent and widespread gender gaps in wage earnings are an illustration of these worsening conditions, which need to be better and more systematically studied.

References

Arab League Secretariat (1998) *Statistical Abstract for Arab Countries*, 8th edn, Cairo.

CAWTAR (2001) *Arab Women's Development Report 2001 – Globalization and Gender: Economic Participation of Arab Women*, Tunis: Centre of Arab Women, Training and Research.

Charmes, J. (1999a) 'Informal sector, poverty and gender: a review of empirical evidence', background paper for the World Development Report 2001, Washington, DC: The World Bank.

Charmes, J. (1999b) 'Gender and informal sector', background paper for *The World's Women 2000, Trends and Statistics*, New York: United Nations, 2000.

Charmes, J. (2000) 'Procedures for compiling data on informal sector from various sources in developing countries', Cairo: Economic Research Forum, and Paris: WIEGO (Women in Informal Employment: Globalizing and Organizing).

Charmes, J. (2002) 'Self-employment, informal employment, informal sector employment: trends and characteristics: a tentative assessment of their statistical knowledge', Paris: WIEGO (Women in Informal Employment: Globalizing and Organizing).

ILO (1990) 'Retrospective edition on population censuses, 1945–89', in *Yearbook of Labour Statistics*, Geneva: ILO.

ILO (1993a) 'Statistics of employment in the informal sector', Report for the XVth International Conference of Labour Statisticians, Geneva, 19–28 January 1993.

ILO (1993b) 'Report of the conference', Report of the XVth International Conference of Labour Statisticians, Geneva, 19–28 January 1993.

ILO (2002) *Women and Men in Informal Employment, A Statistical Picture*, Geneva: ILO.

Institut National de la Statistique (2002) '*Le secteur des micro-entreprises en Tunisie: Analyse des résultats de la seconde enquête nationale sur les activités économiques*' (The micro-enterprise sector in Tunisia: analysis of the results of the second national survey on economic activities), Tunis.

Nour, F. (2000) 'The measurement of place of work in Jordan, based on the employment and unemployment survey, 3rd Round 1999', Department of Statistics, Jordan, paper prepared for the Expert Group Meeting on the Measurement of Place of Work, Geneva, 24–28 August 2000.

PNUD (2000) *La pauvreté aux Comores: concepts, mesure et analyse (Poverty in Comoros: Concepts, Measurement and Analysis)*, République Fédérale Islamique des Comores, Moroni PNUD, BIT.

Royaume du Maroc, Direction de la Statistique (1999) *Les emplois du temps de la femme au Maroc (Time-uses of Women in Morocco)*, Enquête nationale sur le budget temps des femmes, 1997–98, 2 vols, Rabat.

State Institute of Statistics (2001) 'Urban informal sector survey, preliminary results 2000' (in Turkish), *Haber Bülteni*, 31 December 2001, Ankara.

United Nations (1994) *Demographic Yearbook*, 46th edition, population census statistics, special topic, New York: UN, Statistics Division.

United Nations (2000a) *The World's Women 2000, Trends and Statistics*, New York: United Nations.

United Nations (2000b) *Country Report: Palestine, Time Use Survey – A Palestinian Example*, Expert Group Meeting on Methods for Conducting Time-Use Surveys, Statistics Division, New York, 23–27 October 2000, ESA/STAT/AC.79/2.

9 Agricultural intensification and female labour in farm production in north-western Syria

Malika Abdelali-Martini, Elizabeth Bailey, Gwyn E. Jones, and Patricia Goldey

1 Introduction

This chapter presents a case study of the organization of labour in agricultural production in the two provinces (*Muhafazat*) of Aleppo and Idleb in north-western Syria. It examines changes in the constitution and nature of agricultural labour in recent years and analyses labour supply and employment patterns in different farming systems in these two predominantly agrarian areas. It also studies the impact of agricultural intensification on the organization of male and female labour in agricultural production.

The objective of this chapter is to analyse the supply of female labour and employment patterns in different farming systems in north-western Syria. This is achieved through a study of labour requirements for different crops and the impact of intensification on the organization of labour in agricultural production.

2 Agricultural intensification and employment in Syria

There have been far-reaching changes in the farming systems of the study area during the last two decades. The study area is very diversified in terms of agro-ecological conditions, and consequently also in terms of cropping patterns, agricultural techniques, and production technologies. The study area includes three definable agricultural stability zones, based on rainfall and other agro-ecological conditions (Zones 1, 2 and 3 – see Map 9.1, top left corner and discussion of the study area below).

Due mainly to rapid population growth (3.8 per cent annually), Syria has pursued a programme of agricultural intensification since 1975 (AOAD 1975). As a consequence, considerable land reclamations have affected large areas during recent decades, bringing previously uncultivable land into cultivation. These efforts have been implemented in conjunction with the introduction of new technologies (to improve crop production) and new crops (including an increase in tree production). Moreover, during the 1990s, the development of irrigation systems in the study area has been an additional important factor that has impacted the agricultural sector, while mechanization has affected the balance of

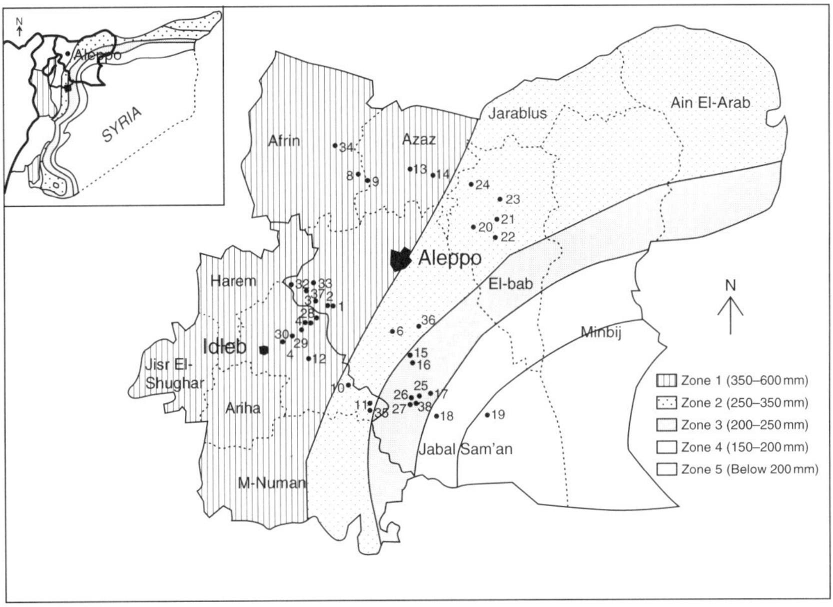

Map 9.1 Villages surveyed in Aleppo and Idleb Muhafazat (Farmers' Informal Survey).

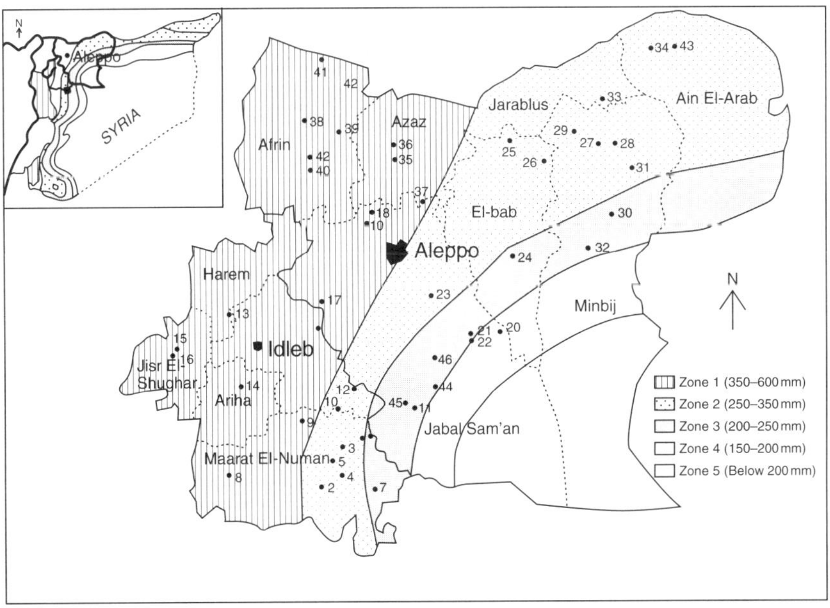

Map 9.2 Villages surveyed in Aleppo and Idleb Muhafazat (Farmers' Formal Survey).

labour demand and supply, decreasing the demand for certain activities, and increasing it for others. Mechanization has also contributed to a decline in male labour demand.

Farmers have responded to these various changes by starting to crop according to expected returns, which are often influenced by market prices. Increasing use of purchased inputs and hired labour also contribute to growing integration of farming households into the market. Some studies have emphasized that farm decisions are increasingly guided by market demand rather than by local needs (Maclachlan 1987). Others have found that the reason behind market integration is increasing reliance on off-farm income (Martini *et al.* 2003).

At the same time, rapid population growth and land subdivision due to inheritance has led to smaller holdings for most households. Farming households have sought additional income from off-farm work to meet their household members' needs. One strategy for men has been to migrate to earn additional income, leaving women on the farm with additional work, as well as working as wage workers on other farms. Traditional Arabic culture, in which a family gains prestige if the women can afford to stay at home attending to domestic duties, is becoming increasingly disregarded. A main social change is, therefore, that women are entering the labour market to become income earners, which allows them to be more involved in decision-making.

Due to the low incomes associated with agricultural activities (especially on small holdings), as well as the decline in the demand for male labour in agriculture, the study area has experienced temporary or semi-permanent out-migration of male members to urban areas (Martini *et al.* 2003). Female household members are then left behind with increased responsibilities for managing farming activities.[1]

There has been a change over the past quarter century, away from the traditional system of labour exchange between farms to a growing reliance on hired labour (Martini *et al.* 1997). Now that production has become increasingly market oriented, and fuelled by population pressure, families of working women are in real need of additional income despite the fact that some or all of their household males are working outside the area (including abroad).

3 The study area

The area under study is located in north-western Syria to the north and south of Aleppo city (Maps 9.1 and 9.2). It is an area where rapid changes in agriculture have been observed, particularly during the last two decades.

In 1975, the Syrian government divided the country into five stability zones based on agro-climatic conditions and rainfall precipitation levels. The characteristics of these zones are at present under review by the government. The 1975 zones were designated 1A, 1B, 2, 3, 4, and 5. The study area falls into three of these zones: 1, 2 and 3. The area is characterized by three different farming systems: (i) wheat-based farming systems; (ii) barley-livestock farming systems; and (iii) mixed farming systems.

The wheat-based farming systems are mainly found in Zone 1B where the average precipitation is above 350 mm annually and not less than 300 mm for two-thirds of the year. This means that with a minimum rainfall requirement of 250 mm, two wheat harvests are possible every 3 years. The mixed farming systems are located mainly in Zone 2, which receives an average rainfall of 250–350 mm annually and not less than 250 mm for two-thirds of the year. The barley-livestock farming systems are found in the area of Zone 3 with an average of 250 mm rainfall for two-thirds of the year. Recent intensification trends are however modifying these systems, particularly during the last two decades.

4 Methodology and data collection

Qualitative and quantitative methods of investigation were used in collecting information, including formal and informal surveys and participant observation.

A rapid rural appraisal was conducted during 1994 in five villages of Zones 1B and 2 (Pratt and Loizos 1992). Key informants from selected villages and farmers were interviewed about the general characteristics of their area. The information collected was used to formulate the questions of the formal survey conducted later during 1996.

Following the initial period of rapid appraisals in Aleppo and Idleb *Muhafazat* (provinces), more focussed and intensive fieldwork that included in-depth interviews was carried out from October 1994 to September 1995. Data were later collected from different locations on labour requirements by crop for different field operations and tasks.

A series of informal surveys guided by a checklist of questions was undertaken in a total of 38 villages (Map 9.1), where about 50 farmers were interviewed either in the Village leader's (*Mukhtar*) guest room or on their own farms. Questions related to agriculture, land use, and changes that had occurred in the area during the past 15–20 years.

The process of information gathering was combined with participant observation to gain information on *who does what activities* and *who controls what resources* (Feldstein and Poats 1990, Rathgeber 1990). Information was collected on the requirements of labour by crop through regular field visits in many locations over the course of an entire annual cycle. One activities analysis worksheet (Feldstein and Poats 1990) was prepared for each crop and completed for all the related activities.

Finally, a formal questionnaire interview was completed with a random multi-stage sample of farming households (Map 9.2). The sample comprised 117 households drawn from 46 villages in the study area in Zones 1, 2 and 3. The farm household survey was conducted from April to October 1996. The questionnaire was developed based on information obtained from the informal surveys.

The qualitative data were analysed using gender analysis tools. The quantitative information was analysed using the Statistical Package for Social Science (SPSS). Descriptive statistical results were generated from the data, using frequencies, means, and standard deviations. Cross-tabulations were used in order to analyse two- or three-dimensional relationships between the variables. The chi-square (χ^2) test was used to test the significance of the relationships between variables.

5 Results and discussion

Our survey results show two types of change: changes in production and changes in labour use. These are discussed below focusing on land use patterns, use of inputs, and land management issues.

5.1 Changes in production

5.1.1 Land use patterns

Table 9.1 shows the diversity of crops grown in the study area, by agricultural stability zones, holding size, and irrigation methods. In terms of land use, the most important crops are cereals (wheat and barley) representing 22 and 26 per cent, respectively, of the total area.[2] Legumes (chickpea, lentil, and faba bean) and cumin, trees, and other crops (such as summer crops of melon, water melon, sesame, sunflower, and tobacco) are next in importance in terms of land area. Table 9.1 also shows that the distribution of crops varies according to agricultural stability zones and irrigation systems. Availability of irrigation determines whether many crops can be grown in the lower rainfall areas. Given its adaptation to dry conditions, 60 per cent of the barley area is found in the area of lower rainfall (Zone 3). However, 29 per cent of the barley area is irrigated. Wheat is distributed across all three rainfall zones, but two-thirds of the area is irrigated. Wheat and barley are sown in the winter wet season, and irrigated wheat and barley includes crops that may receive only one or two supplementary irrigations at times of peak water stress. Both wheat and barley are distributed more or less proportionately across the different holding sizes.

Legumes and cumin are grown primarily in the higher rainfall zones (Zones 1 and 2) and a significant proportion of the area is irrigated. Legumes are among the most labour hungry crops, due to the limited use of mechanization in their production, particularly for weeding and harvest, which are primarily done by hand. Again, these crops are distributed more or less proportionately across different holding sizes.

The principal agricultural changes that have taken place in the area concern mainly intensive crops, and are very much related to the availability of irrigation. This is especially true of the two fully irrigated crops of cotton and potato. Cotton occupies only 2.5 per cent of the total area in the sample and is grown by owners of different holding sizes. However, potato is concentrated on larger holdings and is grown only in Zone 1. During the early informal surveys in 1994, large areas of sugar beet were found in the study area. By the time the formal questionnaire survey was administered in 1996, farmers had progressively replaced sugar beet with cotton in areas that were traditionally growing cotton before the introduction of sugar beet into the government agricultural plans. Both sugar beet and cotton

Table 9.1 Land use patterns in the study area

	Holding size categories (ha)				*Agricultural stability zones*			*Irrigated and non-irrigated*		*Total*
	0–8	*8–20*	*20–40*	*40+*	*Zone 1*	*Zone 2*	*Zone 3*	*Irrigated*	*Non-irrigated*	
Number in sample	39	42	27	9	43	36	38	49	68	117
% of sample	33.3	35.9	23.1	7.7	36.7	30.8	32.5	41.9	58.1	100
% of area in										
Wheat	9.9	26.7	35.5	27.9	39.5	32.7	27.8	66.4	33.6	22.3
Barley	6.6	28.4	45.0	20.0	7.5	32.8	59.7	28.7	71.3	25.9
Legumes[a] and Cumin	6.7	25.2	40.0	28.1	30.0	47.1	22.9	42.3	57.7	13.0
Potato			56.0	44.0	100			100		2.1
Cotton	5.7	30.4	39.3	24.6	35.1	16.5	48.4	98.7	1.3	2.5
Vegetables	8.3	21.1	39.3	30.8	53.4	36.0	10.6	51.6	48.4	2.9
Maize	25.0	75.0					100	100		0.2
Forages		11.8	88.2			23.5	76.5	41.2	58.8	0.4
Trees	21.9	40.1	15.4	22.6	71.2	14.2	14.6	50.5	49.5	15.4
Fallow	5.0	19.7	35.0	40.3	1.1	2.4	96.5	38.8	61.2	13.0
Other[b]	0.5	17.4	21.7	60.4	72.2		27.8	85.5	14.5	19.1
Arable (%)	8.3	21.3	70.4	0.0	31.9	26.2	41.9	48.4	51.6	98.3
Non-arable (%)	8.7	27.5	36.1	27.7	8.3	72.7	19.0	55.3	44.7	1.1
Total (%)	8.7	27.4	36.5	27.4	31.6	26.8	41.6	48.5	51.5	100

Source: Farming household survey conducted by the author in 1996.

Notes

a Legumes include lentils, chickpeas, and faba bean.

b Other crops include melon, water melon, sesame, sunflower, tobacco.

have remained in the government's plans for Zone 1. Both crops are labour intensive, and labour is hired to perform such operations as weeding, harvesting, and sometimes selected post-harvest operations such as potato selection.

Trees (mainly olive) occupy 15 per cent of the total area in the sample. Trees have always been an important crop in Zone 1, but are now expanding to Zones 2 and 3 with lower rainfall (Mazid 1994, Mazid *et al.* 1995). Farmers are progressively shifting from their traditional crops to more profitable crops such as tree crops, which include olive, grape, pistachio, and fruits. Where soil type is suitable, farmers have a strong incentive to increase their tree area.

Olive picking is all done by hand and large numbers of workers are hired in addition to family labour. Olive trees in Syria tend to produce biennially with low production in the 'off year' and high production in the 'on year'. Consequently, labour requirements are very high in alternate years. Moreover, trees do not need the same amount of attention throughout the year as annual crops do. Therefore, farmers who have large areas of trees on their land or whose farm is exclusively planted with trees can devote their time to supplementing their income with off-farm activities, where household members can participate. The tree area is proportionately larger on smaller holdings (0–8 and 8–20 ha).

Other crops (mainly summer crops such as melon, water melon, sunflower, etc.) are more common on larger holdings. Only seven farming households in the sample grow other crops, which include summer crops (melon, water melon, sesame, sunflower, and tobacco). These are mainly large commercial farm operations. Many of the intensive crops were introduced recently in the study area either as a result of irrigation or because of large demand in the market.

The area planted as forage crops is an indication of the importance of animal production. Barley is the major feed crop, but may be grown as a cash crop. Forages, however, are usually grown to supply a farmer's own animals. Forage crops occupy a minimal proportion of the total sample area (0.4 per cent only). They are grown mainly on larger holdings (20–40 ha) and primarily in the lower rainfall area (Zone 3). The main reason for this characteristic is that small farms supplement their income from off-farm activities: they raise animals for household consumption and animal feeding is done on neighbouring fields by grazing crop residues. Large flocks are raised in Zone 3, and consequently more barley is grown in addition to other forage crops to supplement animal feeding. Small flocks were found in all areas of the study sample, particularly in Zones 1 and 2, where animals graze on crop residues of irrigated farms as a result of the decrease of fallow areas and the intensification of agricultural production.

Fallow land represents 13 per cent of the total land area in the sample survey. Almost all the fallow land was found in Zone 3, where large areas of barley are grown. This reflects the crop rotations followed in the lower rainfall areas (Table 9.2). Moreover, the fallow area is proportionately larger on larger holdings (more than 20 ha). On smaller holdings, farmers cannot afford to leave land unplanted; rather, they need to intensify their production in order to meet household needs. Because irrigation has recently spread to Zone 3 in the study area, due to the expansion of irrigation from the Euphrates River, fallow areas on irrigated farms represent 39 per cent of the total fallow land.

Table 9.2 Crop rotations of sample farm households by holding size, agricultural zone, and irrigation (% of sample area in each category)

Rotation[a]	*Holding size categories (ha) (%)*				*Agricultural stability zones (%)*			*Irrigation (%)*		*Total (%)*
	0–8	*8–20*	*20–40*	*40+*	*Zone 1*	*Zone 2*	*Zone 3*	*Irrigated*	*Rainfed*	
CC	12.8	14.3	14.8	—	7.0	30.6	2.6	6.1	17.6	12.8
C/F	10.3	19.0	11.1	22.2	4.7	5.6	34.2	2.0	23.5	14.5
C/Sc	12.8	11.9	11.1	11.1	14.0	5.6	15.8	26.5	1.5	12.0
C/L	25.6	35.7	25.9	11.1	27.9	47.2	10.5	14.3	38.2	28.2
C/L/Sc	7.7	14.3	22.2	33.3	20.9	11.1	13.2	30.6	4.4	15.4
C/L/F	5.1	2.4	14.8	22.2	—	—	23.7	10.2	5.9	7.7
T	25.6	2.4	—	—	25.6	—	—	10.2	8.8	9.4
Total	100	100	100	100	100	100	100	100	100	100

Source: Farming household survey conducted by the author in 1996.

Note

a CC, continuous cereals; C/F, cereals/fallow; C/Sc, cereals/summer crops; C/L, cereals/legumes; C/L/Sc, cereals/legumes/summer crops; C/L/F, cereals/legumes/fallow; T, only trees.

Non-arable land represents only 1 per cent of the total land in the sample. With the introduction of mechanization, previously uncultivated land has been reclaimed. This area does not include common non-arable land within communities, which is used for livestock grazing.

5.1.2 Crop rotation

Crop rotations vary by rainfall zones and to some extent by holding size. The most common rotation in the study area is cereals with legumes. Twenty-eight per cent of the surveyed farms follow this rotation (Table 9.2). It is most common on rainfed land; however, it is not so dominant in the lower rainfall areas (Zone 3) where a cereal/fallow rotation is more common. Cereal/fallow rotations are also more common on the largest holdings (40+ ha). The second most common crop rotation is the three-course rotation of cereals/legumes/summer crops observed in 15 per cent of the total sample farms. This rotation is favoured in higher rainfall areas (Zone 1), on irrigated land, and on larger holdings. One reason for this is the higher labour demands of legumes and summer crops.

Despite efforts by agricultural research institutions to promote the inclusion of legumes in rotations to maintain soil fertility, 13 per cent of farmers follow a continuous cereal rotation. Continuous cereal rotation is more prevalent in Zone 2, where it was found in 31 per cent of the farms. These are mainly poor farmers whose lands are characterized by stony soils and who keep small flocks of sheep. This type of land is suitable only for barley production, which is either grazed by sheep at an early stage or sold for animal feed after harvest. In this situation, household members have more free time to seek off-farm work to secure future assets for the family, such as houses or businesses for their children.

The survey data show that the larger the holding size, the higher the degree of crop diversity, and consequently the higher the level of labour use. Among tree growers, a few farmers grow vegetables between trees for home consumption. These farms, of less than 8 ha, are all located in Zone 1 and make up 27 per cent of the farms located in this zone. These farms employ family and hired labour at harvesting time and supply family labour (household female members) to other farms to work on other crops as wage labour.

Results show that of the households that hire agricultural labour, 40.5 per cent follow a cereals/legumes rotation while a further 19 per cent follow the three-course cereals/legumes/summer crops rotation. It is clear that labour use is closely related to land use patterns. The higher the diversity of crops, and particularly irrigated crops, the higher the labour use of both family and hired labour.

5.1.3 Irrigation

Table 9.3 shows that 40 per cent of the farms in the sample survey area have a source of irrigation. This proportion is higher for larger holdings. Irrigated farms are mainly located in Zone 1, representing 45 per cent of the total irrigated farms, but are also found in Zones 2 and 3 where the drilling of wells for irrigation expanded in the 1990s.

Table 9.3 Importance of irrigation by holding size categories

	Holding size categories (ha)				*Total*
	0–8	*8–20*	*20–40*	*40+*	
Number in sample	39	42	27	9	117
% of holdings with irrigation	38.5	33.3	51.8	44.4	40.2
Irrigated holdings as % of total irrigated holdings	31.9	29.8	29.8	8.5	100

Source: Farming household survey conducted by the author in 1996.

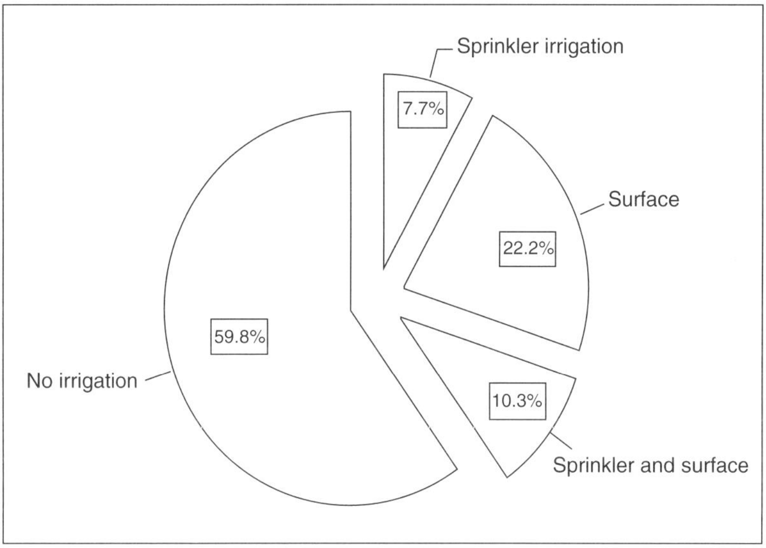

Figure 9.1 Different irrigation systems used in sample farm households (% distribution).

Methods of irrigation differ in the study area (Figure 9.1). The most common is surface irrigation through a system of small channels. Sprinkler irrigation is becoming more widespread in the high rainfall areas, while surface irrigation system is more widely used in low rainfall areas. Some farms use a combination of both systems. Sprinkler irrigation requires capital investment in sprinkler equipment. Surface irrigation is much cheaper, but generally requires more intensive labour both for initial digging of the channels and for diverting the water during irrigation.

Irrigated lands commonly use hired labour, paid on a monthly basis. This cost represents about half the weeding and/or harvesting costs of the crop. Hired labour for irrigation is characterized by its continuity, compared to, say, seasonal operations that use hired labour. Some crops that are intensively irrigated such as cotton, potato, and vegetables involve continuous labour use to maintain the irrigation channels or to move sprinkler pipelines every few hours to irrigate another part of the field.

Information was collected on the actual area irrigated as a percentage of the total farm size. The data show that 23 per cent of farms have the capacity to irrigate all their land, 10 per cent can irrigate more than half their land, 30 per cent can irrigate up to half their land, and 36 per cent can irrigate up to 25 per cent of their land. A few farms are able to supply irrigation to only a tiny proportion of their land, sometimes limited to home gardens producing vegetables for household consumption. Other farms with reliable irrigation sources produce summer vegetables for market sale, particularly in El-Bab district.

5.1.4 Use of fertilizers

The information gathered from the study sample shows that 23 per cent of farming households started using chemical fertilizers back in the 1960s. A larger group of households (45 per cent) started using chemicals, particularly fertilizers, during the 1970s. A further 18.5 per cent of farmers adopted fertilizer in the 1980s and the remaining 13 per cent in the 1990s. Currently, almost all the sample farms obtain their fertilizer through the Agricultural Credit Bank of Syria, while 3 per cent of farmers buy it directly from the free market. Only farmers who hold an agricultural permit can obtain their fertilizer through credit. Fertilizer users have generally decreased the area of land left fallow. More importantly, the rate of fertilizer use has increased considerably from 50 to 200 kg per hectare, mainly for cereals.

5.2 Changes in labour demand and supply

5.2.1 The effect of irrigation on labour demand and supply

Since the early 1980s, rural populations from the drier zones (Zone 3) have supplied irrigated farms in Zone 1 with large numbers of agricultural workers. Recently, farms located in Sfireh and El-Bab districts in Zones 2 and 3 have been supplied with irrigation water by canal from the Euphrates River. In this area, the introduction of irrigation is the main factor driving agricultural intensification. The availability of irrigation in Zone 3 has greatly affected land use patterns in terms of diversification and intensification, with the introduction of irrigated crops that require large numbers of labourers. In the past, these very farms supplied labour to other irrigated farms, particularly in Zone 1. Today, they have stopped hiring themselves out to their distant neighbours and, in fact, have begun to hire workers themselves during the harvest period. This process of intensification has affected the demand for and supply of labour, and also the movement of labour from one area to another.

The introduction of irrigation from the Euphrates to Zone 3, together with the shift from cereal production to more labour-intensive crops, has created continuous employment for individual workers who used to seek work on farms located in the wetter areas. As a consequence, labour is no longer provided from Zone 3 and farmers have started to seek labour from other areas. The change has had wider repercussions. Workers from this area used to move further afield to seek work, particularly to Hassakeh and Raqqa provinces for cotton picking. With the changes brought by irrigation, workers' flow to Hassakeh and Raqqa has decreased considerably and demand is now met mainly by landless households and the remaining small rainfed farm households.

When irrigation from the Euphrates was introduced into areas where land is predominantly State owned, holding sizes were reduced according to the State agrarian law.[3] Farmers in these areas are used to rainfed farming and their experience with irrigation is still limited, which has resulted in loss of production due to over-irrigation or other mismanagement. It is still possible to find farmers who would prefer to return to rainfed farming. The question arises: does irrigation have positive or negative effects on the livelihoods of farming households? On the positive side, farmers are able to diversify their production, increase their farm income, and have additional crop residues to feed their livestock. On the negative side, although partly compensated for by higher income from irrigated crops, their holdings have decreased in size. Also, they have stopped fallowing, which negatively affects the grazing animals on the fallow land. Farmers used to stay on their farms for part of the year, and spend the other part in the steppe grazing animals. Now that irrigation is available, they must spend a greater proportion of the year on the farm, as most of their time is now devoted to producing irrigated crops.

More importantly, on small holdings, the time devoted in the past to off-farm income-earning activities is negatively affected as members of the household cannot now leave their land unattended. The income earned from irrigated crops does not compensate the typical income these small-holders used to earn from off-farm activities, due to their lack of experience in irrigated farming combined with growing population pressures, as well as the higher risk factors now involved and the instability in market prices for agricultural products. The effect of this development is that women undertake less off-farm activities as wage labour in agriculture and men work less in non-agricultural activities. Despite this important change, men have remained active in off-farm activities, which provide higher incomes than agriculture.

5.2.2 The effect of mechanization on agricultural labour

The introduction of mechanization in north-western Syria has had a profound effect on agricultural production. Prior to mechanization, land cultivation was done by animal-drawn ploughs, and most other operations were done by hand. Today, land preparation for all crops is mechanized (except on steep land unsuitable for tractors) and cereal production, including post-harvest operations, is almost entirely mechanized through the introduction of tractors, combine-harvesters, and tractor-powered threshers. This has had an impact on the area devoted to cereals, which has considerably increased during the last few years, and on the amount of labour required in cereal production. However, in other crops, the bulk of the agricultural work, apart from land preparation, continues to be performed manually, and contributes to the high levels of labour demand. Sowing and harvesting of legumes, irrigated crops such as cotton and potato, and summer crops such as melon, sunflower, and vegetables continue to be performed manually. Moreover, olive picking is all performed by hand, although oil pressing is now mechanized.

While mechanization has enabled an expansion in the cereals area and reduced labour demand in cereals production, the introduction of new crops and of other production inputs have considerably increased labour demand for manual operations.

5.2.3 Diversification and intensification of demand for labour in the study area

As a result of land intensification and the new land use patterns, labour is increasingly required to perform a large number of activities in agricultural production. Certain traditional activities (such as manual harvesting and threshing of cereals) have disappeared, while new activities have emerged (such as the application of herbicides, irrigation-related tasks, and activities associated with the new crops introduced).

Commercial farmers hire large numbers of labourers during periods of high labour demand. The survey shows that two-thirds of the farms in the sample hire agricultural labour (Table 9.4). Hired labour use is more extensive in the higher rainfall zones (Zones 1 and 2), where cropping is more diversified, and on irrigated farms. As would be expected, small holdings (those smaller than 8 ha) use less hired labour than larger holdings.

Table 9.4 Farming households using hired labour by holding size, agricultural zones, and irrigation methods

	No. in sample	*Farms using hired labour*	
		No.	*%*
Holding size categories			
0–8 ha	39	20	51
8–20 ha	42	30	71
20–40 ha	27	22	81
40+ ha	9	7	78
Agricultural stability zones			
Zone 1	43	33	77
Zone 2	36	24	67
Zone 3	38	22	58
Irrigated holdings	47	37	79
Rainfed holdings	70	42	60
Total	117	79	68

Source: Farming household survey conducted by the author in 1996.

Casual labour, hired to perform seasonal manual agricultural activities, consists mainly of women and sometimes children. Men normally provide the following services: paid labour for land preparation, cereal harvest by combine-harvester, semi-mechanized activities such as fertilizer application, and regular activities such as irrigation-related tasks. Many of the agricultural operations are highly seasonal, which need to be completed over a short period, and therefore are dependent on casual labour – which consists increasingly of women.

The survey revealed that the frequency of hiring labour gives a more realistic picture of the importance of labour demand. For instance, most farms (both rain-fed and irrigated, and independent of holding size) hire labour for legume harvesting, a labour-intensive activity that takes place over a short period in May. A significant number of farmers, particularly in the higher rainfall zones or in irrigated areas, hire labour throughout the year, for at least 10 months of the year. Variations in demand for labour, and especially casual labour, are largely determined by the agricultural calendar. The changes in production discussed above have all affected the agricultural calendar in the study area, as discussed next.

5.3 The agricultural calendar and demand for women's labour

5.3.1 The agricultural calendar

The agricultural calendar of north-western Syria determines the labour supply and demand for women. The activity calendar shows the timing of different activities at the farm level. In general, production constraints are frequently associated with labour shortages (because particular tasks take place at particular times) due to the need for labour for many crops at the same time (e.g. harvesting one crop, and weeding another). Figure 9.2 shows that the demand for manual women's labour is concentrated in certain peak periods.

The demand for women's agricultural labour gangs is at its highest during legume harvest, which takes place at the same time as the weeding of other summer crops in May–June, and also during olive picking in October–November. During the period May June, many activities pertaining to winter and summer crops are due at the same time, such as weeding, harvesting, irrigating, and roguing.[4] These often need to be completed over a very short period. For instance, once the lentil crop has matured around the end of April and the beginning of May, it must be harvested within 1 week to avoid grain shattering that may cause loss of or damage to the crop. It is mainly during that period that labour demand is at its highest and labour shortages are the most crucial. Moreover, weeding potato and sugar beet is due at the same time as the lentil harvest, which contributes to labour shortages at this time of the year. Due to the vulnerability of legumes to shattering, wages are higher for the legume harvest because this operation cannot be delayed.

By mapping this information on a yearly cycle (the seasonal crops calendar and the labour requirement over the year), periods of heavy work and potential or actual labour shortages are clearly shown. Competing tasks (Table 9.5) by

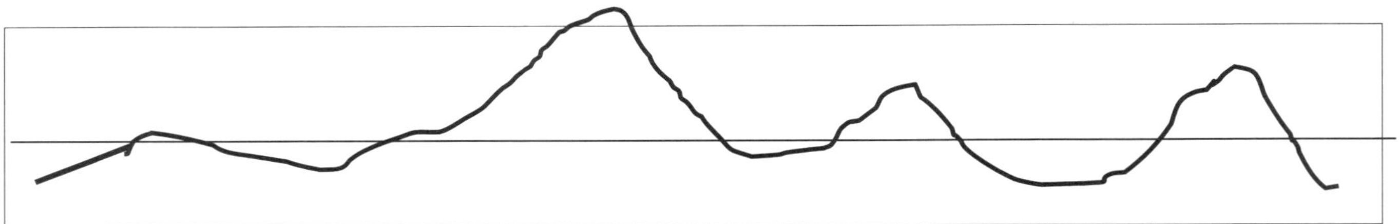

JAN–FEB	MAR–APR	MAY–JUN	JUL–AUG	SEP–OCT	NOV–DEC
Winter crops					
- Weeding cumin in Feb - Irrigating faba bean	- Irrigating cereals, faba bean, soybean, maize and potato - Weeding lentils, faba bean and potato	- Harvesting lentil, cumin, faba bean - Weeding and thinning maize, soybean - Irrigation of wheat, potato, soybean, maize - Roguing wheat - Cutting green of potato	- Potato selection and harvest - Irrigating potato, maize - Harvesting potato, maize, and soybean		
Summer crops and trees (olive and grape trees)					
- Irrigating sugar beet	- Weeding and thinning sugar beet - Cotton irrigation	- Irrigating sugar beet, cotton and soybean - Weeding sugar beet and cotton	- Weeding fall potato - Husking and selecting maize - Sugar beet harvest - Weeding soybean and potato - Sugar beet harvest - Irrigating soybean, sugar beet, cotton, potato - Grape harvest	- Irrigating potato, soybean - Cotton and soybean harvest	- Potato and soybean harvest - Olive picking

Figure 9.2 Labour demand and supply for women and children in north-west Syria for winter and summer crops and trees.

Notes

1 Weeding and harvesting are performed by women and children.
2 Irrigating is performed only by women.
3 Pesticide is applied by women and men.

Table 9.5 Competing tasks by crop during April, May, and June in north-western Syria

Competing tasks by crop	*April*	*May*	*June*
Barley	Irrigation/roguing[a]	Roguing[a]/irrigation	Harvesting[a]
Wheat	Irrigation	Roguing[a]/irrigation	Harvesting[a]
Lentils	Weeding[a]	Harvesting[a]	—
Spring potato	Irrigation/weeding[a]	Irrigation	Irrigation
Sugar beet	Weeding[a]/thinning[a]	Irrigation/weeding[a]	Irrigation
Cumin	—	Harvesting[a]	—
Cotton	Irrigation	Irrigation/weeding[a] and Thinning[a]	—
Faba bean	Irrigation	Harvesting[a]	Weeding[a]
Spring soybean	—	Weeding[a]/irrigation	Weeding[a]
Fall soybean	—	—	Irrigation
Maize	Irrigation	Weeding[a] and thinning[a]	Irrigation

Source: Farming household survey conducted by the author in 1996.

Note

a Tasks performed by hired labour gangs. Other tasks are performed either by family labour or by individual hired workers.

gender are thus identified and described. Non-agricultural activities take place during periods when agricultural work is slack. Therefore, off-farm as well as on-farm activities were investigated in order to evaluate the degree of importance of off-farm activity income for farmers and for hired workers. This process allowed the recording of activities by gender, and permitted the collection of information gleaned from discussions with the principal actors regarding the required time per hectare for different tasks related to the same crop. From this, useful information on the various influences on labour demand and supply trends was derived.

The factors described above all contribute to making the demand for women's labour particularly acute. The seasonal calendar revealed periods of labour shortage and identified all competing tasks by gender in farm production. The competing activities that take place in the same period affect wage rates as workers prefer to supply their labour for higher paid activities such as lentil harvest. During other periods in the year, the need for labour is less urgent. October–November is a period of peak labour demand for fall potato harvest and olive picking.[5] During the period of olive picking large groups of workers are hired over 1–2 months, depending on the size of the planted area. This period is also affected by the variety of olives planted, which results in different timings of maturation in different districts. This assists in spreading demand for labour over a longer period, and provides the opportunity for employment in olive picking in different locations. Most crops require tasks for which women's labour is demanded during the period of April–May. For instance, during that period, workers are roguing wheat and barley fields (mainly in Zone 1), harvesting lentil, faba bean, and cumin, weeding sugar beets and soybean, weeding and thinning cotton and maize.

In Zone 1, where irrigation is available, the demand for labour covers the whole year except December and January when few outdoor activities take place such as mechanized land preparation by men, and fertilizer and pesticide application by a limited number of women and men. On irrigated farms, hired women workers are active during at least 9 or 10 months of the year. Two or three months out of 12 are considered to be the quiet period in the agricultural calendar, usually in winter (December–February), except for cumin, which might require weeding in February. The crops for which labour is most in demand are: lentil, potato, sugar beet, and vegetables on irrigated farms, in addition to olive picking.

As a result of competing demands for labour, wages rise at peak periods – sometimes doubling for a few activities – and working hours extend to the afternoon. In some cases, activities are performed by night, such as activities related to sugar beet harvest and loading.

Competing tasks also affect the composition of labour by age and sex. When demand is at a peak, all available labour sources are used. The information collected during the informal surveys shows that labour during peak periods is composed of workers aged between 9 and 78 years, compared to periods of low labour demand when workers' ages range between 17 and 55 years.

The introduction of mechanization has affected the whole agricultural sector and consequently has affected the demand for and allocation of agricultural labour, as discussed next.

5.3.2 The impact of production changes on labour demand

The gradual introduction of mechanization since the 1950s has resulted in an expansion of cultivated areas and increased production. The use of pumps, tractors, harvesters, threshers, dusters, and sprayers all increased between 1970 and 1997 (MAAR 1997).

As discussed above, many agricultural operations are now mechanized. Cereals production is more or less entirely mechanized; the only operation that is still performed manually is roguing of cereal crops in Zone 1, destined for sale to the General Organization of Seed Multiplication. By contrast, in legume production only land preparation and sometimes fertilizer application are mechanized. Weeding and legume harvest, the most costly operation, is still done manually by women (Martini 1999).

Until the late 1970s and early 1980s, labour shortages were more important in cereal production than in any other crops (Schmid 1980). Today, mechanization has considerably reduced the labour requirements for cereals. As a result, the composition of labour has changed considerably.

These recent changes (mechanization and the introduction of irrigation that supports more intensive cropping) have had both 'labour augmenting' and 'labour saving' effects (Bernstein *et al.* 1992). Mechanization of cereal production has reduced the demand for large numbers of labourers for manual operations, who have been replaced by a smaller number of skilled workers for mechanized operations. On the other hand, the introduction of irrigation has led to greater use of inputs and more intensive cropping or changes in cropping patterns, all of which implies an increase in total labour requirements as well as higher absorption per hectare.

On the sample farms surveyed, mechanization is mainly used for land preparation for all crops, and for harvesting of cereals, in addition to sowing of some crops. It has considerably improved the timing and speed of operations compared to previously, when harvest and post-harvest operations could last the entire summer. The main effect of mechanization on agricultural labour has been in terms of the division of labour between men and women, their organization vis-à-vis the labour market, and resulting wage rates. For instance, mechanization has contributed to shifting the cereal harvest and the related post-harvest operations from a mixed labour force of both women and men to one composed almost entirely of men.

With population growth and agricultural intensification, a gradual division of labour has arisen between men, who perform mechanized activities, and women, who remain involved in manual activities. Socially, rural women stay closer to the household and rarely move beyond their communities; men are more mobile and may move around or travel to urban areas for employment, which gives them a greater opportunity to gain the necessary training and to specialize in mechanized activities. Such specialized labour is more highly paid than manual labour. Burton argues that 'labour intensification is most likely to impact female participation in agriculture if it requires very high labour inputs per day on a seasonal basis' (Burton and White 1987).

The type of qualifications or experience needed for mechanized operations has important implications for the labour market. Farmers need workers who not only know how to operate machinery, but also have associated skills and knowledge in the maintenance of machinery, use of machinery in different soil types and conditions, and can correct fertilizer and chemical use levels. Although these skills are not difficult to acquire, they are restricted to men largely because of the social norms of the region. Consequently, while mechanization has reduced the overall demand for labour in cereal production, it has created jobs for qualified men or has encouraged men to acquire the necessary training in order to take advantage of these new employment opportunities.

In other crops, despite the introduction of mechanization, manual labour is still needed in most operations. In general, mechanization has not resulted in an overall decrease in labour demand because it has led to intensification of agricultural production and created greater demand for manual work, which is dominated by female labour.

Daily wage labour is fast becoming the predominant form of agricultural labour in north-western Syria, especially on large holdings and commercial farms. In the study area, women agricultural workers are not hired individually for most manual activities: they are mainly employed within organized groups, known as 'labour gangs', and led by contractors or 'labour bosses' (Martini 1999) who negotiate contracts and supervise the work. Farmers have direct contact with labour bosses who supply them with women manual workers. The availability of women depends largely on the timing of the operations or tasks for which labour is demanded and on the wages offered for different operations that take place at the same time.

Women constitute most of the agricultural wage labour force as increasingly men are working off-farm in urban areas, earning higher wages than they would in agricultural jobs. There are many explanations as to why women workers have increased. First, wages in agriculture are low, which is why men prefer to seek other work opportunities. Men tend to be hired individually for tasks that are different from those performed by women, usually mechanized tasks such as driving tractors, harvesters, or threshers for which they need some skills and training. Women have limited alternative work opportunities; they work within labour gangs as they need to move together under the leadership of a labour boss, since rural families do not allow their women to work within a mixed agricultural labour force. This represents a significant social development, since an important female labour market has emerged.

5.3.3 Labour shortages

Due to the low wages prevailing in the agricultural sector, a significant proportion of men has left agriculture to seek better-paid jobs in the towns or abroad (Martini *et al.* 2003). Despite these recent trends of male migration, analysis shows no overall farm labour shortages. However, it does show crucial labour shortages at specific times of the year, such as in April–May, July–August, and October–November (Figure 9.2).

Labour shortages occur mainly in manual harvesting and weeding performed by hired female labour gangs. The main crops affected by labour shortages in the study area are lentil, sugar beet, cumin, cotton, faba bean, spring soybean, and maize. Harvesting and weeding of these crops are all due in April, May, and June. To a lesser extent, July and August constitute another period of high labour demand for harvesting spring potato, spring soybean, maize and sugar beet, and for weeding fall potato and fall soybean. During July and August there may be a labour shortage, but only in some areas and it is not as critical as in spring. Olive picking too can cause labour shortages in some areas. Rural populations seek this activity because it is paid in kind (either in olives or olive oil), guaranteeing their annual supply. Also, large numbers of labourers are supplied from the study area to other provinces such as Al-Rakka and El-Hassakeh *Muhafazat* for cotton harvesting in September–October.

6 Conclusion

The case study of north-western Syria offers an example of how rapid agricultural growth accompanied by male off-farm employment has contributed to a considerable increase in female wage labour. The findings contribute to research on the effects of agricultural intensification on labour in different farming systems. Labour demand and supply are very much linked to the systems of agricultural production and thus are affected by the changes that those production systems undergo. Agricultural intensification has considerably altered the division of labour in agriculture, and has drawn more women into the labour force. Mechanization and irrigation have indirectly contributed to increasing the demand for women's labour via the introduction of new crops. Furthermore, the diversification of crops has created new job opportunities throughout the year, from which the organization of women into labour gangs led by labour bosses has emerged as a necessity.

Labour gangs now constitute suitable institutions for rural communities to overcome the social resistance to women working out of the household boundaries. The extent of the increase of agricultural labour, in which women predominate, is likely to be related to important changes in the values of rural communities. These changes have been directed by necessities related to their daily needs. As the need for additional income has become crucial, such communities have gradually started to perceive things differently and to adapt their norms as a response to their pressing needs. The feminization of agricultural labour (Martini *et al.* 2003) is related to the out-migration of men and to the low level of wages in agricultural production, particularly in manual operations. Labour gangs are also important in controlling the agricultural labour market, and their existence has been instrumental in changing the meaning of work for rural communities. They have also led to increasing household incomes. The motivation of rural communities to work via these gangs has increased considerably and work values have developed accordingly. The organization of women's labour has created a female labour market, and greater integration of rural women into the agricultural economy.

Notes

1 Women represented in this study are women of both rural and agricultural households, including female children 12 years and older (children are allowed to participate in agricultural labour markets at the age of 12 in Syria).

2 A study undertaken in 1983 in El-Bab district of north-west Syria found the same percentage areas for wheat and barley (Tully 1984).

3 Before land reform, a non-Syrian (Sultan Abdul Hamid) was the most important landlord. By 1883, about 270,000 ha in 333 villages south of Aleppo were registered in his name. South of Aleppo, the Sultan's land covered 175,000 ha in 234 villages. Most of the land was unregistered and uncultivated until the Sultan ordered tenants to be placed on it. In 1909, the Abdul Hamid estates were declared state property and, after the First World War, were transferred to the Syrian Department of State Domains. During the Agrarian reform, rainfed farms that were supplied with irrigation from the Euphrates were reduced in size by the State as compensation for the irrigation provided to those farms. The land taken from farmers has been redistributed to landless farmers. The land reform has considerably reshaped the social structure of the countryside, and has affected the agrarian economy and the development strategy as a whole in Syria. The main change that occurred through the land reform was the re-distribution of land. Land reform in Syria was introduced mainly in response to the significant disparity in land distribution and holding size, and the number of landless rural families. The reform aimed to create a small-holding peasantry, and to discourage the accumulation of land, diverting private wealth into industrial investment. Thus, this process of expropriation and redistribution transformed the agricultural sector to one dominated by small enterprises and owner-occupied holdings.

4 Roguing is a manual activity that takes place before harvest. It consists of removing the spikes of wheat that are different from the planted variety. These spikes are recognized by the workers as they are longer than the planted variety and they result from a mixture of seeds before planting. These crops are planted under a contract with the Seed Multiplication Organization and should therefore be clean from any other variety.

5 Whole families hired for a period of 1 or 2 months perform olive picking. Women, men, and children all participate in this activity.

References

AOAD (Arab Organization for Agricultural Development) (1975) *The Intensification of Agricultural Production in the Syrian Arab Republic* (in Arabic), Khartoum, Sudan: League of Arab States.

Bernstein, H., B. Crow, and H. Johnson (eds) (1992) *Rural Livelihoods, Crises and Responses*, Oxford: Oxford University Press in association with The Open University.

Burton, M. L. and D. R. White (1987) 'Sexual division of labour in agriculture', in Maclachlan, M. D. (ed.), *Household Economies and their Transformations: Monographs in Economic Anthropology*, No. 3, United States: Society for Economic Anthropology, University Press of America, pp. 107–130.

Fieldstein, H. S. and S. Poats (eds) (1990) *Working Together: Gender Analysis in Agriculture: Case Studies*, Vol. 1, West Hartford, CT: Kumarian Press.

MAAR (Ministry of Agriculture and Agrarian Reform) (1997) *Annual Statistical Abstract for Syria*, Damascus, Syria.

Maclachlan, M. D. (1987) 'From intensification to proletarianization', in Maclachlan, M. D. (ed.), *Household Economies and their Transformations: Monographs in Economic Anthropology*, No. 3, United States: Society for Economic Anthropology, University Press of America, pp. 1–27.

Martini, A. M., R. Tutwiler, and C. Kalume (1997) 'Not for gold, or fine clothes', *Caravan: Review of Agriculture in the Dry Areas*, issue no. 7, Autumn/Winter 1997/1998, Aleppo: ICARDA, pp. 10–13.

Martini, M. A. (1999) 'An analysis of female wage labour in northwest Syria in the context of agricultural intensification', PhD Thesis, Reading University, UK.

Martini, M. A., P. Goldey, G. E. Jones, and E. Bailey (2003) 'Towards a feminization of agricultural labour in northwest Syria', *Journal of Peasant Studies*, 30(2).

Mazid, A. (1994) 'Factors influencing adoption of new agricultural technology in dry areas of Syria', PhD Thesis, University of Nottingham, UK.

Mazid, A., R. Tutwiler, A. Rodriguez, M. Martini, H. Al-Ahmed, and A. Kneifis (1995) 'Agricultural production systems and resource management in agricultural settlement zone 2 in Syria', Farm Resource Management Program (FRMP) Annual Report, Aleppo: ICARDA.

Pratt, B. and P. Loizos (1992) *Choosing Research Methods: Data Collection for Development Workers*, Development Guidelines no. 7, London: Oxfam.

Rathgeber, E. (1990) 'WID, WAD, GAD: trends in research and practice', *The Journal of Development Areas*, 24, pp. 489–502.

Schmid, L. (1980) 'Agricultural Manpower', Syria: Agricultural Sector Assessment, Vol 5: Human Resources and Agricultural Institutions Annex, USDA in cooperation with USAID and SPC, pp. 1–115.

Tully, D. (1984) 'Land use and farmers: strategies in Al-Bab: the feasibility of forage legumes in place of fallow', Research Report no. 13, Aleppo: ICARDA.

Part V

Economic boundaries in flux

10 Defining boundaries

Kuwait's economic reconstruction, 1991–2001

Karen Pfeifer

1 Introduction

Painful and costly as Iraq's invasion and occupation were to Kuwait, the crisis and subsequent liberation offered its government and people a unique opportunity to reinvigorate their previously stagnant economy with new institutions and to creatively redefine their external and internal economic boundaries. Several proposals for serious economic reform had been proffered in the 1980s, and many similar ones were discussed during the years after liberation. However, none of these was seriously undertaken and no fresh ideas came forth in the 1990s. Instead, Kuwait intensified its current and future dependence on the oil sector and on the United States, adjusting its external boundaries to accommodate this policy choice. Furthermore, it rigidified its internal social boundaries instead of relaxing them as part of a reform that might have diversified the economy and enhanced non-state economic activities. Kuwait's weak and erratic economic performance in the decade from 1991 to 2001 reflected these development-constricting decisions.

2 Boundaries of the pre-invasion economy

Before the First World War and the creation of defined nation states in the Arab World, the external economic boundaries of the city-state of Kuwait were fluid. It held a distinct role in the regional economy as a fishing, pearling, and trading hub.[1] Much of its inland trade was with Saudi Arabia and the Ottoman province of Iraq, to which it re-exported a large portion of the goods it imported, and from which it obtained most of its water, food, and crafted goods. With the extension of British influence in the Gulf in the last quarter of the nineteenth century, the weight of trade shifted in favour of the British Empire. However, when the pearling industry collapsed and overseas trade diminished during the 1930s, Kuwait's economic relationships with regional partners again blossomed, with Kuwaiti merchants, for example, investing in date plantations in the Fao Peninsula.

While Kuwait's external boundaries had been fluid prior to the oil era, and it lived in relative peace and prosperity, its internal socio-economic boundaries were strictly delineated. The dominant families who ran the relatively complex productive and commercial economy constituted a wealthy, endogamous, and internally cohesive class.[2] These families had built their fortunes through the pearl-diving and shipbuilding industries, long-distance sea trade around the Gulf and with India and Africa, and entrepot commerce via Kuwait's natural harbour in the north-western *cul-de-sac* of the Arab/Persian Gulf. In the pre-oil era, the Al-Sabah were the leading political family within the ruling elite, considered 'a first among equals' by the other families whose Arabian ancestors had reputedly settled the area in the early eighteenth century. Drawing its income from taxation of trade, the ruling family was beholden to the elite merchant class for its fiscal as well as political support.

2.1 The drawing of external economic boundaries

At the end of the nineteenth century, the Al-Sabah ruler, Mubarak, made a fateful decision without consulting the other elite families. Having usurped the emirship in the only violent political transition Kuwait was to experience before 1990, he secured his rule by signing a secret treaty with Britain giving Kuwait protectorate status in exchange for Britain's assumption of control of its foreign affairs.

In 1922, after Britain gained Mandatory control over Iraq, the British political agent in Kuwait met with the emerging Saudi rulers and a British-appointed representative of Iraq to determine the common boundaries of Kuwait, Iraq, and Saudi Arabia. Without taking account of the views of either Iraq or Kuwait, the British agent drew the boundaries so as to maximize Britain's ability to manage Gulf and peninsular affairs, to exclude other imperial powers, to stabilize Britain's relationship with the Saudis, and, incidentally, to confine Iraq's access to the Gulf to the Shatt al-Arab. These boundaries would also turn out to be advantageous for the British and US energy corporations allowing them later to negotiate oil extractions from the massive reserves of three separate countries with three separate governments.[3]

The city-state of Kuwait had an independent history and its own political dynamics from the early eighteenth century, but the map drawn by the British still conveys the impression that Kuwait had been deliberately scooped out of the narrow southeastern end of Iraq. Post-Mandate Iraqi governments formally recognized these borders during regime changes in 1934 and 1963, but periodically restated the claim that Kuwait should have been an integral part, the 'nineteenth province', of the nation-state of Iraq. British troops remained at the ready to enforce Kuwait's territorial sovereignty when Iraq made military feints in its direction, a role that British and the US military maintain to this day (Cordesman 1997: 3–14).

2.2 Porous boundaries with the international economy

The development of the oil extraction industry by foreign companies during the 1940s drastically transformed Kuwait's comparative advantage. The economy became reoriented around the oil industry, developing within the context of the long wave of US-led growth in an oil-thirsty capitalist world economy from the 1950s until the early 1980s. In effect, Kuwait became a rentier state, with over 90 per cent of government revenues accounted for by oil-extraction royalties (NBK, EFB 1983, 5: 13). Indeed, when oil prices were at their peak in 1980, 71 per cent of GDP originated in the oil sector (NBK, EFQ 1982, 2: 7). Over the 1982–2000 period, when oil prices were more 'normal', oil revenues still accounted for one-third to one-half of GDP (see Table 10.1).

During the development boom years between 1974 and 1982, the national savings rate rose to 50 per cent of GDP, and investment and consumption, public and private, soared. An index of gross fixed capital formation, with a base value of 100 in 1980, shows a rise from 30.7 in 1970 to a peak of 138.0 in 1983 (Al-Yousuf 1990: 72), more than 20 per cent of GDP. In 1983, the GDP per capita of Kuwaiti citizens was $20,300, in the same league as the United States and West European countries, while even the per capita income of *all residents* of Kuwait (citizens and expatriates), at $12,646, was in the middle-income range of the world's economies (NBK, EFB 1985, 8: 6, EIU 1991–2: 10).

Because of its small size and the availability of oil revenues to purchase imports, Kuwait remained open to international trade, with an average tariff on imports of about 1 per cent. Even in the 1980s, when the dinar was allowed to depreciate by 40 per cent in order to discourage imports, tariffs were not raised.[4] Kuwaiti citizens were allowed to freely exchange their dinars for other currencies and to export their savings. Cross-border flows of capital were technically unrestricted, although there were legal limits to ownership by foreign capital (none at all in the oil sector, and no more than 49 per cent for ventures in other sectors), and the net movement of capital, and income therefrom, was deliberately influenced through management of the state's overseas portfolios (Al-Yousuf 1990: 19, 28).

The surplus oil revenues that could not be absorbed by such a small economy were channelled abroad. By the 1960s, the Kuwaiti finance ministry had created an overseas investment portfolio, the General Reserve Fund (GRF), which became a second source of rentier income. The latter accounts for the fact that, since the early 1970s, gross national income has routinely been as much as 20 per cent higher than GDP (NBK, EFB 1983, 5: 6), as indicated in Figure 10.1. Indeed, while Kuwait's official government budget may go into deficit in years when oil prices are lower, its actual (if unofficial) budget is routinely in surplus due to this investment income. Another mainly international portfolio was created in 1976, the unique Reserve Fund for Future Generations (RFFG). The government pledged to add 10 per cent of its non-investment revenues to this fund each year and not to tap the principal for 25 years, that is, until 2001, unless by emiri decree in a national emergency.

Kuwait's foreign aid programmes also expanded as a result of the oil boom, to 4.3 per cent of GDP in the peak year 1982 (Al-Yousuf 1990: 19, 28, EIU 1991–2: 22), significantly higher than the most generous of OECD donors. In addition, the Kuwait Fund for Arab Economic Development undertook the role of a regional

Table 10.1 Composition of GDP by type of economic activity (in %), Kuwait, 1982–2000

	1982	*1988*	*1994*	*1998*	*1999*	*2000*
Crude petroleum and natural gas[a]	44.1	29.5	37.9	29.6	35.6	46.7
Manufacturing	5	13.4	10.5	11.6	11.7	10.2
Hydrocarbon products: chemicals, rubber, and plastics	1.8	9.8	7.3	8.2	8.8	7.9
Construction	4.2	2.4	3.2	2.9	2.4	1.9
Utilities: electricity, water, and gas[b]	−3.7	−0.4	−0.6	−0.3	−0.5	−0.7
Transport, communications, and storage	4.7	4.9	4.9	5.4	5.4	4.6
All services	45.2	49.8	43.7	50.2	45	37
Wholesale and retail trade, hotels and restaurants	11.8	11.3	7.9	8.4	7.1	5.6
Finance, real estate, and business services	18.7	15.3	11.7	14.5	13.6	11.5
Community, social, personal services	14.7	23.2	24.1	27.3	24.3	19.9
Agriculture, fishing, and livestock	0.4	0.5	0.4	0.4	0.4	0.3
Total	100	100	100	100	100	100

Source: National Bank of Kuwait (2002).

Notes

a Crude petroleum is the only subsector under the standard industrial classification category of 'mining and quarrying'.

b Because of subsidies for utilities, the costs of this sector run higher than the value of output, hence the negative entries.

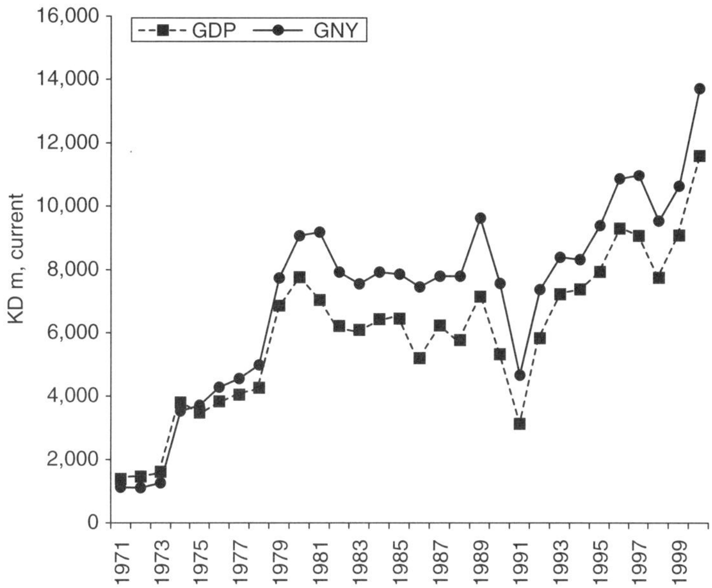

Figure 10.1 Gross domestic product and gross national income, Kuwait, 1971–2000, KD m (current).

Source: IMF, *International Financial Statistics Yearbook* 2001: 632–633.

development bank, providing long-term loans on easy terms for projects in Arab and other countries.

Kuwait was able to benefit greatly from its comparative advantage in world trade as long as oil prices remained favourable. Indeed, by the early 1980s, crude oil and oil products comprised over 90 per cent of all goods exports, including re-exports (NBK, EFQ 1982, 2: 28). Kuwait's direction of trade was also stable and predictable, exporting oil mainly to Europe and, increasingly, to Asia. Japan became the leading purchaser of Kuwaiti exports, taking as much as 20 per cent until 1990, while the United States took less than 10 per cent. Japan was also the leading supplier of imports into Kuwait in the 1980s, its share averaging about 20 per cent, as shown in Table 10.2.

Prior to 1979, Kuwaiti businesses continued their long-held economic relationships with both Iraq and Iran, importing food, serving as the middleman for the re-export trade, and linking businesses among the main cities of the partner countries. The relationship with Iran disintegrated after the 1979 Islamic revolution, especially as the Kuwaiti government fended off demands from its own Shi'a population for increased political representation. It deteriorated further as the 1980–8 Iran/Iraq war ran its course and Kuwait backed Iraq in various ways. Meanwhile, Kuwait's business dealings in and with Iraq continued throughout the 1980s, including government loans for the war effort.

Table 10.2 Top two suppliers of imports to Kuwait, 1983–99

Year	*First (% share)*	*Second (% share)*
1984	Japan 20.1	France 11.0
1985	Japan 26.7	USA 9.6
1986	Japan 24.0	USA 12.8
1987	Japan 19.6	USA 11.6
1988	Japan 12.9	USA 12.2
1989	USA 14.6	Japan 11.4
1990	Japan 11.6	USA 11.1
1991	USA 34.8	Japan 12.4
1992	USA 25.0	Japan 14.4
1993	USA 14.8	Japan 12.6
1994	USA 14.5	Japan 11.7
1995	USA 16.6	Japan 12.1
1996	USA 16.3	Japan 12.0
1997	USA 22.2	Japan 15.1
1998	NA	NA
1999	USA 15.4	Japan 10.2

Sources: EIU, Economist Intelligence Unit Profile (1991–2: 9, 1995–6: 11), Country Report (1995 (4): 3, 1996 (4): 5, 1997 (4): 5, 1998 (4): 5, 1999 (4): 5, 2001 (3): 5).

2.3 The drawing of internal economic boundaries

The advent of the oil economy after the Second World War led to the redrawing of internal economic boundaries and the reconstruction of economic, political, and social pacts.[5] The ruling family negotiated with British and American oil companies to receive all of the royalties into its own hands, making the Al-Sabah financially independent of, and politically superior to, the other elite families, and enabling them to create a redistributive patronage system with the emir at the hub. Upon Kuwait's independence from Britain in 1961, the emir decreed the 'State of Kuwait' to be an hereditary emirate, directed the drawing up of a constitution, and agreed to an elected national assembly that would meet and disband at his discretion.

In exchange for acquiescence to these new realities, the Al-Sabah guaranteed the privileged economic status of their now-dependent clients, the old-merchant families, by creating new methods of capital accumulation – for example, through land transfers and contracts with the government – and by preserving a residual vitality for the now-truncated private-sector economy operating in the shadow of the oil industry. In 1980, at the peak of the oil boom, non-oil activities accounted for just 29 per cent of GDP (NBK, EFQ 1982, 2: 7). The non-Kuwaiti part of the population burgeoned as foreign workers were called upon to fill the growing need for professional and other types of modern labour.

In the 1950s, the ruling family began to distribute shares of its rentier income beyond the elite class to the citizens at large, through public works and the establishment of welfare-state institutions. Between 1954 and 1986, modern infrastructure was developed, including a deepwater port, roadways, communication systems, and public administration. Economic security for Kuwaiti citizens was guaranteed through employment in the public sector, to the extent that, by the early 1980s, wages and salaries constituted 40 per cent of government expenditures. Human services provision expanded broadly to include free education and health care, each of which absorbed about 10 per cent of government expenditures in the 1980s, as well as subsidies for housing, utilities, telephone service, basic food items, and fuels. During this period, expatriates also benefited from a number of these social goods, for example, food and utility subsidies.

Kuwaiti society became more complexly and strictly stratified after the advent of oil wealth. The ruling family sat at the apex, its many members appointed to the top political posts. Just below them was the layer of elite old-merchant families, who staffed the upper reaches of the public sector and pursued private wealth in the economic niches left to them, for example, in real estate, construction, and the import trade. The next layer down was that of the non-elite voting citizens, originally defined as those males whose ancestors had been registered as residents in 1921, mainly descendants of pearl divers, shipbuilders, seamen, and other common folk of the pre-oil era. The ranks of this layer were gradually and selectively enlarged by emiri decree to include naturalized tribal groups loyal to the Al-Sabah who were settled at public expense, with free housing and guaranteed employment. The next layer down were the Shi'a part of the population, mainly of Iranian descent, to whom the emir decreed citizenship rights in order to balance off other political forces in the National Assembly. Next came the 'Bidoon', stateless long-term Kuwaiti residents whose ancestors were presumed not to have been present in 1921.

The expatriate communities were layered by longevity of residence and the nature of their contributions to building the modern Kuwaiti economy. Palestinians were the best established, largest, and economically most significant community.[6] Estimates of the number of Palestinian residents ranged from 350,000 to 500,000, mostly refugee families who had lived in Kuwait as foreign residents for much of their lives and who served as the backbone of the professional middle class and civil service (Crystal 1992: 129–132). Next came Iraqis, Egyptians, and other Arabs, followed by non-Arab unskilled labour at the bottom. Virtually every dimension of the modern Kuwaiti economy, from its financial institutions to its custodial services, was built and catered by expatriates. However, few were offered citizenship and there was little social mobility or intermarriage between the Kuwaitis and non-Kuwaitis, or between the layers of the social hierarchy overall.[7]

The population of Kuwait more than doubled between 1975 and 1990, from 995,000 to 2,130,000. In the first decade, growth came disproportionately from the resident expatriates, whose share of total population rose from 52.5 per cent in 1974 to a peak of 72.3 per cent in 1985. The non-Kuwaiti component of the labour force grew from 70 per cent in 1975 to a peak of 85 per cent in 1990. Until the late 1980s, Arabs made up the majority of the expatriate community, working at all levels in the occupational structure.

By the mid-1980s, the idea began to percolate among the power elite that expatriates, especially political activists, were threatening Kuwait's culture, societal integrity, and political system. The fact that the infrastructure and institutions of a modern society were now fully in place enabled this elite to argue, at least in theory, that Kuwaitis could now replace expatriates in the professional echelons of the occupational structure.[8] A new nationalistic policy was formulated by the Ministry of Social Affairs and Labour in 1983, promoting the 'Kuwaitization' of employment, dispensing with as much skilled and educated expatriate labour as possible, and initiating a series of legal changes that would make it more difficult for expatriate workers to renew their contracts or to bring their families (NBK: EFQ 1982, 2: 8, EFQ 1982, 4: 10, EFB 1984, 7: 8, EFB 1985, 8: 6, 32, EIU 1995–6: 9, 13).

The new policy was directed primarily towards the Arab expatriates and encouraged the recruitment of more non-Arab workers in the mid-1980s. Labourers from Korea and India, for example, took up low-skill, low-pay jobs in construction and services on limited-term contracts. By 1990, prior to any hint of invasion by Iraq, the balance had already been consciously shifted so that Arabs constituted less than 50 per cent of the expatriate labour force, the latter now increasingly made up of single working-age non-Arab males whose only goal in Kuwait was to make, and send home, as much income as possible. Non-Arab female expatriates (also single and temporary) were concentrated in personal and home services, at the bottom of the social hierarchy.

3 Challenges to pre-1990 economic integrity

Attributing Kuwait's troubles to expatriate workers was a reflection of not only an outdated social structure and authoritarian political system, but also a series of seemingly irremediable economic problems. First, there was a sharp reversal of international fortune. The worldwide recessions of 1980–2, the shift towards alternative fuels, and conservation in the oil-consuming countries, and the entry into the oil market of more non-OPEC suppliers, all contributed to a fall in the demand for OPEC oil. Kuwait's 'real' oil revenues (nominal revenues deflated by an import price index) were 13 per cent lower in 1982 than in 1974. Oil prices fell sharply again in 1986 and in 1988, and Kuwait's oil revenues ended in 1988 at 58 per cent of their 1974 value (Al-Yousuf 1990: 6–8). Economic growth in the 1980s was consequently erratic, as is shown in Figure 10.2, with real GDP per capita falling 12.5 per cent in 1985 alone and gross fixed capital formation slipping under 20 per cent of GDP by 1989 (EIU 1991–2: 9–10).

The sense of malaise was underpinned by the failure of the non-oil commodity producing sectors to grow rapidly. Part of this can be accounted for by the Dutch Disease hangover from the oil boom years, and part by the unresolved internal debt crisis created by the crash of the informal Souk al-Manakh stock market in 1982,[9] which undermined confidence in real private investment in the domestic economy (Looney 1992: 566–574).[10] Accordingly, non-oil manufacturing decreased from 3.1 per cent of GDP in 1976 to 2.6 per cent in 1984, and productivity growth stagnated. Indeed, excluding petroleum refining and a few essentially European 'model firms', real value added per worker *fell* from KD 2,836 in 1976 to KD 2,312 in 1984 (Al-Sabah 1988: 26).

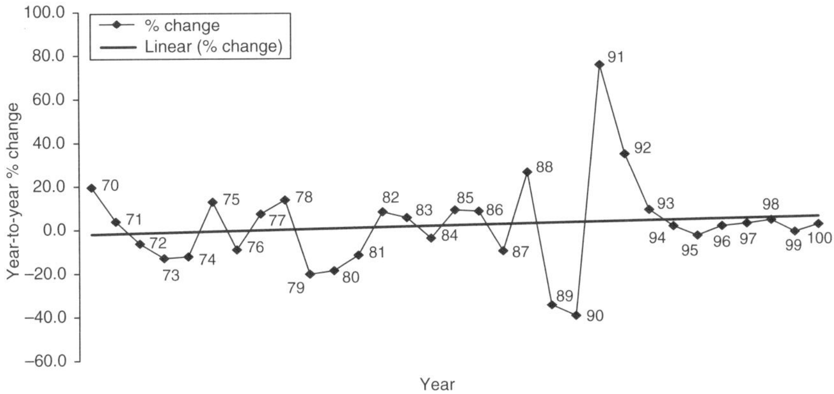

Figure 10.2 Growth rates of GDP, Kuwait, 1970–2001, % change from previous year, and linear trend.

Sources: IMF, *International Financial Statistics Yearbook* 2001: 623–33 and 1999: 573–4 for years 1970–89; *Economist Intelligence Unit* 1995 (4): 3, 1996 (4): 5, 1997 (4): 5, for years 1990–2; IMF, 'Kuwait, Country Report' 2001: 20, for years 1998–2000.

The Kuwait Investment Authority was obliged to liquidate some overseas assets in 1982, 1983, and 1984 in order to cover the shortfall in revenues from oil exports. By 1986, it had taken steps to rebuild that portfolio (NBK, EFB 1983, 5: 30, 1984, 7: 35, 1985, 8: 9), but not enough to withstand another liquidity crisis, now fed by the dead weight of un-collectible loans to other Arab countries (Al-Yousuf 1990: 18–22, 29–30). Iraq, in particular, received $13.2 billion in grants and loans from Kuwait during the war with Iran (Cordesman 1997: 8).

Confronting the vicissitudes of the 1980s, planners and consulting economists repeatedly proposed reform programmes intended to tackle Kuwait's 'structural problems' and to reduce its dependence on oil revenues. In 1985, an 'Economic Activation Committee' argued against building new extractive facilities. Instead, it proposed increasing capacity utilization and efficiency, and expanding and diversifying capital-intensive export industries spinning off from the oil sector (NBK, EFB 1985, 8: 4–5). The next 5-year plan (1985/6 to 1989/90) called for unprecedented public spending reform, bringing excess capacity into use, encouraging private investment, and strictly regulating expatriate labour.

In partial response, the government increased non-oil revenues modestly by imposing user fees on public services (drivers' licenses, vehicle registrations, garbage collection, medical care, education, utilities), and reduced public spending by raising domestic prices (i.e. lowering subsidies) for petroleum products and public housing rentals. These changes threw the burden of adjustment disproportionately onto the expatriate community, since other subsidies for citizens were retained. The treasury began for the first time to issue treasury bills (3-month) and treasury bonds (1–5 year) both to finance budget deficits (Al-Yousuf 1990: 29–30, EIU 1991–2: 8, 11) and to enable the Central Bank to more effectively manage

Table 10.3 Composition of non-oil GDP by type of ownership (in %), Kuwait, 1982–2000

	1982	*1988*	*1994*	*1998*	*1999*	*2000*
Public	23	40	44	44	44	44
Joint + private	77	60	56	56	56	56
Joint	10	5	7	11	11	12
Private	67	55	49	45	45	44
Total non-oil GDP	100	100	100	100	100	100
Non-oil GDP as % of total GDP	55.9	70.5	62.1	70.4	64.4	53.3

Source: National Bank of Kuwait (2002).

liquidity levels and avert crises (Abbas 2002). However, nothing was done to respond to the fundamental problems of lack of investment and productivity growth. As indicated in Table 10.3, the private sector's share of non-oil GDP decreased from 67 per cent in 1982 to 55 per cent in 1988, during a period in which oil revenues had been falling, and continued to decrease until the year 2000.

A third study was undertaken on behalf of the Kuwait Investment Authority in 1988 by a Harvard/MIT think tank posing alternative future scenarios for Kuwait, and serving as the basis for a programmatic document by the Planning Council (Higher Planning Council 1988). The study proposed shifting resources to favour productivity-enhancing, 'high value-added' ventures at home and abroad, such as financial services, education, health care, and design and engineering, all under the control of Kuwaiti citizens.

This study recommended fostering private entrepreneurial activity and shifting the government to more of an East Asian mode of operation, in which it would, for example, provide subsidies to Kuwaiti ventures on the 'reciprocity principle', that is, as rewards for demonstrated performance in productivity growth and export development (Al-Sabah 1988: 22–25, 30–32).[11] The document also mentioned regional economic integration as a desirable means for stimulating economic growth.

In this vision, Kuwait's non-oil exports would become competitive on world markets based on a comparative advantage in its 'human capital' portfolio. Skilled and educated Kuwaitis were to take charge of research and development and oversee the processes of productive labour, quality control, and marketing (Al-Sabah 1988: 2, 14, 27–29). The proposal played to Kuwait's nationalist fears and ambitions, and to the characteristic elitism of the ruling family and merchant class, by promising to reduce reliance not only on oil but also on expatriate labour, which, the report said, 'threatens to corrode Kuwait's cultural and social fabric' (Al-Sabah 1988: 2). Low value-added manufacturing, it stressed, would be done not in Kuwait but in overseas operations employing cheap foreign labour under Kuwaiti supervision (Al-Sabah 1988: 8–14, 19–20, 30–31).

Had these proposals been implemented with success, they would have altered the institutional framework just enough to sustain and fortify existing Kuwaiti socio-economic boundaries: to wit, to keep Kuwait's wealth and as much as possible of its income for the benefit of Kuwaiti citizens alone, to shift management and control into Kuwaiti hands, and to use foreign labour only when needed for menial tasks. The Harvard/MIT study clearly reflects the hostility towards, and fear of, non-Kuwaiti labour that was building during the years of economic decline in the 1980s – a sort of negative nationalism cultivated by the regime to consolidate its narrow political base in times of economic discontent (Ismael 1993: 156, 167).

The reduction in the Arab and professional components of the expatriate labour force was the only aspect of 'reform' actually undertaken. Unconstrained by the National Assembly, which the emir disbanded in 1986, the ruling family chose rather to intensify its pursuit of the course that had brought it wealth and success in the halcyon days prior to 1983. In violation of its OPEC quota, and in competition with other OPEC members similarly seeking to cheat on their agreement, it simply stepped up oil production, from June of 1989 until the invasion by Iraq in August 1990 (EIU 1991–2: 13).

4 Reconstruction and 'boundary adjustment' after 1991

The erosion of the premises underlying Kuwait's economic structure was underway long before the Iraqi invasion in August 1990. While there were equally deep socio-economic problems on the Iraqi side,[12] the emerging conflict was the expression, not the cause, of a shared and growing economic crisis. As devastating as the occupation and war were, liberation and reconstruction were to offer an unprecedented opportunity to Kuwait to address the economic roots of the problem. But this was to be a foregone opportunity.

The Iraqi occupation and the war for liberation caused widespread devastation, especially to infrastructure for communications, electricity-generation, and shipping, as well as directly to oil extraction and processing facilities.[13] An estimated 2 per cent of Kuwait's 100 billion barrel oil reserve went up in flames and up to $10 billion worth of total damage was inflicted (Chalk *et al.* 1997: 3). As GDP plunged by 35 per cent in 1990 and 40 per cent in 1991, the government liquidated $20 billion in assets from the GRF portfolio, indirectly borrowing from the RFFG under an emiri emergency decree. These funds were used to support the royal family and government in exile at Taif, Saudi Arabia, to pay for the war effort, to compensate Kuwaitis returning from abroad, and to finance reconstruction until reparations were forthcoming from Iraq. The fund also helped to compensate Kuwaiti citizens (but not others) who had endured the occupation. Wages of Kuwaiti citizens in the public sector doubled between 1989 and 1992, while those of expatriates in the private sector fell sharply (Mejren 1997: 43–52).

4.1 Stunning recovery – in the oil sector

Sovereignty was restored in February 1991 and the rapidity of recovery in the oil sector amazed observers, while financial support was postponed for other than the most basic infrastructure and for the revival of the private sector (MEED 1991a, 1992). By early 1993, crude oil production had returned to its pre-invasion level of 2 million barrels per day. By 1994, refinery capacity was also restored and the oil sector once again constituted 50 per cent of GDP, over 90 per cent of exports, and 75 per cent of government revenues.

Infrastructure projects in power, road transport, and water facilities were undertaken later in the 1990s. Even so, serious problems, such as plumbing systems and sewage disposal in Kuwait City, remained unsolved as of March 2002, while more glamorous and prestigious infrastructure projects were under discussion. These included the construction of a 'future zone' for cyber industries, a sports stadium, and possibly even a causeway across the Bay of Kuwait (EIU 2001: 11, 27–28).

After a massive surge of recovery-based GDP growth in 1992 and 1993 (by 75 and 34.2 per cent, respectively), economic growth returned to its erratic pre-war pattern (see Figure 10.2). As compared to its typical pre-conflict level (20 per cent) and its surge in 1992 (33.6 per cent), gross fixed investment fell sharply, to 12.6 per cent of GDP in 1999 (EIU 2001: 5, 1993–4: 12). Long-term growth of real GDP remained low, with a compounded average rate of 0.04 per cent per year for the 27-year period 1970–97 (calculated from IMF 2001a: 632–633).

4.2 Sectoral composition of economy

The sectoral composition of GDP also returned to its pattern of wide gyrations, fuelled by changes in the price of oil. As shown in Table 10.1, crude petroleum and natural gas fell from 44 per cent of GDP in 1982 to 27.5 per cent in 1988. Similarly, this sector accounted for 29.6 per cent of GDP in 1998 (low oil prices), 35.6 per cent in 1999 (rising oil prices), and 46.7 per cent in 2000 (the peak of the US-led business cycle and yet higher oil prices). This roller coaster pattern is testimony in itself to the unaltered dependence of the domestic economy on the oil sector, as crude oil and hydrocarbon products continued to account for about 90 per cent of exports (EIU 2001, 2: 5, 1999, 4: 5, 1998, 4: 5, 1997, 4: 5, 1996, 4: 5, 1995, 4: 3).

The share of GDP accounted for by non-oil economic activity continued to vary inversely with the price of oil, while most productive sectors remained weak in the late 1990s. Manufacturing (including hydrocarbon products) ranged from 10 to 12 per cent of GDP, lower than the late 1980s (see Table 10.1). The bulk of manufacturing is accounted for by oil- and gas-related industries (oil refining, petrochemicals, synthetic rubber, and plastics), but even that was lower in 1998–2000 than it had been in 1988 (see Table 10.1). The private sector share of non-oil GDP continued to shrink in the 1990s, even taking joint public/private ventures into consideration, from 77 per cent in 1982 to 56 per cent in 2000 (see Table 10.3).

As shown in Table 10.4, the average growth of GDP in current prices was 7.9 per cent per year from 1995 to 2000 with the productive sectors lagging behind. Financial services grew at an impressive rate of 22.1 per cent. This outcome was facilitated by generous government subsidies to debtors, which restored bank solvency by finally resolving the debt problem carried over from the 1980s (NBK 2002).

The second-fastest growth rate was in transport, communications, and storage, and the third, still above the overall average, was the manufacture of hydrocarbon products. These results were accounted for by a burst of growth of output and

Table 10.4 Growth of gross domestic product, Kuwait, 1995–2000, current prices (average % per year)

Crude petroleum and natural gas[a]	12.2
Manufacturing	6.6
Hydrocarbon products: chemical, rubber, and plastic	8.1
Construction	−0.9
Utilities: electricity, water, and gas[b]	23.1
Transport, communications, and storage	8.5
Services	
Wholesale and retail trade, hotels, and restaurants	1.5
Finance, real estate, and business services	8.9
Financial services	22.1
Community, social, and personal services	5
Personal and household	7.3
Agriculture, fishing, and livestock	2.9
Total Non-oil Sectors	5
GDP at purchasers' values	7.9

Source: National Bank of Kuwait (2002).

Notes

a Crude petroleum is the only subsector under the standard industrial classification category of 'mining and quarrying'.

b The fast rate of growth here is accounted for largely by rising prices (reducing subsidies).

auxiliary requirements from the new Equate petrochemicals plant after 1997. Construction also boomed from 1995 to 1997 as the Equate plant was built, then slumped again, averaging negative growth for the 1995–2000 period as a whole. Personal and household services grew at 7.3 per cent (just under the average), led mainly by the continued importation of servants (NBK 2002). Manufacturing as a whole, as well as real estate and non-financial business services (not shown separately in the Table 10.4), virtually all in the private sector, grew more slowly than the overall average. All available evidence indicates that productivity growth was generally negative, with value-added per worker in many industries significantly lower in 1998 than in 1989 (Mejren 1997: 46, Zind 2001: 167, 169).

4.3 *International income flows*

Despite strong and scandalous evidence of malfeasance and corruption in its main office in London and in Spain, where $5 billion went unaccountably missing (Crystal 1995: 176–177), the Kuwait Investment Authority again undertook to rebuild the depleted overseas funds. Kuwait's investment portfolio income grew during 1994–2000, until it reached its pre-Gulf War level and its customary large current-account surpluses were restored. This income enabled Kuwait's GNP to rise above its GDP by an average of 20 per cent again (see Figure 10.1) and contributed between 10 and 15 per cent of the government's revenue (Chalk *et al.* 1997: 5, EIU 2000, 3: 20, 2001, 2: 18–19).

However, three factors limited the spread of these benefits as of 2001. First, as seen in Figure 10.1, where net income flows account for the difference between GNP and GDP, portfolio revenues fluctuate directly with GDP – that is, with the international business cycle and thus with oil revenues – rather than compensating for declines. Second, of their total private wealth, valued at $172.5 billion in 2002, Kuwaiti citizens were holding $88.6 billion (more than half) in offshore investments, of which $59.8 billion were financial assets.[14] Third, the reduction in the number of the Arab expatriate population led to an outflow of both remittances and unrequited transfers as departing workers sold their belongings and liquidated their savings. The current expatriate population apparently spends less in Kuwait's domestic economy than did its predecessors, further constricting domestic consumption and savings. Reflecting these patterns, the 'current transfers: debit' component of Kuwait's current account, which had averaged $1.38 billion from the period 1985–9, rose to a record $5 billion in 1990 and a peak of $23,798 billion in 1991. It then fell back again to more normal levels, but still averaged over $1.7 billion for the rest of the decade (IMF 2001a: 633).

4.4 External boundary changes

Kuwait's alleged illegal extraction of oil from the Rumailah oil field was one motive for Iraq's invasion. Indeed, pre-conflict resource maps of Iraq and Kuwait show the southernmost tip of the Rumailah field just touching the Kuwaiti border, with no part of this oil field on the southern side of the border (see, e.g. Brawer 1988: 78, 84). However, in 1992, the United Nations Boundary Commission consented to Kuwait's request to move its border with Iraq more than 1850 feet to the north. This gave Kuwait unfettered access to the Rumailah oil field and the Umm Qasr area, where Iraq had built its naval base with access to the Gulf.[15] Control of the new border areas was reinforced by the expulsion of 1500 Iraqis living in the Umm Qasr zone and by the digging of a 130-mile-long trench (Spencer 1994: 87, Cordesman 1997: 13). Newer maps of Kuwaiti oil deposits now include an area called 'Ratqa' (one of the intended targets of Kuwait's oil-expansion programme), which is clearly the southernmost extension of the Rumailah field in Iraq (see Map 10.1).

Other border negotiations, with Saudi Arabia and Iran regarding the 'neutral zone' (see Map 10.1), also serve to consolidate Kuwaiti control over the north-western corner of the Gulf and to virtually eliminate Iraq's already constricted access to its deep waters (EIU 2000, 3: 15).[16] Recent prospecting for oil and natural gas on the island of Bubiyan in that same corner of the Gulf (where none was suspected to exist) was explicitly intended to affirm Kuwait's exclusive political claim here as well. These moves reinforce the ability of Kuwait and its US and British allies to finally and permanently deny Iraq's long-standing application to lease the islands of Bubiyan and Warba for construction of a deep-water port on the Gulf, another Iraqi ambition and bone of contention leading up to the invasion of 1990.

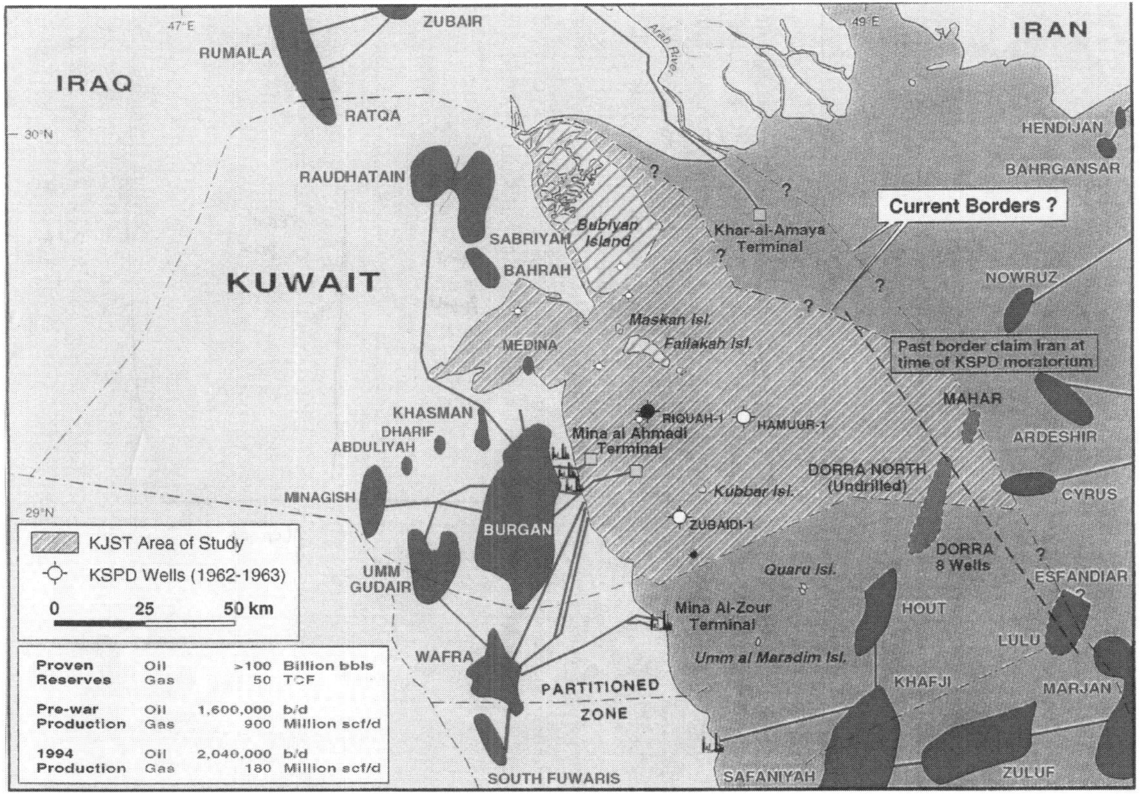

Map 10.1 Distribution of Kuwait's hydrocarbon resources.

Source: Unpublished map, courtesy of Kuwait Petroleum Company, March 2002.

4.5 Direction of trade and capital flows

Kuwait's trade with and financial ties to the United States were strengthened after 1991. While the Kuwaiti government declared its intention to otherwise diversify its trading partners in the direction of the Asian economies, especially in oil refining and petrochemicals marketing, the United States moved into second place as a purchaser of Kuwaiti exports, a shift from less than a 10 per cent share in the 1980s to a share of as high as 20 per cent in the 1990s (see Table 10.2). The United States also replaced Japan as the top supplier of imports to Kuwait, due partly to arms sales that continued throughout the decade.[17] Furthermore, after 1991, the Kuwaiti dinar was formally tied to a 'basket of currencies', predominantly the US dollar, and interest rates in Kuwait now fluctuate in tandem with US interest rates, thus tying Kuwaiti monetary policy directly to US monetary policy (EIU 2001: 9).

Throughout the 1990s and into 2001, on the advice of the IMF and World Bank (MEED 1993, 1994, 1996, *The Middle East* 1997), Kuwaiti officials proclaimed their desire to encourage foreign investment. The first step came in 1995 when the revived stock market was opened to foreign participants (MEED 1996, *The Middle East* 1997, EIU 2001: 22). The second step was to open the petrochemicals industry to foreign capital in 1997, when Union Carbide,[18] now merged into Dow Chemical, took a 40 per cent stake in the 5-year-old joint venture, Equate (EIU 2001, 2: 25–27). The next step would be to allow 100 per cent foreign ownership of firms based in Kuwait (except for oil extraction) and to reduce the top rate of taxation on foreign corporate profits from 55 to 25 per cent (EIU 2001: 20). Then foreign banks would establish branches in Kuwait and the Kuwait Investment Authority (KIA) would expand the scope for foreign capital in the firms under its umbrella (EIU 2001: 21).

4.6 Aggressive oil production and marketing with foreign capital

As of 2001, the Kuwait Petroleum Company (KPC) was undertaking a massive oil development programme, called 'Project Kuwait', at an estimated cost of US$ 7 billion. Its aim was to create 'spare capacity' in its northern oilfields, eventually to 5 or 6 million barrels per day. This is based on the rationale that Kuwait's hydrocarbon technology is 20 years behind its competitors and must improve its efficiency quickly in order to raise production (from about 2 million barrels per day in early 2002 to 3 million barrels per day by 2005). KPC is thus keen to attract foreign capital for participation in this project,[19] which may also help to secure foreign governments' commitment to defending Kuwait and its new borders against any future incursions by Iraq (EIU 2001, 2: 8). European and US multinational energy corporations want to invest directly in 'Project Kuwait' and share profits-per-barrel, rather than conform to the constrictions of service contracts. As of March 2002, a resistant National Assembly had not yet ratified the legal changes needed to make this possible.

4.7 Confronting internal boundaries

Kuwait's economic advisers had long warned that secular stagnation or decline in oil revenues would force the state to renege on its part in the social contract to provide complete welfare for its citizens in exchange for their political quiescence. Nevertheless, the state unilaterally re-established the pre-conflict power-for-welfare trade-off and postponed economic reform that would underpin demands for greater political participation after liberation. Financing this choice was to be made possible primarily from yet higher oil production and higher OPEC quotas for oil exports. More finance was to come from sales to the private sector of public assets held by the KIA, and from the fiscal changes entailed in structural adjustment (MEED 1991a, *The Middle East* 1999).

Although its sizeable capital surpluses make it unlike other countries the IMF advises, the Kuwaiti government agreed in 2001 to undertake domestic 'structural adjustment' reforms similar to those recommended by the IMF to economies facing balance-of-payments or debt-service problems. If the recommended policies were followed, they would reduce the material privileges provided to the Kuwaiti citizenry by the state for the first time since the 1950s. The fiscal components of these policies include curbing the rate of growth of government spending, raising fees for services like medical care and the prices of utilities, reducing public-sector wages and salaries in real terms, reducing subsidies on rents paid by Kuwaiti citizens on publicly owned housing, and possibly introducing an income tax (*The Middle East* 1997, EIU 2001: 9). Aggregate spending on wages and salaries was slated to rise just 2.8 per cent in 2001/2, lower than the 4.5 per cent rate at which Kuwaiti citizens had been entering public employment in prior years (EIU 2001: 20).

Meanwhile, the Kuwaiti labour force has been growing apace. Women constituted 36 per cent of the Kuwaiti labour force by 2001, up from 31 per cent in 1994 (Al-Dàaas 2002: 144). About 10,000 Kuwaiti citizens (both male and female) were entering the labour force annually. This number was clearly too high to be absorbed efficiently into the public sector despite high expectations that the government would hire them. One reason was that the education system was not preparing these entrants with training appropriate to the needs of the private sector.[20] A second reason was many entrants refused to take jobs in the private sector without the incentives of job security, higher salaries, and greater benefits provided by the public sector. The World Bank's advice was to abandon the traditional governmental commitment to furnish jobs to all citizens, and to introduce new education, compensation, and corporate tax policies to shift incentives to private sector employment generation (MEED 1993, 1994, *The Middle East* 1997, 1999, EIU 2001: 8). Similarly, the IMF advised Kuwait to deregulate and desegment the labour market, that is, to harmonize the incentive structure between the public and private sectors (Chalk *et al.* 1997: 7). The desired changes had not been attained as of 2001, when 92.8 per cent of Kuwaitis, and just 8.6 per cent of non-Kuwaitis, were employed in the public sector (Al-Dàaas 2002: 144).

The total population of Kuwait had returned to about 2.2 million by the year 2000, while the composition of the population, the ethnic balance of the labour force and its social and occupational structure had changed marginally. The non-Kuwaiti component of the labour force was 83 per cent in 1994, despite the mass exodus during the Gulf crisis of 1990–1, and over 81 per cent in 2001 despite continued calls for Kuwaitization (EIU 1995–6: 9, 13, EIU 2000, 4: 17, 2001: 5).[21] The numerical majority were contract workers from South and East Asia, mostly single males, concentrated in low-skill, low-pay jobs in construction and services.

The working conditions of expatriate labourers have been roundly criticized, including by the US Labour Department (*Foreign Labour Trends* 1995). As of the mid 1990s, non-Kuwaiti employees of Kuwaiti firms and households were working an average of 51 h per week, as compared to an average Kuwaiti's of 39 h. There was no legal minimum wage in the private sector, where over 90 per cent of non-Kuwaitis are employed, as compared to the Kuwaiti bachelor's minimum monthly KD 226 (US$774) and the Kuwaiti married man's minimum monthly of KD 301 (US$1,031) in the public sector. Some male expatriate workers, such as in the oil sector, have protections like mandatory employer-provided health care and the right to join a union as a non-voting member after 5 years of residence in Kuwait. But no labour laws protect most workers, including the 100,000 female domestic servants.

4.8 Perpetual calls for economic reform

IMF and World Bank proposals for shrinking the government, liberalization, and privatization (e.g. IMF 2001b) have been elaborated by the privately owned National Bank of Kuwait (Al Harun 1999), various economists (e.g. Behbehani 1999), and by some forces in the parliament (Committee on Economic and Financial Affairs 1996, Amuzegar 1999: 83–84). In response, the KIA sold off parts of some of the firms it owns, mainly through issuing shares tradable on the stock market, and created an agency to promote small and medium-sized entrepreneurial ventures. The results remained marginal as of 2002 (*The Middle East* 1999, Al-Tamimi 2002).

Documents from the Higher Planning Council produced in 1994 reiterated the need to diversify the economy and make it more efficient, to encourage private sector and human resource development, to introduce investment in new technology, and to decrease the role of the government as service provider (Higher Planning Council 1994a,b). All of these proposed changes in the 1990s are, as in the 1980s, intended for Kuwaiti citizens only, as conference after conference and paper after paper by Kuwaiti economists criticized the expatriate-dependent labour market and stressed the objective of placing Kuwaitis in jobs in what is supposed to become a thriving private sector (e.g. Al-Salih 1996, Serageldine and Khurshid 1996, Behbehani 1999).

These planners and economists continued to put the onus on the expatriate labour force for Kuwait's poor economic performance, both macro and micro, and for threatening Kuwait's social and cultural identity. Whereas the Palestinian and other expatriate communities were considered a societal threat in the 1980s because they had been too successful, the expatriate communities of the 1990s are condemned for not being successful enough. Many Kuwaiti economists have attributed the weakness of overall domestic demand for housing and manufactured goods to the expatriate community's coming to Kuwait only to work and save, sending the bulk of their earnings to their home countries. They have also attributed the long-term fall in the level of productivity to the generally poor educational and skill levels of this cohort of expatriate workers. Attributing these defects to the workers themselves rather than the policies that created this situation, these economists reiterate the familiar call to 'Kuwaitize' jobs and to reduce the proportion of expatriates in both the workforce and the population at large.

5 Redefining the problem and the solution

Kuwait's economic dilemma revolves around the need to diversify its economy away from oil exportation without losing its cultural and social integrity: the policies pursued in the decade after liberation neither achieved these goals nor restored sustainable economic growth. The resolution of this dilemma may require a paradigm shift in economic thinking, involving a fundamental redefinition of external and internal economic boundaries. Externally, a return to the model of Kuwait's more diversified pre-oil economy, and a more balanced and healthy relationship to the world economy than it has experienced in the 1991–2001 decade, may entail deeper and more extensive regional economic integration than the Gulf Cooperation Council (GCC) can provide.[22] Internally, the key to promoting development on both the demand and supply sides of the domestic growth equation, and indeed securing Kuwait's integrity, may entail the Kuwaitization of persons rather than jobs, that is, a reversal of the policy towards expatriate labour extant since the mid-1980s.

Such a shift in economic thinking may also require the release of political constraints. These constraints emanate from a weak and divided National Assembly and from an arcane ruling regime with a narrow vision of Kuwait's future with itself perpetually at the helm. The ruling family seeks to retain power by fostering Kuwait's oil-dependent status as a US protégé and by smothering the opposition among its citizenry with the gilded-cage privileges of the 'social contract'. This dual strategy requires non-citizen labour to continue its role as the inferior, despised, and excluded 'other'. It entails the reinforcement of the economic boundaries of a socially and politically insular Kuwait, indefinitely postponing pursuit of the goal of sustainable development.

Notes

1 This and the following three paragraphs are from Ismael (1993: Chapters 1–4) and Crystal (1995: Chapters 1–4).

2 It was endogamous in the sense that when Kuwaiti men married Kuwaiti women, those women were chosen within the circle of elite families. However, it was common then, and remains so to the present, that Kuwaiti men who travelled abroad for their work or

education often took foreign wives, whom they brought back with them and integrated into their families and social life.

3 Useful references on this complex set of relationships are: Stork (1989: 31–33), Crystal (1992: 39–44), Ismael (1993: 69–71), and Findlay (1994: 34–43).

4 In the years after its founding in 1981, the members of the GCC agreed to set common external tariffs of a minimum of 4 per cent to a maximum of 20 per cent. However, there were no enforcement mechanisms and countries continued to set their own policy (Al Saqaa 1999).

5 This and the following three paragraphs are from Ismael (1993: Chapters 1–4), Crystal (1995: Chapters 1–4), and Cordesman (1997: Chapter 2).

6 The story of the work and lives of Palestinians in Kuwait has been documented by Ghabra (1987), especially pages 39–52.

7 For example, a 1982 study of 526 heads of households found that 48 per cent were married to relatives and over three-fourths of those to their first cousins (as cited in Al-Mughni 2001: 16). Even in 2001, 'the whole structure of the state is still based on kinship, along the lines of the tribal system of *ashira*.... Kinship loyalty is particularly important for women of the elite classes: their class privileges will survive only as long as their kinship organization' (Al-Mughni 2001: 188).

8 The test of this rationale came after liberation. One source comments, 'the government's ability to handle new project work is anyway in doubt. The loss of expatriate staff – Palestinians, Jordanians, and Iraqis in particular – has left gaping holes in the bureaucracy... Many have little faith in the ability of Kuwaitis themselves to take over the work' (MEED 1992: 2).

9 The government winked as this unofficial market boomed in the heady days of the late 1970s to early 1980s. Because it was based on a pyramidal structure of debt and post-dated checks (rivalling Ponzi-type booms in the West), it collapsed when incomes fell and creditors started calling in payment. The debt and bankruptcy mess undermined the solvency of the banking sector as well and was not resolved until the government bought up the worthless debt instruments from its hapless citizens in the mid-1990s as part of 'reconstruction'.

10 Other factors may have been poor micro-planning by individual firms, overestimating appropriate capacity given limited market size, and the failure of communication and coordination to link complementary industries and to avoid duplication both within Kuwait and in the GCC countries as a group (Looney 1992: 574).

11 Two of the researchers involved in the project, Lance Taylor and Alice Amsden, are well known for their critique of the IMF/World Bank formula and their analyses of the success of the various East Asian development strategies.

12 On Iraq, see Chaudhry (1991).

13 One source suggests that the damage was less than was feared and that the recovery was remarkably rapid (MEED 1991a).

14 Estimate by Azar-Khoury (2002). Another source estimates that Kuwaiti citizens hold \$100 billion in overseas investments (EIU 2001, 2: 20).

15 After the Shatt al-Arab waterway was rendered non-navigable by deposits of silt and explosives during the war with Iran, Iraq built up the connections from Basra to Al-Zubayr to Umm Qasr and linked the naval base at Umm Qasr to the Gulf with a canal (Cordesman 1997: 11–13).

16 Kuwait and Saudi Arabia have negotiated a formal northern border for the neutral zone they jointly control in the Gulf waters east of Kuwait, with Saudi Arabia ceding sovereignty over two islands in the zone to Kuwait. The agreement also entails continued sharing of the extraction of oil and gas between the two countries. This northern border runs along the group of islands around Failaka northeast of Kuwait City. Kuwait has taken up negotiations with Iran on the eastern border of the Neutral Zone. Iraq protested, to no avail, its exclusion from all of these negotiations (EIU 2000, 3: 15).

17 In 2001, Kuwait and the United States signed a new 10-year defence agreement, which keeps 4,500 US troops and US and UK air bases in Kuwait. Kuwait spent $3.3 billion on the military in 1999 (a billion more than had been budgeted) and planned another $2.6 billion worth of military spending in 2000. According to EIU (2001: 8, 17), on a per capita basis, Kuwait's spending, at US$1,440, is almost as high as Israel's, at US$1,465.

18 The author inquired of Kuwaiti Equate managers about their view of Union Carbide's safety record, given the Bhopal disaster. They assured her that Dow would not let such a thing happen in Kuwait.

19 KPC's plans conform to the US energy strategy put forth in the Cheney Report. The report commends Kuwait, among other Arab producers, for having begun to open her energy sector to foreign investment and recommends that the US President support more initiatives in this direction (Cheney 2001: 8.4–8.5).

20 The deficits in the education system were repeatedly brought to the author's attention, for example, by one of the main authors of State of Kuwait, Ministry of Planning, 2001. She argued that all other economic reforms hinged on revamping the educational system, if Kuwaiti citizens were ever to run the country themselves, and bemoaned the failure of the regime and the National Assembly to take the plan seriously (anonymous, interview February 2002).

21 This was a major theme of papers given at conferences organized by the Kuwait Economic Society and published in its journal, *Economic Journal of Kuwait*, in the 1990s.

22 One sign of a possible move in this direction is Kuwait's growing economic relationship with the Islamic Republic of Iran, presumably with US approval, as a bulwark against Iraq. Iran has access to the free zone at Shuweikh Port in Medinat al-Kuwait, and its exports to Kuwait increased by a factor of about 10 in the 5 years after liberation (Cordesman 1997: 14). As of March 2002, Kuwait was negotiating with this former rank enemy over offshore oil and gas rights and the supply of natural gas and water to Kuwait via underwater pipelines, pointedly bypassing Iraq (EIU 2000, 3: 15, 2001, 2: 18). The two countries were also talking of a cross-Gulf rail link. More serious regional integration would be non-viable without the participation of Iraq, which fits with the US goal of replacing Saddam Hussein with a more compliant regime (Fouad 2002: 10).

References

Abbas, H. (2002) Interview, 4 March 2002. (Former Governor of the Central Bank of Kuwait.)

Al-Dàaas, À. À. (2002) 'Performance of the Kuwaiti economy in the year 2001' ('ida' al-iqtisad al-kuwaiti liàam 2001), *Economic Journal of Kuwait* (*majallat al-kuwait al-iqtisadiyya*), 6(12): 109–146.

Al-Harun, A. R. (1999) 'The development role for the private sector in Kuwait in the coming century' (al-dor al-tanmuwi li'l-qitaà al-khas fii al-kuwait fii al-qarn al-qadim), Kuwait Economic Society conference papers, pp. 197–213.

Al-Mughni, H. (2001) *Women in Kuwait, the Politics of Gender*, London: Saqi Books.

Al-Sabah, M. (1988) *Study of the Kuwait Economy: Summary*, vol. 1, Cambridge, MA: CMT International, Inc., and Kuwait Institute of Scientific Research.

Al-Salih, À. G. (1996) 'Population structure and the crisis of employment of the labour force in Kuwait' (al-tarkibah al-sukaniyyah waazmat tauthif al-'amalah fi'il-kuwait), *Economic Journal of Kuwait* (*majallat al-kuwait al-iqtisadiyya*), (1): 35–50.

Al-Saqaa, M. (1999) 'The experiment of the Gulf Cooperation Council: a critical view' (tajribat al majlis at-tàaawun lil-khalij al-àrabi: nathara naqdiyya) *Economic Journal of Kuwait* (*majallat al-kuwait al-iqtisadiyya*), (7): 77–120.

Al-Tamimi, À. (2002) Interview 14 February. (Executive Director, Kuwait Economic Society.)

Al-Yousuf, A. (1990) *Kuwait and Saudi Arabia: from Prosperity to Retrenchment*, Oxford, UK: Oxford Institute for Energy Studies.

Amuzegar, J. (1999) *Managing the Oil Wealth: OPEC's Windfalls and Pitfalls*, London: I.B. Tauris.

Azar-Khoury, R. (2002) Interview, 7 February. (Director of Research, National Bank of Kuwait.)

Behbehani, D. (1999) 'The First Conference for Kuwaiti Businessmen "Welcoming the private sector to perform its economic and social development role" April 1998' (al-mu'tamer al-àwwal li rijal al-àmal al-kuwaitiyin 'ta'hil al-qita'a al-khas làdà dorih al-inma'i al-iqtisadi wa al-ijtimaài' 'ibril 1998), Kuwait Economic Society conference papers, pp. 123–136.

Brawer, M. (ed.) (1988) *Atlas of the Middle East*, New York: Macmillan Publishing Co.

Chalk, N. A., M. A. El-Erian, S. J. Fennell, A. P. Kireyev, and J. F. Wilson (1997) *Kuwait: from Reconstruction to Accumulation for Future Generations*, Washington DC: International Monetary Fund.

Chaudhry, K. A. (1991) 'On the way to market: economic liberalization and Iraq's invasion', *Middle East Report*, 170(21,3): 14–23.

Cheney, R. (2001) 'Strengthening global alliances: enhancing national energy security and international relationships', *National Energy Policy*, Chapter 8: 8.4–8.5. (Vice-President of the United States and Chair, National Energy Taskforce.)

Committee on Economic and Financial Affairs, Kuwait National Assembly (1996) 'Executive summary for the program to transfer property from the public sector to the private sector in the State of Kuwait' (al-mulakhkhas al-tanfeethi li birnamij naql al-milkiyya min al-qitaà al-àm illa al-qitàa al-khaass fii daulat al-kuwait), *Economic Journal of Kuwait*, 1(1): 69–91.

Cordesman, A. H. (1997) *Kuwait: Recovery and Security after the Gulf War*, Boulder, CO: Westview Press.

Crystal, J. (1992) *Kuwait, the Transformation of an Oil State*, Boulder, CO: Westview Press.

Crystal, J. (1995) *Oil and Politics in the Gulf, Rulers and Merchants in Kuwait and Qatar*, Cambridge, UK: Cambridge University Press.

Economist Intelligence Unit (EIU), *Country Report: Kuwait* (quarterly) 2001 (2) and (3); 2000 (3) and (4); 1999 (4); 1998 (4); 1997 (4); 1996 (4); 1995 (3) and (4), London.

Economist Intelligence Unit, *Country Profile: Kuwait* (annual) 1995–6; 1994–5; 1993–4; 1992–3; 1991–2, London.

Findlay, A. M. (1994) *The Arab World*, New York: Routledge.

Fouad, A. (2002) 'Kuwait looks to regain status as regional hub', *The Daily Star* (Beirut), 9 April, p. 10.

Ghabra, S. N. (1987) *Palestinians in Kuwait, the Family and the Politics of Survival*, Boulder, CO: Westview Press.

Higher Planning Council, Kuwait National Assembly (1988) 'Initial imagining of a strategy for the long-run sustainable development of the State of Kuwait' (at-tasawwur al-awwali li istrategiyyah at-tanmiyyah bi 'iyyadat al-madi li daulat al-kuwait), December, unpublished document.

Higher Planning Council, Kuwait National Assembly (1994a) 'Report on financial reform and its directions for development in the Kuwaiti economy' (taqrir bisha'an al-islah al-mali wa taujihat al-tanmiyyah fii al-iqtisad al-kuwaiti), February, unpublished document.

Higher Planning Council, Kuwait National Assembly (1994b) 'Report on the mechanics of implementation of financial and economic reform in the State of Kuwait' (taqrir bisha'an aaliyah tanfeeth al-islah al-mali wa al-iqtisad fi daulat al-kuwait), March, unpublished document.

IMF (1999, 2001a) *International Financial Statistics Yearbook*, Washington DC: International Monetary Fund.

IMF (2001b) *Kuwait: Country Report*, Washington DC: International Monetary Fund.

Ismael, J. S. (1993) *Kuwait: Dependency and Class in a Rentier State*, Gainesville, FL: University Press of Florida.

Looney, R. E. (1992) 'Employment creation in an oil-based economy: Kuwait', *Middle Eastern Studies*, 28(3): 565–576.

Mabro, R. (1999) 'The future of oil in the 21st century: implications for oil-exporting countries', Kuwait Economic Society conference papers, pp. 345–356.

Mejren, A. (1997) 'Labour productivity and wages in the Kuwaiti economy' (intajiyyat al-àmal wa al-'ujur fii al-iqtisad al-kuwaiti), Kuwait Economic Society conference papers, pp. 19–56.

The Middle East (1999) 'Kuwait: financial report (Special Report: Kuwait, Survey of the Kuwaiti Economy) [by] Moin Siddiqi', 287: 27(3) February.

The Middle East (1997) 'Mood of optimism amid economic revival (Kuwait)', 271: 25(4) October.

Middle East Economic Digest (MEED) (1991a) 'Rapid recovery heralds new challenges', 35(51): 12(1), 27 December.

MEED (1991b) 'Economy: a survey of times past (Special Report: Kuwait), 35(19): S19(1), 17 May.

MEED (1992) 'Putting it all back together (Kuwait's reconstruction)', 36(2): III(2), 17 January.

MEED (1993) 'Radical ideas for reforming the system (Kuwait's Economic Strategy)', 37(25): 18(2), 25 June.

MEED (1994) 'Reform tops the post-war agenda (Special Report: Kuwait)', 38(8): 9(3), 25 February.

MEED (1996) 'Taking time to change the tune (Kuwaiti economic policy)', 40(8): 10(3), 23 February.

National Bank of Kuwait (NBK), *Economic and Financial Quarterly* (EFQ), 1982 (2) and (4).

NBK, *Economic and Financial Bulletin* (EFB), 1985 (8) May; 1984 (7) November; 1983 (5) July.

NBK (2002) 'The private sector in Kuwait', *Economic Brief*, 20 February.

Seragaldine, I. and M. Khurshid (1996) 'Basic issues in the development of human resource policy in Kuwait' (qadaiya' assasiyyah fi at-tanmiyyah wa siyasat al-muwadir al-bashiriyyah fi al-kuwait), *Economic Journal of Kuwait* (*majallat al-kuwait al-iqtisadiyya*), (1): 11–34.

Spencer, W. (1994) *Global Studies: the Middle East*, 5th edn, Guildford, CT: The Dushkin Publishing Group, Inc.

State of Kuwait, Ministry of Planning (2001) *Designing the Development Plan for the State of Kuwait, 2001/2002–2005/2006* (proposed).

Stork, J. (1989) 'Class, State and Politics in Iraq', in Berberoglu, B. (ed.), *Power and Stability in the Middle East*, London: Zed Press, pp. 31–54.

United States Department of Labour, Bureau of International Labour Affairs (1994–1995) 'Kuwait', *Foreign Labour Trends*, Prepared by the American Embassy, Kuwait.

Zind, R. (2001) 'Wage structure, technology and productivity in Kuwait and other GCC member states', Kuwait Economic Society conference papers, pp. 159–197.

11 The redefinition of economic boundaries between Israel and the West Bank and Gaza Strip

Leila Farsakh

1 Introduction

Palestinian labour flows have played a key role in integrating the economies of the West Bank and Gaza Strip (WBGS) into Israel since the 1967 occupation. Between 1970 and 1993, Palestinian labour flows to Israel anchored the WBGS' dependence on Israeli goods and trade relations and tied the absorption of the Palestinian labour force to Israeli demand for Palestinian goods and services. Palestinian daily commuters, predominantly unskilled male labourers, represented one-third of the employed population and generated more than a quarter of the WBGS' GNP over most of this period. Their income helped finance the Palestinian trade deficit while at the same time allowing WBGS' per capita income to more than double between 1970 and 1992 (UNCTAD 1993, World Bank 1993, Arnon *et al.* 1997).

With the advent of the peace process, however, labour flows have no longer played the same integrating role. The number of Palestinian workers going to Israel dropped from a peak of 115,600 in 1992 to less than 36,000 in May 1996. After 1997, there was a rise in the recorded number of workers going to Israel and Israeli settlements on the WBGS, but labour flows became highly volatile. In the most recent period since the eruption of the Al-Aqsa Intifada on 29 September 2000, the periodic closures imposed on the Palestinian territories have brought a halt to all movement of labour and goods between Israel and WBGS. Some authors have argued that the role of labour flows in integrating the Palestinian economy with Israel is over, given the political turmoil in the area and the current drop in Israeli demand for Palestinian workers (Arnon *et al.* 1997, Amir 2000).

This chapter maintains that Palestinian employment in the Israeli economy is not over, even if it has changed in form and content since 1993. It argues that Palestinian labour migration continues to be a function of basic economic factors that are, however, conditioned by an Israeli policy of territorial appropriation. Trends in Palestinian labour flows over the past eight years reveal, in particular, a differential process of redefinition of territorial and economic boundaries between Israel *and* the WBGS. In the latter case, labour links between the Gaza Strip and Israel indicate that the two economies are separating, rather than integrating as in the pre-1992 period. In the former, West Bank workers continue to be employed in Israel and on illegal Israeli settlements built in the West Bank, thereby cementing the incorporation of parts of the Palestinian territories into the Israeli State. This process of territorial appropriation and redefinition, which is most evidently manifested in Israel's closure policy and the growth of construction in illegal Israeli settlements in the WBGS, is in violation of the Geneva Convention governing behaviour of an occupying power.[1] It is made possible, in part, via a reliance on Palestinian labour.

2 Integration or separation: Israel and the WBGS since 1993

The Oslo Peace Process initiated in 1993 promised to help the Palestinian economy reduce its 26-year-old dependency on Israel (Diwan and Shaban 1999, Astrup and Dessus 2001). The Economic Protocol (EP), which defines the nature of economic relations between Israel and the Palestinians within the framework of the Israeli–Palestinian Interim Agreement on the WBGS (Oslo II),[2] sought to alter old imbalances between the two economies by promising that 'both parties shall co-operate … to establish a sound economic base for (their) relations which will be governed in various economic spheres by the principles of mutual respect of each other's economic interests, reciprocity, equity and fairness' (EP, preamble).

However, the EP, as with the other parts of the Interim Agreement, did not seek to separate the WBGS from Israel. Rather, it sought to *modify* the nature of economic and territorial relations between Israel and the WBGS. The EP promised to enable the Palestinian economy to grow autonomously, but without clearly demarcating borders between it and Israel.[3]

The EP actually kept the two economies bound in a *de facto* customs union that allowed the free movement of capital and goods between the two areas. Such a customs union was believed to be beneficial to the Palestinian economy, since it permitted the WBGS to build on its 26-year-long trade relation with Israel while at the same time entitling the Palestinian economy to diversify some of its export and import sources to third parties (Kleiman 1994, Astrup and Dessus 2001).[4] Moreover, the agreement allowed for the establishment of a Palestinian National Authority (PNA). This representative authority became responsible for defining Palestinian economic strategy.

Additionally, the EP promised to 'maintain the normality of labour movement between Israel and the WBGS', which was considered to be central to the successful growth of the Palestinian economy, especially in the early stages of its expansion (Kleiman 1994). It was hoped that the peace process would stimulate a rise in domestic investment and industrial growth, an influx of foreign capital and a growth in trade, and thereby cause a rise in local employment that would help reduce the reliance on the Israeli labour market. It was also hoped that a flow of Palestinian labour-intensive goods would eventually replace the flow of workers to Israel (Diwan and Shaban 1999, Arnon and Weinblatt 2001). Essentially, the EP sought to change the pattern of integration between Israel and the WBGS by promising to allow expanded trade links to replace labour ties.

However, the economic record of the past 8 years reveals that the Palestinian economy has failed to grow either steadily or autonomously. It also shows that the WBGS and Israeli economies are separating rather than integrating in this post-Oslo period. Per capita GDP grew by over 6 per cent per annum in Israel between 1992 and 1995 and unemployment rates were lower than 9 per cent in 1996 (Bank of Israel 1999). In the WBGS, by contrast, per capita GNP fell by 15 per cent between 1992 and 1996, and unemployment reached a high of 28.3 per cent in mid-1996 (Diwan and Shaban 1999). GDP growth was negative in 1995 and 1996,[5] and while it recovered after 1997, it remained volatile and a function of Israeli closure policy (IMF 2001). Meanwhile, the WBGS' attempts to integrate into the regional or global economy bore limited results, as trade with Israel still provided a market for 96 per cent of Palestinian exports and a source of 76 per cent of imports in 1998 (Astrup and Dessus 2001). Yet, Palestinian exports to Israel remained volatile and small,[6] growing by less than 0.3 per cent between 1998 and 1999 (UNSCO 2000a). The hope that the export of labour-intensive goods will replace the need to export labour has not been realized. Economic development trends over the past 8 years reveal that trade links have not overtaken the importance of labour flows.

3 Palestinian labour flows to Israel, 1993–2000

Palestinian employment trends in Israel have undergone five major developments since 1993. First, Palestinian labour flows have become erratic. In contrast to the pre-1992 period when labour flows grew steadily (see Table 11.1), the number of workers going to Israel fell from a total of 115,600 workers in 1992 to less than 62,000 in 1996. After 1997, flows started to increase again and overtook the peak touched in 1992, reaching a total of 145,000 workers in mid-2000. Yet, flows remained volatile. By March 2001, total numbers had fallen again to less than 55,000 workers (World Bank 2001).

Second, the Gaza Strip could no longer rely on the Israeli labour market to absorb its labour force, as it did before 1993. Since the signing of the peace process, the Israeli labour market has relied increasingly on West Bank, rather than on Gaza Strip, workers. The Israeli labour market absorbed on average less than 12 per cent of the total Gaza Strip active labour force between 1995 and 2000, compared to 38–45 per cent before 1993 (see Table 11.1). The West Bank, by contrast, still exported 17–25 per cent of its labour force to Israel between 1995 and 1999 (compared with 23–33 per cent in the pre-Oslo period). In mid-2000, a total of 29,600 Gaza Strip workers were employed in Israel, which is close to the total number recorded before 1980. The number of West Bankers was in the range of 116,000 workers in mid-2000 (Table 11.1 and Figure 11.1).

Third, access to Israel has become more restricted and difficult, but more so for Gaza Strip workers than West Bankers. Since the 1970s, Palestinian labour flows to Israel have consisted of both legal and illegal workers.[7] Despite Israel's attempt to regulate all Palestinian workers employed in its economy, 55–70 per cent of all workers were employed illegally up until the late 1980s (Abu-Shokor 1987, World

Table 11.1 Palestinians employed in the WBGS by location of employment (in thousands and %)

	WB workers employed in				*Employed GS workers in*				*Total WBGS*			
	Domestic	*Israel*	*Total*	*% in Israel*	*Domestic*	*Israel*	*Total*	*% in Israel*	*Domestic*	*Israel*	*Total*	*% in Israel*
Yearly averages per period												
1970–3	92.3	28.5	120.8	23.3	49.0	13.6	62.5	21.2	141.3	42.0	183.3	22.6
1974–80	93.3	38.9	132.3	29.4	47.4	29.7	77.1	38.4	140.8	68.6	209.4	32.7
1980–7	103.8	48.9	152.8	31.9	48.5	40.4	88.9	45.4	152.3	89.4	241.6	36.9
1988–93	127.6	62.8	190.4	33.0	65.9	40.6	106.4	38.4	193.5	103.3	296.8	34.9
Yearly averages												
1995	245.8	62.2	308.0	20.2	100.2	3.6	103.8	3.3	346.0	65.8	411.8	16.1
1996	262.7	52.3	315.0	16.6	110.4	10.0	120.4	8.1	373.1	62.3	435.4	14.2
1997	282.6	68.4	351.0	19.5	108.1	14.2	122.3	11.0	390.7	82.6	473.3	17.1
1998	304.0	96.0	400.0	24.0	124.8	24.0	148.8	16.2	428.8	120.0	548.8	21.8
1999	309.7	108.3	418.0	25.9	143.8	26.7	170.5	15.7	453.6	135.0	588.6	22.8
2000	351.1	115.8	466.9	25.0	161.9	29.6	191.5	15.4	513.0	145.4	658.4	22.3
1995–2000	292.7	83.8	376.5	21.9	124.2	17.9	145.3	11.6	416.8	101.7	520.9	19.3

Sources: Calculated from ICBS, *statistical Abstract of Israel*, various issues; PCBS 2000, *Labour Force Survey*, various issues.

Notes

Figures for the West Bank exclude East Jerusalem between 1968 and 1993 and include it thereafter.

Figures refer to total employment (which includes the underemployed, but excludes the unemployed). Figures for 1994 are not available.

PCBS, Labour data refer to yearly averages, except for figures for 2000, which refer to July–September Labour Force Surveys (no. 18).

Figure 11.1 Share of workers employed in Israel in total employment for the WBGS, 1968–2000.

Source: ICBS, *Statistical Abstract of Israel*, PCBS, *Labour Force Surveys*, various issues.

Bank 1993). It was only after 1991, as Israel increased the restrictions on the entry of Palestinian workers into Israeli firms, that the share of legal workers – defined as labourers with work permits – reached 60 per cent of total labour flows. Yet, as can be seen in Table 11.2, Israel has been more successful in controlling the entry of Gaza Strip workers than of West Bank workers. Even after 1997, less than 40 per cent of West Bank workers employed in Israeli enterprises had a permit. In the case of workers from the Gaza Strip, *only* those with permits could work in Israel. Moreover, despite holding such a permit, the access of Gaza Strip workers to Israel was not guaranteed. As Table 11.2 shows, the number of Gaza Strip workers who actually worked in Israeli firms was lower than the number of permits given to workers.

Fourth, employment in illegal Israeli settlements built in the WBGS became important in this period.[8] Available figures on permits for work in Israeli establishments indicate that 30 per cent of permits given to West Bankers since 1994 have been for work in settlements (Table 11.2). In the Gaza Strip, fewer than 12 per cent of permits have been given for work in Israeli settlements and industrial zones. Unfortunately, no accurate data are available on the number of *illegal* workers employed in the settlements, as many workers conceal their employment in such illegal construction activity.[9] However, there are reasons to believe that the actual number of West Bank workers employed in settlements is higher than reported figures indicate and that it has continued to rise (Table 11.1, Figure 11.1). This is partly because Israeli regulations have made access to Israeli settlements far easier than access to Israel, as will be explained below. If we were to assume that one third of those workers are employed in settlements,[10] then an estimated total of 35,000 West Bank workers would have been employed in such illegal settlements in August 2000 compared with 81,000 in Israel.

Table 11.2 Palestinian workers with permits employed in Israel, in Israeli settlements in the WBGS, and in Israeli industrial zones, 1992–2001 (figures in thousands)

Year	*Average number of permits given to*					*Ratio of workers with permits to total workers*		
	West Bank workers	*of which employed in settl.*	*Gaza Strip workers*	*of which employed in settl.*	*WBGS*	*West Bank workers*	*Gaza Strip workers*	*Total WBGS workers*
1992					69.42			0.60
1994	26.20	4.1	25.7	1.3	51.90			
1995	26.80	8.70	17.30	1.30	44.10	0.43	4.81	0.67
1996	26.90	9.10	18.70	1.92	45.60	0.51	1.86	0.73
1997	26.86	7.72	23.59	2.50	50.45	0.39	1.66	0.61
1998	27.50	9.10	27.10	3.70	54.60	0.29	1.13	0.46
1999	27.60	9.50	29.20	3.90	56.80	0.25	1.09	0.42
2000	23.00	9.80	23.50	3.50	46.50	0.20	0.79	0.32
2001	2.10	n.a.	1.90	2.20	4.00	0.06	0.46	0.10

Sources: Israeli Employment Service, unpublished data (for 1992 and 1995, data on workers registered at the employment office); PCBS (2000), *Labour Force Survey Annual Report*, 1999. Ramallah; Palestinian Ministry of Labour, 2000, *Work Permits to Israel and Settlements*, Ramallah; UNSCO (2000b), *Labour Data Base on West Bank and Gaza Strip Work Permits to Israel, the Settlements and Industrial Zones*. Ramallah; UNSCO (2001), *Impact on the Palestinian economy of confrontation, mobility restriction and border closures, 1 October–31 January 2001*. Ramallah.

Notes

Figures refer to yearly averages, except for 2000 where they refer to mid-year numbers, and for 2001, which refer to the January 2001 data only.

Figures on permits for work in settlements refer also to permits for work in Israeli industrial zones.

Fifth, the characteristics of Palestinian workers employed in Israel and the settlements have changed over time. On the one hand, flows continue to be dominated by male, unskilled, and semi-skilled, workers. However, the average age of workers employed in Israel in 1999 was higher than in 1980. Between 1975 and 1987, over 42 per cent of WBGS workers in Israel were under the age of 24 (Farsakh 1998). By mid-2000, this share had dropped to less than 31.4 per cent for West Bank workers and 7 per cent for Gaza Strip workers (PML 2001). Yet, as can be seen in Table 11.3, workers in settlements are found to be younger, less educated and predominantly less skilled compared with workers in Israel. In terms of sectoral concentration, over 55 per cent of WBGS workers in 1998 and 2000 were employed in the Israeli construction sector, which includes construction beyond the Green Line as well as in the settlements (Table 11.3).

Table 11.3 Economic characteristics of WBGS workers employed in Israel compared with those employed on Israeli settlements in the West Bank (WB), 1998 and 2000

Distribution (%)	*1998*		*2000*	
	WBGS workers in Israel and settlements	*WB workers in settlements only*	*WBGS workers in Israel and settlements*	*WB workers in settlements only*
Age distribution				
15–24	29.9	40.2	24.9	43.4
25–34	26.4	38.5	24.0	34.6
35–44	23.6	14.8	23.3	17.7
45 and older	25.8	6.5	25.8	4.3
Years of schooling				
0–6	36.0	24.2	33.8	21.6
7–9	28.7	35.0	31.8	43.2
10–12	25.0	32.5	24.5	31.6
13	8.1	8.3	7.9	3.6
Sectoral distribution				
Agriculture	10.2	23.1	9.0	19.5
Industry	12.2	18.6	14.5	17.1
Construction	55.2	42.1	55.5	52.9
Services	22.4	16.2	21.0	10.5
Occupation				
Skilled	44.1	39.2	48.3	37.3
Unskilled	47.3	54.1	41.1	58.4

Sources: PCBS (2001), *Labour Force Survey*, no.18, 2000, at www.pcbs.org/english/labor/round18/lbr18_05.htm; lbr18_07.htm, lbr18_09.htm; lbr18_11.htm; PCBS (2001), *Selected data on West Bank workers in Israeli settlements*, unpublished data.

Notes

'Skilled workers' refers to those defined as craft workers and machine and plant operators (PCBS definition).

Data refers to July–September labour survey in 1998 and 2000.

4 The determinants of WBGS labour flows since 1993

The persistence and fluctuations of Palestinian labour flows over the interim period indicate that there are strong economic forces inducing people to move. These forces remain circumscribed by Israeli political considerations, though. Three factors in particular continue to determine the prospects for Palestinian employment in the Israeli economy. These include the nature of Palestinian labour supply and incentives to migrate, Israeli regulation of Palestinian labour mobility, and Israeli demand for Palestinian workers, particularly in the construction sector.

4.1 Palestinian labour supply and incentives to migrate

The incentives to seek employment out of the WBGS economy have remained strong, especially in view of the fact that the Palestinian labour force has been growing by over 4.1 per cent per annum since 1993 and is expected to grow by 4.4 per cent per annum over the next decade (IMF 2001). By end of 2000, a total labour force of 732,000 persons was reported to be working or seeking work, which is the equivalent of 45.2 per cent of the working age population (defined as those 15 years old and above). Labour participation rates have been particularly low, recorded at an average of 41.7 per cent in the Gaza Strip and 46.9 per cent in the West Bank (PCBS 2001c). This implies that a relatively small working force is sustaining a population growing at more than 5.1 per cent per annum, which is one of the highest population growth rates in the world today (IMF 2001).

The WBGS economy has also faced a significant unemployment problem since 1993. In contrast to the period between 1970 and 1993, when unemployment rates in the WBGS remained lower than 7 per cent (Farsakh 1998), unemployment rates in the post 1993 era have been between 15.1 and 37 per cent in the Gaza Strip and between 10.1 and 24.2 per cent in the West Bank (PCBS 2001b). The number of jobless workers increases particularly in years of intensive closures, especially in 1996, and after September 2000 (see Figure 11.2). Unemployment usually increases the incentive to seek a job outside the domestic economy (Harris and Todaro 1970, Massey *et al.* 1998). As can be seen from Figure 11.2, unemployment rates and levels of participation in the Israeli labour market are inversely related: they both depend on the level of access to Israel.

Figure 11.2 also indicates important differences between the Gaza Strip and the West Bank. It shows that unemployment rates in the Gaza Strip remain higher than the percentage of workers employed in the Israeli economy, which is another indication of the degree of separation taking place between the Gaza Strip and Israel. If we were to look at the situation in the West Bank, we find that unemployment rates have been typically lower than those reported in the Gaza Strip. They have also been lower than the share of the labour force employed in Israel, indicating a continuous trend of integration between the Israeli and the West Bank economies. Figure 11.2 highlights the fact that the Gaza Strip could not rely on the Israeli labour market to the same extent as the West Bank, post 1993.

The ability of the domestic WBGS economy to generate enough jobs to absorb its growing labour force, and thereby to reduce the incentives to migrate, has been

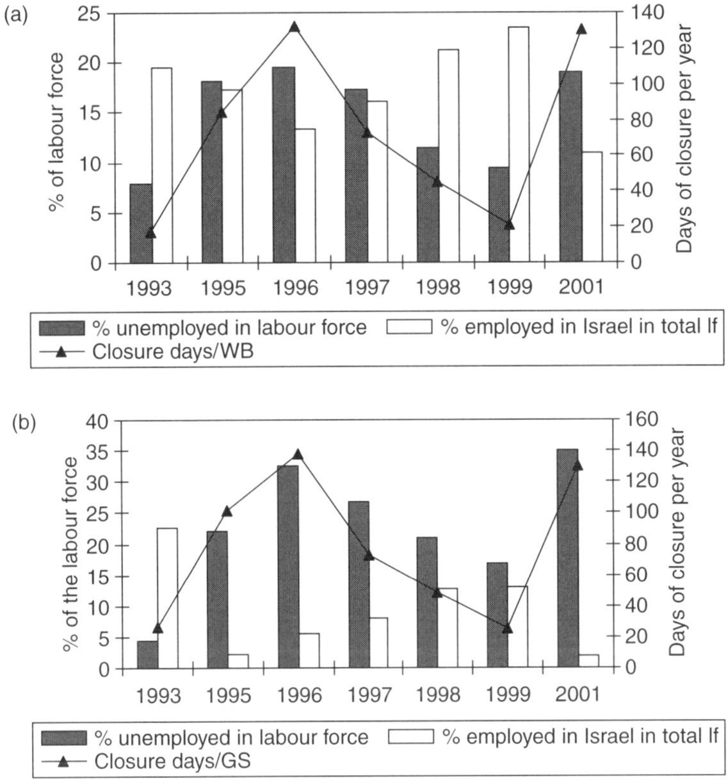

Figure 11.2 Share of unemployed and of workers in Israel in (a) total West Bank labour force and (b) total Gaza Strip labour force, 1993–2001.

Source: Calculated from Table 11.1, PCBS (2001b) and UNSCO (2000b).

Notes
The right axis refers to the number of days of closure per year. The left axis plots the percentage of those unemployed and of those employed in Israel. Figures for days of closure in 2001 refer to the period between January and June only.

mixed. Between 1995 and 2000, the domestic economy succeeded in generating a total of 309,000 new jobs (Farsakh 2002). These outpaced the growth of Palestinian employment in Israel and helped reduce unemployment rates between 1997 and 1999. The domestic labour market has been responsible for more than two thirds of total employment in the past five years. Conversely, between 1967 and 1993 it was the Israeli labour market that was the source of two-thirds of total employment growth (Farsakh 1998).

However, domestic employment growth in the post 1993 period has remained dependent on Israeli closure policies. The intermittent closures imposed on the Palestinian territories since the beginning of the Al-Aqsa Intifada have led to massive layoffs and high unemployment rates (see Figure 11.2). Moreover, employment generation capacity varies between the West Bank and Gaza Strip. In the Gaza Strip, most of the jobs created since 1993 have been in the public sector. This sector has absorbed 25–30 per cent of the domestically employed workforce since 1995. In the West Bank, by contrast, the public sector generated only 18 percent of total employment since 1995 (MAS 2000). The productivity of these jobs remains highly questionable, in view of the drain that they represent on fiscal revenues and their concentration in the police forces.[11] Meanwhile, the growth in West Bank domestic employment has not always been substantially higher than the number of jobs created in Israel (Farsakh 2002). Between 1998 and 1999 in particular, the West Bank absorbed less than 45 per cent of the increase in total employment. In the Gaza Strip, by contrast, growth of employment in the domestic economy was more important than that in Israel. The domestic market accounted for 77 per cent of all employment over this period (Farsakh 2002). The large presence of West Bank workers in Israeli establishments in the period 1997–9 (see Table 11.1), years with few closure days, reflect an increase in Israeli demand for such labour as well as relative ease of access.

The third factor influencing migration incentives are wage levels. Judging from aggregate data, wages of Palestinians in Israel are nearly double those that are earned in the domestic economy (see Figure 11.3). Looking at wages of male workers in the construction sector, where over 50 per cent of WBGS workers in the Israeli economy are employed, we find that the wage gap between Israel and the Gaza Strip remains significant, reflecting the lack of integration between the

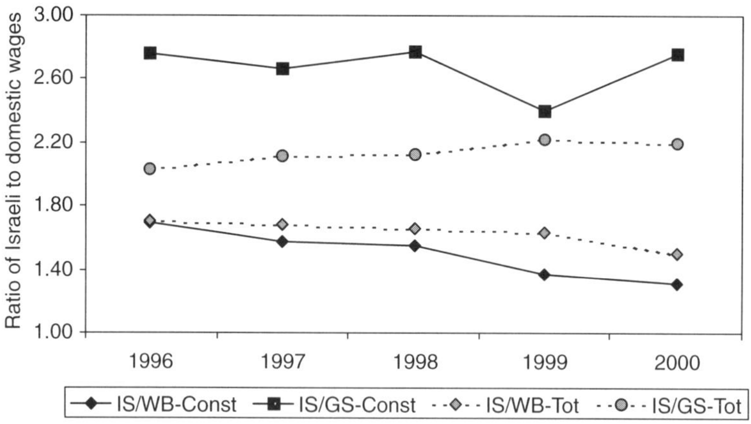

Figure 11.3 The ratio of domestic to Israeli-sourced wages for male Palestinian workers employed in the domestic and the Israeli construction sectors respectively and the economy at large, 1996–2000.

Source: PCBS, *Labour Force Survey*, various issues.

Notes

Israel/WB-const, Israel/GS-const: wages earned in Israel as a ratio of wages in the West Bank and in the Gaza Strip in the construction sector. Israel/WB-Tot, Israel/GS-Tot: wages in Israel as a ratio of wages in the West Bank and the Gaza Strip in all sectors.

two economies. Gaza Strip workers employed in Israel earn more than double what they would earn in the domestic construction sector (Figure 11.3). The situation for West Bank workers is, however, different. The wage differential for construction workers employed in Israel versus those employed domestically has converged over the years, indicating the growing integration between the West Bank economy and Israel. By 2000, the wage premium for West Bank workers employed in Israel was only 30 per cent (Figure 11.3).

4.2 Economic versus political considerations

Palestinian employment in Israel since 1993 has become dependent on Israeli regulatory constraints, and particularly on Israel's permit and closure policies. Israel's permit policy consists of regulating the entry of workers into its territory on the basis of security considerations, rather than on the basis of supply and demand.[12] Imposed since 1991, the permit policy has made entry of WBGS workers into Israel conditional on obtaining a security clearance from the Israeli military establishment, as well as on acquiring a request of employment from an Israeli employer (PHRIC 1992, Law 1999). The Oslo Process institutionalized this system, and complicated it still further. Since 1993, Israel has restricted permits to married men over the age of 28. It has also shortened the duration of the permit to a period of 2 months: and permits are not always renewable. Moreover, these permits bind workers to a specific firm and place of employment, thereby restricting their mobility.

In principle, the permit policy is applied to workers seeking a job on the settlements as well as in Israel. However, since 1993, Israel has made the conditions for issuing a permit for work *in the settlements* easier than for work beyond the Green Line. Workers seeking a job in a settlement do not need to be married or older than 18 years. They are also not restricted to specific hours of work. Moreover, from the employer's point of view, workers' permits for settlements are cheaper than for those employed beyond the 1967 borders. This is because Israeli employers in the settlements are exempt from paying Palestinian workers social security benefits to which they are entitled if they are employed in Israel. These amount to 25–30 per cent of gross wages paid for legal Palestinians working in Israel (Kav Laoved 1997, Farsakh 1999).

The efficacy of the permit policy in regulating labour flows depends heavily on Israeli *closure* policy. Imposed since 1993 as a security measure against suicide attacks, Israel's closure policy consists of cutting the flow of goods and labour between the WBGS and Israel as well as between the WBGS and the rest of the world. In a situation of internal closure, Israel restricts mobility between the various parts of the West Bank itself and prevents any contact between the West Bank and the Gaza Strip. Between 1993 and 2000, Israel closed its borders with the WBGS for 484 effective days, which is the equivalent of nearly 3 months of closures a year (UNSCO 2001). During such periods no worker could get to their job in Israel, or in the settlements. As can be seen from Figure 11.2, the number of Palestinian workers with jobs in Israel decreased as days of closure increased.

Israel's imposition of the closure policy has been the most effective measure to date in restricting the mobility of workers and in demarcating boundaries between Palestinian and Israeli areas.

Israeli permit and closure policies alone, however, do not explain why West Bank workers have found it easier to access Israel and the settlements than Gaza Strip workers. The key reason for the West Bank's greater accessibility to the Israeli labour market compared to the Gaza Strip is tied to Israel's *territorial* policy in these two Palestinian areas. From 1978, it can be seen that Israel has fostered territorial and economic ties with the West Bank rather than with the Gaza Strip.[13] These differing Israeli territorial interests are best reflected in its settlement policy. Between 1972 and 1993 Israel built more than 123 settlements in the West Bank, hosting 120,000 Israelis. In East Jerusalem a total of 126,000 Israelis live in ten settlements surrounding 130,000 Palestinians (FMEP 1999). In the Gaza Strip, by contrast, Israel has built 16 settlements and the settler population did not exceed 4,800 Israelis in 1993. Following the Oslo Process, Israel enhanced its territorial claim over the West Bank (including East Jerusalem) by building over 49 new settlement posts and by increasing the settler population, from 246,000 to 360,000 between 1993 and 1999 (FMEP 2001). In the Gaza Strip, instead, the settler population increased by less than 2,000 persons over the same period. The expansion of settlements in the West Bank had an important role in fostering demand for Palestinian labour, and thereby encouraging labour links between the West Bank and Israel. At the same time, the growth of settlements jeopardizes the territorial contiguity of the West Bank and weakens the territorial and economic possibilities for its separation from Israel (see Map 11.1).

The fact that Israel is more interested territorially in incorporating larger parts of the West Bank than of the Gaza Strip is also reflected in the way the Oslo Process addressed each of the two Palestinian areas. The Oslo Process gave the Palestinian Authority greater control over the Gaza Strip compared to the West Bank. By mid-2000, the Palestinian Authority controlled 85 per cent of the land and 98 per cent of the population in the Gaza Strip compared with 41 per cent of the area in the West Bank (i.e. areas A and B) (FMEP 2000). Israel, by contrast, continued to fully control area C, which cut 59 per cent of the West Bank into various cantons that cannot easily dispense with their links to Jerusalem, to Israeli settlements, or to building sites on the 1967 Green Line border (see Map 11.1). Meanwhile, Israel chose to demarcate its border more clearly with the Gaza Strip by establishing the Eretz and Karni checkpoints and by meticulously monitoring any illegal crossing. In the West Bank, Israel chose to keep the borders porous, thereby enabling West Bank workers to sneak illegally to work beyond the 1967 borders (see Table 11.2).

4.3 Israeli demand for Palestinian workers

Despite their importance, Palestinian labour flows to the Israeli economy are not solely determined by political parameters, but are also conditioned by the nature of Israeli demand. In the 1980s, various segments of the Israeli economy became

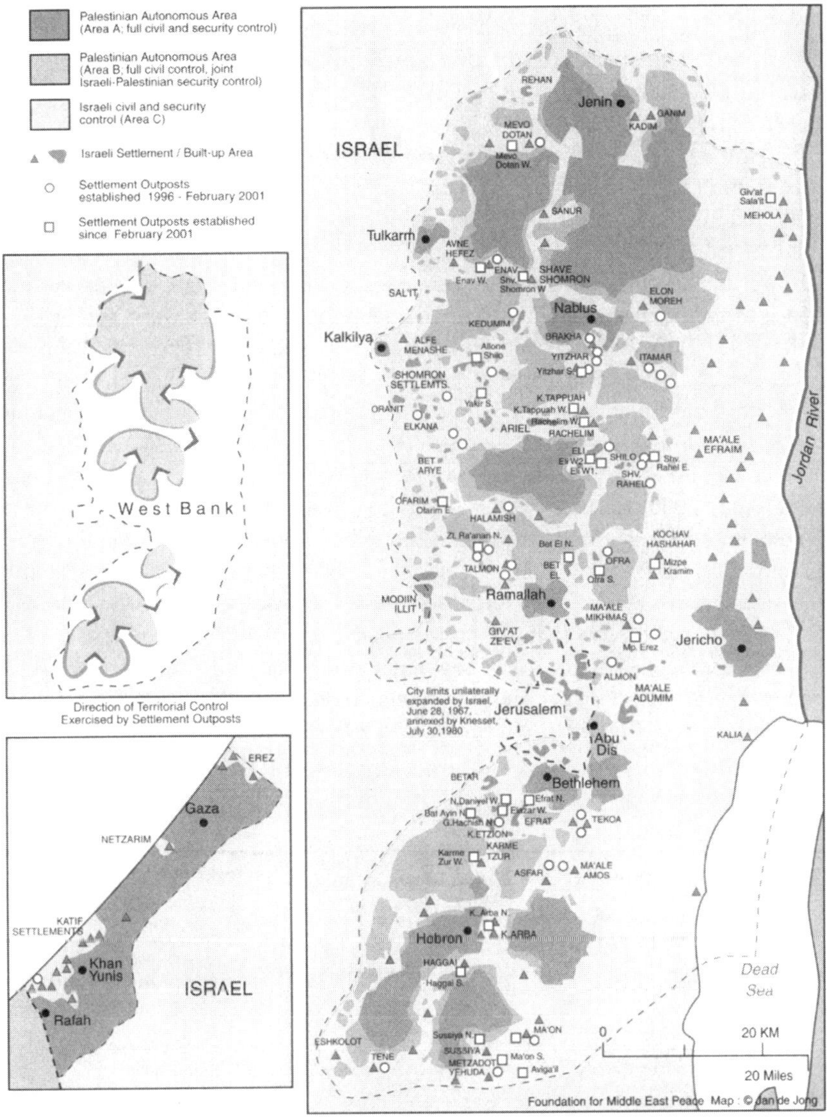

Map 11.1 Israeli settlement outposts – January 2002.

Source: Foundation for Middle East Peace/Jan de Jong (Washington).

dependent on the supply of low-cost Palestinian labour, especially as WBGS workers tended to be concentrated in low skill occupations that were shunned by Israelis, such as those in agriculture, services and construction (Semyonov and Lewin-Epstein, 1987; Farsakh 1998). The wages of a Palestinian worker were typically 20–40 per cent lower than the wage of an Israeli employed in the same job (Kleiman 1992). At the sectoral level, WBGS workers represented nearly one-third of all construction sector employees during the 1980s and early 1990s (see Table 11.4). They occupied an important niche by dominating low and semi-skilled elementary construction jobs (also referred to as wet jobs). Their availability contributed to keeping construction costs low and the sector labour intensive (Bar-Nathan *et al.* 1998, Amir 2000). The presence of WBGS workers in the Israeli construction sector is particularly significant in view of its importance to the Israeli economy. It represented 9–12 per cent of Israel's GDP since 1990, and has had strong multiplier effects on the rest of the Israeli economy (Bank of Israel 2000).

However, the entry of overseas workers into the Israeli labour market since 1991 is argued to have reduced Israeli demand for Palestinian workers. By 1998, a total of 150,000–200,000 overseas workers, with and without permits, were estimated to be employed in Israel (Gesser *et al.* 2001). This is nearly double the number of Palestinian workers that were employed in Israel in that year. Foreign workers are argued to provide a substitute to Palestinian workers since they tend to be concentrated in low-skilled jobs which WBGS workers previously dominated (Amir 2000, Bartram 1998). According to the limited figures available on workers with permits, foreign workers tend to be heavily represented in the Israeli agricultural sector and in domestic services.[14] Furthermore, 42–50 per cent of legal overseas workers were reported to have worked in the construction sector in the 1990s (Farsakh 1998), similar to the percentage of WBGS workers in Israel. However, given the absence of disaggregated data on skills, educational background, and productivity of foreign workers compared with Palestinians, it is not possible to assess to what extent the former are substitutes of the latter. What is

Table 11.4 Workers employed in Israel's construction sector, 1975–2000 (figures in thousands)

Year	*Number of workers (in thousands)*			*% of total employed workforce in Israeli construction*	
	Israelis	*West Bank and Gaza Strip*	*Overseas*	*Palestinians*	*Overseas*
1975	90.1	36.0		28.5	
1980	79.2	35.5		31.0	
1985	72.2	42.4		37.0	
1992	107.5	85.9		44.4	
1993	118.0	61.0	4.1	34.1	2.2
1994	139.5	46.5	21.2	25.0	10.2
1995	144.1	38.0	62.1	20.9	25.4
1996	150.5	33.1	59.7	18.0	24.5
1998	131.4	60.4	43.5	31.5	18.5
1999	120.7	64.6	56.3	34.9	23.3
2000	116.4	59.1	55.7	33.7	24.1

Sources: ICBS, *Statistical Abstract of Israel*, various issues, Tables 12.9, 12.7: Bank of Israel (2000), *Annual Report 1999*, Table 2.A.38; Bank of Israel (1999), *Annual Report 1998*, Table 2B.38.

clear, is that the intake of overseas workers is tied to the closures imposed on the WBGS: it was seen to increase in years in which closures were most intensively exerted on the WBGS. Conversely, the number of permits issued to overseas workers in all sectors dropped from 90,192 to 70,172 in 1999, a year in which less than 24 days of closures were imposed on the Palestinian territories (IMOL 2001, UNSCO 2001).

In order to understand the reasons behind the continuous absorption of Palestinian workers in Israel in the 1990s, it is necessary to analyse Israeli demand, particularly in the construction sector, where the majority of WBGS workers are concentrated. The demand for Palestinian workers in the Israeli construction sector has been tied to the overall growth of the sector, its geographic distribution and the ability of cheap labour to access places of work.

Available data reveal that the growth of the Israeli building industry has been fast enough to stimulate the demand for *all* types of workers. Between 1990 and 1998, the building industry grew by over 8.7 per cent per annum, faster than the growth of the country's GDP.[15] Its growth was mainly instigated by the intake of over 980,000 new immigrants in this period, arrivals that had led to an increase of 31 per cent in the total Israeli population by the end of 1999. While construction output fell after 1997, in comparison to 1995 figures, the number of new dwellings constructed continued to be twice as high as in 1989.[16]

As can be seen from Table 11.4, the growth of Israeli construction in the 1990s led to an increase in the number of Israeli as well as non-Israeli workers. The number of foreign workers tripled between 1994 and 1996, while the number of WBGS workers fell, representing half of all employed foreigners by 1996: this was a period marked by intensive closures. Yet after 1997, the flow of West Bank workers recovered, while the number of foreign and Israeli workers dropped. After 1998, Palestinian workers came to represent over 31 per cent of all employees in the Israeli construction sector, while foreign workers represented less than 24 per cent of the total workforce in construction (Table 11.4). While Palestinian workers did not reoccupy the central role that they had in 1992, they were clearly still in demand.

The geographic distribution of Israeli construction has contributed to the continuous absorption of Palestinian workers. Since 1992, over 50 per cent of total new houses built by Israeli contractors were in areas that are adjacent to the West Bank (e.g. the Central District in Israel) or within the Palestinian Territories (namely Jerusalem and the settlements) (see Table 11.5). Table 11.5 shows that construction in the Central District in particular represented 27–41 per cent of all newly built houses. Access by Palestinian workers to construction sites in this area has been relatively easy, as they are at a 5 km distance from parts of West Bank towns and villages.[17] The expansion of the Central District is linked to the government's 1991 plans to shift the economic and demographic weight of the country away from Tel Aviv and the coastal axis, towards the centre of the country and around Jerusalem (Dunsky and Golani 1992).[18] The development of the Central District is also part of a 1990 plan to absorb the growing Israeli immigrant population as well as to integrate the 'rocky hills in the East of the Central

Table 11.5 Annual number of housing units built in Israeli-controlled areas, by region, 1990–9

Year	*Total (number)*	*Figures in percentages*						
		Jerusalem	*Northern*	*Haifa*	*Central*	*Tel Aviv*	*Southern*	*WBGS*
1990	42,360	9.1	16.7	9.4	22.9	10.3	27.1	4.4
1991	83,700	7.3	20.3	9.0	14.7	5.2	34.3	9.3
1992	43,420	6.1	20.8	10.1	17.6	8.8	21.8	14.6
1993	35,800	7.2	15.7	12.6	35.4	11.4	11.5	6.3
1994	43,560	9.8	11.6	11.2	36.5	11.8	16.2	2.9
1995	62,620	6.5	13.8	8.8	41.2	8.8	17.1	3.9
1996	55,940	10.5	17.9	12.2	28.6	8.7	19.1	3.0
1997	50,930	9.2	18.2	9.6	27.3	8.5	23.4	3.7
1998	42,920	6.4	17.0	8.5	27.7	9.9	21.3	9.1
1999	37,210	6.6	19.6	12.1	27.8	9.6	17.5	6.7

Sources: ICBS, *Statistical Abstract of Israel*, 1993, 1996, 1999, Tables 16.4 and 16.5.

Note
The data refers to the number of dwellings where construction has begun.

region' within Israel's metropolitan areas of Tel Aviv and Jerusalem (Shahar 1992). These 'rocky hills' refer to the West Bank.

Construction of Israeli settlements in the West Bank and East Jerusalem has also perpetuated demand for Palestinian workers (Table 11.5, Figure 11.4). Settlements are of relatively easy access for Palestinian workers, particularly in periods without closures. Contractors and workers do not have to cross check-points or wait hours to reach their places of work in the settlements. Indeed, an average of 2,300 new housing units per year were built in the WBGS between 1993 and 1999 (FMEP 2000, see also Figure 11.4), and in East Jerusalem a similar number of houses has been built annually over the same period. Construction growth has been fastest in major settlements that are less than 15 km away from the 1967 borders, particularly in places such as Ariel and the Shomron area along the Green Line, as well as around metropolitan Jerusalem, in places such as Maale Adumim and Gush Etzion (FMEP 2000).[19] Moreover, over 186 miles of Israeli bypass roads were paved and completed between 1994 and 1997 (Peace Now 2001). Since 1995, the annual number of new dwellings under construction in the settlements has continued to grow, while Israel itself has witnessed a fall (see Figure 11.4). In 1998, 9 per cent of all Israeli construction was undertaken in the settlements, even though the Israeli settler population in the West Bank (including East Jerusalem) represents less than 4.2 per cent of the total Israeli population.[20] The expansion of these building sites fundamentally undermines the territorial contiguity of the West Bank, while simultaneously incorporating certain parts of the West Bank into the Central District in Israel (see Map 11.1). Interestingly, the number of new houses under construction in the settlements peaked in the years preceding the initiation of the peace process in 1993 and peaked again during the (failed) negotiations for the final status agreement in 1998–9 (Figure 11.4).

Demand for Palestinian workers is also linked to their comparative cost (the closest substitutes being other foreign workers). It is not obvious, though, that foreign workers can meet the demand for Palestinian workers, for three main reasons. Firstly, foreign workers are not always cheaper than Palestinian workers. While available data indicate that it is cheaper for an Israeli employer to hire a *legal* overseas worker (i.e. with a permit) rather than a Palestinian worker – because Israeli regulations deprive overseas workers of social security benefits to which legal Palestinian workers in Israel are entitled (Kav Laoved 1997)[21] – foreign workers are *not* cheaper than Palestinians who are employed in Israeli settlements in the WBGS, for whom such benefits are not available.[22]

Amir (2000) argues that the foreign workers' wages in construction are on average lower than the wage of an Palestinian worker (with and without a work permit). The average hourly wage of a WBGS worker (both legal and illegal), was of the order of $2.5 in 1997 (PCBS 1998), while foreign workers are reported to earn effectively $1.96–$2.5 per hour (Amir 2000: 8). On the other hand, Palestinians employed in the settlements earn on average $2.2 per hour.[23] In other words, they are cheaper than Palestinian workers in Israel, but not necessarily more expensive than foreign workers. Moreover, the transaction costs involved in employing Palestinians in the settlements is lower than those incurred by employing Palestinians in Israel. Workers commuting to the settlements do not have to queue for hours at checkpoints nor travel long distances to get to their place of work. Thus, from an Israeli employer's point of view, a Palestinian worker

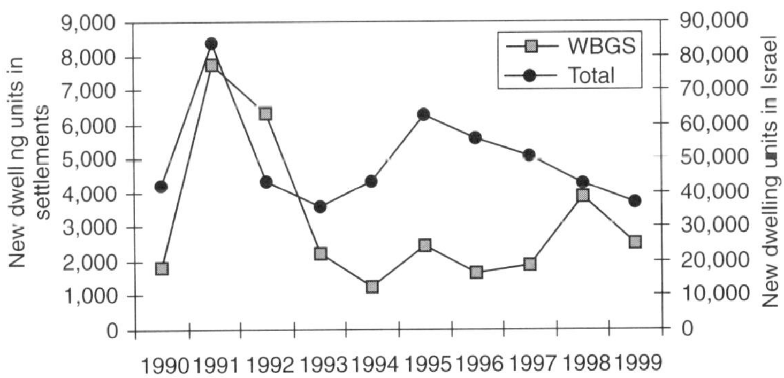

Figure 11.4 New dwelling units constructed in Israel and in Israeli settlements in the WBGS.

Source: ICBS, *Statistical Abstract of Israel*, 1993, 1996, 1999, Tables 16.4 and 16.5.

Notes

The data refers to number of dwellings where construction has begun. The left axis refers to the number of new dwellings constructed in the settlements on the WBGS. The right axis refers to the number of total houses constructed in Israeli controlled areas.

remains attractive, particularly for jobs on settlement construction sites, as the cost of his employment is not higher than that of a foreign worker and has other added advantages.

The second element that explains why foreign workers cannot totally substitute Palestinian workers has to do with the geographic distribution of Israeli construction and with the accessibility of workers to work sites. There is reason to believe that Palestinian and overseas workers are distributed in different geographic areas. Overseas workers are concentrated in major Israeli cities such as Tel Aviv (Gesser *et al.* 2001). Moreover, Israeli regulations facilitate the supply of Palestinian workers to settlements and border regions, while making it more costly for them to get to Tel Aviv or Northern areas of Israel. Palestinian contractors and workers have found it easier to access Israeli construction sites within the West Bank, or along the Green Line which juxtaposes the Central District of Israel, especially in years of limited closures (see Map 11.1). As previously mentioned, construction in the settlements, Jerusalem and the Central District represents over 50 per cent of all growth in this sector since 1992.

The final factor determining the prospects for West Bank employment in Israel is tied to the pattern of labour recruitment in the Israeli construction sector. Foreign workers have not always been accessible to all types of Israeli construction firms. The Israeli Ministry of Labour regulates the supply of overseas workers in close coordination with the Israeli Association of Contractors and Builders. This Association, which defines the recruitment and terms of employment of these workers, has directed overseas labourers mostly towards large construction firms, thereby depriving smaller construction companies of such workers (Amir 2000). Many smaller firms thus have to resort to illegal channels of recruitment of foreign labour, mainly through illegal labour recruitment firms, or, alternatively, continue to employ Palestinian workers. Illegal hiring of foreign workers, though, entails a number of risks, especially in view of the Israeli government's decision to impose heavy fines on enterprises hiring illegal workers (Kav Laoved 2000).

The supply of Palestinian workers to Israeli construction firms does not pass through private recruitment firms. Rather, it is organized through a decentralized system of Palestinian subcontractors, who have come to play a pivotal role in the completion of low skilled subcontracted projects since the 1980s, particularly in providing what are termed 'skeleton work' and 'wet jobs' (Amir 2000). These subcontractors provide their main Israeli contractor with workers, while at the same time freeing the Israeli construction firm from the responsibility of paying the workers directly or keeping them on site once the project is over. While foreign workers are also increasingly involved in subcontracting arrangements with Israeli firms (Amir 2000), it is not yet clear to what extent they can replace Palestinian subcontractors and workers. Palestinian subcontractors often speak Hebrew and have established long-standing relations of trust with Israeli contractors: foreign companies cannot offer the same advantages, at least not immediately. From the Israeli government's point of view, Palestinian subcontractors and workers are preferable to foreigners because they return home at the end of a day's work, and thus do not burden Israeli society with costs of accommodation or integration as foreign workers do.

5 Conclusions

Palestinian labour flows to the Israeli economy since 1993 show that a process of redefinition of economic and territorial boundaries has been taking place between Israel and the WBGS. This process is pre-empting the political negotiations that seek to reach a viable final status peace agreement between the Palestinians and the Israelis. Trends in Palestinian labour flows, which continue to be determined by structural economic and political factors, also suggest that the Palestinian territories have been turned into *de facto* labour reserves, which are dependent on the Israeli economy, and yet are increasingly unable to access it.

The contradictory processes of separation and integration, that shape the prospects for Palestinian employment outside the domestic economy, are best demonstrated in the evolving labour and land relations between Israel and the WBGS. On the one hand, the labour links between Israel and the Gaza Strip have been severed and the two economies are in the process of separating. This separation is not the result of a greater internal capacity of the Gaza Strip economy to absorb its growing labour force or to reduce its dependence on Israeli product and labour markets, but is the outcome of Israel's successful restriction of Gaza Strip labour outflows. The success of Israeli restrictions is attributed not only to Israel's permit and closure policies, but also to its clear demarcation of its borders with the Gaza Strip.

On the other hand, labour links between Israel and the West Bank have been maintained and the two economies have not yet separated. The West Bank continues to rely on the Israeli labour market to absorb its growing labour force, albeit at fluctuating levels and with a continuing dependence on Israel's closure policy. The fact that Israel has not defined its borders clearly with the West Bank, as with the Gaza Strip, also helps explain why the flow of West Bank workers has persisted during the Oslo period. Meanwhile, the growth of the construction sector in Israel, particularly around Jerusalem, in Central areas that border the West Bank, and in the settlements, has maintained a demand for West Bank workers despite the arrival of overseas workers. The expansion of these areas will determine the final status borders between Israel and the West Bank. Until these are defined, Israeli demand for Palestinian workers may well continue.

The Al-Aqsa Intifada begun in September 2000, and the closures imposed thereafter, have accentuated the process of territorial redefinition and the transformation of the WBGS economy into unviable labour reserves. Palestinian GNP per capita is estimated to have decreased by 27 per cent in 2001, dropping to a total of $1,630, lower than 1994 figures (World Bank 2001). The unemployment rate rose to over 28 per cent in July 2001, and poverty increased to 60.4 per cent of total Palestinian households (PCBS 2001a,c).[24] Meanwhile, Israel has continued to expand its illegal settlements, often through the use of West Bank labour. In the last quarter of 2000, after the Al-Aqsa Intifada had erupted, 954 new publicly funded housing units were initiated in the settlements, which accounts for over 10 per cent of all public housing starts in Israel (FMEP 2001). In the first half of 2001, construction in the settlements represented nearly 33 per cent of nationally tendered projects and 9.5 per cent of all private housing starts (FMEP

2001). Between July and September 2001, Israel announced the construction of another ten settlements in the area and a total of 40,100 Palestinians were reported to be working in Israeli areas.[25] Such developments indicate that the process of territorial appropriation and integration through the use of cheap Palestinian labour is not yet over. They also suggest that the ability of the Palestinian economy to successfully separate from the Israeli economy and to create the foundation for a viable and contiguous Palestinian State might have been irrevocably compromized.

Acknowledgement

The author is grateful to the Foundation for Middle East Peace/Jan de Jong (Washington) for permission to reproduce Map 11.1.

Notes

1 According to the Fourth Geneva Convention, an occupying power has no right to change the demographic character of the area it occupies or to incorporate part of the land it controls. Israel's annexation of East Jerusalem and the construction of Israeli settlements in the rest of the West Bank and Gaza Strip are thus illegal from an international legal perspective. They also compromise the territorial integrity of the WBGS, which the Oslo Process promised to preserve (Article IV, Oslo I). Closure policies are also illegal, since they are a form of collective punishment that imposes a *de facto* siege on Palestinian areas and prevent local inhabitants from reaching their places of work and residence.

2 The Economic Protocol, referred to as the Paris Protocol, forms Annex V of the Interim Agreement signed on 28 September 1995 (Oslo II). The Palestinian–Israeli Declaration of Principles on Interim Self-Government Authority (DOP, or Oslo I) signed on 13 September 1993, and the Interim Agreement on which it is based, are the central documents of the Oslo Peace Process.

3 These issues were deferred to the final status negotiations. See article V.3 of the Palestinian–Israeli Declaration of Principles on Interim Self-Government (DOP).

4 The list of goods that the Palestinian economy is allowed to import from non-Israeli sources includes lists A1, A2, and B.

5 It grew by –2.4 per cent in 1995 and –3.2 per cent in 1996. In 1999, it was recorded at 6.0 per cent (IMF 2001).

6 Palestinian exports represent less than 23 percent of total trade with Israel (UNSCO 2000a).

7 The category 'legal' workers refers to those registered with the Israeli Employment Service and receiving basic social security benefits. Illegal workers are those recruited through illegal channels.

8 According to the Fourth Geneva Convention governing the behavior of an occupying power, Israeli settlements in the WBGS are illegal because they change the demographic and territorial character of the land occupied in 1967.

9 Workers are reluctant to admit that they work in settlements, ever since the PNA declared in 1996 that such work is illegal and will be penalized.

10 This is the ratio given for workers with permits, see Table 11.2.

11 It is estimated that 55,000 out of 80,000 jobs created in the public sector between 1994 and 1999 were in the police force (IMF 2001).

12 Until 1988, Palestinian workers entered Israel freely and worked wherever they found a job (see Farsakh 1998, 1999).

13 Ever since the Drobles Settlement Master Plan in 1978 and the Camp David Agreement in 1979, Israel decided to consolidate its settlements in the East Jerusalem and in its metropolitan area, as well as in the rest of the West Bank (Aronson 1996).
14 Official data also reveal that 25 per cent of all overseas workers are concentrated in the agricultural sector (ICBS 2000, Table 12.6). This is higher than the share occupied by WBGS workers (legal and illegal). PCBS (2000b) reports that only 12 per cent of all WBGS workers employed in Israel work in agriculture. Overseas workers are also found to be concentrated in the service sector, particularly in domestic services as well as in semi skilled jobs such as nursing (Gesser *et al.* 2001). These are sectors in which Palestinian workers are not present.
15 Based on data calculated from the Bank of Israel (2000: Table 2.A.37). Construction output is defined as residential and non-residential buildings measured in square metres, where construction has begun.
16 Nineteen Thousand new dwellings were built in Israeli in 1989 compared with over 35,000 units after 1990 (Bank of Israel 1999: Table 2.A.37); see also Table 11.5.
17 Particularly in the case of towns such as Qalqilia, Tulkarem, villages in the Latrun area and around Modiin along the Green Line.
18 These plans are referred to as the 'Seven Stars' and 'Hill Axis' plans (see Dunsky and Golani 1992).
19 In Maale Adumin over 700 new units were accepted for construction in November 2000. This settlement had a total population of 22,000 settlers in 1999 (FMEP 2000).
20 Calculated from ICBS, *Statistical Abstract of Israel* 2000, Tables 2.2 and 5.5.
21 These benefits represent 27 per cent of legal workers' gross wages in Israeli construction (Kav Laoved 1997).
22 Overseas workers and Palestinians employed on Israeli settlements in the WBGS are not entitled to pensions and end of service bonuses to which Palestinian workers in Israel are entitled. They are given basic national insurance coverage, which is paid by the employer, and which amounts to less than 1 per cent of gross wages. Workers also get health insurance, which is mainly paid from their share (Kav Laoved 1997).
23 PCBS (2000a,b), unpublished data on workers' wages in the settlements.
24 The figure for those unemployed refers to all those who did not work for an hour during the week of the survey (this is the ILO definition). If the number of workers discouraged from searching for jobs were added to this figure, the total share of unemployment would be of the order of 35.5 per cent in June 2001 (PCBS 2001c). Poverty is defined as all households (two adults and four children) earning less than $1,642 per month (PCBS 2001a)
25 See Peace Now (2001) and PCBS (2001c).

References

Abu-Shokor, A. (1987) *Socio-Economic Conditions of West Bank and Gaza Strip Workers in Israel*, Palestine: Najah University (in Arabic).

Amir, S. (2000) 'Overseas foreign workers in Israel: policy aims and labour market outcomes', Maurice Falk Institute for Economic Research in Israel, discussion paper A00.01.

Aronson, G. (1996) Settlements and the Israel–Palestinian negotiations: an overview, Final Status Issues Paper, Washington, DC: IPS.

Arnon, A. and J. Weinblatt (2001) 'Sovereignty and economic development: the case of Israel and Palestine', *The Economic Journal*, 111, 291–308.

Arnon, A., I. Luski, A. Spivak, and J. Weinblatt (1997) *The Palestinian Economy: Between Imposed Integration and Voluntary Separation*, Leiden: Brill.

Astrup, C. and S. Dessus (2001) 'Trade options for the Palestinian economy: some orders of magnitude', MENA Working Paper Series no. 21, Washington, DC: World Bank.

Bank of Israel (1999) *Annual Report 1998*, Jerusalem.

Bank of Israel (2000) *Annual Report 1999*, Jerusalem.

Bar-Nathan, M., M. Beenstock, and Y. Haitovsky (1998) 'The market for housing in Israel', *Regional Science and Urban Economics*, 22, 21–49.

Bartram, D. (1998) 'Foreign workers in Israel: history and theory', *International Migration Review*, 32(2), 36–51.

Diwan, I. and R. Shaban (1999) *Development under Adversity: The Palestinian Economy in Transition*, Ramallah: MAS-World Bank Joint Report.

Dunsky, N. and Y. Golani (1992) 'The Star plan – the hills Axis,' in Golani, Y. *et al.* (eds), *Planning and Housing in Israel in the Wake of Rapid Changes*, Israel: Ministry of Interior and Ministry of Construction and Housing.

Farsakh, L. (1998) *Palestinian Employment in Israel 1967–1997: A Review*, Ramallah: MAS.

Farsakh, L. (1999) *The Implementation of Labour Related Articles in the 'Protocol on Economic Relations between Israel and the PLO': A Critical Assessment*, Ramallah: MAS.

Farsakh, L. (2002) 'Palestinian labour flows to Israel since Oslo and beyond?', paper presented at the MEEA/AEA meeting, Atlanta, 3–5 January, 2002, at http://gsb.luc.edu/depts/economics/meea/volume4/Farsakh.htm.

Foundation for Middle East Peace, FMEP (1997) 'Report on settlements in the Occupied Territories, 7/3 (April–May), Washington, DC.

FMEP (1999) 'Report on settlements in the Occupied Territories', 9/3 (April–May), Washington, DC.

FMEP (2000) 'Report on settlements in the Occupied Territories', 10/4 (July–August), Washington, DC.

FMEP (2001) 'Report on settlements in the Occupied Territories', 11/6 (November–December), Washington, DC.

Gesser, S. C., R. Raijman, A. Kemp, and J. Reznik (2001) 'Making it in Israel: Latino undocumented migrant workers in the Holy Land', *Estudios Interdisiplinario de America Latina y el Carribbe*, 11(2), July–December, 1–40.

Harris, J. and M. Todaro (1970) 'Migration, unemployment and development: a two-sector analysis', *The American Economic Review*, 60, 126–142.

ICBS (2000) *Statistical Abstract of Israel*, Jerusalem.

ICBS *Statistical Abstract of Israel*, various issues, Jerusalem.

IMF (2001) *The West Bank and Gaza Strip: Economic Performance, Prospects and Policies*, Middle Eastern Department, Washington, DC: IMF.

Israeli Central Bureau of Statistics, ICBS (1998) Report to the Press, July.

Israeli–Palestinian Interim Agreement on the West Bank and the Gaza Strip, (Oslo-II), (and its Protocols). Washington, 28 September 1995.

Israeli Ministry of Labour, IMOL (2001) 'Israeli employment office foreign labour data', unpublished data, Jerusalem.

Kav Lavoed (Workers' Hotline) (1997) 'Palestinians return to the work force, Newsletter', March.

Kav Lavoed (1998) 'Palestinian workers in Jewish settlements', August.

Kav Lavoed (2000) 'Numbers can be deceptive: non-Israelis in the Israeli labour market', Newsletter', May.

Kleiman, E. (1992) 'The flow of labour services from the West Bank and the Gaza Strip, Working Paper no. 260, Jerusalem: Hebrew University.

Kleiman, E. (1994) 'The economic provisions of the agreement between Israel and the PLO', *Israel Law Review*, nos 2–3: 347–373.

Law (1999) 'Right to work: economic rights under military occupation', November, Jerusalem.

MAS-Palestine Economic Research Institute (1999 and 2000) *The Economic Monitor*, nos. 6 and 7, respectively, Ramallah.

Massey, J. A., G. Hugo, A. Kouaouci, A. Pelligrino, and J. E. Taylor (1998) *World in Motion: Understanding International Migration at the End of the Millennium*, Oxford: Clarendon Press.

PCBS (1998) 'Labour force survey annual year Report', 1997.

Palestinian Central Bureau of Statistics, PCBS (2000a) 'Labour force survey, no. 18', Ramallah.

PCBS (2000b) 'Labour force survey annual year Report', 1999.

PCBS (2001a) 'Impact of Israeli measures on the economic conditions of Palestinian households', July–August 2001, Ramallah.

PCBS (2001b) 'Labour force data', at http://www.pcbs.org/labourforce.html

PCBS (2001c) 'Labour force survey', April–June, no. 21, http://www.pcbs.org/labourforce.html

Palestine Human Rights Information Centre, PHRIC (1992) 'The impact of the work permit system on Palestinian workers in Israel', Jerusalem, September.

Palestinian Ministry of Labour, PML (2001) 'Work permits to Israel, Israeli settlements and industrial zone's', Ramallah.

Peace Now (2001) Report on settlements activities, www.Peacenow.org/nia/pr/10042001.html

Roy, S. (2001) *Gaza Strip: The Political Economy of De-Development*, Washington, DC: Institute of Palestine Studies.

Semyonov, M. and N. Lewin-Epstein (1987) *Hewers of Wood and Drawers of Water: Noncitizen Arabs in the Israeli Labour Market*, New York: Cornell University Press.

Shahar, A. (1992) 'Developing plan for Jerusalem–Tel Aviv Intermetropoliltan Region' in Golani, Y. *et al.* (eds), *Planning and Housing in Israel in the Wake of Rapid Changes*, Israel: Ministry of Interior and Ministry of Construction and Housing.

UNSCO (2000a) 'Report on the Palestinian economy: with special report on Palestinian merchandise trade', Jerusalem.

UNSCO (2000b) 'West Bank and Gaza Strip work permits to Israel, Israeli settlements and industrial zones', Ramallah.

UNSCO (2001) 'The impact on the Palestinian economy of the recent confrontations, mobility restriction and border closures', 1 October 2000 31 January 2001, www.arts.mcgill.ca/mepp/unsco/unfront.html

United Nations Conference on Trade and Development, UNCTAD (1993) *Economic Development in the Palestinian Economy*, Geneva: UNCTAD.

World Bank (1993) *Developing the Occupied Territories: an Investment in Peace*, six volumes, Washington, DC: World Bank.

World Bank (2001) *The West Bank and Gaza Update*, the World Bank Group Quarterly publication of the West Bank and Gaza office, June.

12 Turkey after Helsinki

Economic challenges

Sübidey Togan

1 Introduction

After pursuing inward-oriented development strategies for 50 years, Turkey switched to outward-oriented policies in 1980. The policy of 'opening up' was pursued with the aim of integration into the European Union (EU). At the current time, all industrial goods circulate freely between Turkey and the EU; that is, no quotas and tariffs are imposed on imports of industrial goods. Turkey is also currently implementing the EU's Common Customs Tariffs on imports of industrial goods from third countries and has adopted most of the preferential trade agreements the EU has concluded over time. On the commercial policy side, the country is implementing measures similar to those of the EU's commercial policy – it has adopted EU competition law, established a Competition Board, adopted EU rules on protection of intellectual and industrial property rights, established a Patent Office, and adopted most of the EU's product standards.

These are considerable achievements. Yet, trade liberalization has been restricted to industrial goods only. In 2000, agriculture still constituted 13.5 per cent and services 58.2 per cent of GDP. Thus, trade liberalization is yet to affect approximately three-fourths of Turkey's GDP. This may change, however, as recently Turkey was officially recognized as a candidate state for EU membership.[1] With accession to the EU, Turkey will liberalize its trade with the EU in agricultural commodities and services, and it will become part of the European single market. Furthermore, EU membership will require Turkey to adopt and implement the whole body of EU legislation and standards – the *Acquis Communautaire* – and also participate in European Monetary Union (EMU).

The purpose of this chapter is to highlight selected aspects of Turkish accession, emphasizing problems related to joining the single market, adopting the *Acquis Communautaire*, and meeting the Maastricht criteria for fiscal and monetary policies. The final section considers issues related to the costs and benefits of Turkish accession.

We argue that Turkey will derive welfare gains from integration with the EU, but will also incur costs associated with the adoption of the Common Agricultural Policy (CAP), liberalization of services, attainment of macroeconomic stability, and complying with EU environmental directives. However, gains from integration are expected to exceed by far the costs of adjustment.

2 Single market effects

In this section, we consider issues relating to technical barriers, liberalization of agriculture and services, and issues relating to state aid.

2.1 Technical barriers

Technical barriers to industry are said to exist as long as the EU and Turkey impose different standards as conditions for entry, sale, and use, and have different legal regulations on health, safety, and environmental protection, as well as different procedures for testing and certification of conformity to existing regulations or standards. Under the EU's new approach to removing technical barriers, essential policy requirements for particular products are set out, while the development of technical standards conforming to the requirements has been entrusted to standardizing bodies. In 1989, the European Community, as it was then, put in place the 'global approach to testing and certification', which is based on mutually acceptable auditing procedures. Goods manufactured pursuant to the requirements of the global approach are permitted to display a generic mark of conformity – the 'CE' mark. All goods displaying that mark are entitled to circulate freely within Europe and are exempted from further conformity assessment by an importing nation.

On the other hand, according to Decision 1/97 of the EC-Turkey Association Council, establishing the Customs Union, Turkey had to harmonize its technical legislation to that of the EU, and according to Decision 2/97 of the Association Council, it was supposed to incorporate into its internal legal order 324 instruments that correspond to various EEC or EC Regulations and Directives on technical legislation before the end of 2000. But the work has not been completed until now. In addition, in order to participate in the free circulation of goods in the enlarged European single market, Turkey has to align its national quality infrastructure, which is a generic term encompassing the operators and operation of standardization, testing, certification, inspection, accreditation, and metrology, to the European one. Products manufactured in Turkey must satisfy the same requirements as those prevailing in the EU, and the demonstration of conformity to these requirements must be done in the same 'harmonized' way and according to the same principles as those in the EU. Recently, Turkey has taken major steps in this direction. But it still has to establish the necessary structures on conformity assessment and market surveillance.

2.2 Agriculture

Joining the EU will require Turkey to extend the customs union to agricultural commodities and also to adopt and implement the CAP. Since currently there are substantial border controls between the EU and Turkey, and external tariffs applied by each to third countries' imports differ significantly, adopting the CAP will imply the abolition of all these border controls in agricultural commodities trade between the two as well as the adoption of the EU's external tariffs with regard to third countries. As a result, the gap between the prices of agricultural products in the EU and Turkey will narrow, with any remaining differences reflecting quality and transportation and/or marketing costs.

Although agricultural price policy will be harmonized between the two parties, different levels of direct support policies and input subsidies in Turkey and EU could, in principle, remain. Current EU support policies continue to be based on market price support provided through administered prices, export subsidies, and tariffs. Price support policies are combined with production quotas and/or land set-asides. Three years ago, a package of measures called Agenda 2000 was agreed by EU Heads of State at the March 1999 European Summit in Berlin.[2] The aim of the agricultural policy reform was to meet the goals of budget reduction and to prepare for enlargement. The reform package can be viewed as continuing the shift that began with the 1992 CAP reform package from support prices to direct payments. Support prices are expected to approach world prices over time.

In Turkey, support was provided in a variety of ways: through guaranteed or minimum prices, via the provision of subsidized loans, and direct agricultural inputs subsidies. Under the price support scheme, the public sector was committed to purchasing products through public marketing agencies and agricultural sales cooperatives at support prices announced by government decrees annually. Moreover, short-term investment credit for agriculture has been subsidized by the government at interest rates well below inflation and commercial rates. Interest rates on loans from the Agricultural Bank have been significantly negative in real terms. Finally, subsidies for fertilizers, pesticides, and irrigation have also been significant in Turkey. According to an OECD estimate (2000), total support to the agricultural sector as a percentage of GDP over the period 1997–9 was just over 8 per cent. The corresponding estimate for the EU in the same period is only 1.53 per cent. Also, between 1997 and 1999, the total support per capita amounted to US$245 in Turkey and US$344 in the EU, while estimates of producer support per hectare of agricultural land amounted to US$295 in Turkey and US$845 in the EU. It follows, therefore, that other OECD countries give even larger transfers per farmer – although compared to Turkey, they have fewer farmers and higher incomes.

Table 12.1 lists the institutional prices for cereals and sugar in Turkey and the EU. It shows that the prices of the commodities under consideration here are

Table 12.1 Selected institutional prices in Turkey and the EU (US$/tonne)

	Turkey			*EU*	
	1998	*1999*		*1998*	*1999*
Wheat			Wheat		
Durum, Anatolian	277	220	Durum	133	127
Durum, other	235	201	Common	133	127
Hard, white	223	192			
Hard, red Anatolian	204	192			
White Barley	150	144	Barley	133	127
Rye	159	136	Rye	133	127
Maize	175	155	Maize	133	127
Sugar beet	68	66	Sugar beet (Italy)	52	50

Source: Various issues of the Official Gazette and European Commission (2000).

higher in Turkey than in the EU. Under a Customs Union between Turkey and the EU, commodity prices in Turkey should move closer to those in the EU. Hence, for those commodities, producer prices in Turkey will have to decline considerably after the formation of a single market in agricultural commodities with the EU. Furthermore, with the implementation of Agenda 2000 in the EU, the prices of these commodities are expected to fall to their world price levels, and as a result Turkish prices will have to fall even further.

Recently, the Turkish authorities decided to phase out agricultural support mechanisms, a condition of the stabilization programme agreed with the IMF and signed on 22 December 1999. The government introduced instead a 'decoupled' direct income payments system as used in the EU. As prices of major agricultural commodities fall towards world price levels in Turkey and the system of subsidized loans and direct subsidization of agricultural inputs is abolished, the country is intending to offset the accompanying reduction in farmers' incomes through an increase in direct aid payments as in the EU. Such a move would help to provide farmers with a fair standard of living.

Recently, the EU declared that farmers from Central and Eastern European (CEE) countries will not be excluded from direct income support payments. It also stated that direct payments would be introduced in CEE countries equivalent to 25 per cent of the present system in 2004, 30 per cent in 2005, and 35 per cent in 2006. After 2006, these payments would increase incrementally in such a way as to ensure the new Member Sates reach in 2013 the support level then applicable. Since by 2013 support could absorb a high percentage of the EU budget, it is likely that the support system will change by then. Since Turkish farmers will face a similar situation, Turkey will have no choice but to finance the direct income support expenditures from its own budget until it is eligible for direct payments from EU. This will place a heavy burden on the Turkish budget and the policy will also have high administrative costs. This can be regarded as one of the costs of joining the EU.

2.3 Services

Services cover a wide range of activities such as financial services, transportation, and telecommunications, and accounted for 58.2 per cent of Turkey's GDP in 2000. Nevertheless, trade liberalization in this sector was not on the agenda in Turkey until the beginning of the Uruguay Round of multilateral trade negotiations. Thereafter, it has been discussed mainly within the Undersecretariat of the Treasury, the organization responsible for carrying out negotiations regarding services.

2.3.1 Financial services

Currently, in the EU, citizens and firms are free to invest their money, open accounts, take out loans, issue securities, and buy insurance and securities wherever they choose to do so within the Union, and banks, insurance companies, and security firms are free to offer their services without restriction in all EU countries.

An essential requirement for the achievement of this liberal regime is freedom for financial agents within the EU to establish branches in all Member States, and to offer their services throughout the EU whether they have established a presence in each country or not, as well as complete capital liberalization. For this purpose, the EU has harmonized basic standards for supervising financial institutions and protecting investors, depositors, and consumers, mutually recognized the Supervisory Authorities' competence and the manner in which they apply those standards, and introduced the principle of 'home country control'. The latter principle means that the EU branches of a financial institution established in one Member State will be subject to prudential supervision by the Authorities in its host country, and likewise the services which it provides throughout the EU will be subject to home country prudential supervision.

In Turkey, the new banking law of June 1999 mandated the creation of a new independent Banking Regulatory and Supervisory Agency (BRSA). The BRSA takes over banking regulation and supervision responsibilities previously fulfilled by various departments. The limits imposed on a single borrower and to related parties were tightened, banks' exposure to non-financial participations were limited, and minimum capital requirements were increased. Furthermore, the new Banks Act introduced higher minimum capital requirements for new banking licenses, and urged implementation of operational policies in line with the Basle Accord. According to this Act, the establishment of a bank, founded as a joint stock company, or opening of the first branch of a bank based in a foreign country, is subject to authorization from the Council of Ministers of a proposal endorsed by BRSA. With the amendment of the Banks Act in December 1999 the BRSA became the sole authority able to grant permission for the establishment of a bank. After receiving the permission to found a bank or open a branch office in Turkey, an additional license from the BRSA is required to accept deposits or engage in other banking operations. Banks are free to open additional branch offices provided they comply with the principles set by the BRSA and they have achieved the standard ratios introduced. If necessary the BRSA may subject the opening of additional branch offices to authorization. Any new bank must have a minimum of $30 million in capital, payable in cash and upfront. Banks established abroad, which are willing to open branch offices in Turkey, must have the same amount of paid-in capital allocated to Turkey. Any amendments to the articles of association of a bank shall require the approval of the BRSA. In addition to the above mentioned regulations, the government has recently taken steps to correct the weak loan loss provisioning rule and the lenient large exposure and connected lending limits. With the December amendments to the Banks Act, tighter limits were imposed on both on- and off-shore balance sheet commitments to related parties and especially to companies belonging to the same group. Furthermore, in June 2000, a plan for the gradual reduction of deposit insurance was put into operation. Finally, on 11 May 2001, Parliament amended the Banking Law. The amendment changes regulations governing the protection of investors, mergers and acquisitions, and competition; accelerates legal proceedings for troubled banks taken over by the Savings Deposit Insurance Fund; and allows the seizure of assets of owners and administrators of failed banks.

With the relaxation of entry barriers to the banking sector during the 1980s, the number of foreign banks in Turkey increased from four in 1980 to 15 in 2002. However, in terms of their shares in total assets, credits, and deposits, foreign banks still remain insignificant. Foreign banks are less active in collecting deposits and extending loans, but play a relatively larger role in offering financial services that are accounted for under off-balance sheet items.

The above considerations indicate that the Turkish financial reform programme was quite successful in transforming the Turkish financial system into a modern one. The objective of the legislative and regulatory reform is to bring the regulatory and supervisory regime for the Turkish financial sector up to the level of international practice and in line with EU standards. The objective has been achieved to a large extent but more still needs to be done. After Turkish accession to the EU, citizens and firms in the EU and Turkey will be free to invest their money, open accounts, take out loans, issue securities, and buy insurances and securities wherever they choose within the EU and Turkey, and banks, insurance companies, and security firms will be free to offer their services without restriction in all EU countries, including Turkey. As a result, competition in the Turkish financial sector will increase, Turkey will recognize the Supervisory Authorities' competence of EU Member States, and introduce its legislature to the principle of home country control. Competition will lead to lower prices for consumers as well as to a larger variety of financial instruments. Some Turkish banks will benefit from larger markets by concentrating on activities in which they have comparative advantage, while other banks may be forced to merge with foreign firms or exit from the market. Adjustment will certainly be costly for both the winners and the losers.[4] This cost can again be regarded as a cost of joining the EU.

2.3.2 Telecommunications

Since its inception in the mid-1980s, the EU's telecommunications policy has focused on two main objectives: economic efficiency and the guarantee of universal service. The achievement of these aims has been pursued through the application of a set of complementary principles: market liberalization and harmonization of conditions for a common regulatory framework. The regulatory framework promoted by the European Commission has now been adopted to achieve these aims. Since 1 January 1998, the EU has had fully competitive telecommunications markets in all Member States but five; Portugal, Spain, Greece, Ireland, and Luxembourg have derogations and have postponed the introduction of full competition until 2002 at the latest.

The EU's experience demonstrates that competition is the best way to ensure efficient operation and sufficient technological innovation to keep up with the pace of global change, that regulation is vital, and that privatization combined with the establishment of conduct regulation has a positive impact on performance.

Turk Telecom dominates the Turkish telecommunications sector, a national monopoly that has exclusive rights to all fixed line voice operations. In January 2000, Parliament approved legislation to reform the telecommunications sector, which initiated the process of deregulating the sector over the medium term. A regulatory authority has been established and a new regulatory board has been appointed. The reforms have led to the establishment of private mobile telephone companies and of a series of companies providing value added services such as internet access and cable television under revenue sharing agreements. On 12 May 2001, the Turkish Parliament passed the new Telecommunications Act, which aims to end the state monopoly on landline telecom services by privatizing most of Turk Telecom.

When Turkey accedes to the EU, it will have to introduce full competition in telecommunications. In particular, the country will have to adopt and implement the EU's legislative measures, centring on liberalization of all telecommunications services and infrastructure; adoption of open network provision measures to ensure a competitive environment; maintenance and development of minimum supply of services and the definition of common principles for financing the universal service; the establishment of a common framework for the interconnection of networks and services; and the approximation of general authorization and individual licensing regimes to those in the EU.

2.3.3 Electricity and natural gas

An important accession requirement in the electricity sector is compliance with Directive 96/92/EC, which concerns the rules of the internal market in electricity, adopted on 19 December 1996 and effective from February 1997.[4] Most member states have 2 years to bring this into effect. The Directive establishes common rules for generation, transmission, and distribution of electricity, and offers a variety of alternative ways of meeting the criteria. Its fundamental aim is to achieve a competitive market in electricity. Similar considerations apply in the case of natural gas. The 1998 European Gas Directive provides for the gradual opening of the natural gas market to competition over a 10-year period to reach 33 per cent of total gas consumption.

In Turkey, the electricity sector is dominated by state-owned enterprises, although there are privately owned firms accounting for about 21 per cent of electricity generation. Under the current regulations, the private operator signs a long-term power purchase agreement with the state-owned generation enterprise in which the latter commits itself to buy the output of the plant for a period of, say, 20 years at a fixed price in foreign currency. This contract, guaranteed by the Turkish Treasury, assures the investor that the project will be profitable irrespective of future demand for power. As a result, the government retains the commercial risks.

The Turkish government has recently passed a new Electricity Law,[5] which attempts to introduce a market model similar to the EU's. This will transfer most of the task of supplying and distributing electricity and the associated market risks to the private sector, eliminate the need for additional state-guaranteed power purchase agreements, and minimize costs through competitive pressures on producers and distributors along the EU model. The government's future role will be largely confined to determining sector policy, owning the transmission system, and setting up an independent regulatory body to ensure that the rules are respected and that prices are competitively determined.

On the other hand, the current market structure in the Turkish gas sector is based on monopoly provision. BOTAS, the state-owned enterprise, has a monopoly on imports of gas, and is the only transmission company. Local companies – owned either by the municipalities or by BOTAS – provide distribution and supply. Recently, the government passed a new Gas Law (2 May 2001). With this law the government plans to establish a competitive market as in the EU and encourage private sector participation through a phased policy. As in the case of electricity, an independent regulator for the gas industry has been established. This authority determines the transmission and distribution access rules and tariffs and the methodology for the regulation of retail prices.

2.3.4 State aid

During the 1980s, Turkey used three different tools of industrial policy intensively: investment incentives, export incentives, and policies targeted at state-owned enterprises. In each case, the government tried to obtain a preferred allocation of resources through the use of subsidies. Investment incentives, regulated by laws and decrees, have been directed to reducing the cost of investment, reducing the need for external financing, and increasing profitability. On the export side, using various types of incentives during the 1980s, governments have been able to increase profitability.

However, regarding policies for state-owned enterprises, we should note that the Turkish public enterprise sector is still very large. The state-owned enterprises have shown in general poor economic performance due to the soft-budget constraints they faced.[6] They are not subject to market discipline and as such escape bankruptcy laws. Moreover, they receive subsidies from the government through direct transfers, equity injections, and debt consolidation.

Turkey has recently eliminated most of its investment and export incentives. Within this context, GATT-legal subsidies such as those for Research and Development (R&D) and to facilitate the adaptation of plants to new environmental regulations have been introduced. Export subsidies in Turkey are now restricted to subsidies provided for R&D activities, to environmental projects, and to financial assistance for export promotion.

Although considerable progress has been achieved in the fields of investment and export incentives, similar progress has not been made in the case of public enterprises. This means that even though privatization was a prominent part of the Turkish structural adjustment programme since 1983, it did not gain momentum until very recently. Turkey recognizes that it will have to stop subsidizing public enterprises, align its state aid policies to those of EU, apply the same competition policies to all firms whether private or public, and to privatize the public enterprises.[7]

3 Economic challenges

In this section, we consider issues related to macroeconomic stability, labour markets, and compliance with EU environmental directives.

3.1 Macroeconomic stability

The Treaty of Maastricht, signed in December 1991, laid the groundwork for the process leading to the EMU. The Treaty outlined three successive stages. The first stage began with the removal of the remaining capital controls in July 1990 and an enhanced commitment by Member Countries to fixed parities within the European Monetary System (EMS). The second stage began in 1994 with the setting up of the European Monetary Institute in Frankfurt, which prepared the practical steps required to establish an integrated system of European Central Banks, including the partial pooling of foreign exchange reserves and the development of common operating procedures. The third stage started on 1 January 1999 with the irrevocable fixing of exchange rates among the countries admitted to the Monetary Union. It was accompanied by the creation of the European System of Central Banks. At the centre of this system lies the European Central Bank, a new institution that determines monetary policy across the EMU. National banks survive as local subsidiaries, mostly in charge of bank supervision and operational aspects. The common currency, the Euro, began circulating on 1 January 2002, gradually replacing national currencies.

Before entering the Monetary Union, a country has to satisfy the convergence criteria summarized under five headings: (i) member country's inflation may not exceed the average of the three lowest inflation rates in the EMS by more than 1.5 per cent; (ii) its long-term interest rate must not exceed the average of the interest rates in the three countries with the lowest inflation rates by more than 2 per cent; (iii) its exchange rate must have been in the 'normal' band of the Exchange Rate Mechanism (ERM) without devaluation for at least 2 years; (iv) its public debt cannot exceed 60 per cent of its GDP; and (v) the budget deficit must not exceed 3 per cent of its GDP. These criteria are meant to guarantee that the countries that join EMU will be able to sustain a low rate of inflation.

Table 12.2 shows the EMU convergence criteria for Turkey and the CEE countries. It can be seen that the CEE countries are close to satisfying the criteria, but by contrast Turkey is still far away from satisfying the conditions. Indeed, Turkey is in the midst of a determined campaign to turn around decades of weak economic performance, reflected in pervasive structural rigidities and weak public finances. The past few years have witnessed three major attempts at addressing these underlying weaknesses. The first was during 2000 under the 3-year Standby Agreement initiated in December 1999. Despite some notable achievements, a worsening current account and a fragile banking system led in late 2000 to a liquidity crisis, which turned into a full-blown crisis in February 2001. The government decided to abandon the crawling peg regime and floated the currency. In May 2001, IMF increased its assistance under a new stand-by arrangement. Just as the revised programme was beginning to show results, the 11 September events triggered the re-emergence of serious financing problems. In February 2002, IMF approved a new 3-year stand-by credit for Turkey to support the government's economic programme. With the implementation of this stabilization programme Turkey envisages a gradual but steady improvement in its economic conditions.

Table 12.2 EMU convergence criteria

	Inflation rate, %		*Budget deficit, % of GDP*		*Government debt, % of GDP*		*Interest rates, 10 year bonds*	*Exchange rate stability, deviation from parity*		*Currency regime*
	2000	*2001*	*2000*	*2001*	*2000*	*2001*	*Last*	*Last*	*Max (2Y)*	
Bulgaria	10.1	7.9	−1.1	−1.0	83.8	72.5	5.2	0.0	−1.3	Currency Board (EUR)
Czech Republic	3.9	4.7	−4.0	−3.2	29.2	29.0	5.5	14.0	−6.0	Managed Float (EUR reference)
Estonia	4.0	5.8	−0.7	1.1	6.6	6.2	4.7	0.0	0.0	Currency Board (EUR)
Hungary	9.8	9.2	−3.5	−5.0	56.1	51.5	6.7	5.4	−4.5	Crawling peg (EUR)
Latvia	2.7	2.5	−2.8	−1.9	10.0	12.2	10.7	2.6	2.6	Peg (SDR)
Lithuania	1.0	1.3	−2.8	−1.4	28.3	29.0	7.9	8.1	8.1	Currency Board (EUR)
Poland	10.1	5.5	−2.7	−6.3	43.8	38.0	8.3	8.4	−8.7	Float
Romania	45.7	34.5	−4.1	−3.7	29.2	31.2	34.9	−31.4	−31.5	Managed Float (USD reference)
Slovakia	12.0	7.3	−6.8	−7.2	32.9	42.7	7.8	4.0	−2.0	Managed Float (EUR reference)
Slovenia	8.9	8.5	−1.4	−1.3	25.1	25.4	na	−7.1	−7.1	Managed Float (EUR reference)
Turkey	54.9	54.4	−19.6	−17.6	57.4	93.3	56.5	56.9	93.3	Float
Reference value	2.8	3.3	−3.0	−3.0	60.0	60.0	7.3		±15%	

Sources: Deutsche Bank Research (2002), Turkish State Planning Organization, Central Bank of Turkey and Turkish Treasury (2002).

Note
Parity refers to the last 3-year average exchange rates against Euro. In the case of Turkey, the interest rate is annual compound interest rate on government bonds of 8 months' duration obtained in the latest auction of treasury bills.

During the period leading up to adoption of the Euro there are three steps that Turkey must consider. Until entry into the EU is secured, Turkey retains control of its exchange rate policy, implying freedom over its monetary framework and the exchange rate regime. Upon accession, the exchange rate policy of Turkey becomes a common concern for the EU. Turkey will be expected to join the Exchange Rate Mechanism (ERM-II) at some point after accession for a period of at least 2 years. Finally, after fulfilment of the Maastricht criteria, Turkey will have to adopt the Euro.

3.2 Labour markets

According to Togan (2000), the Turkish labour market is extremely flexible. The reason behind the flexibility lies in the fact that it is not homogeneous. It has different wage setting mechanisms in the formal and informal sectors. The informal sector is largely free from most types of labour regulation and is not subject to taxes and related charges. Activities in this sector rely mostly on provision of labour services without formal employment contracts. Job insecurity is pervasive and workers get very few benefits from their employers. Labour regulations are observed by the formal sector and this sector also pays all taxes and related charges such as social security contributions and payments to various funds. According to Togan (2000), the share of informal sector in total employment is about 60 per cent. The reasons for this relatively high share are: (i) the very high tax rates on wage income, high tax related charges, and substantial payments to various funds that have to be paid in the formal sector as a requirement of social security law and the laws regulating the taxation of personal incomes; (ii) the relatively high firing costs imposed by, and the stringency of the various clauses of, the labour law; and (iii) lack or weakness of enforcement mechanisms for respective laws in the economy.

Studies reveal that the Turkish population increases on average by one million persons a year. Thus, Turkey has to create new jobs on a continual basis. In the past, Turkey has successfully solved its unemployment problem through the existence of a large, flexible informal sector where wages are free to equilibrate demand and supply, and via labour migration from Turkey. Table 12.3 shows the number of Turkish citizens and workers abroad. As one can see, 89 per cent of Turkish workers living abroad work in Europe. Moreover, 732,000 workers of the entire 1.2 million working abroad (over 60 per cent) are employed in Germany.

With Turkish accession to the EU, Turkey will have to introduce a comprehensive labour market reform. After the reforms have been passed, the authorities will have to enforce the rule of law uniformly, but this will have to be done without increasing the unemployment rate in the economy. Hence, these labour market reforms will probably entail substantial reductions in tax rates on wage income, tax-related charges, and payments to various funds, as well as reductions in firing costs and making various clauses of the labour law less stringent.

Table 12.3 Labour migration from Turkey (Cumulative, 2001)

	Citizens living abroad		*Workers abroad*	
	Number	*%*	*Number*	*%*
Europe	3,127,691	88.85	1,047,842	88.76
Germany	2,053,600	58.34	732,189	62.02
France	311,356	8.85	76,122	6.45
Netherlands	299,909	8.52	51,000	4.32
Austria	134,229	3.81	57,098	4.84
Belgium	70,701	2.01	25,874	2.19
Other Europe	257,896	7.33	105,559	8.94
Middle East and North Africa	117,180	3.33	100,480	8.51
CIS countries	53,050	1.51	15,895	1.35
Other countries	222,119	6.31	16,333	1.38
Australia	52,620	1.49	13,500	1.14
USA	130,000	3.69	—	—
Canada	35,000	0.99	—	—
Japan	1,729	0.05	1,729	0.15
Other countries	2,770	0.08	1,104	0.09
Total	3,520,040	100	1,180,550	100

Source: State Planning Organization.

3.3 Compliance with EU environmental legislation

Joining the EU will require Turkey to adopt and implement the entire body of EU legislation and standards on environmental protection. This means that Turkey will have to bring its environmental protection system, infrastructure, and standards up to Western European levels, which, in turn, will require substantial investments by both the public and private sectors as well as changes in regulations and supporting institutions.

Consider the EU regulations on wastewater collection and treatment. According to the urban wastewater directive (91/271/EEC), all urban areas with a total wastewater discharge equivalent to 2000 population are required to be connected to a sewer system, and the discharges of collected sewers must receive at least secondary treatment. The directive allows for exceptions for towns with a population of less than 10,000 in cases when sewers would produce no environmental benefit or would involve excessive cost.

According to the 1997 general census of population, the total population of Turkey is approximately 62.87 million. Of this figure, 13.75 million live in areas with populations of 2,000 and less, 49.12 million live in areas with populations of more than 2,000, 22.57 million live in areas with population of 10,000 and less, and 40.3 million live in areas with populations of more than 10,000. In 1997, there were 2,835 municipalities with a total population of 48.2 million. Moreover, 7.3 million lived in rural municipalities. According to the State Planning

Organization, 72 per cent of the population living in municipalities were not connected to sewer treatment. For an additional 23 per cent of the population, sewer systems were under construction. Upon the completion of these systems, the percentage of population connected to sewer systems will rise to 51 per cent of the population living in municipalities. Furthermore, 2 per cent of the municipalities have wastewater treatment facilities, and 14 per cent of the population living in villages have sewer connection with septic tanks.

Assuming that the sewer systems under construction will be completed during the coming years we could conclude that out of the 48.2 million living in municipalities, 24.5 million will be connected to sewer systems in the near future, leaving 23.7 million with no connection to sewer systems. In the villages, a further 11.8 million people have no sewer connection.

The costs for new sewerage systems will depend on three parameters: (i) the proportion of the rural population living in towns that would be classified as agglomerations, with a population of more than 2,000 population equivalent; (ii) the proportion of towns with between 2,000 and 10,000 residents that will be exempted from constructing sewer systems on the grounds of no environmental benefit or excessive costs; and (iii) the proportion of the rural population that must have sewer systems. Once the Commission and Turkey have reached an agreement on these parameters during the entrance negotiations, the cost of compliance with the EU directive can be determined. Rough estimates of investment costs to comply with the directive are in the region of some US$16 billion (Togan 2001). Additional operating, maintenance, and replacement costs would increase this even further.

The above considerations reveal that environmental protection presents challenges for Turkey. These are likely to be even more substantial when one adds to the costs of compliance with regulations on wastewater collection and treatment, the costs of compliance with EU regulations on drinking water, industrial pollution, dangerous chemicals, fuel standards, air quality, and waste management. Again, these costs are best considered as the 'price' of joining the EU. One can also argue that Turkey would have had to bear these investment costs in any case. Only the timing of the investments would be different, as EU directives do not necessarily correspond to Turkey's priorities at this stage of its development.

4 Costs and benefits of Turkish accession: towards an appraisal

Following accession to the EU, Turkey will produce and export those goods and services in which it has comparative advantage. Furthermore, with the increase in market size and elimination of trade barriers, integration will lower prices of different commodities by increasing competition and spurring efficiencies via better exploitation of scale economies. A larger variety of products will be offered in the Turkish market and intra-industry trade with the EU will increase. In cases where larger Turkish firms are operating on a more efficient scale and competing more effectively, liberalization may lead to higher sales and higher employment.

But in other industries restructuring may be accompanied by a sizable re-allocation of employment as firms cut back on redundant workers and close inefficient plants and offices. In those sectors the number of firms will probably be reduced through mergers and bankruptcies. Thus, integration will remove the distortions in the price system, which, in turn, will boost the allocative efficiency of the Turkish economy. As a side-effect, this heightened efficiency will make Turkey a better place to invest, causing investment generally to rise, and with it foreign direct investment. Thus, the allocative efficiency gains from integration will be boosted by induced capital formation. While investment increases above its normal level, the Turkish economy will experience a growth effect. All this means improved welfare for Turkish people in the long term.[8]

Besides the free movement of goods and services, EU membership would involve the free movement of capital and labour with Turkey. Although the 1995 Customs Union decision is silent on the movement of capital, it should be noted that as of 2002 there are no restrictions on capital movements either in the EU or in Turkey.

As for the movement of labour, there is currently a ban on the recruitment of migrant workers from Turkey in EU countries and Turks visiting EU countries face visa restrictions. With accession Turkish workers are expected to migrate to EU countries. Given the current relative wage situation, opening EU labour markets to Turkish workers might increase the wages of Turkish migrants and lower western wages for unskilled workers. The extent of likely Turkish migration is difficult to estimate. Labour mobility between Turkey and the EU will probably be achieved after a relatively long transition period after accession. By that time it is possible that the expected increase in Turkish welfare due to static and dynamic effects of integration may have caused the wage differential between Turkey and the West to decrease. This may, in turn, lead to a reduction in potential migration from Turkey.

Furthermore, with accession Turkey will be eligible for EU structural funds. As a result, infrastructural investments will increase, which, in turn, will contribute to economic growth as emphasized by Canning (2000). Finally, within a few years of EU accession Turkey will abondon its national currency and adopt the Euro. Belonging to the currency union will reduce the costs of international transactions and promote trade and openness. According to Frankel and Rose (2002), joining a currency union can tripple a country's trade with other currency union members. They also argue that there is no evidence of trade diversion, and that each 1 per cent increase in the country's overall trade relative to GDP raises income per capita by at least one-third of a per cent.

Comprehensive and up to date quantitative analyses of the effects of accession on the Turkish economy are not available. Harrison *et al.* (1997) have analysed the economic implications for Turkey of a Customs Union with the EU. The authors show that Turkey would gain between 1 and 1.5 per cent of GDP annually from this type of arrangement depending on the complementary policies it adopts. But the study abstracts from a consideration of the liberalization of trade in services between Turkey and EU, perfect mobility of capital and labour between the two sides, and fails to assess the different costs of adjustment mentioned above.

Welfare gains for Turkey from integration with the EU will have a price, no doubt. That price will be the adjustment costs associated with the adoption of the CAP, liberalization of services, attainment of macroeconomic stability, reform of the labour market, and compliance with EU environmental directives.

From the opposite perspective, gains will accrue to current EU members with Turkish accession. One set of gains would come from standard comparative advantage sources. There are also political gains to be derived from Turkish membership. Turkey is a large and fast expanding market. In terms of GDP, in fact, it is the largest market in the Middle East, Balkans, and Caucasus. As incomes in Turkey and Eurasia increase, the EU will derive potential gains from increased trade. Through increased stability and security in the Balkans and the Caucasus, the EU's energy security can improve and its defence expenditure may decrease, leading to further potential savings.

Since Turkey's integration into the EU will have budgetary implications for the latter, we now turn to a consideration of this effect. In the EU budget, two items dominate the spending side: the CAP and structural spending. On the other hand, two items dominate the revenue side of the EU budget: the fourth resource and VAT. According to the agreed rules, the Union gets a share of each member's national VAT receipts. The fourth resource is based on members' GNPs and is used to balance the accounts.[9]

According to the financial prospects for the EU 15 in the period 2000–6, as determined by the EU Heads of State at the March 1999 European Summit in Berlin, the pre-accession EU financial transfers to the CEE countries cover PHARE,[10] agricultural and structural support. The aim of the PHARE program is to focus resources on the institution building required for the adoption of the *Acquis Communautaire* by the CEE countries, where institution building implies the strengthening of democratic institutions, public administration, and organizations that have a responsibility in implementing and enforcing Union legislation. Approximately 30 per cent of PHARE funds are allocated to institution building and the rest to investment support. On the other hand, support under SAPARD (the Special Accession Program for Agriculture and Rural Development) aims at helping to finance projects in various fields of agriculture and rural development, while support under ISPA (the Instrument for Structural Policies Pre-accession) is designed to help in the fields of environmental protection and infrastructure. Entitlement to EU support from these pre-accession funds calls for co-payment by the recipient country. SAPARD differs from the PHARE scheme in that the selection of projects is the task of the recipient country and the EU participates only in *ex post* control. With ISPA, projects have to be coordinated with the European Commission from the outset. In addition to these pre-accession EU financial transfers to the CEE countries, the after accession transfers of agricultural and structural funds from the EU to the CEE countries offer greater prospects, but their magnitude is not certain yet.

Assuming that the EU will follow a similar budgetary strategy for Turkey, we can estimate that annual PHARE funds to Turkey during the pre-accession period could amount to around Euro 900 million, annual SAPARD funds to Euro 400 million, and annual ISPA funds to Euro 800 million. Thus, during the pre-accession period, which may start in 2007, Turkey could receive from the EU a total of Euro 2.1 billion annually. After accession, the funds allocated for Turkish agriculture and structural policies could be increased gradually as in the case of CEE countries. Such policies would be feasible as the total amount of appropriations for payment as a proportion of GNP would not exceed the critical value of 1.27. Once a member of the EU, Turkey will also contribute to the EU budget. Turkey's contribution to the EU's budget, forming 1 per cent of its GDP, could amount to about Euro 2 billion annually. As a result, the net budgetary cost of Turkish membership to EU will be reduced accordingly.

The above considerations reveal that the conditions for EU accession can be grouped into two categories. The first involves a number of specific and absolute requirements for membership, where Turkey generally has little or no choice as to the form or type of compliance. The second category covers a range of conditions and guidelines, often in the form of minimum standards, but where Turkey retains some choice about where it positions itself prior to and following accession. Key examples of the former are the requirements regarding the Customs Union, CAP, health of the financial sector, and EMU. Key examples of the latter set of conditions are the requirements regarding the environment and labour markets. It seems that Turkey will have to satisfy, as soon as possible, the former set of conditions and with some time lag the latter set of conditions.

The whole process will be costly to both parties, but it will be beneficial in the end.

Notes

1 See the Presidency Conclusions of the Helsinki European Council held on 10–11 December 1999.

2 See Presidency Conclusions, Berlin European Council, 24–25 March 1999.

3 Claessens *et al.* (1998) define foreign banks as those banks that have at least 50 per cent foreign ownership. According to the authors, the share of foreign bank assets in total bank assets averaged over the period 1988–95 was 77 per cent in Greece, 31 per cent in Spain, 61 per cent in Hungary, 51 per cent in the Czech Republic, and 1 per cent in Turkey. With liberalization in financial markets the penetration rates of foreign banks in Turkey are expected to increase substantially. As some of the Turkish banks merge with foreign banks or exit from the market, employment in the sector will be adversely affected.

4 For a summary of the Directive, see http://www.europa.eu.int/en/comm/dg17/elec/memor.htm

5 Law Number 4628, published in the Official Gazette on 3 March 2001.

6 For a recent analysis of State-owned enterprises in Turkey, see Arslan and Celasun (2000).

7 Turkish Competition Law is silent with regard to public undertakings. It does not contain a clause such as Article 86 (ex Article 90) of the EEC Treaty, which explicitly brings public undertakings within the scope of competition policy. Moreover, it is worth noting that state aid in Turkey has recently taken the form of injections to private banks under the management of Savings Deposit Insurance Fund. These are mainly banks hit by capital losses during the November 2000 and February 2001 crises due to the sharp decline in the market value of government securities holdings and capital losses arising from the sharp depreciation of its exchange rate. According to EU regulations, state aid to the banking sector is subject to the same conditions as any other state aid and as such it should be avoided.

8 The process described above corresponds to the experience of EU membership for Spain, Portugal, and Ireland.

9 The Union's own resources consist of agricultural duties and sugar and isoglucose levies, customs duties, VAT resources, and the fourth resource. The fourth resource is a variable, budget balancing resource for which the call-in rate is calculated during the budgetary procedure in such a way as to cover the amounts not yielded by other budget revenue. The own resources ceiling was raised in 1999 from 1.21 per cent of GNP in 1995 to 1.27 per cent of GNP.

10 PHARE is the European Union initiative that supports the development of a larger democratic family of nations within a prosperous and stable Europe. It was initially developed as an immediate response to challenges facing the countries of central and eastern Europe.

References

Arslan, I. and M. Celasun (2000) 'State-owned enterprises and privatization in Turkey: policy, performance and reform experience, 1985–95', in Celasun, M. (ed.), *State-Owned Enterprises in the Middle East and North Africa: Privatization, Performance and Reform*, London: Routledge.

Canning, D. (2000) 'The contribution of infrastructure to aggregate output', World Bank Working Paper, Washington, DC: The World Bank.

Central Bank of Turkey, http://www.tcmb.gov.tr, accessed during 2002.

Claessens, S., A. Demirgüç-Kunt, and H. Huizinga (1998) 'How does foreign entry affect the domestic banking market?' World Bank Working paper, Washington, DC: The World Bank.

Deutsche Bank Research (2002) *EU Enlargement Monitor*, http://www.dbresearch.com: April.

European Commission (2000) *The Agricultural Situation in the European Union: 1999 Report*, COM (2000) 485 Final, Brussels: European Commission.

Frankel, J. and A. Rose (2002) 'An estimate of the effect of common currencies on trade and income', unpublished paper.

Harrison, G. W., T. F. Rutherford, and D. G. Tarr (1997) 'Economic implications for Turkey of a customs union with the European Union', *European Economic Review*, 41: 861—870.

Organization for Economic Co-operation and Development (2000) *Agricultural Policies in OECD Countries: Monitoring and Evaluation*, OECD: Paris.

Togan, S. (2000) 'The unreported labour market in Turkey', paper presented at the Conference on Unreported Labour Market, State Institute of Statistics, 6 December 2000, Ankara.

Togan, S. (2001) 'Turkey and the European Union', unpublished paper, Bilkent University, Ankara.

Turkish Treasury, http://www.treasury.gov.tr, accessed during 2002.

Turkish State Planning Organization, http://www.dpt.gov.tr, accessed during 2002.

13 Economic foundation for peace?

The case of trade policy in the Oslo Agreement

Nu'man Kanafani

1 Introduction

The Middle East has been the burial ground for several reconciliation and peace attempts in the past 100 years. The fate of the latest attempt, the Oslo Process, is probably the most tragic in the exhaustingly long list of missed opportunities. The Oslo Process, or the collection of security, political and economic agreements signed between the Palestinian Authority (PA) and Israel during the period 1993–2000, triggered great hopes and received unprecedented support, both locally and internationally, in its early stages. Yet, the process did not only fail in realizing its ends, it has also deepened the mistrust and bitterness between the two nations. A great deal has been and will be written, I am sure, on the roots of this failure. In this article I shall deal exclusively with the part of the Oslo accords which addressed the economic relations between Israel and the West Bank and Gaza Strip (WBGS). My aim is to investigate the principles upon which the trade agreement was based and to shed light on how the agreement was implemented and subsequently failed long before the total collapse of the political process. I shall try to use this case to draw some lessons for the future.

2 Background

Immediately after the occupation in 1967, the WBGS was cut off from their previous trade relationships and forced into new and asymmetrical economic ties with Israel. The Palestinian areas became 'partners' with Israel in a *de facto* one-sided customs union: Israeli products had free access to the WBGS markets while Palestinian products were subjected to a wide range of restrictions. Agricultural exports from the WBGS to Israel were practically prohibited, except as a buffer to meet any shortages in supply from Israeli sources, while manufactured exports were subject to multiple administrative controls and non-tariff barriers (NTBs). Israel's trade policy, well known for its high degree of protectionism and its innovative use of NTBs (GATT 1995), applied automatically to the WBGS without any allowance for the particular needs and potential of the Palestinian economy. Strict administrative controls on water and land use, licensing requirements for the cultivation of certain crops and regulatory restrictions on the establishment of firms and investment projects effectively held back production in the WBGS, especially in fields where competition with Israeli products was possible. There was practically no formal financial system (Hamed 1996) and Palestinian farmers and manufacturers were effectively excluded from the various forms of public subsidies extended so generously to their Israeli counterparts. The new geopolitical realities, along with restrictions on the activities of foreign agents and the lack of scale economies, put an end to the WBGS's earlier direct trade relationships with the outside world. In effect, all direct external relationships were transformed into indirect relationships operating through Israeli entry points, and through Israeli import and export agents.

On the other hand, almost all direct and indirect taxes imposed on the inhabitants of the WBGS were transferred to the Israeli treasury: direct and indirect taxes were collected on the basis of 'origin' or place of payment rather than on the basis of 'destination' and residency. Thus, Palestinian workers in Israel were obliged to pay national insurance contributions without being entitled to most of the corresponding benefits. Import taxes and excise paid on goods consumed by the Palestinians in the WBGS, but imported via Israeli ports, were also retained by Israel. The procedure was the same for purchase taxes and other charges imposed on Israeli products that were paid for by the WBGS's Palestinians.

During the occupation period, the economy of the WBGS became firmly locked into a position of excessive resource deficit, becoming to an even greater extent totally dependent on labour exports – now mainly to Israel – and on non-requited transfers from abroad. The WBGS ended up with the peculiar economic structure of an extremely poor productive base, weaker than in typical 'low-income countries', but with a per capita GNP at the top of the range for the 'lower middle-income countries'. The Occupied Territories have since become the second most important single market for Israeli exports (after the United States). More than 90 per cent of the total WBGS's imports of goods (US$1,050 million) came from Israel, while only three quarters of their minuscule exports (US$385 million) went to Israel. The vulnerability that dependence on a single market for trade and employment inevitably brings was clearly demonstrated in the early 1980s, when the Israeli economy fell into a relatively recessionary period and remittances from the Arab Gulf countries stagnated. By the late 1980s, and after the outbreak of the first *Intifada*, per capita income declined sharply with a dramatic increase in unemployment and poverty (World Bank 1993).

3 The Economic Protocol (EP 1994)

The short description above depicts the background to the economic relations between WBGS and Israel, which presumably one of the Oslo Accords' documents, the Protocol on Economic Relations between Israel and the Palestinian Authority (29 April 1994), sought to address. The Protocol's attempt to establish new trade relations based on 'mutual respect of each other's economic interests, reciprocity, equity and fairness' was embodied in three basic principles:

- Free access for WBGS agricultural and industrial products to the Israeli market (with the exception of five agricultural commodities on which increasing quotas were imposed up to 1997).
- The right of the WBGS to undertake independent and direct trade relations with the outside world, either via its own special crossing points (to Jordan and Egypt) or via Israeli international ports where Palestinian goods 'will be given equal trade and economic treatment.' Furthermore, it was agreed that the WBGS's external trade would be subject to Israel's trade policy and regulations except in two cases. First, the PA has the right to its own import policy (including customs and other import charges as well as standard specifications) on quantities designed to meet the WBGS's own market needs of specified goods (lists A1 and A2). Second, the PA has the right to impose its own import charges (but not standards specifications) on imports from a second list of goods (list B).
- The introduction of the principle of 'destination' rather than 'points of entry' for the reimbursement of all import taxcs (as well as VAT). Thus, article III, 15 states: 'The clearance of revenues from all import taxes and levies between Israel and the PA will be based on the principle of the place of final destination'. The Article confirms that this will be the case even if Israeli agents carried out importation, as long as the final destination of the said goods is the WBGS.

4 Customs unions versus free trade areas

There are two standard forms of preferential trade arrangements: free trade areas (FTAs) and customs unions (CUs). Both incorporate free trade between the participating countries, but while in an FTA each country maintains its own policy on imports from the rest of the world, members of a CU adopt a common trade policy towards third countries. In order to allow for free trade between countries with different external tariffs, an FTA requires the existence of customs borders between members. This is necessary to prevent trade 'deflection' whereby goods are imported via the country with the lowest external tariff and then sent tariff-free to the markets of other members of the FTA. Together with the adoption of specific rules of origin, the customs borders ensure that only products with confirmed domestic origins are eligible for free movement within the FTA.

Since the seminal work of Viner in the 1950s, it has been well established in theory that both FTAs and CUs are only second-best solutions, which do not necessarily lead to welfare improvement in the countries concerned. This is because trade liberalization within blocks leads to two opposing effects with respect to resource reallocation: trade *creation* (where demand shifts from local production to more efficient producers in a partner country) and trade *diversion* (where the shift is from more efficient producers outside the CU/FTA to less efficient producers in a partner country). While trade creation increases consumer and producer surpluses, trade diversion leads to a net loss. The question as to whether the static effects of trade integration will bring about an improvement in welfare depends on whether trade creation is stronger than trade diversion. The answer to this question is largely empirical and differs from one case to another. It depends on the particular production and demand structures and the relative volume of external trade and the tariff rates, as well as the type and degree of trade distortions that remain after the establishment of the preferential arrangement.

Along with the static or resource reallocation effects, trade integration has potential dynamic benefits. These include the various possible effects on growth such as scale economies, externalities, and technology spillover. Although the positive nature of these effects is usually emphasized, economists are still unable to provide satisfactory estimates of their empirical significance (El-Agraa 1989).

The comparison between a CU and an FTA, from a welfare perspective, is, then, largely an empirical issue. Although trade diversion may be lower in an FTA than in a CU (because countries can select their own external tariffs to preserve the competitive edge of efficient third country producers) the dynamic effects are probably stronger in the CU. In fact, recent studies within the political economy school stress the advantages of CUs over FTAs for a variety of other reasons as well (Panagariya and Findlay 1994, Krueger 1995). The use and misuse of rules of origin, which are necessary in FTAs, play an important role in the analysis of this school. However, the risk of 'polarization', or what Brown (1961) calls 'back wash' (tendency for economic activities to concentrate in one region only) is probably stronger in CUs than in FTAs. This is particularly important in the case of preferential trade arrangements, which involve developed and underdeveloped economies.

5 The Palestinian debate

The EP envisaged a specific 'hybrid' preferential trade agreement between Israel and the WBGS: a regime which combines elements of a CU (absence of customs border between Israel and the WBGS) as well as elements of an FTA (different tariff and regulations on imports from third countries, albeit only on specific goods).

Preferential trade agreements are usually assessed on the basis of their positive effects on bilateral trade. However, this is clearly not the appropriate criterion in assessing the success or failure of the EP. From the Palestinian perspective, the EP provided an opportunity to reduce the WBGS's dependency on the Israeli market, at least with regard to imports. In that sense, the EP reverses the usual role of a trade agreement, as pointed out by Fassberg (1996). Rather than bringing two independent economic systems together and imposing reciprocal limitations on them, the EP was designed to establish a sphere of independence for a new economic entity. 'Economic union', Fassberg (1996: 169) concludes, 'is not the objective, but rather a very clear point of departure'.

The Palestinians were particularly interested in the opportunity, which the EP provided, to revive the WBGS's old trade relations with neighbouring markets and to reduce the trade diversion that took place during the *de facto* economic annexation by the Israeli economy. Thus, the paradox referred to earlier: the extent of the reduction in Israel's share in total WBGS imports and that of the expansion of WBGS exports to other markets are more relevant criteria for the success of this particular 'preferential' trade agreement. The PA saw the EP as a contractual document, which would replace the forced economic annexation of the previous period with cooperative relations.

Palestinian economists and politicians were divided in their evaluation of the new trade regime. One group (e.g., El-Musa and El-Jafari 1995) stressed the very narrow margin left open by the EP for the PA's own import policy. It questioned whether the WBGS's economy would be able to revive under a trade policy that was tailored to the needs of an economy as advanced and structurally different from the WBGS as that of Israel. Based on such scepticism, along with a fear that polarization would reinforce the WBGS's status as a labour reservoir, this group favoured a standard free trade relationship or an even more distant trade relationship with Israel. The fact that an FTA implies a higher degree of political autonomy was also an important element in the argument of this group. In fact, some PA politicians saw the three lists as a first step and believed that the likely, albeit contentious, process of enlargement of these lists would eventually lead to a standard FTA arrangement.

Another group (e.g. Abed 1996, Kanafani 1996) argued that although the WBGS's potential benefits from preferential trade with Israel were reduced because of Israel's commitments to liberalization within the WTO, the economy of the WBGS could still draw important gains from free access and proximity to the huge Israeli market. This group stressed that the old trade structure had been created by imposed constraints and that a properly functioning customs union should not, in principle, prevent the WBGS from restructuring its trade and reviving the old regional relations. Finally, this group pointed out that the absence of customs borders with Israel could be beneficial for the WBGS, in that it secured a smoother flow of trade, increased the dynamic benefits and eliminated the need to introduce rules of origin that could be harmful for Palestinian exports.

Notwithstanding this difference of opinion, the EP triggered high hopes, and it was left to empirical experience to demonstrate how much benefit the new trade regime would bring, and whether this would justify more or less trade integration with Israel after the end of the 5-year transitional period.

6 Dashed hopes

The WBGS's economic performance since the signing of the EP has been extremely disappointing. In spite of the overall optimism generated by the peace process, the considerable inflow of foreign aid and the very low starting point of the economy after the harsh years of the first Intifada, real per capita GDP and GNP actually declined between 1993 and 1998. Gross fixed investment dropped, after an initial rise, by about 7 per cent between 1995 and 1998 (Kessler 1999). The performance of the external trade sector was particularly discouraging. Up to

1997, the overall value of WBGS exports hardly even returned to the level attained a decade earlier; while imports more than doubled during the decade, leading to a $1.8 billion trade deficit, a little less than one-half of the GDP in 1997 (PCBS 1999). The collapse in living standards and the dramatic increase in poverty are thoroughly documented in Diwan and Shaban (1999).

What went wrong? Available data reveal that the WBGS's economic performance in this period closely followed the cycle of the 'closures'. Closure is a code name for an Israeli practice of collective punishment which includes a variety of measures leading to the effective and comprehensive physical siege of the WBGS, whereby all movements of goods, vehicles and people outside (and sometimes even within) the WBGS are totally banned. Between 1993 and 1999, the WBGS were subject to 311.5 days of comprehensive closure (UNSCO 1997–9). The figure refers only to 'actual' working days (i.e. excluding the days of closure which occur during Muslim and Jewish holidays, Saturdays and half of Fridays). In 1996 alone there were 27 days of 'internal closure' (i.e. the banning of movement within the West Bank itself). The closures were imposed not only in response to suicide bombs exploded by Palestinian extremists, but also on a recurring basis as a 'pre-emptive' measure in advance of some alleged threat.

It is hardly surprising that, for areas as small as the WBGS and as dependent on Israel for employment and trade, the physical siege would lead to a standstill of economic life. It is, therefore, tempting to argue that the dismal economic performance of the WBGS was due to the closure policy. It is tempting, in other words, to claim that progress was hindered by purely politically volatile circumstances, rather than by any shortcomings in the EP as such. However, some economists maintain that the failure is precisely due to the fact that the Protocol was never properly implemented: 'the political impasse made all arrangements, including the economic agreement, unworkable' (Kleiman 1997). Whilst not denying the crucial effect of the political environment on economic performance, I believe that it is misleading to suggest that the failure was exclusively due to factors external to the EP. The logical implication of such a claim is that similar economic arrangements between the two parties would be workable in the future provided that political goodwill prevails on both sides. I shall argue here that this is not the case.

The EP's design for trade relations in particular was, in fact, exclusively dictated by political considerations. Economics was totally subordinated to politics. I shall argue that the trade regime of the EP was unnecessarily complicated and it lacked essential elements to allow it to fulfil its promises. The economic regime seems to have been carefully tailored to safeguard, and to enforce, the strict limits imposed on the PA's political sovereignty. As a direct result, the arrangements did not only fail in bringing economic benefits but also contributed in clouding the process of reconciliation even further.

7 A level playing field?

The fact that it was so easy to make the EP's trade provisions inoperative, by issuing a simple military order of closure, indicates their inherent weakness rather than lack of culpability. The Israel–PA agreements, to which the EP was attached, distinguishes between 'functional jurisdiction' and 'territorial jurisdiction'. The PA was granted both jurisdictions in specified small areas (Areas A), but only functional jurisdiction in other areas (Areas B) and neither in Areas C. Areas C are neatly spread out and cover all of the WBGS's access points to Israel as well as to the outside world. This peculiar situation meant that in reality the PA could be easily stripped of any effective jurisdiction in any area. For example, building a housing complex in Gaza depends on permission from Israel to allow cement to pass through 'C' Areas on its way from Egypt or Israel. The idea of slicing a small geographical region into pieces and expecting these isolated islands to operate as a cohesive economic structure (Art. I, 4 of the EP) was never convincing. Its inadequacy was probably one of the core reasons for the sad fate of the EP as a whole and its trade provisions in particular. Not surprisingly, therefore, Israel's army personnel did not worry about the commitments to free access and free trade, so frequently cited in the EP (Halevi 1999). The EP simply failed to provide the necessary assurances for truly free access and for reciprocal and equal treatment of trade.

Israel recognized the extreme economic hardships imposed on the Palestinians by the closures but maintained that these were unintended effects of a policy that was made necessary by security reasons. The Palestinians have, however, frequently stressed that the heavy-handed measures were probably motivated by reasons other than genuine security: Israel was applying economic strangulation as blackmail for political ends. Here again, the EP was utterly useless in helping to find a middle way where trade could flow freely without undermining security. After all, the inevitable clashes of interests must have been expected from the start: the EP was not a document institutionalizing cooperation between two friendly nations, but a 'treaty' with an ambitious aim of replacing the old 'captive-market' relations with equal and partner-like relations.

Although Israel's trade policy has witnessed substantial changes during the 1990s, there are still strong reasons to suspect that technical and non-technical standards, sanitary and veterinary requirements, and packing and labelling specifications are actively deployed to put imports at a disadvantage. The GATT Secretariat has pointed out frequently (see, e.g. GATT 1995) that Israel's mandatory specifications are tailored to serving the interests of local producers and giving them an edge over imports. Required standards for agricultural and food products are particularly strict, especially those for dairy products and meat imports. Even the United States has frequently complained that many standards requirements in Israel 'are drawn up so as to favour local products with no relation to performance safety' (Aminoff 1991: 33). In addition, there are strong indications that purchase and excise taxes are deployed in a manner which discriminate against imports. Furthermore, Israel still has strong co-operative marketing boards, which, again according to the GATT Secretariat, play an important role in impeding free market mechanisms (especially in poultry markets), along with a wide range of direct and indirect state subsidies to agriculture and manufacturing. The latter includes support for both research and new technology, tax holidays, export guarantees and other incentives related to regional development, while direct subsidies to agriculture take the form of subsidies on inputs (such as water) as well as subsidies on exports such as flowers, citrus fruits and vegetables. All of these constitute serious and potentially explosive issues for any trade integration agreement.

Israel's 'formidable' NTBs – as aptly described by Rivlin (1992: 98) – have been particularly harmful to the WBGS's agricultural exports to Israel (PA 1997). They not only affect the WBGS's potential exports but also increase trade diversion and, consequently, the cost that the WBGS bear from trade integration with Israel. It is obvious that securing 'fair' economic relations between the two parties requires that all these issues should be tackled, perhaps by the provision of some sort of compensation to the WBGS economies. However, the EP was totally silent on this point, except for pointing out that the 'Palestinian side has also the right to employ other methods of encouraging industry resorted to in Israel' (Art. IX, 2a). Clearly, since the PA could hardly be expected to have the resources and administrative structure to extend a comprehensive programme of subsidies similar to that in Israel, this formulation served only to legitimize free-trade violations and to institutionalize 'unfair' trade.

8 The implementation vehicle

As highlighted earlier, the EP did very little to secure fair and equal treatment of trade. It called for the establishment of a Joint Economic Committee (JEC) 'to follow up the implementation of this Protocol and to decide on problems related to it' (Art. II: 1). The JEC was entrusted with a long array of duties and was made the main vehicle for implementation. Naturally, the guarding of the implementation of a cooperation agreement between old and bitter enemies requires strict rules of conduct, clear guidance for dispute resolution and an efficient enforcement mechanism. This is particularly important in this case because, perhaps intentionally, many aspects in the EP were left vague, and because the EP's proposed trade regime was an innovation that was bound to bring about numerous conflicts. However, none of these necessary elements to ensure proper implementation were provided. Apart from pointing out that the JEC shall consist of equal numbers of delegates and that it shall reach its decisions by agreement, nothing else was specified about the JEC's working procedures. The JEC was given the mandate to determine its own 'rules of procedure and operation', but up to 1998 the Committee operated in a totally informal manner, without even a schedule of regular meetings or official minutes.

The two contracting parties to the EP are, of course, vastly unequal on all levels. Yet, the success of any contractual agreements requires some reasonable distribution of bargaining power between the parties to secure balanced implementation and to maintain the incentives for continued co-operation. Clearly, though, the structure and working methods of the JEC demonstrate that the EP not only deprived the weaker party of all its bargaining power, but it also left it hopelessly dependent on the mercy and goodwill of the stronger one. Moreover, the EP's provisions give the impression that the JEC's working procedures would be loose and very informal, which inevitably works to the advantage of the stronger party. The hegemony is set in stone by the EP's declaration that delegates to the JEC shall 'reach their decisions by agreement.' The absence of any reference to arbitration, which is a standard clause in trade agreements, was a recipe for failure and stalemate. The weaker party would inevitably be left with a chronic sense of being both impotent and ill treated, while the other party was bound to fall into the trap of the arrogance of power.

9 The three lists

The novelty of the EP's trade regime lies in the design of the three lists of goods and commodities. The main objective was to allow the two parties to have different import and/or customs policies on these goods, without the need of customs borders between them. To avoid trade deflection (whereby all imports come in via the country with the lowest external tariff), quantitative restrictions were imposed on the importation of these goods. Thus, the PA was allowed to have its own tariffs on specified goods provided that those were imported in specified quantities to meet the WBGS's market needs. Obviously, this novel regime was constructed in order to accommodate contradictory political aspirations. A standard FTA between the two parties was ruled out because it would require the existence of customs borders. Israel's concern with the political significance of any sort of 'borders' with the WBGS was so strong that it even rejected the idea of having 'moving customs borders', that is, customs borders which are moved from time to time within a large zone. The PA, on the other hand, saw a standard customs union as an arrangement that offered little, if any, autonomy in trade policy. The EP proposed a regime which combines elements from both worlds: the PA was allowed some limited say in trade policy with respect to the WBGS's own imports of certain goods, while Israel secured the absence of borders with the WBGS.

The EP's trade regime was, perhaps, innovative in 'solving' a political dilemma. Yet, the more important question is whether this complicated and untried arrangement makes economic sense and contributes to the process of development and reconciliation. The answer, alas, is no! A trade regime that was invented exclusively to provide a cover for a vague, imprecise, and unfinished political compromise was inevitably bound to be obscure, and lead to unfortunate economic consequences. Moreover, turbulent relations on the trade front eventually fuelled the political conflict: the EP became a conflict-generating document that complicated further, rather than facilitated, the process of political reconciliation.

The EP specified three lists. List A1 includes 29 items, 13 of which can only be imported from Jordan and Egypt, and the rest from any Arab country. List A2 includes 18 items, 12 of which also figure in A1, which can be imported from anywhere in the world. Finally, list B covers a relatively large number of specific tools and equipment. Unlike lists A1 and A2, there are no quantitative restrictions on the WBGS's imports under list B, but these imports have to meet Israel's own standards and specifications for imports. Aside from the way in which certain goods appear, peculiarly, in more than one list, the reasons as to why these particular goods were selected are far from obvious. The selection seems to be arbitrary and does not serve a clear development purpose. Although the disaggregated data for the WBGS's imports are unreliable, it appears that the goods and commodities listed in lists A1 and A2 accounted for less than one-fourth of the WBGS's total imports in 1992. In any case, the real scope for the PA to operate its own import policy with respect to these goods is very limited indeed. It is obvious that the PA's option to impose higher import tariffs on these goods compared to Israeli tariffs is meaningless, since this would encourage the WBGS's imports to be registered as imports into Israel. The PA's option is therefore limited to imposing lower tariffs than Israel's. However, a detailed analysis of Israel's customs book for 1996 shows that tariffs on the vast majority of A1, A2, and B goods were either zero or very low; in fact, many of the goods in the A1 and A2 lists are also exempt from standard specifications (Kanafani 1996).

But even if there were considerable scope for reducing import taxes on A1 and A2 goods, the merits of such a policy would be questionable. The WBGS, as pointed out earlier, suffers from a chronic trade deficit, and lowering tariffs would aggravate the deficit. On the other hand, it is hardly conceivable that the newly created PA would give up revenues from import tariffs. The PA has actually imposed identical import charges on A1 and A2 goods to those imposed by Israel, presumably for fiscal reasons. This, in fact, is not regrettable: there is no reason to assume that lowering or abolishing import duties on goods subject to quotas would have been beneficial to the WBGS economy, that is, that the lost import revenues would have been balanced by equal or greater benefits to WBGS consumers in the form of lower prices. Reducing customs imports on goods subject to quotas would most probably have generated increased rents for those with access to the import licenses.

Indeed, the whole concept of introducing import lists and quotas is problematic, given the requirements for its proper functioning – regular estimation of domestic market needs (on the basis of what prices?); the operation of two customs books at the crossing points; keeping a track of licences – especially since these tasks would have to be carried out by the newly created PA bureaucracy which had no previous experience or administrative tradition.

It is hardly surprising that some of the quotas in the lists have never been fixed due to irreconcilable controversies between the two parties. The PA was in a never-ending battle to enlarge the lists, to prove that the fixed quotas were smaller than market needs, and to keep track of the difference between what had been licensed for import and what was actually imported, etc. Insofar as an assessment can be made under the extraordinary conditions of closure, actual experience with the lists suggests they contributed to the existence of excessive regulation and strong monopolistic trends in the WBGS's trade. Indeed, in some cases the quotas were used as bargaining tools in monopolistic arrangements between major Israeli suppliers and semi-official Palestinian distributors, as in the case of cement (Kanafani *et al.* 1998).

10 Third party relations

The PA was able, however, to derive two major benefits from the existence of these lists and the trade regime that they incorporate. The first was probably unintended, while the second is more political than economic. I have already pointed out that Israel's stringent specifications and standards on imports act as powerful NTBs. The WBGS's imports via the quotas in lists A1 and A2 could, at least in theory, escape these stringent requirements: thus the lists were useful in a roundabout way. This explains why the significance of list B was minimal, since imports from B have to conform to Israel's standards. Additionally, purchase taxes paid on imports via the lists were acquired by the PA, unlike the taxes on other imports into the WBGS.

The second major benefit from the lists was that they allowed the PA to sign separate international trade agreements. Bilateral trade agreements in the Middle East have traditionally been based on reciprocal trade concessions on specified goods, and the EP's lists were convenient as such to allow the PA to enter into preferential trade arrangements with neighbouring Arab countries.

The PA's scope for entering into international agreements was set out in Article IX of Oslo II. The Article made clear that, in as far as trade policy is concerned, any international agreement signed by the PA should be in line with the framework laid down in the EP. The PA has signed a number of trade agreements with other countries on the basis of the three lists. The agreement with Jordan in 1995 is the most important example of these. The PA also signed a trade agreement with the EU in 1997; however, unlike the agreement with Jordan, this was not explicitly based on the EP's lists but was virtually a standard Association arrangement within the EU's Mediterranean Initiative. The agreement was strongly disputed by Israel but the PA and the EU used the existence of the lists as a principle in their legal argument: since the PA was allowed to have its own import policy on the goods included in the three lists, then the WBGS can be considered a separate 'customs territory'. Israel maintained that the Med Association agreements implicitly constitute contractual relations between independent entities with defined geographic sovereignty and communicated its reservations on the PA–EU agreement to the WTO's Council on Trade in July 1997.

The root of the dispute can, in fact, be traced back to the EP itself (as well as other PA–Israel agreements). The ambiguity of the true nature of the trade regime is at the heart of the dispute: is it a standard customs union or not? Most experts accept that the EP's regime is not, *and interestingly, the term 'customs union' does not exist in any of the signed documents between the two parties*. The question then is whether the scope of deviation from the standard customs union is wide enough to consider the WBGS as a separate 'customs territory'. A customs territory, according to Article XXI B2 of the GATT Charter, is any territory with separate tariffs or other regulations of commerce on a 'substantial' part of its trade with other territories. The European countries (EU and EFTA) as well as Canada have considered the scope provided in the EP wide enough to justify separate contractual agreements with the WBGS, rejecting Israel's claim of a 'single customs envelope'.

On a purely technical level, however, Israel's concerns boil down to whether the PA has offered more generous trade concessions to the EU than what the EU already has through its own free trade agreement with Israel. A detailed investigation (Kanafani 2000) has documented that this is actually not the case. Obviously, the real reason for Israel's anxiety is the significance of the EU–PA agreement as a *de jure* recognition of the separation between Israel and Palestine. Free trade accords, under the WTO rules, are agreements between autonomous customs territories. This explains the significance of the United States' decision to 'extend' its FTA agreement with Israel to incorporate the WBGS rather than signing a separate trade accord with the PA.

Nor should one underestimate the relevance of economic motives behind Israel's fierce opposition. Recognizing the WBGS as a separate customs territory provides yet another reason for putting an end to Israel's practice of 'smuggling' the products of its illegal settlements in the WBGS (as well as in East Jerusalem) into the EU. Being in one 'customs envelope' with the WBGS can be misused to warrant the tariff-free access of the settlements' products into the EU markets.

The numerous trade agreements signed separately by Israel and the PA with third party countries overlap each other and have created a chaotic and highly problematic trade setting: the benefits from the novel trade regime were mainly political in nature. This reaffirms the argument that when a trade design is constructed solely to resolve a tactical political dilemma, the parties will continue fighting their political battle using economics and trade as tools.

11 Import tax clearance

The clearance of import taxes between Israel and the PA has probably been the most successfully implemented aspect of the trade arrangements. The amounts transferred to the PA gradually increased and the money clearance sub-committee met regularly even during periods of acute tension. Israel withheld the reimbursement of funds on a number of occasions, but this led to widespread international condemnation. Nevertheless, the procedure of tax clearance became a source of chronic and heated dispute between the two parties. Eventually, indeed, the disputes about which of the charges paid by Palestinian consumers, but collected by Israel, should be reimbursed and whether the WBGS was receiving its fair share, turned out to be the most controversial issue in the EP. The EP's procedure for import tax clearance had unfortunate consequences for the PA's commercial policy and contributed to the development of an atmosphere of suspicion and distrust with Israel.

The EP states that 'the clearance of revenues from all import taxes and levies between Israel and the PA shall be based on the principle of the place of final destination.' Thus, all import taxes and levies on goods purchased and consumed by WBGS Palestinians would be reimbursed to the PA. This is regardless of the nationality and/or place of registration of the importing agent, and regardless of the crossing points through which these goods enter the WBGS (via Israel or directly). The EP also specified that reimbursement would be conducted on the basis of monitoring and documenting actual transactions: all invoices would be collected and clearance would be based on documentary evidence that import taxes and levies had indeed been paid to the 'wrong' side, an approach that can conveniently be referred to as a *'micro'* approach.

The actual implementation of this rather complicated and highly bureaucratic procedure has resulted in the PA losing the revenues of the following import taxes and levies, which were paid by the Palestinian consumers but collected by Israel:

- Customs duties and the relatively high purchase taxes paid on foreign goods that were first imported to Israel and then re-imported by the WBGS (with the exception of excise on fuel). It is a well-established fact that virtually all of the WBGS' imports from overseas used to arrive via this channel.
- Purchase taxes on Israeli-manufactured products that were paid for and consumed by the WBGS' Palestinians. These taxes were not refunded to the PA even when they were duly invoice-documented.
- All customs and other import taxes and levies paid on the imported-content of Israeli manufactured goods sold in the WBGS.
- All customs and other import taxes and levies (and VAT) imposed on the purchases of the WBGS from Israel that are *not* documented by invoices.

Several attempts have been made to estimate these lost revenues, the so-called 'fiscal leakages': the PA's (1998) estimates put the figure as high as $380 million annually. Dumas (1999) applied three different estimation methods and concluded that the PA's losses amounted to $90–140 million in 1997 (some one-fourth of what was actually reimbursed, or 2.6–4.2 per cent of WBGS' GDP). Remarkably, Dumas excluded from his calculation the revenues lost due to non-documented direct purchases. One can only guess at the amount of these non-invoiced purchases by Palestinians in the Israeli market: the PA put it at about 30 per cent of total registered imports from Israel.

The PA's reaction to the chronic, and probably substantial, fiscal leakage came in stages. First, in October 1996, a notification was issued stating that Israeli import agents of international suppliers or Israeli manufacturers were banned from supplying local (WBGS) retailers as well as from selling directly in the WBGS. Foreign and Israeli producers were required to have their own domestically registered agents in the WBGS. Clearly, the aim was to prevent sales of goods in the WBGS that were not clearly and specifically imported directly to a locally registered business. The second major step came in June 1997 and was designed specifically to stop the leakage of customs and excise duties on new and second-hand cars purchased by Palestinians from Israel. Finally, since August 1997, the PA's Customs Authority has started to undertake raids on retailers' shops to enforce the implementation of these regulations. Shops selling goods with high purchase taxes (electrical equipment and installations, chemical products, perfumes, and spare parts for cars) were particularly targeted.

The PA also experimented with other, more sophisticated ways to circumvent the leakage: for example, cutting purchase taxes in half to make direct imports (within the quotas of the lists) more competitive than to re-import via Israel. In this way the PA's treasury was able to collect at least half of the purchase taxes, which is better than losing them entirely.

Israel reacted strongly to these measures and considered them a breach of the principles of the CU. However, soon thereafter Israel started to ask Palestinian importers to sign pledges making them legally responsible for guaranteeing that their imported goods would not leak in any way to Israeli customers. This was, perhaps, a mere over-reaction, but it also reflects Israel's concern over the remote possibility of 'reverse' fiscal leakage, since import taxes and levies paid on *direct* Palestinian imports are reimbursed to the PA. Needless to say, both the PA and Israel's measures implied in reality that goods could no longer be freely exchanged and were, as such, in sharp contravention to the wording, not to mention the spirit, of the EP.

The above exposition makes it clear that the way in which the procedure of import tax clearance was designed and applied turned it into a source of continuous conflict of interests and simply led to higher costs of trade diversion, making the WBGS's losses higher and more tangible: purchase of Israeli rather than foreign products involved not only the loss of customs duty but also loss of the relatively high purchase taxes. Re-import from Israel, rather than direct import from overseas, also involved losing the purchase taxes paid. In fact, the system ensures that it is nearly always more preferable for the PA to favour direct imports over re-imports from Israel, to favour imports over Israeli-manufactured goods (on which high purchase taxes are imposed) and to limit, as much as possible, direct non-recorded purchases (including weekend family shopping). In the absence of reciprocal trade diversion in favour of the WBGS, therefore, the PA has had a clear commercial incentive to deploy administrative measures to reduce trade with Israel.

Israel, on the other hand, has had just as obvious an incentive to restrict direct Palestinian trade relations with the outside world: the WBGS is an extremely important market for Israeli products. Israel's vested interest in limiting the WBGS's direct imports can be served either by deploying the usual NTBs, or by other means disguised as 'security' measures.[1]

The micro approach to import tax clearance, which is based on complicated and excessively bureaucratic procedures of invoice documentation, has led to unfortunate tendencies in the WBGS markets. Confronted with the almost impossible task of collecting all invoices and bills from small retailers to reclaim customs duties (and VAT), the PA found it much easier to deal with just a few major importers. This has provided an argument, or a pretext, for encouraging monopolization of the Palestinian market. Poor administrative skills and lack of bookkeeping traditions in the bazaar have enhanced this tendency. The PA's eagerness to reduce the fiscal leakage and increase its revenue encouraged it also to interfere in the daily life of businesses and created a peculiar black market for 'smuggled' goods from Israel. Note also that WBGS traders have had no direct commercial interest in delivering the invoices to the PA to allow it to reclaim import taxes and levies (unlike with respect to VAT).

Many of these problems could have been avoided if a true revenue sharing or 'macro' approach had been adopted instead of clearance on the basis of invoice documentation. Revenue sharing is a system where all fiscal charges, including customs, import taxes, and levies in both countries are redistributed on the basis of some aggregate variables related to income and consumption. Such an approach has been successfully applied in the Southern Africa Customs Union (SACU).

One can only speculate as to why the 'micro' approach was chosen for import tax clearance while the same EP made use of the 'macro' approach for estimating the WBGS's Balance of Payments surpluses *vis-à-vis* Israel (for the purpose of allowing the PA to convert the excess amount of Israeli currency into foreign currency, Art. IV: 16). It must have been clear in advance that the PA would need a very long time to establish the administrative structure needed for the working of invoice-based clearance, but perhaps the PA may have thought that such a system was more attractive because of the greater autonomy it provides. Israel, on the other hand, may have considered the approach a convenient way of prolonging the period of resource drain from the WBGS. The micro approach was, perhaps, also chosen because it gives a superficial appearance of 'fiscal independence', permitting Israel to dismiss the Palestinian demand for compensation for the past, present, and future cost of trade integration. A true revenue-sharing approach should incorporate a mechanism to redistribute the overall benefits from trade integration fairly among the participating parties. This would imply that the WBGS's share of the total pool of imports and other indirect taxes should be increased to compensate for the unequal distribution of the costs of integration. In the SACU, for example, the pool of all import taxes, surcharges and excises is initially distributed among the five member countries in proportion to each country's consumption (of imports and of other goods subject to excise taxes). The share of each of the four poorer members of the union (Botswana, Lesotho, Namibia, and Swaziland) is then increased by a factor of 42 per cent to compensate them for various types of losses which arise from joining a CU with an advanced economy such as the Republic of South Africa: losses due to trade diversion in favour of the more advanced economy due to the 'polarization effect' and losses due to giving up the option of having trade policy and fiscal discretion.

12 Concluding remarks

The relationship between the political settlement and economic prosperity was ambivalent from the outset of the Oslo Process. It was not clear which of them would drag the other along in its wake, that is, whether peace would secure improvements in the living standards of the Palestinians or whether substantial foreign aid was needed to improve their condition and lure them into a fragile political settlement. This is not a trivial issue, because it has significant implications for how much the political arrangement should make allowances to ensure an adequate base for economic progress and prosperity. It is crucially important for determining to what extent a political arrangement can continue ignoring the elementary prerequisites for an economy to function in a proper fashion.

It is safe and rather uncontroversial to claim that the failure of the EP was exclusively due to a turbulent political environment and lack of political will. In fact, the shortage of political will was already manifest in the design of the EP and not merely confined to its implementation. Any future economic arrangements will have to confront this point. Any political compromise, which ignores the economic prerequisites for securing sustainable improvements in the Palestinians' living standards and their access over their resources, will be founded on sand.

I have attempted, in this chapter, to show that the trade regime of the EP was designed solely to serve tactical political purposes and that a great deal of the economic problems of the WBGS in the past years can be traced back to this unfortunate and short-sighted decision. While the political design was obscure, partial and temporary, the EP exhibited the same characteristics in the economic sphere. The degree of uncertainty that it has created would make it impossible for any economy to function properly. Along with this, the complex trade arrangements and disagreements regarding the lists and tariff refunds have become new sources for additional disputes, stoking the political conflict even further.

Recent experience shows that the reasons behind the failure of trade go beyond the issue of physical siege. The implementation of the EP on the ground, or lack of it, has exposed four major weaknesses that should be avoided in any future arrangements, as outlined below. But even before considering these points, a fundamental element must be made very clear: it goes without saying that if Israel's practice of 'closure' over the WBGS is permanent, occasional, or even probable in future, then there will exist no grounds whatsoever for cooperation between Palestine and Israel, be that economic or otherwise. The Palestinians would then be forced to work for a total cut-off from Israel and to invent alternative routes for economic progress.

Of those four major weaknesses, the first is that interim, unfinished and half-hearted economic arrangements have had catastrophic economic consequences, if only for the fact that they are synonymous with uncertainty about the future. Uncertainty is probably the single most important factor in explaining the dismal economic performance of the WBGS, especially with respect to productive investment. The Israeli policy of closure is particularly harmful because it is totally unpredictable. It is time to realize that any political settlement that does not ensure economic viability and improvements in standards of living, undermines its own foundations.

Second, the absence of a real enforcement mechanism and of effective arbitration between the parties is one of the major defects in the EP in general and its trade arrangements in particular. The arbitration body should have full competence to deal with all trade disputes no matter what their origins are (security or mere customs valuation problems), and to do so with an undisputed enforcement mechanism. Both Israel's notorious record of creative use of NTBs and the PA's brief experience of trade matters promise endless trade disputes in the future.

This, along with the vast discrepancy in the bargaining power of the two contracting parties, implies the need for an effective arbitration mechanism and a permanent arbitration body. Special arrangements could probably be made to assign this role to the WTO, although the WBGS is not yet a member of this organization.

Third, the trade regime envisaged in the EP was unnecessarily complex in its structure, imprecise and not always fair. Given the special circumstances of the region, the parties would certainly be better off with as simple, as straightforward and as fair a trade regime as possible. As I have argued at some length, the hybrid trade regime envisaged in the EP was an unfortunate novelty. It was basically a political creature that allowed the parties to continue their political battle by economic means. It established a costly regime of double bureaucratic layers, double trade policies and customs books, and countless overlapping preferential trade agreements with third parties. At the same time, the Palestinians lost the potential gains from a properly designed customs union without benefiting much from FTA concessions.

Finally, with regard to future arrangements, if a customs union is chosen, then some macro-formula for revenue sharing should be seriously considered. It is well established, both in theory and from actual experience, that potential benefits from trade integration are not necessarily equally distributed between the participants. A future CU between Israel and the WBGS should incorporate a mechanism for compensating the poorer and weaker members of the union. If an FTA is chosen, there will be an even stronger need for an enforcement mechanism and arbitration to solve the problems related to rules of origin and to smooth the flow of trade on the customs borders. Special non-reciprocal trade concessions should then be carefully negotiated to give the WBGS economy a chance to restructure itself and develop its productive base.

Acknowledgements

An earlier version of this article was published in *Economic Journal* (vol. 111, June 2001). The author and editors are grateful to Blackwell Publishers for permission to reproduce it here.

Note

1 The Federation of Israeli Chambers of Commerce, in a letter dated 25 January 1996, argued that since the EP did not create customs borders, any Israeli importer, distributor, or agent of foreign manufactured goods should have the full right to distribute and sell these goods in the WBGS. Furthermore, Dan Gillerman, from the Federation President's office, made it clear that the services of the army would also be deployed to guarantee the interests of Israeli importers: 'In our effort to avoid further damage… we are active together with the Israeli Government and army representatives to stop the impact of the [PA's decisions].'

References

Abed, G. (1996) 'The prospects for long-run sustainable growth', paper prepared for a conference:*The Palestinian Economy – Towards a Vision'* June 9 –12, Ramallah, West Bank: Birzeit University and the Arab Economists Association.

Aminoff, N. (1991) 'The US–Israel free trade agreement of 1985: in theory and practice', *Journal of World Trade,* 25: 1.

Brown, A. (1961) 'Separation versus a common market in developing countries', *Yorkshire Bulletin of Economic and Social Research,* 12 (1 and 2): 33–40 and 88–96.

Diwan, I. and R. Shaban, (eds.) (1999) *Development Under Adversity – The Palestinian Economy in Transition*, Ramallah, West Bank: Palestine Economic Policy Research Institute (MAS) and the World Bank.

Dumas, J.-P. (1999) 'Fiscal leakage in the West Bank and Gaza Strip' MEDA Programme of the EU, MEDA Team, The EU's Directorate General 1 B (April).

El-Agraa, A. (1989) *The Theory and Measurement of International Trade Integration*, London: Macmillan.

El-Musa, S. and M. El-Jafari (1995) 'Power and trade – the Israeli-Palestinian Economic Protocol', *Journal of Palestine Studies*, 24: 20–31.

EP (1994) 'Protocol on economic relations between the government of the State of Israel and the PLO, Representing the Palestinian People', Paris.

Fassberg, C. (1996) 'Legal aspects of Israeli–Palestinian economic relations', in Cotran, E. *et al.* (eds), *The Arab–Israeli Accords – Legal Perspectives* London: SOAS.

GATT (1995) 'Trade policy review mechanism – Israel,' *World Trade and Arbitration Materials*, 7(1): 59–77.

Halevi, N. (1999) 'Trade and the Paris Protocol', MEDA Programme of the EU, MEDA Team, The EU's Directorate General 1B (April).

Hamed, O. (1996) *The Palestinian banking system – reality and potentials*, Ramallah, West Bank: Palestine Economic Policy Research Institute (MAS).

ICBS (1996) *National Accounts of Judea, Samaria and the Gaza Area 1968–1993*, Jerusalem: Israel Central Bureau of Statistics.

Kanafani, N. (1996) *Trade Relations between Palestine and Israel – Free Trade Area or Customs Union?*, Ramallah, West Bank: Palestine Economic Policy Research Institute (MAS).

Kanafani, N. (2000) 'Associating Palestine with the European Union – the present framework and the way ahead', Working paper series 9937, Cairo: Economic Research Forum for the Arab Countries, Iran, and Turkey.

Kanafani, N., C. Woodcraft, and A. Daoud (1998) 'Implementation of trade-related articles of the Protocol on Economic Relations between Israel and Palestine', Brussels: A Report to the European Commission, Directorate General 1 B.

Kessler, V. (1999) 'Palestinian's external trade performance under the Paris Protocol – hopes and disillusions', MEDA Programme of the EU, MEDA Team, The EU's Directorate General 1B (April).

Kleiman, E. (1997) quoted in *The Economic Pulse* Ramallah: The Arab Economic Association, September–October.

Krueger, A. (1995) 'Free trade agreements versus customs unions', NBER Working Paper No. 4198.

PA (1997) 'Non tariff barriers imposed on Palestinian trade', Ramallah: The Ministry of Agriculture, Palestinian National Authority.

PA (1998) 'Financial losses', A letter from the Palestinian Ministry of Finance to the JEC's Palestinian coordinator, the Deputy Minister's Office (15 March).

Panagariya, A. and R. Findlay (1994) 'A political economy analysis of free trade area and customs union', World Bank Policy Research Working Paper No. 1261, March.

PCBS (1999) *Foreign Trade Statistics – Main Results*, Ramallah: Palestinian Central Bureau of Statistics.

Rivlin, P. (1992) *The Israeli Economy*, Westview: Boulder.

UNSCO (1997–9) 'Report on economic and social conditions in the WBGS', Quarterly Reports, Jerusalem: The UN Office of the Special Coordinator in the Occupied Territories.

UNSCO and the World Bank (1997) 'Closure of the West Bank and Gaza – August–Sept', Jerusalem: Fact Sheet.

World Bank (1993) *Developing the Occupied Territories – An Investment in Peace,* six volumes, Washington, DC: World Bank.

Index